Business to Business Marketing

Business to Business Marketing

A Value-Driven Approach

Wim G. Biemans

 **McGraw-Hill**
Higher Education

London   Boston   Burr Ridge, IL   Dubuque, IA   Madison, WI   New York   San Francisco
St. Louis   Bangkok   Bogotá   Caracas   Kuala Lumpur   Lisbon   Madrid   Mexico City
Milan   Montreal   New Delhi   Santiago   Seoul   Singapore   Sydney   Taipei   Toronto

Business to Business Marketing: A Value-Driven Approach
Wim G. Biemans
ISBN-13 978-0-07-712189-1
ISBN-10 0-07-712189-9

McGraw-Hill
Higher Education

Published by McGraw-Hill Education
Shoppenhangers Road
Maidenhead
Berkshire
SL6 2QL
Telephone: 44 (0) 1628 502 500
Fax: 44 (0) 1628 770 224
Website: *www.mcgraw-hill.co.uk*

British Library Cataloguing in Publication Data
A catalogue record for this book is available from the British Library

Library of Congress Cataloging in Publication Data
The Library of Congress data for this book has been applied for from the Library of Congress

Acquisitions Editor: Rachel Gear
Senior Development Editor: Leonie Sloman
Marketing Manager: Alice Duijser
Production Editor: Louise Caswell

Text Design by Hard Lines
Cover design by Ego Creative
Printed and bound in the UK by Bell and Bain Ltd, Glasgow.

The McGraw-Hill Companies

Mixed Sources
Product group from well-managed
forests and other controlled sources
www.fsc.org Cert no. TT-COC-002769
© 1996 Forest Stewardship Council
FSC

To Simonique

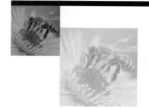

Brief Table of Contents

Detailed Table of Contents

Insights and Mini Cases

Preface

Business to consumer (B2C) marketing may be more visible through supermarkets, television advertising and all kinds of magazines, but the driving force behind a developed country's economy are the millions of business transactions taking place off stage. This book introduces readers to the fascinating and complex world of business to business (B2B) marketing.

This book is based on the successful Dutch book *Business Marketing Management*, published by Noordhoff Uitgevers since 1992. It uses a managerial perspective and focuses not on abstract constructs but on state-of-the-art ideas and techniques that have proven their worth in practice. In writing this book, I combined the latest concepts and theoretical developments with a down-to-earth perspective that helps managers to implement them. Many of the concepts and techniques described in this book have been developed and used in executive training sessions and applied to real-life B2B marketing situations. This provides the student of B2B marketing with a window on how firms are applying B2B theory in practical situations. All but one of the cases included in this book, for example, are based on interviews and training sessions with real B2B firms and the questions included in the cases describe the real-world problems these managers are struggling with.

Origins of business to business marketing

In the 1960s, a new marketing discipline, called industrial marketing, was born when people started to develop several frameworks describing the buying behaviour of organisations. Together with traditional concepts and techniques from B2C marketing, such as target customers, positioning and the 4 Ps (product, promotion, price, place), this helped firms to apply marketing to the complexity of industrial markets. In the late 1970s, European academics began to question the existing conceptualisation of industrial marketing and emphasised the importance of relationships and networks. These concepts were developed for industrial markets, but were later also applied in the field of consumer marketing. Gradually, the field of industrial marketing morphed into B2B marketing as people began to realise that it encompasses not just for-profit industrial firms, but all kinds of business customers, including hospitals, universities, municipalities and charities. Now, in the twenty-first century, B2B marketers are at the forefront of developing new concepts and applying new marketing techniques. B2B marketers, for instance, take the lead in experimenting with social media like LinkedIn and Twitter to communicate with customers.

As this brief biographical sketch illustrates, B2B marketing has evolved into a mature marketing discipline, with its own theoretical concepts and techniques and an identity distinct from B2C marketing. This is consistent with the fact that B2B marketing represents the majority of a developed country's economic activity.

Why a value-driven approach?

Successful B2B marketers contribute to the success of their customers by delivering superior value. This idea is the central theme of this book. Value is defined as the benefits minus costs that a customer receives and this value should be superior in the sense that it is more than that of the next-best alternative. This book shows how firms can develop effective value propositions and translate them into the familiar marketing tools of products and services, sales and delivery channels, communication and pricing. In so doing, it uses a European perspective throughout the book with numerous examples and cases from European B2B firms.

Structure of the book

The book starts by defining the field of B2B marketing, describing the nature of B2B customers and B2B markets and introducing the concept of value (Chapter 1). The rest of the book uses the following reasoning:

- Successful B2B marketing is based on a detailed understanding of B2B customers and B2B markets (Chapters 2 and 3).
- These insights are combined with the firm's capabilities to design creative strategies that allow it to deliver superior value to customers (Chapter 4).
- This value is summarised in the firm's value proposition and translated into the various marketing instruments, such as its products and services (Chapter 5), sales and delivery channels (Chapter 6), communication (Chapter 7) and pricing (Chapter 8).
- To stay competitive, B2B firms need to constantly monitor and improve their performance and marketing capability (Chapter 9).
- To make all this possible, a B2B firm should be designed with the needs of the customer and the value offered to them in mind (Chapter 10).

Just like any B2B product, this book has to offer superior value to its customers. The book has several key characteristics that set it apart from the competition and offer superior value for its users:

- a combination of state-of-the-art knowledge about value creation with more traditional marketing frameworks
- a process-driven managerial approach that shows how firms can systematically design, develop and implement superior value creation
- a European setting, with many real-life examples and cases from European B2B firms
- an accompanying website that offers several useful resources to both lecturers and students, such as PowerPoint presentations for all chapters, multiple-choice questions, suggestions for additional readings and executive exercises.

Guided Tour

Chapter contents

1.1 The nature of B2B marketing
1.2 B2B customers
1.3 B2B products

Chapter Contents
A brief list of key chapter contents is highlighted at the start of each chapter.

Introduction

O riginally, business to business of marketing, heavily borrowi marketing. But during the last 20 y concepts, methods and technique of B2B markets. As a result, B2B discipline, with a distinct ident he importance of B2B marke cial case of marketing developed

Introduction
Each chapter opens with an introduction, which sets the scene and introduces you to the issues that will be addressed in the chapter.

spend. Three co orporate purchase card, o

MINI CASE: KLM SAVES ON PURCH,

D utch airline KLM initiated its th KLM's Top 10 cost reductions a costs, (3) fewer company cars, (4) re (6) standardisation of software, (7) offices, (9) fewer courses for pers The largest opportunities for of €4.7 billion represen l). The largest

Mini Cases
Each chapter provides several short cases, illustrating how the concepts introduced in the chapter have informed decisions in real companies.

computers, c al services and cereals

INSIGHT: B2B applications for fr

Fragrances are typically associated with names like Calvin Klein, Chanel and Dior. generated by smells, fragrances are also our emotions and buying habits; for inst nd stimulate workers and by hospita ant ones. Other firms use fr visitor numbers and

Insight Boxes
These help readers see the real-life application of ideas in broader contexts: issues and trends in industry sectors or business marketing as a whole.

Summary of Key Concepts

These bullet points review the 'take-away' messages from the chapter and are a helpful revision aid.

Summary of Key Concepts

■ B2B customers are not interes
these products. B2B products
value creation for their own c
contribute to the success of t

■ B2B vendors can only hel
their customer's busines
derstand how the

Key Terms

All key terms are highlighted where first discussed in each chapter to emphasise their importance. They are also listed at the end of each chapter so that readers can test their understanding.

olete. At the heart
making, which encompas
their motivations and intera
a more detailed description o
making process results in the
presented in Figure 2.2.
    Each **customer-activity cycl**
A problem may arise because o
has become obsolete and need
to manufacture a new produc

Discussion Questions

Each chapter includes ten questions designed to encourage you to review and apply the knowledge you have acquired from the chapter.

sion-making un
E-procurement, p. 52

Discussion questions

1   A vendor may create value th
    Explain how each of these th
    a consulting firm.

Further Reading

These suggestions have been chosen as the ideal starting point for any additional reading or further research on the chapter's themes.

Further reading

Anderson, James C. and **James A**
    what customers value, *Harvar*
Ellram, Lisa (1993) Total cost of
    International Journal of Pur
Kraljic, Peter (1983) Purchasi
    Business Review, 61(5): 1
    dermerwe, Sandra (
    Sloan M

Technology to enhance learning and teaching

Visit **www.mcgraw-hill.co.uk/textbooks/biemans** today

 Online Learning Centre (OLC)

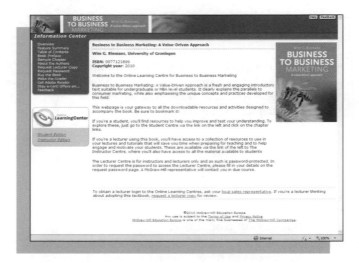

For Students

The Online Learning Centre (OLC) is your gateway to the following activities designed to accompany the book:

- **Self test questions** provide immediate feedback on your understanding.
- **Internet marketing exercises** show you how to use companies' websites to gain insights into their digital marketing strategies and activities.

For Lecturers

This collection of resources has been put together to help lecturers adopting this text save time when preparing their teaching and to help them engage and challenge their students so that they get more out of their course.

- **Teaching notes for the cases** help guide discussion around the case questions.
- **Example solutions** to the discussion questions at the end of each chapter and the Internet exercises.
- **PowerPoint slides** covering the main concepts in each chapter.
- **Artwork from the book** to illustrate lecture presentations or handouts.
- **Real world exercises** require students to gather information from real companies and develop their understanding of how B2B marketing principles explored in the book are applied in practice. They are designed to be used either on work placements or as assignments.

EZ Test Online

This easy-to-use online testing tool is accessible to busy academics virtually anywhere – in their office, at home or while travelling – and eliminates the need for software installation. Lecturers can choose from question banks associated with their adopted textbook or easily create their own questions. They also have access to hundreds of banks and thousands of questions created for other McGraw-Hill titles.

A bank of multiple choice and short answer questions is available to lecturers adopting this book. Multiple versions of tests can be saved for delivery on paper or online through WebCT, Blackboard and other course management systems. When created and delivered though EZ Test Online, students' tests can be immediately marked, saving lecturers time and providing prompt results to students.

To register for this FREE resource, visit **www.eztestonline.com**

Custom Publishing Solutions: Let us help make our content your solution

At McGraw-Hill Education our aim is to help lecturers to find the most suitable content for their needs delivered to their students in the most appropriate way. Our **custom publishing solutions** offer the ideal combination of content delivered in the way which best suits lecturer and students.

Our custom publishing programme offers lecturers the opportunity to select just the chapters or sections of material they wish to deliver to their students from a database called CREATE™ at **www.mcgrawhillcreate.com**

CREATE™ contains over two million pages of content from:

- textbooks
- professional books
- case books – Harvard Articles, Insead, Ivey, Darden, Thunderbird and BusinessWeek
- Taking Sides – debate materials

Across the following imprints:

- McGraw–Hill Education
- Open University Press
- Harvard Business Publishing
- US and European material

There is also the option to include additional material authored by lecturers in the custom product – this does not necessarily have to be in English.

We will take care of everything from start to finish in the process of developing and delivering a custom product to ensure that lecturers and students receive exactly the material needed in the most suitable way.

With a Custom Publishing Solution, students enjoy the best selection of material deemed to be the most suitable for learning everything they need for their courses – something of real value to support their learning. Teachers are able to use exactly the material they want, in the way they want, to support their teaching on the course.

Please contact your local McGraw-Hill representative with any questions or alternatively contact Warren Eels **e:** warren_eels@mcgraw-hill.com.

Improve Your Grades!
20% off any Study Skills book!

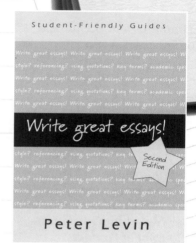
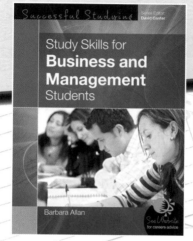

Our Study Skills books are packed with practical advice and tips that are easy to put into practice and will really improve the way you study. Our books will help you:

- Improve your grades
- Avoid plagiarism
- Save time
- Develop new skills

- Write confidently
- Undertake research projects
- Sail through exams
- Find the perfect job

Visit our website to read helpful hints about essays, exams, dissertations and find out about our offers.

www.openup.co.uk/studyskills

Special offer!
As a valued customer, buy online and receive 20% off any of our Study Skills books by entering the promo code *BRILLIANT!*

About the Author

Wim G. Biemans is Associate Professor at the Faculty of Economics and Business of the University of Groningen, and has also taught as guest professor at several universities (Ghent, Aarhus, Manchester, Beijing, Pisa, Ljubljana). He teaches in the areas of B2B marketing, business development, product development and services marketing.

The focus of both Wim's teaching and research is on the development and marketing of technological innovations in B2B markets. His PhD was awarded in 1989 for research on cooperation between firms in developing new B2B innovations. In the following 25 years, his research resulted in more than 100 scientific papers and articles, published in journals such as *Journal of Product Innovation Management, Industrial Marketing Management, Journal of Business and Industrial Marketing, International Journal of Innovation Management* and *R&D Management*.

In 2008 he was awarded the 'Thomas P. Hustad Best Paper Award for Outstanding Professional Contribution for 2007' for an article published in *Journal of Product Innovation Management*. His expertise has also been recognised through membership of the editorial board of the two leading academic journals on B2B marketing: *Industrial Marketing Management* and *Journal of Business and Industrial Marketing*. In addition, he is a frequent reviewer for *Journal of Product Innovation Management, European Journal of Marketing* and several other scientific journals.

Based on his research, Wim has authored or edited several books, including *Product Development: Meeting the Challenge of the Design–Marketing Interface* (1995) and the Dutch bestselling title about B2B marketing, *Business Marketing Management: Strategy, Planning and Implementation* (in Dutch), the fifth edition of which was published in 2008 and inspired this book. He is also a frequent speaker in executive training programmes, where he helps B2B firms to increase their market orientation, improve their marketing efforts and structure their innovation processes.

Acknowledgements

Although writing is a lonely process of turning an empty screen into another useful chapter, many people have contributed to this book. The material presented in this book is the result of more than 20 years of experience studying, researching and teaching B2B marketing and a large number of people have contributed to my understanding of the field. Numerous students and managers challenged my thinking during lectures and seminars and helped me to improve my ideas. Many colleagues contributed by acting as a partner in researching B2B marketing, co-authoring academic papers or by responding to them. Several managers contributed to this book by allowing themselves to be interviewed for the cases, providing images to be used as illustrations or giving permission to reprint material from their websites. A special word of thanks goes to the lecturers who acted as beta testers for this book and provided numerous useful comments and suggestions on earlier drafts. The people from McGraw-Hill were helpful in guiding me through the process of writing the book and making it as good as possible. Finally, Simonique and Lotte gave me the space that I needed to get this book finished and provided all the distractions that I needed to keep my sanity during this project.

Wim G. Biemans

Publishers' Acknowledgements

Our thanks go to the following people for their feedback at various stages in the text's development:

-Joep Arts, *Vrije University, The Netherlands*
-Nicolas van Dijl, *Fontys Hogeschool Venlo, The Netherlands*
-Peter Erdelyi, *Bournemouth University, UK*
-Rebecca Hughes, *University of the West of England, UK*
-Gert Human, *University of Cape Town, South Africa*
-Mercy Makhita, *Vaal University of Technology, South Africa*
-George Masikunas, *Kingston University, UK*
-Erik Rasmussen, *University of Southern Denmark*
-Ellen Roemer, *University of Bradford, UK*
-Sicco Santema, *Technische Universiteit Delft, The Netherlands*
-Haseeb Shabir, *University of Leeds, UK*
-Graeme Stephen, *Robert Gordon University, UK*
-Frederick Thomson, *University of Kent, UK*

Every effort has been made to trace and acknowledge ownership of copyright and to clear permission for material reproduced in this book. We are grateful to the following organisations for their permission to reproduce advertising or product images, we would will be pleased to make suitable arrangements to clear permission with any copyright holders whom it has not been possible to contact.

Chapter 1: p.5 Vekoma Rides Manufacturing, BV, p.15 De Boer. **Chapter 2**: p.38 ABB, p.40 Massachusetts Insitutue of Technology, p.55 Dell Inc. **Chapter 4**: p.116 Rolls-Royce Plc., p.121 Bridge House Studio and GXS Ltd. **Chapter 5**: p.140 McGraw-Hill, p.143 GXS Ltd., pp.145,147 &152 Elsevier, p.167 Microban International Ltd. **Chapter 6**: p.180 & p.182 McGraw-Hill, p.198 Elsevier.
Chapter 7: p.213 Elsevier, p.215 Nokia Corporation, p.219 M.H. (Mac) McIntosh at www.sales-lead-experts.com, p.225 The McGraw-Hill Companies, p.228 BtoB & Media Business magazines, p.229 McGraw-Hill, p.232 ON24 Inc., p.236 McGraw-Hill.
Chapter 8: p.260 McGraw-Hill, p.271 Engine Lease Finance Corporation.
Chapter 9: p.287 American Marketing Association, p.290 Elsevier, p.292 Nedstat, p.294 Dundas Data Visualisation Inc., p.295 Institute for Operations Research and the Management Sciences, 7240 Parkway Drive, Suite 300, Hanover, Maryland 21076. **Chapter 10**: pp.307 & 310 McGraw-Hill, p.315 Elsevier.
Cases: pp.329 & 331Vekoma Rides Manufacturing, BV, pp.345–347 NNZ.

PART 01
Understanding Business to Business Marketing

CHAPTER

01

B2B marketing

Introduction

Originally, business to business (B2B) marketing started as a special case of marketing, heavily borrowing concepts and techniques from consumer marketing. But during the last 20 years academics and business people developed concepts, methods and techniques that are tailored to the unique characteristics of B2B markets. As a result, B2B marketing has evolved into a mature marketing discipline, with a distinct identity, separate from consumer marketing. The importance of B2B marketing is often underestimated. Rather than being a special case of marketing, B2B marketing represents the majority of economic activity in developed countries.

Successful application of B2B marketing concepts and methods requires insight into the characteristics of B2B markets and how they shape B2B marketing approaches. This chapter defines the field of B2B marketing and emphasises the key objective of all B2B marketing: 'contributing to the success of your customers'.

The chapter presents the broad range of B2B customers, which includes commercial enterprises, government agencies and institutions. In addition, it shows the variety of B2B products, which range from fasteners, printed circuit boards and office supplies to printing presses, aircraft and nuclear plants. The practice of B2B marketing is strongly determined by the characteristics of B2B markets, such as derived demand and complex buying behaviour. To illustrate that B2B marketing is both influenced by and influencing consumer marketing, the link between both marketing disciplines is also discussed. The chapter concludes by explaining that successful B2B marketing revolves around the creation of superior value for customers.

1.1 The nature of B2B marketing

The sleepy little town of Vlodrop, The Netherlands, is home to the headquarters of Vekoma Rides Manufacturing, one of the largest roller-coaster manufacturers in the world and a market leader in the amusement industry. Here, engineers design the latest thrills with brand names like Boomerang, Invertigo and Stingray that evoke the smell of popcorn and candyfloss and the screams of excited children. Vekoma's products are often repackaged by its customers to further increase their appeal and differentiate them from the competition. Walibi Belgium, for instance, painted a Vekoma Suspended Looping Coaster bloodred and renamed it 'Vampire'; other Vekoma roller-coasters received the colourful names Cobra, Werewolf and Invertigo (Figure 1.1).

Vekoma started as Veld Koning Machinefabriek in 1926, building agricultural machinery, moved into mining after the Second World War and entered the amusement industry around 1980. During the last three decades it has become a world-leading supplier of family coasters, thrill and mega coasters, indoor and custom-designed coasters, and several other attractions and specialities. The company is relentlessly focused on the success of its customers: 'Whenever you are looking for a new unique roller-coaster or attraction, or new trains for an existing ride, our concept design department is enthusiastic to build your dream and create an unforgettable experience for your guests' (www.vekoma.com). But how do you keep innovating on the basic concept of a roller-coaster? How do you convince theme parks of the safety and potential of new designs? How do you figure out what the end customers (the theme park's visitors) want? How do you keep up with the ever-increasing demands for new thrills? How do you segment your markets according to thrill levels that are still acceptable? How do you combine the company's need for standardised products with the customer's need for customisation and uniqueness? Welcome to the wonderful world of B2B marketing...

Most people associate marketing with familiar consumer brands, such as McDonald's, iPod, Nokia and Heinz. But while these brands are quite ubiquitous and hard to ignore, they only represent the more visible tip of the iceberg. Most marketing efforts concern products and services that are sold to organisations

FIGURE 1.1 Vekoma's Invertigo

Source: Vekoma Rides Manufacturing. Used with permission.

instead of consumers. The volume of transactions in business markets has been estimated as two to four times as much as the transaction volume in consumer markets. This means that most marketing is B2B marketing and that students of marketing are most likely to end up working for a company that sells to business customers!

B2B marketing is the marketing of products or services to companies, government bodies, institutions and other organisations that use them to produce their own products or services or sell them to other B2B customers. This definition of B2B marketing emphasises the nature of business customers and the purpose for which B2B products are bought. B2B customers are organisations instead of consumers, varying from small family-operated local companies to large multinational conglomerates with several business units and gigantic purchasing budgets. General Motors' global parts purchasing budget for 2006, for example, was $85 billion! B2B customers are not always for-profit firms, but also include schools, hospitals, courthouses, political parties, zoos, ministries and libraries. A courthouse buys photocopiers, computers, desks and filing cabinets, for example, while a zoo purchases cages, building materials, animals and fresh produce. According to Jim Marlett, assistant director of the Sedgwick County Zoo (USA), their yearly purchases include 1,500,000 crickets, 25,000 rats and mice, 48 tons of acid digestible fibre and even daily rations of cow's blood for their vampire bats.[1]

The second characteristic of B2B marketing is that B2B customers buy products for the operation of their business – either by using them to manufacture their own products and services (Wilkinson Sword buys steel and plastics to manufacture razors), to support their business processes (Akzo Nobel purchases office supplies and furniture to be used in their offices) or to sell them to other B2B customers (Ottevaere is one of Belgium's largest suppliers of building materials). This implies that a product is only a B2B product when it is bought by an organisation for one of these three purposes; not every purchase by an organisation belongs to the realm of B2B marketing. When Twinings, a producer of tea with a 300-year history, sells its famous teas through Sainsbury's to consumers, it engages in consumer marketing. But Twinings selling tea to Sainsbury's for use in its company restaurant is an example of B2B marketing. Similarly, Sainsbury's uses consumer marketing to sell Twinings tea to consumers (this particular type of consumer marketing is also called *retail marketing*), but B2B marketing to sell the tea through its online groceries store to small local businesses. In addition, Twinings' marketing directed at Sainsbury's is called *trade marketing*. These different types of marketing are graphically depicted in Figure 1.2.

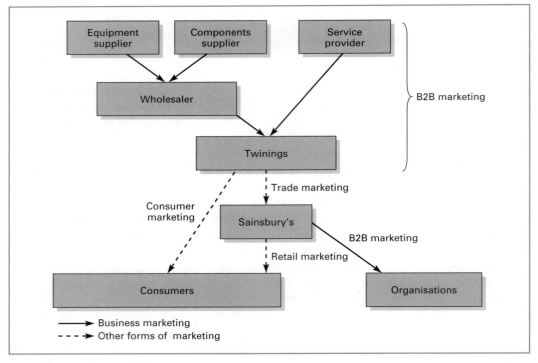

FIGURE 1.2 Positioning of B2B marketing

> ### ᏺ INSIGHT: B2B marketing for consumer marketers
>
> Knowledge about B2B marketing is also relevant to manufacturers of consumer products, such as Unilever and Procter & Gamble. Although these manufacturers use consumer marketing to sell their consumer brands through various retail chains, these retail chains are large organisations whose buying behaviour is often quite similar to that of B2B customers. They employ professional purchasers, negotiate about delivery and payment conditions and sign long-term blanket contracts with suppliers. Indeed, large retailers frequently want to participate in their suppliers' product development. This means that marketers working for manufacturers of consumer products would clearly benefit from knowledge about organisational buying behaviour and effective B2B marketing strategies.
>
> But there is a second reason why insight into B2B marketing is useful for manufacturers of consumer products. These manufacturers buy large quantities of materials and components to manufacture their consumer products that are marketed by their suppliers using B2B marketing. If the purchasers at manufacturers like Unilever, Procter & Gamble and Nestlé are familiar with B2B marketing strategies and techniques, they are better equipped to negotiate good business deals and develop effective relationships with their suppliers.

It could be argued that there is no such thing as a B2B product. After all, a product is only a B2B product when it is bought by an organisation for a specific purpose. When a self-employed consultant buys a new mobile phone, the phone is a B2B product. But when the same person buys the same phone for private use, it is a consumer product. The phone is identical, but it is a different customer (consulting firm versus consumer), using different buying motives. This means that manufacturers of mobile phones must use different marketing approaches for the two groups of customer, for instance offering attractive tariffs, handsets and group conferencing and billing services to business customers and emphasising the available memory, built-in camera and sound quality to consumers.

While many products may be sold to both consumers and business customers (see Section 1.5), in practice many products are bought exclusively by organisations. Products such as fighter jets, printing presses and speciality chemicals are clearly developed for business applications. Because many of these products are used in manufacturing or other business processes, these B2B vendors are less familiar to the general public. The average consumer has no problem recalling the brand of car she drives or the mobile phone that is used daily, but will probably be stumped when asked about the manufacturer of the tyres on her car or the battery in her mobile phone. B2B vendors are like the submerged part of the proverbial iceberg: invisible, but providing the foundation for their more visible consumer marketing counterparts.

1.2 B2B customers

B2B customers can be categorised into three groups: commercial enterprises, government agencies and institutions. Each of these three groups of B2B customer has its own characteristics and should be approached differently by vendors.

Commercial enterprises

There are three types of commercial enterprise: users, original equipment manufacturers and resellers.

Users

Users purchase business products or services to produce their own products or services that are sold to business customers and/or consumers. Users purchase these products to set up or support their manufacturing processes; for instance, Volkswagen buys photocopiers, computers, office supplies and automated manufacturing systems to manufacture cars. These products do not become part of the car, but are used to manufacture them.

Original equipment manufacturers

Original equipment manufacturers (OEMs) buy B2B products to incorporate them in their own products, which are subsequently sold on business or consumer markets. Volkswagen, for instance, buys suspension and steering parts, seating systems, brakes, door handles and thousands of other parts to manufacture cars with the familiar Volkswagen brand. All these products become part of the end product that is sold to consumers and business customers. Sometimes, the purchased B2B product that becomes part of the car is branded and visible to the end user. Examples are shock absorbers (Bosch), car radio systems (Philips) and tyres (Michelin). This strategy of *ingredient branding* was made famous by Intel when it introduced its Intel Inside campaign to convince consumers that a computer's performance is basically determined by its microprocessor.

Some vendors develop and manufacture the complete product and sell it to a B2B customer, who then markets the product under its own brand name. This strategy is quite usual in the computer market, where Taiwanese manufacturers like Quanta and Compal produce computers that are sold with familiar brand names such as Hewlett-Packard and Dell.

Resellers

Resellers purchase business products and sell them to B2B customers. They do not really change the physical product but may add value by bundling products into systems and by offering several support services (such as advice, installation, maintenance and training). Finning Ltd (UK) is the world's largest Caterpillar heavy and general equipment dealer. In addition, it is also the leading provider of Cat, MaK and Perkins Sabre Power and Energy Systems to marine, power generation and industrial and OEM customers. To support its products it offers a menu of services, including preventive maintenance, emergency repair, breakdown cover, financial services, warranties, professional advice on whether to recondition, repair or overhaul when problems occur, and contamination control programmes to keep the equipment running and thus reduce downtime and maintain productivity.

Government agencies

A significant number of B2B products and services are bought by government agencies. This includes various agencies at both central and local government levels. In addition, state-owned companies, such as utilities and national railway companies, frequently display similar purchasing behaviour. Public authorities spend some 16 per cent of the EU's gross domestic product, which is equivalent to half the gross domestic product (GDP) of Germany. The purchasing process of government agencies is often characterised by complex decision making, comprehensive procedures, national and European rules and guidelines, and much bureaucracy. The European Commission, for example, published a brochure on green public procurement (GPP), which offers guidelines for government agencies to purchase goods and services that respect the environment. Examples are energy-efficient buildings, office equipment made of environmentally sustainable timber, organic food in canteens and electricity from renewable energy sources. The European Union also published public procurement directives that apply to all contracts above a specified threshold.

All this regulation, procedure and bureaucracy frequently results in extremely ineffective and inefficient buying behaviour and outcomes. The press regularly reports examples of taxpayers' money being spent on products that are inadequate, too expensive or both. In 2008, *The Guardian* reported on a series of abandoned government IT projects since 2000, costing the British taxpayer almost £2 billion. The projects included the Department for Work and Pensions squandering more than £1.6 billion by abandoning three major schemes: a new benefit card which was based on outdated technology, an upgrade to the Child Support Agency's computer which could not handle 1.2 million existing claims, and £140 million for a streamlined benefit payment system that never worked properly.[2] In Australia, a 1999 report on the management of major equipment acquisition projects revealed 'systemic problems' involving more than 200 projects worth almost $43 billion.[3] Large government projects are almost systematically over-budget and suffer extensive delays.

Despite all the bad press, many governments have invested in improved purchasing functions and procedures, resulting in more professional purchasing that is increasingly similar to purchasing by commercial firms. For example, in the UK, Buying Solutions is an Executive Agency of the Office of Government Commerce (OGC) in the Treasury that defines its role as "to maximise the value for money obtained by Government departments and other public bodies through the procurement and supply of goods and services" (www.buyingsolutions.gov.uk). It provides economies of scale and helps public organisations to save time and costs on the pre-purchase stages by offering a set of pre-tendered contracts with a range of vendors and several services to facilitate the purchasing process. Buying Solutions is available to central and local government organisations, but also to the wider public sector comprising health, education and emergency services, utilities and not-for-profit sectors.

Institutions

A third group of B2B customers encompasses the numerous institutions purchasing B2B products to perform their function. This includes hospitals, nursing homes, blood banks, schools, universities, politial parties, museums, labour unions, trade organisations, churches and the Red Cross. This very diverse group of customers includes both small local organisations and large national organisations with more formalised purchasing functions; for instance, hospitals and universities use sophisticated purchasing procedures.

The buying behaviour of institutions is characterised by inadequate cost control, limited purchasing proficiency, the use of budgets that need to be depleted at the end of the year, limited focus on price and decentralised purchasing. Frequently, there are also significant differences between the people buying the products and the ones actually using them. Smart vendors benefitted from this less-than-professional buying behaviour. Manufacturers of hospital equipment, for example, reaped huge profits by selling their equipment at low prices and making money on the sale of expensive supplies (such as sensors) that are needed to use the equipment. Many institutions, however, have now developed more professional purchasing functions. Nowadays, the decision to purchase new medical equipment is no longer made by a single doctor, but by a group, involving the doctor and nursing staff that will use and operate the equipment, someone from the technical department who needs to maintain and repair it, and someone from finance who monitors the total budget. Vendors need to track such changes in buying behaviour because they influence the effectiveness of marketing strategies and tactics.

1.3 B2B products

The diversity of B2B markets is also reflected in the broad range of **B2B products**, varying from office supplies, lubricants and electronic tools to welding robots, printing presses and roller-coasters. Table 1.1 classifies B2B products into several categories, each with its own characteristics and marketing implications.

Raw and processed materials

Raw materials are farm and natural products that are used by customers with little or no alteration, such as corn, wheat, milk, iron, oil, copper, chemicals, natural gas and compressed air. These materials become part of the customer's product or are used in some other part of the customer's operations (for instance, in an engineering laboratory). Processed materials are raw materials that have undergone some sort of conversion (such as plastics produced in granular form).

TABLE 1.1 Categories of B2B products: buying approaches and marketing implications

Category description	Buying approach	Marketing implications
Raw and processed materials		
Materials that are used in manufacturing. Raw materials are not altered by the vendor (corn, iron, oil, natural gas), while processed materials have undergone some conversion (plastics)	Purchasing and manufacturing are the key departments, focusing on securing a dependable source of supply	Large-volume and customised items are sold directly; lower-volume and standard items are sold through channel partners. Customisation allows for premium pricing, but standard items are sold at low or competitive prices
Component parts		
Fabricated products that are bought by customers and become part of their end product (tyres, windows and batteries become part of a car)	Engineering is the primary decision-maker in selecting vendors, because the parts have to conform to performance specifications. Purchasing plays a key role when it comes to securing supply and negotiating price and delivery schedules. Other departments, such as manufacturing and quality control, may also be involved	Components are marketed like materials: either sold directly or through channel partners, depending on the nature of the component and the quantity bought. When the components have a competitive advantage, premium pricing is possible, otherwise low prices
MRO supplies		
Supplies for maintenance, repair and day-to-day operations (lubricants, spare parts, soap, office supplies)	For several standardised, low-importance items (such as office supplies), purchasing is the key decision-maker and price the primary buying motive. For more specialised items, users are most important, focusing on quality of the items and support services provided by the vendor	MRO items are typically sold through channel partners or through the internet, but large-volume buyers are sold to directly. Most supplies are homogeneous; to avoid price competition vendors should identify and emphasise non-price differences (for instance, unique support services)
Capital goods		
Facilities and fixed equipment used by customers in their manufacturing process or generally to run their business (offices, warehouses, elevators, computer systems)	Because of the significant expenditures, top management is the primary decision-maker, closely followed by the intended users of the capital goods. Top management will assess ROI and evaluate the trade-off between make or buy. Users will emphasise the required performance of the capital goods	Capital goods are typically sold directly, because of the large amount of money involved, extended decision making and their complex technical aspects. Vendors should emphasise non-price factors, such as technology, delivery and pre- and post-sale services
Tools and accessories		
Light equipment and tools that are less expensive than capital equipment and typically bought in larger quantities (trucks, office equipment)	Key decision-makers are purchasing (focusing on price and the vendor's overall services) and users (emphasising quality and support services)	Tools and equipment that are standardised and/or bought in small quantities are sold through channel partners or directly through the internet, while major customers are sold to directly. Vendors should emphasise quality and innovation. Both vendors and channel partners must offer superior services

TABLE 1.1 *Continued*

Services		
Activities performed by third parties (catering, management consultancy, transportation, security)	Users of the activity's results are the primary decision-makers and they will select service providers based on their capability to provide the service. Purchasing may be involved to negotiate prices. As an alternative, the customer also assesses the costs and benefits of performing the activity in-house	Because the service is mostly intangible, the service provider must communicate the benefits of using the service (strong focus on advertising and the use of reference customers). Because services are less easily copied, there may be opportunities to charge premium prices
Systems		
Combination of products and services into a complete system, offered as a solution to customers (computer systems, drilling systems)	The customer's top or mid-level management are the primary decision-makers, focusing on ROI and evaluating make-or-buy decisions. The intended users emphasise the required performance of the system	Systems are sold through extended marketing and negotiation processes. Relationship marketing plays a key role, both in acquiring projects and in managing the relationships with partners. Systems sellers must focus on integration, offer a broad range of services and use flexible pricing schemes

Several parties may be involved in the customer's buying process. Marketing forecasts sales of the end product, engineering provides the specifications of the required products, manufacturing wants a flexible supplier and purchasing looks for reliability in a vendor. Customers buying large volumes or custom items usually negotiate long-term contracts and are supplied directly by the vendor. Naturally, the tighter the specifications, the less standard the product and therefore the higher the price that can be commanded.

Component parts

Fabricated products that become part of the customer's end product are component parts. They are identifiable products of varying complexity and include items such as integrated circuits, switches, motors, sensors, displays, monitors and tyres. Sometimes, these component parts are visible to the user of the end product and branded by the supplier; for instance, a car contains branded tyres (Michelin, Pirelli), sparking plugs (Bosch, Champion) and a battery (Varta, Hoppecke). Another example is Dolby noise reduction technology in audio equipment.

Component buying is similar to the purchasing of materials. Component parts are often distributed through specialised channels. Large volume buyers of component parts negotiate long-term contracts guaranteeing delivery of quality products at an acceptable price.

MRO supplies

All organisations need numerous products to make their organisations and manufacturing processes run smoothly. These so-called maintenance, repair and operating (MRO) supplies include paints, coatings, sealants, chemicals, lubricants, paper, office supplies, spare parts, packagings, lamps, uniforms, cleaners, degreasers, cutting fluids, adhesives and fasteners. Spare parts are usually supplied by the equipment manufacturer, but many other MRO items can be bought in supermarkets and hardware stores or from specialised distributors. Dutch-based *FABORY* is the leading distributor of industrial fasteners, such as bolts, nuts, screws, pins and nails, in the Benelux region. In addition, the company also distributes chemical fasteners (tapes, adhesives, sealants) and tools.

Due to the simple nature of MRO items, the customer's purchasers are the key decision-makers and price is a key buying motive. Many resellers use dedicated software or the internet that allows their customers to efficiently order MRO products online. Efficient ordering and delivery systems keep them out of price wars.

Capital goods

This category includes all facilities and fixed equipment that are used by customers to conduct their business. Capital goods are generally depreciated over a number of years and include buildings, HVAC installations, elevators, telephone exchanges, computer servers and printing presses. All of these products involve major financial decisions that require extended negotiations between buyer and seller. Negotiations may take many months and involve top executives from both organisations.

Because of the large amount of money involved, vendors have direct contact with customers. Capital goods are not primarily sold on price, but on special services, delivery schedules and offered options to finance the deal. Many vendors offer leasing, for example, which allows customers to deduct the leasing costs as an operating expense and to periodically upgrade to a new generation of the product.

MINI CASE: BOSCH – A LEADING SUPPLIER OF COMPONENTS, CAPITAL EQUIPMENT AND SYSTEMS

German-based Robert Bosch GmbH is well known as a leading supplier to the automotive industry, supplying a broad range of components, such as electric motors, fuel filters, brake systems, drive belts, windshield wipers, sensors, sparking plugs, horns, batteries, steering systems and lighting systems. In addition, it offers a range of diagnostic instruments for repair shops. But Bosch has several other divisions as well:

- *Bosch Security Systems* offers a wide range of fire, intrusion, social alarm, CCTV, management and communication systems and components.
- *Bosch Communication Services* offers inbound, outbound, front- and back-office customer communication to a wide range of industries. In addition, it runs one of the largest monitoring centres in Germany, offering remote monitoring services to monitor buildings, machines, containers, vehicles and people.

▶
- *Bosch Packaging Technology* designs, manufactures and installs complete filling, process and packaging lines for manufacturers in the pharmaceutical, confectionery and cosmetics industries. It also offers a range of services including complete service packages, customised systems and all-in-one solutions.
- *Bosch RexRoth AG* develops, produces and sells complete systems for industrial and factory automation. Company teams find solutions for every customer problem, using hydraulics, electrics, pneumatics and mechanics to develop cross-technology solutions.

Source: www.bosch.com

Tools and accessories

The tools and accessories bought by B2B customers are used for similar purposes as capital goods. The difference is that tools and accessories are generally less expensive and bought in larger quantities. While a B2B customer needs only one telephone exchange, they may require dozens of personal computers. This category of B2B products includes generators, pumps, trucks, portable drills, cement mixers, personal computers, desks and filing cabinets.

Purchasers and users are the most important decision-makers when it comes to buying tools and accessories, with quality and price being the key buying motives. Most manufacturers collaborate with local distributors, with the manufacturers supplying the tools and the distributors providing local inventory and service.

Services

B2B services are all activities performed by third parties on a contractual basis; for example, management consultancy, advertising, insurance, communication, web design, legal advice, financial services, market research, design, catering, gardening, security and cleaning. The Dutch firm De Boer is one of the leading providers of turnkey temporary accommodation solutions, including tents for exhibitions, trade shows, festivals, product launches, parties and sport events, but also business continuity through temporary restaurants, distribution centres, prisons, showrooms and supermarkets. Its accommodation solutions have been used for music festivals, Olympic Games, G8 meetings and Mobile World Congresses. Its business space solutions, in particular, often look like real buildings (Figure 1.3).

The customer's key decision-makers depend on the nature of the service; for instance, management consultants are hired by top and mid-level managers, while caterers can be selected by purchasers or facility managers. The purchasing department is usually involved in negotiations with service providers. Service providers must convince their customers that they are able to deliver what is promised. Good communication programmes help service providers to enhance the perceived uniqueness of their services and allow them to charge higher prices. Services are discussed in more detail in Chapter 5.

FIGURE 1.3 De Boer, provider of quick-to-build accommodation
Source: De Boer. Used with permission.

Systems

Systems combine separate products and/or services into a complete working system. An integrated computer system may, for example, consist of hardware, software, a comprehensive programme for maintenance and upgrades, and the training of personnel. National Oilwell Varco in Norway is the leading supplier for the worldwide oil and gas industry. It provides comprehensive drilling solutions that include technically advanced, field-proven equipment integrated into systems. These drilling solutions are supported by life-cycle management services, including e-business solutions, spare parts distribution systems and strategically located repair and service facilities. All these elements are combined to increase drilling efficiency, minimise environmental impacts and maximise customers' life-cycle economics.

Systems buying is similar to the purchasing of capital goods. Systems sellers typically need to customise, compete on services offered and use flexible pricing schemes.

1.4 Characteristics of B2B markets

The effectiveness of marketing strategies and tactics depends on the characteristics of the markets targeted. In B2B markets, one or more of the following characteristics may be important: (a) the demand for B2B products depends on the demand for other downstream products (derived demand); (b) the demand for B2B products is related to the demand for other B2B products (joint demand); (c) there are few, geographically concentrated, customers; and (d) organisational buying behaviour is complex. The rest of this section discusses these characteristics of B2B markets and their implications for vendors' marketing efforts.

Derived demand

All B2B markets are characterised by **derived demand**: the demand for the B2B product depends on the demand for downstream products. The demand for steel, for example, depends on the demand for products that are (partly) made of steel, such as cars, airplanes, building products, drills, pipes, gears, springs, drums, rails, ships, and various packagings for consumer products like tins, cans, and battery and lipstick cases. This means that B2B marketing is all about contributing to the success of your customers. Vendors must create value for customers by offering products or services that help their customers to increase the value they in turn offer their customers. B2B vendors should not focus on their products, but on their customers' key success factors and how they can help them to become more successful. Finning, the UK distributor of Caterpillar, formulates its vision succinctly as follows: '[Our] job is to make our customers and company successful.' It puts the success of its customers before its own success; when its customers are successful, its own success will follow. This key notion is also communicated by DHL, global market leader in the international express and logistics industry – 'Our customers' success is our success' (www.dhl.com) – and reflected in the pay-off used in its advertising: 'We help you keep your promises.'

The key marketing implication of derived demand is that B2B vendors must closely monitor the developments in their downstream markets. But this basic principle is hard to implement for B2B vendors near the beginning of the supply chain, such as vendors of steel, chemicals and fibres. Typically, the products from these firms are used in a wide range of applications; for instance, plastics from GE Plastics are used for products such as the Smart Forfour, INSORB surgical skin staplers, Philips tanning units and Varox water purifiers. It is simply impractical and too expensive for these companies to monitor all downstream markets. In practice, marketers solve this dilemma by identifying key applications and assigning priorities: only a limited number of applications or markets are closely watched, while others are reacted to as soon as market changes manifest themselves.

MINI CASE: B2B FIRMS FEEL THE EFFECTS OF REDUCED CONSUMER DEMAND

In 2009, numerous B2B firms were confronted with the effects of the global financial crisis. Maltha is a leading European industrial organisation specialised in the processing of glass waste into a valuable raw material for the glass processing industry.

Every year, Dutch consumers throw approximately 420,000 tons of glass into glass containers, which is collected and recycled for glass manufacturers, who then sell the recycled glass to manufacturers of consumer products such as Heineken. But, while the used bottles keep coming, the demand for recycled glass has dropped significantly because consumers buy fewer products. American demand for Heineken beer has gone into a slump, which means that Heineken needs substantially less glass for the production of beer bottles. In addition, the costs of energy and sand have dropped to such an extent that glass manufacturers find it less attractive to use recycled glass for their manufacturing processes. Using glass shards requires less energy in the manufacturing process, but the lower energy prices have changed the economic dynamics. As a result, Maltha has 30 per cent more glass waiting to be recycled and has started to renegotiate with municipalities about price reductions. Some municipalities do not accept the lower prices and sell their glass to companies in Portugal instead. Apparently, consumers still buy enough port to maintain stable prices in the Portuguese glass industry...

Source: *nrc•next*, 14 July 2009, pp. 12–13

But even when a vendor focuses on just a few supply chains, marketing may be complicated because there are several levels of **downstream customer**. Imagine a fibre manufacturer dealing with a supply chain consisting of weavers, pressers, helmet manufacturers and Ministries of Defence. At the same time, the weavers also sell their cloth to polyester manufacturers, who sell strengthened polyester to boat manufacturers, who in turn sell their boats to consumers (Figure 1.4).

The fibre manufacturer will typically only have developed relationships with its **direct customers**, the weavers. All downstream customers operate in totally different markets and are not part of the fibre manufacturer's traditional customer base. The longer the chain, the more difficult it is for a B2B vendor to identify where critical decisions are made concerning its product, the major players at this level, key decision-makers in individual firms, their buying motives and the best strategy to approach them. After all, each downstream level is an unfamiliar market to the vendor! With multiple value chains the problems quickly become all but insurmountable. But successful upstream vendors manage to develop good working relationships with critical downstream customers. DSM, a major supplier of chemicals, plastics and other materials, talks directly with Volkswagen and General Motors about the development of new plastic components. This marketing directed at downstream customers is largely invisible to the general public. But some B2B vendors use communication programmes targeted at consumers. By branding their material or component, they make their products visible to consumers and generate a pull effect through the entire value chain (McCarthy and Norris 1999; Simon and Sebastian 1995). This strategy was made famous by Intel, with its Intel Inside campaign, but is also used by Teflon (non-stick coatings for carpet protectors

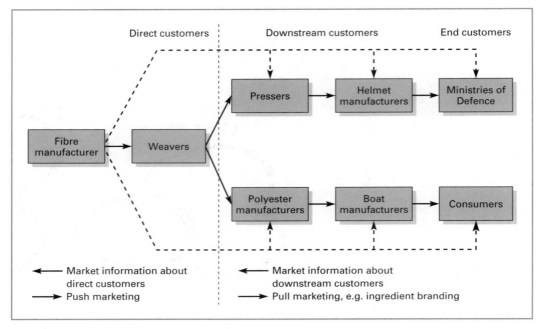

FIGURE 1.4 Marketing to direct and downstream customers

and cookware), Tetra Pak (carton packagings), Kevlar (boats, bulletproof vests), Gore-Tex (waterproof protection for outdoor clothing), Shimano (brakes for bicycles) and Microban (antimicrobial protection of numerous consumer products). But such pull strategies do not always work. Downstream customers may fail to grasp the component's contribution to the value of their own product, while direct customers may resent the vendor communicating with their customers.

Another consequence of derived demand is that demand fluctuations are amplified through the supply chain. B2B vendors over-react to observed demand fluctuations and tend to increase their orders more than the demand for their products has increased. Thus, changes in consumer demand result in delayed and amplified changes in the demand for B2B products (a phenomenon known as the *bullwhip effect*). This is evident for materials and components that enter downstream products, but also goes for capital equipment and MRO items, although in these cases the delay is usually longer. If consumer demand for air travel goes up, for example, it will take a while before an airline orders additional aircraft and needs more spare parts and lubricants to service them.

Joint demand

The demand for B2B products frequently depends on the demand for other related B2B products. For example, to build computers a manufacturer needs a specific combination of casings, microchips, monitors, disk drives and fans. As the demand for computers increases, the demand for all these components increases as well.

On the other hand, if there is a temporary shortage of disk drives, the manufacturer might decide to temporarily stop buying fans and microchips as well until the disk drives become available again. **Joint demand** may also be caused by the desire of B2B customers to buy related products and services from one supplier. Such one-stop shopping reduces procurement costs and improves the relationship with the vendor.

Few, geographically concentrated customers

Many B2B markets consist of relatively few, large customers. Tetra Pak, for example, is a major supplier of processing and packaging solutions to the food industry and supplies not just packaging materials, but also complete integrated processing, packaging and distribution lines and stand-alone equipment. One of its key markets is the dairy industry. But, because of increasing consolidation in the European dairy industry, Tetra Pak has only a limited and slowly dwindling number of dairy customers in each country. Similarly, aircraft manufacturers have only a few customers worldwide; half of the world's fleet is operated by just 17 large airlines.

But while B2B customers may be few in number, they often purchase in large quantities. Steel producer Corus spends several hundred million euros per year just on energy. This purchasing power makes it interesting to pursue them as individual accounts, but also increases the impact of a lost customer on the vendor's bottom line.

In addition, B2B customers are frequently geographically concentrated. Government agencies are typically located in the same city. Petrochemical companies are located near harbours and related infrastructure. Attractive tax regimes caused IT companies, such as Intel, IBM, SAP and Dell, to establish themselves in Ireland. And several high-tech firms are located close to leading universities that supply them with high-quality employees and collaborate in research. A geographical concentration of customers may result in a concentration of vendors. Sometimes one customer may be important enough to influence location decisions; for instance, manufacturers of steel drums build production facilities on the sites of petrochemical customers and paint manufacturers integrate their paint operations with the production lines of car manufacturers. Geographical concentration lowers the costs of logistics, but may also lead to a high level of mutual dependency. When General Motors threatened to close several major plants in December 2008, a large number of specialised local suppliers faced bankruptcy.

Complex buying behaviour

B2B customers buy B2B products for the operation of their businesses, which results in **buying behaviour** with several specific characteristics. The key characteristic of organisational buying behaviour is that several individuals may be involved in the buying decision, combining different backgrounds, perspectives and buying motives. The decision to buy a new-generation printing press, for example, may involve users (functional specifications), maintenance workers (ease of servicing the press), someone from finance (price and operating costs), a purchaser (relationships with potential vendors) and a business unit manager (opportunities for competitive advantage). This group is called a **buying centre** or **decision-making unit (DMU)**. It is the supplier's job to identify the buying centre members, determine their roles in the decision-making process, determine their buying motives, and translate all this information into an effective marketing approach. An effective marketing approach combines different communication means and messages targeted at all key buying centre members. When the buying centre includes people with a technical background, with much specialised expertise, for example, a vendor may have someone from R&D join the salesperson making the sales call.

Organisational buying processes may involve long, complex decisions with several stages and milestones. A McGraw-Hill study found that it takes four to four-and-a-half sales calls to close an average business sale. In the case of capital equipment sales, the sales cycle is often measured in years.[4] Vendors of products with a low buying frequency need to keep track of their customers in between purchases and monitor when customers are getting ready for a new purchase. In between purchases they can maintain the relationship with their customers by offering product upgrades, selling support services or leasing the product. This strategy results in a constant stream of revenues and establishes an ongoing relationship, thus giving the vendor an edge over the competition when it is time for a new purchase.

In addition, B2B customers may use prescribed procedures and systems, such as *approved vendor lists* that include all pre-approved vendors. To keep these approved vendors on edge, many customers require that at least three competitive offerings are compared for all major purchases, using *vendor rating systems*. In these situations, an *in supplier* (the current vendor) will use a very different marketing approach from an *out supplier* (a competitor trying to get the customer's business).

Finally, because B2B customers need the purchased products and services for their business processes, their demand is relatively inelastic. Even at high prices, they still need the materials, components and products to stay in business. But B2B customers do compare prices with the prices of acceptable alternatives. Therefore, the demand for steel is partly determined by the price for aluminium.

Market characteristics drive marketing strategy

Together, these characteristics of B2B markets determine the vendor's marketing approach. When there are only a few B2B customers, each of them representing a significant transaction volume, vendors develop close personal relationships with key DMU members. Supported by product brochures and a company website, personal selling is used to create superior value for customers. Supported by technical employees, salespeople educate customers in how to use the product to their best advantage. In these close relationships, a vendor's offering is frequently customised, while key customers are involved in the vendor's product development. In developing such close relationships, vendors emphasise their *share of customer*, rather than market share (Anderson and Narus 2003).

But not all B2B markets are like that. Vendors like Microsoft, Xerox, Hewlett-Packard and Office365 sell standardised products to a large number of customers, varying from small family-owned businesses to large globally operating firms. Branding, advertising and the internet are their key marketing instruments and prices are very competitive and closely matched to the competition. Microsoft, for example, has sold its ubiquitous Office software at premium prices for years, but this may change with the increasing use of open-source software offered for free by Google and Linux. The marketing strategies and tactics of these firms closely mirror the strategies and tactics used on consumer markets and have caused some authors to question the underlying logic of a distinction between consumer marketing and B2B marketing (Fern and Brown 1984; Wilson 2000). But even though several B2B markets closely resemble consumer markets and consumer marketing approaches may also be useful for B2B markets, this does not negate the inherent differences that often exist between both types of market. And these differences result in different marketing approaches.

In addition, one must realise that the large majority of companies (both vendors and customers) are small or medium-sized firms. These firms frequently lack the resources to develop a professional marketing or purchasing capability. A small manufacturer with 35 employees will typically not even have a marketing manager and be very much sales-oriented and focused on short-term results. But the approaches, principles and techniques described in this book can be applied by all B2B vendors. Even small firms without a marketing department stand to benefit significantly from the basic principles and approaches of B2B marketing.

1.5 Link with consumer marketing

Over the years, B2B marketing has evolved into a mature marketing discipline with a distinct identity, separate from consumer marketing. But this does not mean that these two marketing disciplines are unrelated. Indeed, several links exist between consumer marketing and B2B marketing.

Same basic concepts and tools

Consumer marketing and B2B marketing use the same basic marketing concepts, such as market segmentation, target customers and value proposition. Consumer marketing techniques are also used in B2B marketing. Relationship marketing, for example, was developed by local retailers with intimate knowledge of local customers and subsequently applied to buyer–seller relationships in B2B markets. But consumer marketing also borrows from B2B marketing: tour operators apply the buying centre concept to target different household members who influence the selection of a holiday destination. Changing market conditions also stimulate cross-fertilisation between the two disciplines. Because key decision-makers are increasingly difficult to reach, some vendors have turned to television to communicate with these hard-to-reach buying influences.

Derived demand

The demand for all B2B products ultimately depends on the demand for consumer products. B2B vendors must monitor the developments in key consumer markets and translate them into effective marketing approaches. Large manufacturers of soft drinks, fruit juices and snacks focus on marketing their brands and leave the development of new products to flavour manufacturers. Manufacturers of flavours conduct their own market research to investigate consumer preferences and translate these into exciting new products. Some B2B vendors use this link between consumer marketing and B2B marketing to target consumers directly.

MINI CASE: INTEL'S FIRST EXPERIENCE WITH CONSUMER MARKETING

When Intel started its famous Intel Inside campaign in 1990, it transformed the firm from a component supplier little known outside the PC industry into a household name. Intel's brilliant strategy consisted of convincing consumers that the performance of PCs is determined by the PC's microprocessor, thus creating a significant pull effect in the market for PCs. With this strategy, Intel engaged in consumer marketing, in addition to its regular B2B marketing efforts directed at PC manufacturers. But Intel failed to realise that consumer markets have their own rules, with a game very different from that played in B2B markets.

This lesson was driven home when Intel experienced problems with its Pentium chip. In June 1994, Intel engineers discovered an error in the new chip. Under certain conditions this error could result in much larger errors in subsequent calculations. When flaws are discovered, it is industry practice for chip manufacturers to publish errata to warn their customers. But Intel characterised the design flaw as 'minor' and 'not warranting an erratum'. It corrected the error in a future chip revision, but continued to sell hundreds of thousands of flawed chips already produced. This could still be acceptable practice in B2B markets, considering the characterisation of the design flaw as only 'minor'.

In October 1994, Doctor Thomas Nicely, a professor of mathematics, independently discovered the bug and reported it to Intel. When he received no response, he posted a message on the internet. Word spread quickly on the internet and was picked up by the industry press. On 27 November 1994, Andrew Grove, CEO of Intel, posted a response on the internet that acknowledged the problem. However, he emphasised its minimal significance and offered to replace the chip only for 'users of the Pentium processor who are engaged in work involving heavy duty scientific/floating point calculations'. This qualified offer inflamed many consumers. National newspapers like the *New York Times* started to report the story and the discussion grew progressively worse. When Intel was increasingly criticised it offered, on 20 December 1994, to replace the chip for all its end-users, 'no questions asked'.

On 17 January 1995, Intel issued a press release that mentioned a charge of $475 million against earnings for the fourth quarter of 1994 to pay for the replacement program.

Role of individuals

B2B marketing is about transactions and relationships between organisations, but organisations are organised collections of individuals. This means that all organisational buying decisions are made by individuals, who are susceptible to personal relationships and emotions (despite all corporate purchasing procedures and guidelines). Personal relationships are critical in many B2B markets. In some industries, the network of relationships is a salesperson's most valuable asset and orders are often awarded to a vendor because of the personal relationship with the sales representative. A Dutch brewery once purchased a very sophisticated access control system for its computer room, while a much simpler and cheaper solution would have sufficed. Why? Because its CEO was very impressed by a striking product demonstration at a trade show. Savvy sales representatives use insights from behavioural psychology to appeal to their customers' emotions. They realise that corporate buyers are consumers in their spare time and cannot just turn off their emotions at work.

Selling to consumers and B2B customers

Many companies sell more or less the same product to consumers and B2B customers (**dual marketing**; Biemans 2001; Quelch 1987). Car manufacturers sell their cars to consumers and fleet owners. Manufacturers of food products sell their products to consumers, institutional customers (hospitals, schools) and companies. And airlines sell seats to tourists and business travellers. The list of products that can be sold to both types of customer is almost endless, varying from paint, insurance, computers, carpets and toilet paper to energy, flowers, shampoo, financial services and cereals.

⌇⌇ **INSIGHT: B2B applications for fragrances**

Fragrances are typically associated with consumer products, marketed with famous brand names like Calvin Klein, Chanel and Dior. But because over 70 per cent of our emotions are generated by smells, fragrances are also increasingly used by B2B vendors to subliminally affect our emotions and buying habits; for instance, fragrances are used by manufacturers to de-stress and stimulate workers and by hospitals to mask unpleasant odours and replace them with pleasant ones. Other firms use fragrances to stimulate a positive 'buying reflex'. Shopping malls increase visitor numbers and customer spending by using different fragrances at different times of the day; for instance, the smell of coffee in the morning and of pastries in the afternoon. And casinos use fragrances that encourage clients to stay at the tables longer and be more adventurous.

In the continuous search for new customers and additional revenues, companies are increasingly turning to dual marketing; for instance, many theatre operators started to target businesses to use their theatres for meetings, conferences and product presentations. Most applications of dual marketing concern products that were first sold in B2B markets; when later product generations became more user-friendly and affordable, they were sold to consumers as well. Examples are computers, mobile phones, cameras and car navigation systems. Even such familiar household goods as typewriters, sewing machines, frozen foods and zips once started out as B2B products. But dual marketing also works in the other direction. IKEA, for example, actively targets small business owners with the tagline 'A better life at work'. Similarly, vacuum cleaners were developed around 1900 for households. When manufacturers discovered that they were also used to clean offices, they began to target business firms as a separate market.

Dual marketing offers the advantages of increased sales, economies of scale, opportunities for synergy (for instance, when consumers are attracted to the professional image of professional tools or kitchen appliances) and better market information. Unfortunately, there are also potential pitfalls: companies lack the knowledge required to target both markets, problems in one market spill over into the other one, or the markets are not easily separated, resulting in confused customers. Vendors that want to sell their products to both consumers and B2B customers must make two kinds of marketing decision:

1 *How will we target both markets?* Can we sell the same product in both markets or should we offer two versions of the same product? Which sales channels are most appropriate for both markets? How can we prevent overlap between both markets? Which prices can be charged in both markets? Which communication messages, media and strategies are most appropriate for both markets?

2 *How will we organise the marketing function internally?* Should we create two separate marketing departments? Which market gets priority in case of product shortages? How can we coordinate marketing decisions to create synergy? Do we need different people for each marketing group?

While the marketing literature treats consumer marketing and B2B marketing as two distinct disciplines, many companies manage to combine them by successfully applying dual marketing.

1.6 Creating value for customers

Business marketing is helping your customers to be successful by delivering superior customer value. It is not about selling products, but about helping your customers to succeed. After all, B2B customers do not need products, but they do need the value offered by these products to produce their own products and services. Value is defined as the benefits minus costs that customers receive in exchange for the purchase price. Every customer will assess whether the net benefits offered by the vendor outweigh the purchase price that has to be paid to enjoy them.

In addition, customers will compare the net value offered by alternative vendors. Thus, successful B2B marketing depends on a vendor's detailed understanding of what customers value. Successful B2B vendors understand the key success factors of their customers and are always looking for better ways to contribute to their success. Unfortunately, many B2B vendors are strongly focused on their products and cannot explain why a customer should do business with them rather than one of their competitors.

This book addresses this problem by making the notion of value creation central to all chapters. Chapter 2 focuses on the basic building block of a vendor's market knowledge: the individual customer. The chapter presents the customer-activity cycle as a useful tool to understand B2B customers and their relationship with a specific product or service. Chapter 3 expands these concepts by looking at the broader picture of markets. The chapter shows how firms combine information about customers with information about all other relevant market players and factors. The resulting market pictures are used to make marketing decisions and initiate marketing actions. For example, firms make sense of B2B markets by looking at customers, grouping them into segments and taking competitors into account. Next, the resulting market pictures are used to craft strategies aimed at creating superior value for customers. Chapter 4 shows how firms select target customers and determine the value offered to them. It combines the opportunities identified in the market with the competences of the firm, and demonstrates how firms capture their superior value in a competitive value proposition. The firm's value proposition summarises the value offered to customers and this value is deconstructed in the next four chapters. Chapter 5 discusses the products and services offered by the firm. Chapter 6 presents the major options for reaching customers; for instance, through a dedicated salesforce or through independent channel partners. Chapter 7 focuses on communicating with customers and Chapter 8 discusses how vendors set prices to capture value from customers. Because effective marketing is a continuous process, Chapter 9 discusses the processes of marketing evaluation and control. Finally, Chapter 10 combines several key concepts by describing the characteristics of a value-creating organisation and strategies to implement value creation as the firm's guiding philosophy.

Online
Learning **Centre**

When you have read this chapter, log on to the Online Learning Centre website at ***www.mcgraw-hill.co.uk/textbooks/biemans*** to explore chapter-by-chapter test questions, further reading and more online study tools.

Summary of Key Concepts

- B2B marketing is the marketing of products or services to companies, government bodies, institutions and other organisations that use them to produce their own products or services or sell them to other B2B customers.

- B2B customers can be categorised into three groups: commercial enterprises, government agencies and institutions. Each category of B2B customer has its own characteristics.

- There are three kinds of commercial enterprise: users, original equipment manufacturers and resellers. Most B2B customers are users who use B2B products for the production of their own products.

- B2B products can be classified into: raw and processed materials, component parts, MRO supplies, capital goods, tools and accessories, services and systems. Each type of B2B product has specific characteristics and requires a different marketing approach.

- The nature of B2B marketing is determined by the nature of B2B markets, which have certain characteristics that set them apart from most consumer markets.

- The most important characteristic of B2B markets is that the demand for B2B products is derived from the demand for downstream products. Derived demand complicates B2B marketing, especially for firms near the beginning of the value chain.

- Other key characteristics of most B2B markets are joint demand, a limited number of customers and complex buying behaviour (multi-person decision making).

- Not all B2B markets have these characteristics. Products such as office supplies, insurance and mobile phones are sold to a large number of B2B customers and the marketing of these products often closely resembles the marketing of consumer products. But when these products are sold to large B2B customers, different approaches may be required (such as long-term contracts and automatic online ordering).

- B2B marketing is related to consumer marketing because (a) both use the same basic concepts and tools, (b) they are linked through derived demand, (c) organisational buying behaviour is done by individuals who may act like consumers, and (d) the same product may be sold to both consumers and organisations.

- All B2B marketing has the same key objective: to create superior value for customers. This concept of value creation drives all major B2B marketing decisions and actions.

> **? Key Terms**
>
> B2B customers, p. 8   Derived demand, p. 16
> B2B marketing, p. 5   Direct customers, p. 17
> B2B products, p. 10   Downstream customers, p. 17
> Buying behaviour, p. 19   Dual marketing, p. 23
> Buying centre, p. 20   Joint demand, p. 19
> Decision-making unit (DMU), p. 20   Original equipment manufacturers, p. 8

Discussion questions

1 Some people think that the distinction between consumer marketing and B2B marketing does not make much sense. They feel that the marketing discipline is better served by focusing on the similarities between the two areas. Can you provide reasons for this position? Do you agree?

2 The purchasing behaviour of organisations is usually more rational than the purchasing behaviour of consumers. Why is that? Describe two specific situations where an organisation's purchasing behaviour is expected to be dominated by emotional buying motives. How can a vendor effectively deal with this?

3 The purchasing behaviour of institutions and government bodies is becoming increasingly professional. Do you think that their purchasing behaviour will become indistinguishable from the purchasing behaviour of commercial firms? Justify your answer.

4 Vendors of B2B products typically find it more difficult than vendors of consumer products to identify customer needs. What are the reasons for this? How can this problem be solved?

5 A key problem in B2B marketing is dealing with downstream customers. Why is this so difficult for most B2B firms? How can firms initiate a marketing programme aimed at downstream customers?

6 B2B marketing frequently borrows concepts and techniques from consumer marketing. Describe several concepts and techniques from consumer marketing that have been (or can be) applied by B2B firms. Explain, for all of these concepts and techniques, whether they can also be used by small B2B firms.

7 The marketing literature uses several terms, such as business marketing, business-to-business marketing, industrial marketing and organisational marketing. What are the advantages and disadvantages of each of these terms? Which term do you prefer? Why?

8 Imagine that a manufacturer of beds wants to sell its beds to both hotels and hospitals. What are the major differences between the marketing approaches for each market?

9 Some products that are sold to both business customers and consumers originate in consumer markets, while others were first sold to business customers. What are the advantages of starting to sell business products to consumers? What are the potential pitfalls? What are the advantages of starting to sell consumer products also to business customers? What are the potential pitfalls?

10 Several B2B firms try to improve their marketing by hiring marketing managers with much experience in consumer marketing. In which situations do you think that this strategy will work? In which situations will this strategy probably turn out to be not very effective?

Further reading

Anderson, James C. and James A. Narus (2003) Selectively pursuing more of your customer's business, *MIT Sloan Management Review*, 44(3): 42–49.

Biemans, Wim G. (2001) Designing a dual marketing program, *European Management Journal*, 19(6): 670–677.

Fern, Edward F. and James J. Brown (1984) The industrial/consumer marketing dichotomy: a case of insufficient justification, *Journal of Marketing*, 48(2): 68–77.

References

Anderson, James C. and James A. Narus (2003) Selectively pursuing more of your customer's business, *MIT Sloan Management Review*, 44(3): 42–49.

Biemans, Wim G. (2001) Designing a dual marketing program, *European Management Journal*, 19(6): 670–677.

Fern, Edward F. and James J. Brown (1984) The industrial/consumer marketing dichotomy: a case of insufficient justification, *Journal of Marketing*, 48(2): 68–77.

McCarthy, Michael S. and Donald G. Norris (1999) Improving competitive position using branded ingredients, *Journal of Product & Brand Management*, 8(4): 267–283.

Quelch, John A. (1987) Why not exploit dual marketing?, *Business Horizons*, 30(1): 52–60.

Simon, Hermann and Karl-Heinz Sebastian (1995) Ingredient branding – Reift ein Junger Markentypus [Is a new type of branding being used]? *Absatzwirtschaft*, (6): 42–48.

Wilson, Dominic E. (2000) Why divide consumer and organizational buying behaviour?, *European Journal of Marketing*, 34(7): 780–796.

Notes

[1] http://findarticles.com/p/articles/mi_qa3698/is_200610/ai_n17196136.

[2] www.guardian.co.uk/technology/2008/jan/05/computing.egovernment.

[3] www.smh.com.au/articles/2004/04/30/1083224588493.html.

[4] Collins, Michael (1996) Breaking into the big leagues, *American Demographics*, January: 24.

PART 02
Making Sense of Customers and Markets

CHAPTER 02

Understanding B2B customers

Introduction

The key to successful B2B marketing is a detailed understanding of B2B customers. B2B customers buy B2B products and services to create value for their own customers. Successful vendors help B2B customers to be successful with their customers. This requires an intimate knowledge of B2B customers and how they use the vendor's products and services to create value for their customers. A useful tool to gain this detailed understanding is the customer-activity cycle, which maps the relationship customers have with the vendor's product. The customer-activity cycle describes all customer activities related to the product, starting with need identification and ending with disposing of the product. Thus, the customer-activity cycle is broader than the customer's buying process and can be used to identify opportunities for value creation.

This chapter starts by defining the concept of customer value as all benefits minus costs that the customer receives in exchange for the purchase price. It discusses the various components of benefits and costs and explains how customers use the concept of value to determine the most attractive offering. Next, it describes the customer-activity cycle and presents the organisational buying process in greater detail. Organisational buying decisions are often made by buying centres, consisting of several individuals, each with their own background and buying motives. The chapter also discusses how organisational purchasing is becoming increasingly professional and efficient, especially because of the internet. But the customer-activity cycle goes beyond the traditional purchasing process. After the vendor's product has been installed, the customer-activity cycle continues with the use, maintenance and repair, expansion and upgrading, and disposal stages. Each of these stages is discussed and may present opportunities for innovative vendors.

2.1 Customers want value to help them create value

Most B2B firms use a product-oriented perspective on B2B marketing and selling: their B2B customers offer products to their customers and, to manufacture these products, they need all kinds of materials, components and capital goods (derived demand). A manufacturer of golf carts, for example, needs a large number of products to manufacture them, such as engines, shock absorbers, batteries, chassis, braking systems, steering assemblies, wheels, body panels and transmissions, but also machinery for welding, roll forming, automatic assembly and painting. Numerous vendors offer the various components and manufacturing machinery that are needed to manufacture golf carts. But successful B2B vendors realise that the core of business marketing is to help your customers to be successful in creating superior value for their customers. These vendors use a value perspective on B2B marketing: they create value for their customers by helping them to offer superior value to the customers' customers. Thus, a vendor of components and systems for golf carts understands the needs and requirements of golfers (the downstream customers), and thus what makes golf cart manufacturers (the immediate customers) successful, and translates these insights into superior value offered to golf cart manufacturers. Using a product perspective, a B2B vendor would ask which products the customer needs to manufacture their own products. Using a value perspective, a B2B vendor uses their knowledge of how the customer creates superior value for their customers to identify opportunities to help the customer be more successful in this creation of value (Figure 2.1). When he was still Vice-President and General Manager of GE Plastics, Jeffrey Immelt concluded that GE Plastics' most important product is 'customer productivity': 'Selling is dead. These days, account managers have to be customer-productivity experts. That's what we're really selling' (Wiersema 1996: 93–94). And Swedish Tetra Pak proclaims succinctly on its website: 'Our business is making your company more profitable' (www.tetrapak.com).

The starting point: customer needs

Successful business marketers understand the needs of their customers and are able to translate these needs into superior value. There are three types of **customer needs** (Thompson 2000):

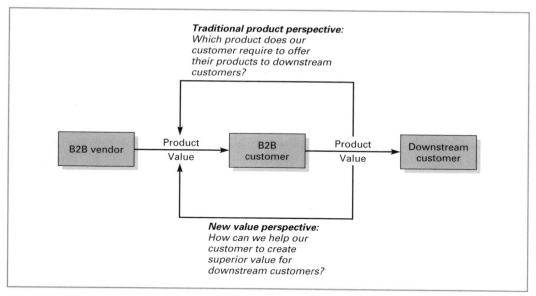

FIGURE 2.1 B2B marketing: product versus value perspective

- *Basic needs* are the basic requirements that each vendor needs to meet to be in business (such as answering the phone and having a reliable system for delivering goods and services). Doing the basics poorly will drive customers away. Doing them extremely well, however, will not significantly increase customer satisfaction or cause competitors' customers to switch vendors. A firm's first priority should be to improve the must haves for which the firm does not meet customers' minimum expectations or which are performed below the industry average of all successful competitors.

- *Satisfier needs* are needs that a customer would like to see fulfilled but which do not impact customer buying behaviour (such as leather chairs in the lobby and sparkling clean washrooms). Offering these nice to haves is the least important: doing them well puts a smile on the customer's face but does not lead to higher customer satisfaction. Many firms mistakenly invest a lot of resources in needs that are satisfiers and do not impact buying behaviour.

- *Attractor needs* are needs that, if performed best in the industry, deliver such superior value to customers that they are willing to switch vendors (such as efficient online ordering procedures, which saves costs for the customer). These are the needs that, assuming that the basic needs are met, deserve the highest priority from management and hold the greatest potential.

Because customers get used to certain levels of performance and competitors continuously improve their own performance, the classification of needs into basics, satisfiers and attractors is continuously changing. In 2000, efficient online ordering was an attractor in many industries, but nowadays it is often considered to be a basic need.

> $\mathcal{G}\mathcal{J}$ **INSIGHT: Many B2B firms do not know what their customers want**
>
> A customer has many interactions with vendors and each interaction serves as a moment of truth. At each moment of truth, the vendor must deliver the expected level of performance or run the risk of losing business. Many B2B marketers are convinced that they know what their customers want. But do they really?
>
> Both IBM and a large commercial bank wanted to understand and ensure customer satisfaction regarding the accuracy of their financial statements and invoices. Both companies assumed that customers would only be interested in having the statements and invoices mention correct prices. But when they asked customers about the ideal invoice or statement, the results were eye-opening.
>
> The bank's customers valued correct charges, but mentioned many additional attributes of accuracy. According to their perception, for example, an accurate statement reflects the customer's full relationship. So, rather than receiving multiple statements, customers want one overall statement that reflects all transactions with the bank. In addition, an accurate statement must have the same cut-off date for all charges appearing on the statement so that customers can determine their complete financial status as of a single day.
>
> Similarly, IBM's customers wanted invoices that facilitate ease of reconciliation by the customer and that match the original deal. Current prices are irrelevant: invoices should include the price that was quoted originally. These examples once again show that managers are quick to think that they know their customer; but they should beware of thinking on the customer's behalf. There is just no substitute for the voice of the customer!
>
> *Source*: Thompson (2000).

The final result: superior customer value

Insight into customer needs must be translated into superior value offered to a specified group of customers. A key marketing principle states that customers are interested not so much in a vendor's products, but in the value they derive from using the products. Basically, customers hire products to perform a specified function (Christensen et al. 2005). Value is the difference between the perceived benefits and costs (net benefits) that a customer receives in exchange for the purchase price (Anderson and Narus 1998). These benefits may be derived from three different sources:

- *The vendor's product or service*, such as quality, safety, ease of use, design, ease of installation, modularity, existence of upgrades, durability, sturdiness, speed, power, compatibility with other products and estimated operating costs. Services offer similar benefits. A customer looking for a transportation company will be interested in its speed, flexibility, reliability and the possibility of checking the status of orders online.
- *The vendor's employees*, who have characteristics such as friendliness, empathy, flexibility, communication skills, technical expertise, problem solution skills

and integrity. In many industries, personal relationships are of critical importance and make the difference between winning or losing an order.

- *The vendor's organisation*, which offers benefits because of its geographical location, local presence, certificated business processes, help with product development, experience with partnering, and favourable ordering and payment systems. The insurance industry periodically measures the 'ease of doing business' (EDB) of insurance carriers, which is a critical variable for agents representing them. EDB in the insurance industry encompasses criteria such as: understands and acts on the needs of agency personnel, is responsive in underwriting, is flexible in underwriting, provides accurate, timely policy services, and has effective user-friendly technology.[1] Some organisational benefits may actually be delivered by the vendor's business partners; for instance, fast problem solving and speedy delivery of replacement parts may be taken care of by local distributors.

Whatever the source of the benefits offered to customers, vendors must realise that what counts are the benefits as *perceived* by the customer. Different customers value different elements of a vendor's offering and, even when they value the same elements, they may perceive that value differently. While this complicates research into customer needs, it also creates opportunities for effective market segmentation.

The costs from the value equation refer to all costs that the customer must incur to enjoy the benefits from the vendor's offering. Some customers only look at the offering's purchase price or its direct costs, but more sophisticated customers calculate all costs involved in acquiring, using and disposing of the product. The **total cost of ownership** encompasses (Ellram 1993):

- *Pre-transaction costs*, which include all costs that are incurred before placing the order. Frequently overlooked pre-transaction costs are the costs of identifying and qualifying vendors, visiting vendors, educating vendors regarding the firm's systems and expectations, and adapting to the systems, styles and delivery methods of new vendors. Vendor selection and the addition of a new vendor are often incorrectly considered to be 'free'.

- *Transaction costs*, which consist of all costs of ordering and receiving the product, such as the costs of preparing and placing the order, following up on the order, expediting the order, receiving, matching receiving data to the invoice, paying the bill, inspecting the product, and returning products. Especially the costs of preparing the purchase order and correcting incorrect documents are frequently forgotten.

- *Post-transaction costs*, or all costs that occur after the purchased product is owned by the firm. Some of these costs may not occur until years later when the purchased product is modified or disposed of, and are thus frequently forgotten. Post-transaction costs include the costs of field failures, defective finished goods rejected before sale, repair and replacement in the field, and the costs of maintenance and repair. Some post-transaction costs may even occur further down the supply chain; for instance, problems with the customer's product may cause loss of goodwill or damage to the firm's reputation. These costs may be considerable; for production machines the post-transaction costs are typically more than 50 per cent of total costs.

MINI CASE: ABB'S AZIPOD® OFFERS SIGNIFICANT BENEFITS FOR CUSTOMERS

Source: ABB. Used with permission.

In 1990, ABB Marine launched the Azipod® electric propulsion system for ships. The Azipod® unit is fixed outside the ship and combines the functions of a propulsion motor, main propellor, rudder and stern thruster. These traditionally separately installed units are no longer needed, which saves machinery space and weight on board and increases design flexibility. The Azipod® systems have been shown to reduce fuel consumption in cruise ships by about 10 per cent when compared to diesel-electric propulsion systems with a conventional shaft-line arrangement (which represents savings of approximately 40 tons of fuel per week!). In 2004, ShinNihonkai, Japan's leading ferry operator, bought two ferries equipped with the Azipod®. The company reported fuel savings of 20 per cent, as well as 15 per cent more transportation capacity, compared with ships of a similar size using diesel engines.

In addition, the Azipod® can revolve 360 degrees, which significantly increases manoeuvrability and allows large cruise ships to enter small harbours without the help of towing boats. Because the Azipod® eliminates the stern thrusters, external shaft supports and rudders, it reduces vibration and noise levels, which improves passenger comfort. After the installation on board the cruise ship MS *Elation* in 1998, the benefits of the Azipod® propulsion system were so convincing that the podded propulsion system became a standard for most new cruise ships. Azipod® systems are now used on nearly all large cruise ships, but also on ferries, yachts, rescue boats, arctic tankers and icebreakers. Almost 20 years after its introduction, Azipod® is a well-established product, with approximately 4,500,000 accumulated hours of operation.

Vendors must offer **superior customer value**, in the sense of superior to competitive offerings. In evaluating a vendor's offering, B2B customers will always make two comparisons. To determine the vendor's 'value for money' or 'net value', they will compare the value of the vendor's offering with the price they have to pay to obtain the offering. To identify the best deal available to them they will compare a vendor's net value with that of the next-best alternative. These comparisons are also captured in the following value equation:

$$(\text{Value}_V - \text{Price}_V) > (\text{Value}_A - \text{Price}_A)$$

In this equation, Value_V and Price_V represent the value and price of a particular vendor's offering, while Value_A and Price_A are the value and price of the next-best-alternative offering. Although many vendors present their offering as unique, there is *always* an alternative. The alternative may be an offering from a competitor that uses a similar solution for the customer's problem, the most recent offering from the same vendor, the customer's decision to make the product themselves or the customer's decision to maintain the status quo (that is, to do nothing). The difference between value and price represents the customer's *incentive to buy*. It is essential to realise that raising or lowering the price of an offering does not change the value of that offering to the customer, but only changes the customer's incentive to buy the offering. Thus, price does *not* create value, but should reflect value (see Chapter 8).

In practice, customers will always introduce price into the discussion. Many salespersons are frustrated by customers complaining that their product is too expensive. They complain that their product is a commodity and the only strategy available to them is to compete on price. But for most vendors, this is not a viable long-term strategy. There can be only one vendor with the lowest price! Discussions about price are part of the game between buyers and sellers. Vendors who cannot explain the value of their offering in terms that matter to customers will be forced to compete on price. And lower prices directly impact the firm's profitability. Customers only select on price when they perceive the offerings from alternative vendors to be more or less identical. Successful vendors deal with this situation by demonstrating the superior value of their offering (see Chapter 4). But this requires customer research to measure the value of their offering to specific customer segments.

2.2 The customer-activity cycle

Effective B2B vendors understand how the value delivered through their products and services contributes to their customers' value-creation processes. Thus, their focus is not just on how their customers buy their products, but also on how their customers experience problems and use the value offered by products as a solution to these problems. This process is captured by the *customer-activity cycle*. Every B2B customer-activity cycle consists of three broad stages: (1) the customer decides what to do, (2) the customer does it, and (3) the customer keeps it going (Vandermerwe 2000). Whether a customer buys office supplies, catering services or a turn-key process installation, all activities can be categorised according to these three categories. For a hospital purchasing medical equipment, for example, the pre-, during and post-stages of the customer-activity cycle include: (1) defining the need for medical equipment, selecting and evaluating potential vendors, and purchasing the medical equipment from the preferred vendor; (2) having the equipment delivered and installed, and using the equipment; and (3) maintaining and repairing the equipment, purchasing related products and services, upgrading the equipment through new software releases, and disposing of the equipment when it becomes obsolete. At the heart of the customer-activity cycle is the customer's decision making, which encompasses the decision-making process, the people involved, and their motivations and interactions. Combining this basic concept of three stages with a more detailed description of customer activities and the customer's decision-making process results in the 'hub-and-spoke' model of the customer-activity cycle presented in Figure 2.2.

Each **customer-activity cycle** starts with a definition of the problem to be solved. A problem may arise because of internal factors (for instance, a piece of equipment has become obsolete and needs to be replaced, or new parts or materials are required to manufacture a new product) or external factors (for example, when a competing

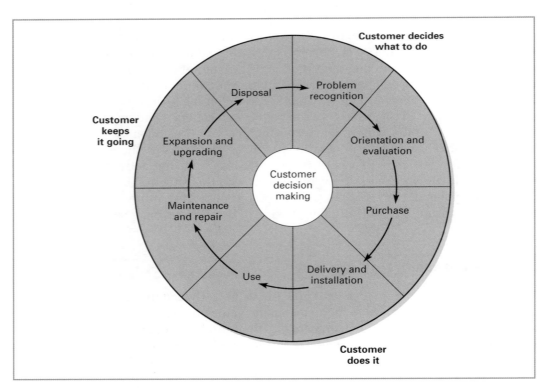

FIGURE 2.2 The customer-activity cycle

Source: Adapted from Vandermerwe (2000).

vendor launches an attractive offering or the customer is no longer satisfied with the performance of the current vendor). Current vendors (the so-called **in suppliers**) have an advantage because they already have a relationship with the customer and are thus in a better position to learn about new opportunities at an early stage. Next, the identified problem is translated into specifications of the required product. Functional specifications describe what the product needs to do, while technical specifications define product characteristics in great detail. Again, current vendors have an advantage because they may be able to influence product specifications in a favourable direction.

However, B2B vendors must be aware that B2B customers do not always have to purchase the products that they need. An alternative option is to make the required products themselves. Henry Ford used to make all components and material needed to build his famous Model T; he even bred his own sheep because he needed the wool to produce the car's upholstery. Multinational companies such as IBM and Philips used to proudly proclaim that they produced everything needed for the production of their products. But, with improved flexible manufacturing techniques, the availability of cheap vendors and strategic thinking in terms of key competencies, these firms have reconsidered their approach. Nowadays, the **make-or-buy decision** is one of the key strategic decisions a firm has to make.

A make-or-buy decision is usually triggered by developments in the firm's environment; for instance, increasing price competition forces a firm to reduce costs, which may be achieved by using external sources for specific products or components. Basically, firms will decide in favour of in-house production of all items and processes that are critical to the success of their product, require specialised design and manufacturing skills or equipment, or belong to the firm's core competencies (either current or planned). All other items and processes may be outsourced to external vendors – **out suppliers**. Sometimes, this make-or-buy decision is very straightforward. Processes such as catering, security and cleaning are frequently outsourced. For other items and processes the make-or-buy decision may be quite complex, with its outcome depending on a host of factors, such as the costs of in-house production, availability of excess plant capacity, need for control over production, availability of capable vendors, need for a second source, and availability of expertise.

For many make-or-buy decisions the key variable is cost, but this goes beyond a comparison of production and purchase costs. When a firm decides to make a product, the costs include incremental inventory-carrying costs, direct labour costs, incremental factory overhead costs, delivered purchased materials costs, and incremental purchasing costs. Similarly, when it decides to purchase a product, the costs encompass purchase price, transportation costs, handling and inspection costs, incremental purchasing costs, and incremental quality control costs.

Apart from short-term cost savings or quality improvements, make-or-buy decisions also have long-term strategic consequences. The decision to buy an item from an outside source may result in dependence on a dominant vendor or the loss of essential skills. In some cases, it may even contribute to the creation of a competitor. Make-or-buy decisions should not only address short-term cost reductions but also include these long-term effects on the firm's strategic market position.

2.3 The organisational buying process

While consumer products are bought by individuals or households in a relatively short period of time, buying processes for business products may be complex, extensive and involve several individuals and procedures. The **organisational buying process** consists of a series of activities that can be grouped into three stages (Figure 2.3):

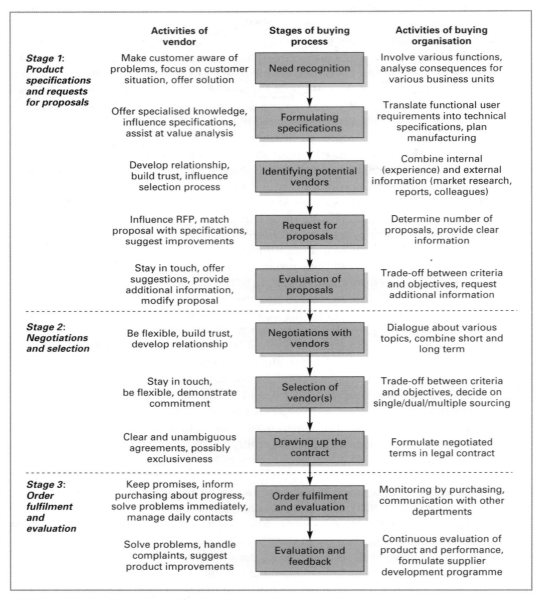

FIGURE 2.3 Stages of the organisational buying process

1 *Product specifications and request for proposals*, where product specifications are formulated and vendors invited to submit proposals.

2 *Negotiations and selection*, where the organisation negotiates with potential vendors and selects the most promising one.

3 *Order fulfilment and evaluation*, where the order is fulfilled and the vendor's performance evaluated.

Stage 1: Product specifications and request for proposals

The organisational buying process starts with the buyer acknowledging and defining the need for a product or service. Such a need may be caused by internal factors (when the currently used product has become obsolete and needs to be replaced or when new parts are required for a newly developed product) or the result of external factors (when a competing vendor makes an interesting offer or when the buying organisation is dissatisfied with the current vendor's performance). Depending on the situation, the need for a product may be recognised by a purchasing agent or the intended user of the product. Current vendors have an advantage because they already have a relationship with the customer and are thus in a better position to learn about new opportunities at an early stage.

Next, the buying organisation translates the defined need into specifications of the required product. Functional specifications describe what the product needs to do, while technical specifications define the product's characteristics in great detail. Again, current vendors have an advantage because they may be able to influence product specifications in a favourable direction. Subsequently, the buying organisation identifies a number of potential vendors. The organisation's purchasing department plays a key role at this stage because of their knowledge of and relationships with potential vendors. The product's intended users and other customers may also provide useful information at this stage; for instance, trade-sponsored online communities are a valuable tool to obtain objective information about customers' experiences with products and vendors (similar to the book reviews posted by consumers on Amazon.com). Many business customers use *approved vendor lists* that list all vendors per product specification that meet the customer's requirements and are accepted as vendors (some organisations also use *preferred vendor lists*). Many business customers publish their approved vendor lists on the internet. Approved vendor lists restrict the number of vendors and thus reduce costs. However, they are also said to stifle competition, which may increase costs in the long run. For potential vendors, the first priority is to be included on the list. Information about the customer's selection criteria, the evaluation process and the people and departments involved help a vendor to design the appropriate strategy.

After a number of potential vendors have been identified, a limited number of them are asked to submit a detailed proposal. The *request for proposals* (RFP) contains detailed product specifications and background information. Potential vendors must realise that a proposal is an important means of communication. A professional layout, clear language and explicit link between required specifications and offered characteristics contribute to success. All proposals are compared and discussed internally. For standardised products, a vendor can usually be selected based on the submitted proposals. For more complex products, one or more vendors may be asked to provide additional information. Whatever the situation, vendors are advised to focus on the customer's requirements, rather than their own products.

Stage 2: Negotiations and selection

When several vendors appear to fit the bill, negotiations will follow about prices, discounts and delivery terms. For more complex products, these negotiations also include the vendor's technical support, installation, training, maintenance and upgrades. Vendor negotiations are typically directed by purchasing personnel, but may include people from other departments such as manufacturing, logistics and maintenance. Potential vendors must be flexible, build trust and develop a relationship with the customer. A list of reference projects or customers is often important at this stage.

Eventually, the most suitable vendor is selected. Customers that do not want to depend on one vendor (*single sourcing*) may select several vendors and award each vendor a part of their business (*multiple sourcing*). Some customers work with multiple vendors, but always use just one vendor for each manufacturing plant (*multiple single sourcing*). This results in economies of scale and stimulates competition among the selected vendors. The results from the negotiations are formalised in a contract. Depending on the nature of the product and the buying situation, such a contract may refer to a one-time delivery or regulate prices and deliveries for a number of years. In the latter case, the contract can usually be terminated each year.

Stage 3: Order fulfilment and evaluation

After the contract has been signed, the customer's purchasing department needs to ensure that the vendor lives up to the contract. Inadequate vendor performance hurts the relationship and reduces the chances of future business. When problems occur, vendors should inform their customers as soon as possible and help identify an acceptable solution. Many B2B customers use comprehensive vendor rating systems to evaluate the vendor's performance. In case of inadequate performance, the customer may start looking for an alternative source or award a larger percentage of its business to a competing vendor. Customers may provide their vendors with continuous feedback because this helps them to initiate corrective measures and improvement programmes.

2.4 Organisational decision making

Organisational buying behaviour may be very complex and vendors need detailed information to design effective marketing and sales strategies. Vendors must: (1) identify the key individuals involved in the buying decision; (2) determine each individual's role and influence during the buying process; (3) determine each individual's buying motives and communication preferences; and (4) translate all this information into an effective selling approach.

Buying centre composition: who is involved?

One of the key pieces of information that a vendor needs is information about who is involved in the organisational buying process. Many organisational buying decisions require input from various parts of the organisation and are thus conducted by a group of individuals. All individuals involved in the buying decision are called the **buying centre** or **decision-making unit** (DMU). A buying centre is not a fixed organisational unit, but a loose structure to deal with a specific purchasing situation. However, large multinational firms frequently establish formal buying teams for specific product categories. Buying centres may also include members that are not part of the buying organisation; for instance, firms purchasing a new telephone exchange often hire telecommunication consulting firms to help them identify the best offering. Other examples of outside buying centre members are engineering firms, architects, insurance firms, government agencies, test laboratories and other customers in non-competitive industries. Even competitors may be part of the buying centre for non-strategic purchases that benefit the whole industry.

Roles and influences: how are they involved?

Having identified the members of a buying centre, a vendor needs to determine each member's role and influence during the buying process. Buying centre members play one or more roles, defined as follows (Webster and Wind 1972):

- *Initiator*: first recognises the need, opportunity or problem that could be solved with a purchase and thus sets the buying process in motion.

- *Buyer*: is formally responsible (but may have limited authority) for selecting vendors and consummating the purchase. Responsibilities include evaluating vendors, requesting proposals, conducting negotiations, drawing up the contract and placing the order. Buyers are usually purchasing officers.

- *User*: will use the product to be purchased. Users tend to have little authority and often also play the role of initiator. In addition, they are frequently involved in specifying minimum performance requirements that the product must meet. The influence of users varies from minor to major.

- *Influencer*: does not select the product or vendor but significantly influences the decision made, for instance by providing specifications or evaluation criteria. Examples of influencers are product developers, quality control engineers, manufacturing employees and external experts.

- *Decider*: makes the actual buying decision by ultimately approving all or any part of the buying decision; whether to buy, what to buy, how to buy and where to buy.

- *Gatekeeper*: controls or filters the flow of information regarding products and vendors to members of the buying centre, for instance by controlling salespeople's meetings with buying centre members. Purchasing officers frequently play the role of gatekeeper.

It is important to distinguish between **buying centre roles** and individuals. One individual may play several roles and one role may be played by several individuals. In a large firm, for example, the buying centre for a complex product may be comprehensive, including representatives from several departments, each playing a distinctive role. But in a small firm buying a relatively simple product, the buying centre consists of just one or two individuals playing multiple roles.

Vendors must also determine each individual's influence and power within the buying centre. There is no correlation between an individual's functional background and their role or influence. Instead, a person's power depends on factors such as the type of purchase, the time pressure involved, the number of alternatives to be considered and the perceived risk of making a wrong decision. Power within a buying centre may be the result of an individual's hierarchical position, expertise or personality. It is often very difficult and time-consuming to develop an understanding of the relative positions of power and the changing interactions and relationships between buying centre members during the buying process. But simply drafting a table that lists the key individuals involved as well as their roles in the buying decision often goes a long way to understanding the customer's buying behaviour.

Buying motives: how do they decide?

 To a large extent, **buying motives** can be derived from each buying centre member's functional area. Table 2.1 provides an illustrative example. Usually, each buying centre member is interested in just one (or only a few) of the benefits offered by the vendor. But organisational buying decisions are not made by organisations or departments, but by individuals. And each individual has their own background, experience, risk aversion, personality and perception of how organisational objectives are best realised. This means that buying centre motives are partly related to the buying task at hand and partly caused by each individual's background and personality. It also implies that buying motives are not always rational. Even though an organisation needs products for rational economic purposes, emotional motives

TABLE 2.1 Functional areas and their key concerns

Functional area	Key concerns in buying decision
Purchasing	Obtaining the lowest possible price at acceptable quality levels; maintaining good relationships with vendors; standardisation of purchased items to realise purchasing efficiencies
Design and development	Name and reputation of vendor; especially the ability of vendors to meet design specifications; flexibility to meet specific requirements
Manufacturing	Reliable delivery of purchased items in order to ensure uninterrupted manufacturing; standardisation of purchased items to increase manufacturing efficiency
Quality control	Assurance that purchased items meet formulated specifications, tolerances and governmental regulations
Maintenance	Degree to which purchased items are compatible with existing facilities and equipment; maintenance services offered by vendors
Sales/marketing	Impact of purchased items on the attractiveness of the company's products to customers
Finance/accounting	Effects of purchases on the company's cash flow, balance sheet and income statement; differences between costs and budgets; feasibility of make-or-buy and lease options over outright purchasing
General management	Contribution of the purchased items to the firm's competitive position

may influence the buying decision; for instance, the personal relationship between purchaser and salesperson often strongly influences the outcome of the buying decision. In the words of a key decision-maker: 'I know that buying from vendor A, instead of from vendor B, will cost €50,000 extra per year, but I'd rather have lunch with the salesperson from vendor A than the one from vendor B!' This is not surprising: buying centre members are individuals and, like everybody else, they are also susceptible to emotions. A customer's decision-makers may present their buying decision as rational, but that is only a rationalisation after the fact. In reality, organisational buying decisions are influenced by all kinds of emotional motives.

✍ INSIGHT: Organisational buying behaviour may be less rational than it appears

Customers often present their buying behaviour to vendors as a very rational process; for instance, many customers explain to salespeople that they use a *weighted factor score method* to determine the best vendor. With this method, the customer (1) identifies the criteria to be used in the buying decision, (2) determines the relative weights to be assigned to all criteria, (3) determines for each vendor under consideration the score on all identified criteria, and (4) multiplies the scores with the weights, which are then summed to identify the best vendor. An example is provided below.

Criterion	Weight	Vendor A	Vendor B	Vendor C
Quality	0.3	$8 \times 0.3 = 2.4$	$7 \times 0.3 = 2.1$	$6 \times 0.3 = 1.8$
Conformance to specifications	0.2	$8 \times 0.2 = 1.6$	$8 \times 0.2 = 1.6$	$6 \times 0.2 = 1.2$
After-sales support	0.1	$5 \times 0.1 = 0.5$	$7 \times 0.1 = 0.7$	$6 \times 0.1 = 0.6$
Reliability	0.1	$7 \times 0.1 = 0.7$	$7 \times 0.1 = 0.7$	$7 \times 0.1 = 0.7$
Just-in-time delivery	0.1	$5 \times 0.1 = 0.5$	$7 \times 0.1 = 0.7$	$6 \times 0.1 = 0.6$
Price	0.2	$6 \times 0.2 = 1.2$	$7 \times 0.2 = 1.4$	$6 \times 0.2 = 1.2$
Total score		**6.9**	**7.2**	**6.1**

In this particular case, the customer uses six criteria to identify the best vendor out of three alternatives: A, B and C. Of these criteria, quality, conformance to specifications and price are considered to be the most important. Vendors A and B offer a high-quality product with good conformance to specifications. Vendor C's offering is rather average on almost all criteria. Using this method, the customer would select vendor B. Vendor A would be given the message that its offering is quite similar to vendor B's in terms of the most important criteria, but its after-sales service and just-in-time delivery are inadequate. As a result, vendor A decides to invest in improving its after-sales support and just-in-time delivery performance.

But this method appears to be much more rational and objective than it really is. To understand this, consider the following questions: How were the six criteria determined? And what about the weights for each criterion? And the scores for each vendor? All too often the presented results from a rational weighted factor score method hide a messy, emotional buying process. Often, what *really* happened is the following. Company procedures required the buying

▶

centre members to consider three alternatives. But they already knew that vendor B was their favourite vendor. To comply with their organisation's procedures, they filled out the table for the three vendors under consideration and changed the weights and vendor scores until vendor B ended up as the best alternative. While the very rational weighted factor score method appears to be very objective, it was only used to comply with company procedures and justify a buying decision that was strongly influenced by emotional motives. It is not a description of a rational buying process, but an after-the-fact rationalisation of very messy and emotional decision making.

Buying situations

In practice, organisational buying behaviour depends on the nature of the buying situation. There are three basic **buying situations**: straight rebuy, modified rebuy and new task (Robinson et al. 1967).

Straight rebuy

The majority of organisational purchases are straight rebuys: the product has been bought before, the requirements are the same and there is little need to evaluate alternative offerings. The buying process is optimised, frequently using established buying routines; for instance, when a manufacturer purchases roller bearings for the production of motorcycles it probably has a long-term contract with a supplier. To increase efficiency, the manufacturer of roller bearings may use the internet to link with the motorcycle manufacturer's production facilities so that bearings can be delivered just-in-time. Another example is when purchasing selects a vendor from a list of pre-approved vendors. In straight rebuys, the selection criteria are clear and there is a strong disposition to do business with specific vendors. Straight rebuys usually involve standard products that are bought frequently. But this depends on the size of the organisation: the purchase of a number of notebook computers may be a straight rebuy for a large manufacturing firm but a new task for a small consulting agency. Current and pre-approved vendors have a clear advantage and invest in efficient ordering and payment procedures to increase the customer's switching costs.

Modified rebuy

In other situations, the buying organisation thinks it is beneficial to re-evaluate alternatives. For example, because of dissatisfaction with the current vendor, an alternative vendor presents an attractive offer, new vendors have entered the market or product requirements have changed. In a modified rebuy, the customer collects information about alternative offerings and evaluates them together with the current vendor's offering to identify the most attractive option. With modified rebuys, the purchase is important enough to warrant a more extensive buying process. But because the customer is already familiar with the product, information about alternative offerings can be collected relatively quickly. Modified rebuys are also used to test if the current vendor still has the most attractive offering. Whatever the reason, in modified rebuys the current vendor must go to great lengths to demonstrate the superior value of their offering. Competing vendors will try to lure the customer away with all kinds of attractive offerings. A vendor of waste water treatment equipment found that customers building new plants often prefer to do business with their current vendors. Even though they compare different vendors, they recognise the advantages of staying with their current vendor. A customer building a new plant with the same waste water treatment equipment can train its personnel on the existing installation. Some customers stick to their current vendors despite the problems they have experienced with them. According to their reasoning, it is better to deal with familiar problems for which solutions have already been identified than with totally new problems.

New task

The most extensive buying process occurs with new tasks: the customer has no experience purchasing the product and requires extensive problem solving to identify the most attractive offering. New tasks occur when the customer needs new parts or materials (*judgemental new task*), but also when the decision is extremely important to the firm (*strategic new task*). Because the buying criteria are unclear, the buying process is often dominated by one or a few individuals. An example of a new task is a manufacturing firm purchasing an industrial robot to perform a function that is currently done manually. Current vendors of other products who are also able to offer the new product are at an advantage because they are already familiar with the organisation's structure, buying procedures and decision-making processes and may already have relationships with key decision-makers.

> *⌒⌒* **INSIGHT: European rail companies face new task in buying new-generation fast trains**
>
> European travellers increasingly prefer trains above airplanes for trips between cities that require up to four to six hours. Cars get stuck in traffic and airplanes require a lot of time for check-in, safety checks and boarding, and are plagued by delays. But train manufacturers have recently launched a new generation of super-fast trains that offer an attractive alternative for short trips between major European cities. Before the introduction of fast trains on the Madrid–Sevilla line, for example, airplanes had 67 per cent and trains 33 per cent market share of travel between these two cities. After the introduction of fast trains on this line, the market share of airplanes dropped to 16.4 per cent, while the share of trains increased to 83.6 per cent.
>
> In February 2008, Alstom launched the AGV (Automotrice Grande Vitesse): the successor of the TGV that can travel at up to 360 km/h. These new-generation trains are powered by wheel trucks that are distributed along the train (instead of concentrated in the front and rear cars), which frees up 20 per cent extra space for passengers. In addition, the trains weigh significantly less, resulting in 30 per cent reduction in energy consumption.
>
> But to enjoy the benefits of these new trains, national rail companies need to build new tracks and harmonise their signalling and control systems. The European Commission backs the development of the European Rail Transport Management System (ERTMS), which should create a European-wide standard for signalling. ERTMS equipment encompasses both on-track gear and on-train gear. The buying process for these new-generation fast trains and related equipment is very complex and comprehensive, involving many departments and individuals as well as coordination between national rail companies.

The vendor's response

Thus, buying centre membership, roles and interaction are influenced by a host of factors. It is critical for a vendor to determine a customer's buying centre composition, dynamics and the underlying drivers. Buying centre composition and interaction patterns may change over time; for instance, new departments may become involved in the buying decision or one department may gain influence. Sometimes, these changes may be very sudden; for instance, when a customer gets a new CEO or a key decision-maker leaves the firm. Vendors must constantly monitor buying centre complexity at the level of individual customers or market segments.

Vendors must use their insight into buying centre composition, interaction patterns and buying motives to determine the appropriate selling approach. Buying centre members must be addressed with the right message, using the right communication channels. Kone, the Finnish manufacturer of elevators, used to sell its products using price as the sole differentiator. But when it was about to launch the MonoSpace elevator in Germany in 1996, it discovered that purchasing decisions about elevators were made jointly by owners, architects, structural engineers and building contractors. Kone launched a marketing campaign to educate owners about the MonoSpace's lower operating and maintenance costs and to explain its design benefits to architects. The architects sold the product's value to owners, and together they convinced contractors to install the new product. Using this differentiated benefit-oriented sales approach, Kone doubled its share in the German market in three years (Narayandas 2005).

Some suppliers create sales teams, consisting of representatives from various departments (such as sales, marketing, R&D), whose composition mirrors the composition of the customer's buying centre. The sales team's key member is the sales representative, who has relationships with both current and potential customers, but they are assisted by specialists from other disciplines when necessary. Thus, someone from R&D may discuss technical issues with a customer's production manager. Joint customer visits by a salesperson and someone from R&D boost the quality of the sales call and give R&D employees a better understanding of the customer's problems and product application.

Just like buying centres, sales teams are usually temporary and may include outside members, such as satisfied customers who demonstrate the product in their own organisation, vendors of complementary products and independent laboratories that have tested the product. Use of a sales team, consisting of individuals with different backgrounds, requires that all customer communications are carefully coordinated. Communication by a maintenance engineer should not contradict the promises made earlier by a salesperson. The sales representative is typically responsible for coordinating all customer contacts, but for large projects this is usually done by a sales manager, account manager, project leader or marketing manager.

2.5 Professional and efficient procurement

Not all products and vendors are equally important to a buying organisation. Frequently, 80 per cent of the purchased volume is bought from 20 per cent of the vendors. Professional customers use a differentiated purchasing approach, with the purchasing strategy depending on the type of product. A well-known classification uses two variables to distinguish between different types of product. The first variable is the *influence of the product on the customer's financial performance*, which is high when much money is spent on purchasing the product, the product represents a large part of the cost of the end product, the product has a large influence on the quality of the end product and price elasticity is high. The second variable is the *purchasing risk*, which is high when there are only a few vendors, many competitors need the product as well, it is expensive to switch vendors, the product has a high inventory risk and there are only limited substitution products. Together, these two variables result in a **purchasing portfolio** with four types of product, each with its own characteristics and purchasing strategy (Kraljic 1983).

Non-critical products are standard products of low value, resulting in a small impact on financial performance. They are typically purchased frequently and there are many vendors available, which implies a low purchase risk. Non-critical items are typically purchased by a purchasing officer and the emphasis is on reducing costs by increasing the efficiency of the buying process (for instance, through product standardisation or e-procurement). *Leverage products* represent a high percentage of the buyer's profits, but there are still many vendors available. In addition, these products are standardised, allowing for substitution. This makes it easy to switch vendors and provides customers with an attractive bargaining position. Customers may focus on negotiating attractive deals. An alternative strategy is to invest in vendor development, intensify the relationship and transform the leverage product into a strategic product. This allows for customisation, but also increases dependency on the vendor. *Strategic products* are critical for the buyer's process or product and represent a high supply risk (because of scarcity or delivery problems). Strategic products are typically customised or built to specification. The purchasing strategy for these products is to develop long-term cooperation with vendors, emphasising the co-creation of long-term value. Naturally, customers would run the risk of becoming too dependent on one vendor. Products that are protected by patents or brands that are demanded by users are also strategic products. Intel stimulated this situation with its famous Intel Inside campaign. Finally, *bottleneck products* have a limited impact on financial results, but are problematic because there is a relatively high purchasing risk (because there is just one vendor or delivery is unreliable). Many customers deal with this problem by keeping extra stock or signing long-term contracts, but this does not eliminate the root cause of the problem. A better strategy would be to find a more standardised product or alternative vendors (which means that the product becomes non-critical). Some products are only bottleneck products because they are overspecified; loosening the specifications would increase the number of available vendors.

In addition to developing appropriate purchasing strategies for different types of product, customers can also use the purchasing portfolio to determine the type of purchaser that is needed. Non-critical products require cool analytical thinkers who know how to streamline the purchasing process. Leverage products need sharp negotiators who can negotiate the best deal. Strategic products need empathetic thinkers who are able to take a long-term perspective and establish cooperative relationships. Bottleneck products need purchasers who are creative in identifying alternative products or vendors.

Purchasing efficiency and e-procurement

For manufacturing firms, purchasing represents 50–60 per cent of sales, while for trading firms this may be as much as 90 per cent. So, firms may realise significant savings by reducing purchasing costs, which contributes directly to the firm's profits. A small reduction in purchasing costs results in a significant increase of return on assets. Firms use several strategies to reduce purchasing costs, such as pooling purchases for energy and demanding lower prices. But the benefits are largest when firms take a critical look at their whole purchasing function. A detailed analysis of the purchasing function typically finds that 60 per cent of the invoices account for only 5 per cent of total spend. Streamlining the purchasing process reduces costs and frees purchasing managers to focus on the remaining 40 per cent of invoices that represent 95 per cent of total spend. Three common strategies to implement more efficient purchasing are a corporate purchase card, outsourcing of purchasing and **e-procurement**.

MINI CASE: KLM SAVES ON PURCHASING COSTS

Dutch airline KLM initiated its third round of cost reductions in the summer of 2003. KLM's Top 10 cost reductions are: (1) faster billing, (2) increased control of travel costs, (3) fewer company cars, (4) reduced spending on marketing, (5) fewer phone calls, (6) standardisation of software, (7) outsourcing of salary administration, (8) better use of offices, (9) fewer courses for personnel, and (10) merging of departments.

The largest opportunities for cost reductions are thought to be in purchasing. Purchasing costs of €4.7 billion represent 70 per cent of the total costs (the other 30 per cent are costs of personnel). The largest single item is fuel (€1 billion per year). Apart from fuel, KLM purchases a large variety of products, such as stationery, airplane engines and ground handling services at foreign airports. Part of KLM's strategy is to change specific fixed costs into variable ones. From 2002 onwards, for example, KLM leases the trucks that pull the airplanes to the runways, so that they only incur costs when the trucks are actually used. In addition, KLM terminated subscriptions to several magazines, and outsources internal publications to specialised external sources. Even the familiar KLM blue is no longer required: pens, writing blocs and cars can be any colour that happens to be cheapest.

Source: NRC Handelsblad, 19 July 2003

Corporate purchase card

A corporate purchase card (CPC) is issued by a bank or card company and used by organisations to purchase products of low value more efficiently. In most organisations, 80–90 per cent of the purchasing budget is spent on non-critical items such as stationery, spare parts, temporary workers and courier services and the average cost of each purchasing transaction is €75–100. CPCs make use of electronic invoice presentment and payment to streamline the purchasing process by seamlessly integrating all parties involved in the transaction without manual handling of data entry. Vendors also benefit from a CPC through faster payments, reduced administration costs, lower risks and increased customer loyalty. Next-generation CPCs further increase the benefits for both buyers and vendors; for instance, through integration with ERP and payables/receivables systems and reducing the risks of fraudulent merchants and non-received goods.

When implementing a CPC, the organisation first analyses its vendors and makes agreements about delivery and price with a few selected vendors. Next, the firm's employees receive a CPC, which can be used to purchase a prescribed set of products from pre-approved vendors at negotiated prices within authorised credit limits. Note that CPCs are issued to an organisation's end-users, thus bypassing the purchasing function and leaving purchasing professionals to focus on high-value, strategic products. US Postal Services implemented 18,000 cards and saved €21 million per year! CPCs have become quite popular; some 1,500 organisations in Britain use a total of 50,000 cards. CPCs are most beneficial to large and medium-sized firms making numerous small-value transactions. Small businesses may also benefit from a CPC but their savings will be more modest.

Outsourcing of purchasing

Purchasing costs may also be reduced by outsourcing the purchasing of non-critical products. Specialised organisations pool the purchasing of many clients and can obtain 15–40 per cent lower prices from vendors. Such a specialised organisation takes over the whole purchasing process for specified non-critical products, including the formulation of specifications, vendor selection, negotiations, order fulfilment and evaluation. Through outsourcing firms enjoy lower prices and better delivery conditions, limit the number of vendors that they have to deal with, save time and eliminate processing costs. Purchasing service providers use a fee structure based on flat management transaction fees or retainer fees plus profit sharing on the savings accrued. Outsourcing of purchasing is frequently found in healthcare, because hospitals often lack a professional purchasing department, and small firms that do not have the required expertise.

MINI CASE: BUYING SUPPORT AGENCY OFFERS PURCHASING SERVICES

Established in 2002, the UK-based Buying Support Agency (BSA) does just that: it supports organisations in their buying functions. Founder and Managing Director, Matthew Roper, says: 'Our mission is to significantly reduce client costs by boosting their purchasing power. But we're much more than just an overheads cost reduction company – we have a pool of procurement experts who are as comfortable building a Procurement Audit Toolkit for the National Audit Office, training a team of buyers or developing procurement strategies for Government Agencies in Bosnia as they are cutting routine business costs for SME businesses.' BSA offers three types of service:

- *The BSA Consortium*: a buying group developed to deliver maximum buying power to its clients. The realised cost savings are up to 35 per cent (on average 15–25 per cent). The product groups covered include stationery and office supplies, cleaning supplies, catering supplies, vending services, parcel courier services, gas and electricity, print and packaging, telecoms and workwear.

- *Procurement consultancy and audit*: a function-wide review of purchasing strategies, policies, processes, systems, organisational structure, contract and supplier management and skill sets, which are then benchmarked against best practice.
- *Purchasing training*: several programmes to train employees in best practice purchasing, effective negotiations, import duty cost reductions and dealing with customs.

BSA has worked with numerous clients in the private and public sectors.

Source: www.buyingsupport.co.uk

E-procurement

Recent developments in ICT created many opportunities to drastically change the face of purchasing. The rise of the internet, in particular, allowed many firms to realise significant savings on purchasing costs. The major advantages of e-procurement are time savings, access to new vendors, easy comparison of alternative offerings, lower prices, lower costs, increased control over spending and inventories, and more efficient use of personnel. But not all products are suitable for online purchasing. The most likely candidates are low-value products and services with high transaction costs, such as cleaning products, office supplies, software, computers, catering services, electrical components, chemicals and other materials. There are four types of e-procurement: electronic data interchange (EDI), vendor website, virtual private network and electronic marketplace.

The oldest application of online purchasing is EDI, a proprietary network that connects a buyer with a vendor through a one-to-one data connection. EDI was widely used before the internet arrived on the scene and many firms had made substantial investments in these closed networks. EDI technology has recently been superseded by internet applications of online buying. Over a period of 18 years, only 70 of Boeing's 700 customers established an EDI connection with Boeing. But when the airplane manufacturer opened a website that could be used to order components, 334 customers used the website in its first year of operation. Nevertheless, many EDI systems exist and EDI is still used for a large number of electronic commerce transactions.

With the growing popularity of the internet, many vendors opened websites where customers could look at and order products. The most famous example of a vendor website is www.dell.com, where customers can configure and order computers. As early as 2001, Dell received online orders of $50 million each day (!) and its website generated 40–50 per cent of its total sales. An important contributor to Dell's success is its launch in 1997 of Premier Pages, which can be used by corporate customers to build their own Dell portal where employees can order pre-approved Dell products at prenegotiated prices (Figure 2.4). Currently, there are thousands of companies that have built their own personalised Dell website using Premier Pages, saving them millions of euros per year and freeing purchasing personnel for more important tasks.

Some organisations create a proprietary purchasing portal behind their organisation's firewall. Such a virtual private network (VPN) is developed and maintained by the buying organisation, connects the organisation with several pre-approved vendors and directs the organisation's online purchasing through

FIGURE 2.4 Dell's Premier Pages
Source: Dell Inc. Used with permission.

procedures and buying conditions. While this gives the buying organisation complete control, the costs of such a VPN can be quite substantial. Schlumberger, the world's largest supplier to the oil industry, employs some 60,000 buyers who purchase pens, desks and spare parts for oil field equipment. At the end of the 1990s the company switched from an EDI system to a VPN, which allowed purchasers to buy products from hundreds of pre-approved vendors at prenegotiated prices. This resulted in lower purchasing costs and lower prices, but also established a uniform system throughout the global company (transferred employees no longer need to learn to work with a new system). Volkswagen Group's VWGroupsupply.com handles 90 per cent of the firm's global purchasing volume, including all automotive parts, indirect materials and components, amounting to more than €50 billion annually, more than 70 per cent of the Group's annual revenue.

The next step in the evolution of e-procurement was the establishment of electronic marketplaces that connect multiple buyers with multiple vendors. During the 1990s, e-marketplaces grew rapidly in industries such as chemicals and metals. It is estimated that more than 1,000 e-marketplaces are in operation, with some of them trading a substantial amount of business. An overview of e-marketplaces can be found on www.emarketservices.com. There are four types of e-marketplace (Kaplan and Sawhney 2000). *MRO hubs* bundle the offerings of a large number of vendors of MRO products. These hubs focus on improving the efficiency of the procurement process for operating supplies for a diverse set of industries. Examples are the websites of W.W. Grainger and Staples. *Yield managers* focus on on-time ad hoc procurement of operating supplies. Buyers and sellers use the sites to adjust their operating resources upwards or downwards at short notice. Examples are Employease (for human resources) and eXcesstrade.com (electronic components). *Exchanges* create spot markets for manufactured inputs in specific industries. The exchange maintains relationships with buyers and sellers, but buyers and sellers meet in the virtual marketplace to conduct one-time transactions to smooth out peaks and valleys in demand and supply. Examples are e-Steel, ChemConnect, European Energy Exchange and the business pages on eBay. *Catalogue hubs* organise the systematic sourcing of manufactured inputs and services for specific industries.

Examples are Achats-Industriels.com (industrial equipment and components, French-speaking countries), Canalmetal (industrial machinery and machine tools, Spain), Idrogest (equipment and services for pipelines, water systems, sewerage, irrigation, Italy) and industritorget.se (workshop machinery and tools, Sweden). Most e-marketplaces also offer services, such as job listings, news, advertisements, industry reports, trade show listings and discussion groups.

MINI CASE: GRAINGER EXPANDS ITS ONLINE CATALOGUE

Grainger's 2007 catalogue featured no fewer than 138,000 MRO products, an increase of 23,000 products over the company's 2006 record offering. 'Our customers count on us to be a one-stop shop for a broad selection of MRO supplies so they can efficiently manage their facilities,' says Kevin Peters, senior vice-president of supply chain management. 'We bolstered our offering in several key categories including plumbing, material handling, fasteners and security products, and we're excited to announce that we are poised to serve even more of our customers' needs.' In response to customer feedback, Grainger added more than 7,000 plumbing products (high-grade pipes, valves, fittings), 4,000 material handling supplies (conveyors, hoists, casters), 5,000 fasteners (nuts, bolts, screws) and 1,600 security products (locks, hinges).

The new catalogue offers more than 3,000 pages of product and technical information, as well as enhanced search and selection tools to help customers find the products they need. 'Our customers told us they turn to our catalogue as a reference tool for sourcing MRO products, even when making a purchase over the phone or online,' says Peters. 'As Grainger broadens its product line, we're also enhancing our catalogue to help customers find the right products as quickly and conveniently as possible.'

Source: *Purchasing*, 1 February 2007

E-marketplaces create value through aggregation or matching. Using aggregation, e-marketplaces bring a large number of buyers and sellers under one roof and reduce transaction costs through one-stop shopping at prenegotiated prices. This works best when the cost of processing a purchase order is relatively high compared to the cost of the product procured, products are specialised and the number of products is very large. E-marketplaces that use the matching principle create value by bringing buyers and sellers together to negotiate prices in real time. This is most appropriate when products are relatively standardised, trading volumes are massive relative to transaction costs, and demand and prices are volatile.

Despite the often-proclaimed advantages of e-procurement, there are also disadvantages. Many managers emphasise that online buying can only replace face-to-face interaction for specific types of product and situation (such as buying large amounts of standardised products at low prices). A 2007 eMarket Services report shows that nearly 40 per cent of companies in the European pharmaceutical sector state that they use the internet or other IT networks to purchase goods or services. But only 7 per cent of all pharmaceutical companies in the seven largest European countries purchase more than 25 per cent of their purchases online.

Strategic purchasing

Organisations increasingly realise that they spend a lot of money on purchasing and substantial benefits may be gained by streamlining the purchasing process and transforming purchasing into a strategic activity. Purchasing is no longer an operational activity; it is a strategic function that uses vendors to contribute to the creation of superior value for customers. Many firms have expressed this changed perspective by appointing a *chief procurement officer* and making purchasing a strategic function that directly contributes to the firm's profits. With **strategic purchasing**, the organisation focuses on its core activities and outsources everything else to specialised vendors. In addition, firms significantly reduce the number of vendors they do business with, often by 50–90 per cent (for instance, by encouraging preferred vendors to broaden their product lines). Such drastic reductions of the vendor roster reduce the costs associated with selecting, developing and maintaining vendors, and stimulate the remaining vendors to reduce costs by sharing designs and production resources. In addition, shipping costs are also lower when similar parts are made in the same plant. Drastic reduction of the vendor base also allows firms to develop close relationships with the remaining vendors (for instance, through joint product development). Firms such as Océ, DSM and BMW increasingly purchase complete systems from vendors, resulting in a vendor hierarchy: (1) co-developers, who develop new products together with the customer (gross margin: 30–50 per cent); (2) main contractors, who supply complete subsystems (gross margin: 20–30 per cent); (3) co-makers, who supply components (gross margin: 15–20 per cent); and (4) jobbers, who assemble products (gross margin: 10 per cent). In close buyer–supplier relationships both parties freely exchange information about demand forecasts, production planning, cost structures and marketing plans. Vendor development programmes may be used to further improve the selected vendors' performance. But there are also disadvantages to this strategy of vendor rationalisation and reduction; for instance, it may prevent the customer from benefiting from the expertise of a niche supplier.

MINI CASE: AIRBUS SLASHES ITS VENDOR LIST

In November 2006, Airbus announced that it would axe more than 80 per cent of its supply base, reducing the number of vendors from its current 3000 to just 500. This would reduce material costs by £1 billion over the next three years and cut administrative costs by an additional £235 million. According to Matthias Gramolla, Vice-President of Sourcing Strategy at the European Aeronautic Defence & Space Co. (EADS; Airbus' parent organisation), 'the intention is not to take any suppliers out of the industry or our supply chain. But we do want to focus more on a limited number of systems and equipment suppliers. And we want our Tier One suppliers to manage overall systems and the sub-tier suppliers that support them.' Decisions about which vendors will be considered for this meta-integrator role will be based on the following:

> - a vendor's willingness and ability to share market risk
> - ongoing performance
> - system capabilities (including the criticality and uniqueness of the system or service provided by the vendor)
> - financial strength.
>
> Airbus executives have commented that the remaining vendors will be expected to provide additional price and cost concessions. Surviving vendors will continue to be measured on the metrics that are used in all EADS business units: commercial, technical, quality, logistics and customer support performance. In addition, metrics will be added to measure vendors' future health and capabilities (supplier capabilities, financial health, corporate and social responsibility and how well the vendors manage their own supply chains).
>
> *Source*: www.supplyexcellence.com

A strategic purchasing function is more connected within the organisation, provides a clear contribution to the firm's strategy and performance, and interacts closely with other business functions. Transforming a firm's purchasing department into a strategic function is a complicated process that changes relationships with suppliers, is supported by information systems and requires new skills. Such a transformation has consequences for all parties involved.

For the buying organisation, it means that purchasing must be positioned as a strategic function, both in terms of hierarchical position, relationship with other business functions and involvement in business processes. In addition, the firm must analyse its vendor base, reduce the number of vendors and develop close relationships with the remaining vendors. This may require investments in vendors to develop new capabilities or products that will improve cost or quality.

For the purchasing function it means that employees need to develop new skill sets. Instead of just negotiating with suppliers, purchasing officers also need to discuss with other business functions at early stages of specification development and contribute specialised knowledge about material availability, cost drivers and delivery reliability. In addition, purchasing officers must be able to initiate supplier development programmes and contribute to product and process innovation. Strategic purchasing tasks are similar to the strategic tasks of account managers, which explains why strategic purchasing is also being referred to as *reverse marketing* (Leenders and Blenkhorn 1988). This new cooperative skill set may be problematic for purchasers that have spent the last 20 years focusing on obtaining the lowest purchase price. Many firms have discovered that they need to replace 20–45 per cent of their employees because they do not fit in the changed corporate culture.

Finally, strategic purchasing also has consequences for the vendors' marketing strategies. Vendors persisting in product-oriented thinking will be delegated to one of the lower tiers, suffering reduced margins. Vendors who want to position themselves as potential partners need to analyse their customers' buying orientation, calculate profitability per customer, and use account management to target the appropriate customers.

2.6 Expansion, upgrading and disposal

More than 25 years ago, Theodore Levitt (1983: 87) wrote that 'the relationship between a seller and a buyer seldom ends when a sale is made'. He compared the relationship between seller and buyer with a marriage and stated that the quality of the marriage depends on how well the seller manages the relationship. A product such as automated machinery needs to be installed and serviced to keep it running smoothly as part of the customer's operations. Sometimes, the vendor's product needs to be modified to optimise the fit with the customer's business processes. In the customer-activity cycle (Figure 2.2), this is expressed by the 'maintenance and repair' stage, which is a direct consequence of the equipment sale and typically part of the vendor's total offering. Paques, the Dutch manufacturer of purification systems for water, gases and air, for example, offers a wide range of services for optimal operation of the customer's treatment plant, including remote monitoring, troubleshooting, audits and technical support. These types of service are aimed at getting the best out of the vendor's product as part of the customer's operations.

In contrast to these after-sales services, the subsequent 'expansion and upgrading' stage of the customer-activity cycle refers to all customer activities aimed at expanding the benefits from the vendor's offering. A university may, for example, initially contract with a caterer for only one of its faculties and only when the experiment turns out to be a success expand the caterer's business to other faculties. The vendor's objective during the 'expansion and upgrading' stage is to increase the bond with the customer in order to lock in the customer and secure future business. For example, a vendor may increase the customer's longevity of spending (that is, the length of the customer relationship) by offering product upgrades. Some equipment vendors make it easy for their customers to switch to more state-of-the-art products and enjoy increased benefits, such as reduced downtime and repairs, lower costs of ownership, new warranties, more effective use of capital, enhanced equipment capacity and improved operating safety. Xerox's website contains a Product Upgrade Centre, where customers can look up the equipment they own and find product and upgrade recommendations. Computer vendors often sign contracts with customers that specify the conditions allowing customers to upgrade to a newer system. But product upgrades do not always require that the old product is traded for a new one. Vendors may also replace specific product components or change the old product's software to bring its performance to a higher level. Some vendors offer customised equipment upgrade kits, consisting of all components tailored to specific customer upgrade needs, as well as a service technician who will install the components and provide the required documentation. When the product upgrade only requires new software, customers can often easily download the software from the vendor's virtual private network (VPN) together with detailed instructions for installation.

From the customer's perspective, expansion may also refer to increasing the diversity of spending by purchasing completely new offerings from the same vendor. This further cements the relationship and increases the customer's switching costs.

Finally, the customer-activity cycle concludes with disposal of the product. There may be many different drivers of disposal; for instance, a customer may redesign its own product and no longer need specific components or raw materials. New government regulations may require manufacturing firms to eliminate materials that are harmful to the environment. Or a new strategic direction may cause a firm to divest certain businesses and therefore specific pieces of equipment. PC manufacturers offer their customers help with disposal of technology equipment because many customers are unaware of environmental regulations concerning the disposal of IT equipment and underestimate data security and privacy issues. Financial institutions and hospitals, for example, may face severe fines for unlawful dumping of IT equipment containing confidential information. Hewlett-Packard has established HP Technology Renewal Centres which receive end-of-life customer equipment and reconfigure all equipment with remaining value. All identifiable customer data are cleared using an intensive, HP-designed process.

Online *Learning* Centre

When you have read this chapter, log on to the Online Learning Centre website at ***www.mcgraw-hill.co.uk/textbooks/biemans*** to explore chapter-by-chapter test questions, further reading and more online study tools.

Summary of Key Concepts

- B2B customers are not interested in products, but in the value they derive from these products. B2B products and services must help customers in their own value creation for their own customers. This means that B2B vendors must contribute to the success of their customers.

- B2B vendors can only help their customers if they are intimately familiar with their customer's business processes and key success factors. They need to understand how their products and services contribute to the value creation processes of their customers.

- Value is defined as all benefits minus costs that a customer receives in exchange for the purchase price.

- In making their purchase decision, customers will (a) assess whether a vendor's net value exceeds the purchase price and (b) select the vendor that offers the highest net value.

- A useful tool that helps vendors to understand their customers is the customer-activity cycle, which maps the total relationship between customers and the vendor's product. The customer-activity cycle describes all of the customer's product-related activities, starting with identification of need and ending with disposal of the product. Mapping the customer-activity cycle can help vendors to identify opportunities for value creation.

■ The core of the customer-activity cycle is the organisational buying process, which consists of three broad stages: product specifications and requests for proposals, negotiations and selection, and order fulfilment and evaluation.

■ Organisational decision making frequently includes several departments or individuals (the buying centre), each with their own background and buying motives. Vendors must assess buying centre composition, the interaction between buying centre members and the key buying motives.

■ The nature of a customer's buying process depends on the buying situation. There are three buying situations: straight rebuy, modified rebuy and new task. Most organisational buying decisions are straight rebuys.

■ Organisational buying behaviour is becoming increasingly professional and efficient. Internet technology, in particular, helps customers to increase the efficiency of organisational buying.

■ The customer-activity cycle does not end with the delivery and installation of the product. Customers may, for example, require repair and maintenance, upgrade the product over time, expand use of the product and eventually dispose of the product. Each of these activities offers innovative vendors new opportunities to create value.

🔑 Key Terms

Buying centre, p. 45	In suppliers, p. 41
Buying centre roles, p. 45	Make-or-buy decision, p. 41
Buying motives, p. 46	Organisational buying process, p. 42
Buying situations, p. 48	Out suppliers, p. 41
Customer needs, p. 34	Purchasing portfolio, p. 51
Customer-activity cycle, p. 40	Strategic purchasing, p. 57
Decision-making unit, p. 45	Superior customer value, p. 39
E-procurement, p. 52	Total cost of ownership, p. 37

Discussion questions

1 A vendor may create value through its products, employees or organisation. Explain how each of these three may be a critical source of customer value for a consulting firm.

2 Effective value management starts with charting the customer-activity cycle. Describe the key activities for a theme park buying roller-coasters. Also describe the key activities for a small manufacturer buying fasteners from a local vendor. Explain the differences. What are the consequences for a vendor's opportunities to create value in both situations?

3 Several vendors find themselves in commodity markets, with customers buying the lowest-priced offerings. The way out of this commodity trap is to identify, develop and offer superior customer value. But customers frequently persist in their habit of buying on price. Describe several different strategies to deal with these customers.

4 What are the key differences between the purchasing behaviour of consumers and organisations? What are the implications of these differences for the vendor's marketing strategy?

5 In influencing buying processes, members of a firm's buying centre may have power and influence for all kinds of reasons. Describe the different bases of power and influence. How can buying centre members use their power during the buying process? How should a vendor deal with this?

6 Several different employees of a vendor may interact with customers. Describe a few specific examples. How can a firm coordinate and manage all these different customer interactions?

7 What are the advantages and disadvantages of single sourcing, dual sourcing and multiple sourcing? Which strategy would you prefer?

8 How can vendors use the concept of buying situations to design effective marketing and sales strategies and tactics?

9 Business customers increasingly buy products online. What are the consequences for a vendor who considers selling its products online, in addition to selling through distributors?

10 The implementation of strategic purchasing also has significant consequences for vendors. Describe the major consequences for vendors who are increasingly faced with customers who are transforming their purchasing function into a strategic business function.

Further reading

Anderson, James C. and James A. Narus (1998) Business marketing: understand what customers value, *Harvard Business Review*, 76(6): 53–65.

Ellram, Lisa (1993) Total cost of ownership: elements and implementation, *International Journal of Purchasing and Materials Management*, 29(4): 3–11.

Kraljic, Peter (1983) Purchasing must become supply management, *Harvard Business Review*, 61(5): 109–117.

Vandermerwe, Sandra (2000) How increasing value to customers improves business results, *Sloan Management Review*, 42(1): 27–37.

References

Anderson, James C. and James A. Narus (1998) Business marketing: understand what customers value, *Harvard Business Review*, 76(6): 53–65.

Christensen, Clayton M., Scott Cook and Taddy Hall (2005) Marketing malpractice: the cause and the cure, *Harvard Business Review*, 83(12): 74–83.

Ellram, Lisa (1993) Total cost of ownership: elements and implementation, *International Journal of Purchasing and Materials Management*, 29(4): 3–11.

Kaplan, Steven and Mohanbir Sawhney (2000) E-hubs: the new B2B marketplaces, *Harvard Business Review*, 78(3): 97–103.

Kraljic, Peter (1983) Purchasing must become supply management, *Harvard Business Review*, 61(5): 109–117.

Leenders, Michiel L. and David L. Blenkhorn (1988) *Reverse Marketing: The New Buyer–Supplier Relationship*, New York: Free Press.

Levitt, Theodore (1983) After the sale is over . . . , *Harvard Business Review*, 61(5): 87–93.

Narayandas, Das (2005) Building loyalty in business markets, *Harvard Business Review*, 83(9): 131–139.

Robinson, Patrick J., Charles W. Faris and Yoram Wind (eds) (1967) *Industrial Buying and Creative Marketing*, Boston, MA: Allyn and Bacon.

Thompson, Harvey (2000) *The Customer-Centered Enterprise: How IBM and Other World-Class Companies Achieve Extraordinary Results by Putting Customers First*, New York: McGraw-Hill.

Vandermerwe, Sandra (2000) How increasing value to customers improves business results, *Sloan Management Review*, 42(1): 27–37.

Webster, Frederick E., Jr. and Yoram Wind (1972) *Organizational Buying Behavior*, Englewood Cliffs, NJ: Prentice Hall.

Wiersema, Fred (1996) *Customer Intimacy: Pick Your Partners, Shape Your Culture, Win Together*, Santa Monica, CA: Knowledge Exchange.

Note

[1] Salz, Nort (2005) Ease of doing business survey sets benchmark for carriers to follow, *Insurance Journal*, 5 December.

Making sense of B2B markets

Introduction

To craft effective marketing strategies, B2B vendors must have an intimate understanding of their customers and the markets they are a part of. While the focus is on understanding the wants and needs of customers, these must be placed in a broader context that includes all relevant market players and market forces. The ability to sense developments in the market and translate them into effective marketing strategies is the key capability that helps firms to create a competitive advantage. Successful firms use a market orientation to collect market information, disseminate this information within the firm and use the information to initiate marketing actions.

This chapter first explains the process of market sensing and describes how firms collect market information to construct market pictures that are used to make marketing decisions. The most critical market information concerns the wants and needs of customers. B2B vendors employ a variety of sources to collect customer information, ranging from published sources and market research to interaction with customers. In addition, vendors gather information about other market parties, such as suppliers, competitors, government agencies, channel partners and vendors of complementary products. This chapter describes how managers combine all this information to make sense of their markets and construct market pictures that represent their perception of the market. This process of sense-making is strongly influenced by the mental models that exist in the organisation. Mental models influence the kind of information managers look for, and how collected information is interpreted and used to make marketing decisions. A well-known example of a mental model is the firm's market segmentation scheme, which simplifies the complexity of business markets into a limited number of easily understood market segments.

3.1 Market sensing

To offer superior value for customers, firms must be intimately aware of their customers' wants and needs and use this knowledge to guide their actions in the marketplace. In other words, firms must be market oriented, both in how they think and how they act.

Being market oriented

Market orientation is generally defined in terms of a firm's behaviour and consists of three components (Kohli and Jaworski 1990): collecting market information, disseminating market information within the organisation, and using market information as the basis for coordinated action in the marketplace. The concept of market orientation emphasises that market information is the cornerstone of effective B2B marketing. Market information is defined as all information about current and future wants and needs of current and potential customers, as well as all factors influencing these wants and needs (ibid.). The factors that influence customer wants and needs include competitor offerings and actions, technological developments, regulations, channel partners, vendors of complementary products and changes taking place in the firm's downstream markets. New EU directives regulating wastewater treatment, for example, impose treatment standards and influence organisations' buying decisions about wastewater treatment equipment, systems and services. Thus, firms must collect information about all key market players:

- *Customers*, which in business markets refers to both immediate and downstream customers (for instance, through a continuous dialogue with key customers).
- *Competitors*, because customers will always compare a firm's offering with alternative offerings (for instance, a firm may employ *reverse engineering* to get detailed information about a competitor's products).

- *Suppliers*, whose materials and components influence the quality of the firm's offering.

- *Other market parties*, such as channel partners (who advise customers, install products and provide after-sales service), government (which issues regulations) and research institutes (which develop new technologies that may be applied in new products).

To collect all this information firms use a wide range of strategies, such as buying industry reports that describe market trends, looking at competitors' websites, analysing customer complaints, analysing sales data and recording customer visit reports from salespeople. But a maintenance engineer who hears from a customer about problems with a competitor's product also contributes to the firm's market knowledge when that information is communicated to the firm's marketing or R&D manager. Effective dissemination of market information ensures that information actually reaches the people who need it. As part of this internal dissemination process, market information is being sorted, combined with other information, analysed to identify relationships between variables and interpreted to attach meaning for specific contexts. Thus, new market information is used by individuals to continuously update their market pictures. In practice, many B2B firms are plagued by inadequate communication between departments and business units. Consider the following typical examples:

- The list of reference projects in a tender does not even mention a project that was done three years ago for the same client.

- Two business units from the same firm send out completely different tenders competing for the same project.

- Employees do not share market information because they feel more powerful when they know more than their colleagues.

The process of collecting market information and making sense of all this information is called **market sensing** (Day 1994). Effective market sensing requires open-minded inquiry, widespread information distribution and mutually informed mental models that guide interpretation (see also Section 3.5). But many B2B firms are too focused on their internal processes or they feel that they already know all about their markets and the best way to serve them. As a result of this complacent attitude they often miss significant changes in customer requirements or a competitor's strategy. A 2002 survey of 140 corporate strategists found that fully two-thirds admitted that their organisations had been surprised by as many as three high-impact competitive events in the past five years. Moreover, a staggering 97 per cent of the respondents stated that their companies have no early warning system in place (Fuld 2003).

> ⌐⌐ **INSIGHT: Using peripheral vision to identify hidden opportunities and threats**
>
> An increasingly important capability concerns the firm's use of peripheral vision. While much market activity occurs within easily defined borders and frameworks, many weak signals are less easily visible. Good peripheral vision involves knowing where to look for these signals, knowing how to interpret them, knowing when to turn one's head in a new direction, and knowing how to act on these weak signals when they are still ambiguous. The opportunity of white LED lighting, for example, was recognised by LED companies, but completely missed by lightbulb manufacturers. The five components of a capability for peripheral vision are: (1) vigilant leadership that encourages a broad focus on the periphery, (2) an inquisitve approach to strategy development, (3) a flexible and inquisitive culture that rewards exploring the edge, (4) knowledge systems for detecting and sharing weak signals, and (5) organisational configuration and processes that encourage exploration of the periphery.
>
> *Source*: Day and Schoemaker (2006)

The collected and disseminated market information contributes to managers' perception of customers and markets. The resulting market pictures are subsequently used to design and implement marketing strategies and activities; for instance, underperforming products are compared with similar products, historic sales numbers and information about recent market developments to initiate appropriate actions in the marketplace (such as increasing the support offered to channel partners, modifying the product's characteristics or changing its pricing structure). This three-stage process of collecting market information, internally disseminating market information, and using market information to develop and implement marketing strategies and activities is depicted in Figure 3.1.

The importance of market information and how organisations handle information have changed drastically during the last two decades. Many industries are characterised by increasing clockspeeds: new technologies and new product generations are introduced faster than ever, putting pressure on firms to keep up with the changes. Increased clockspeeds go hand in hand with increased uncertainty and a need for more market information. While the internet helps by making unheard-of amounts of information available, for example through portals with business information, it also contributes to information overload and many managers are looking for new tools to make sense of all the available information (such as intranets, knowledge exchange communities and literature alert services).

The effects of being market oriented

The concept of market orientation is not free of criticism. Detractors claim that it results in incremental, trivial product development, reduced industry competitiveness and a loss of industry leadership. Obviously, a market orientation is no guarantee of success; it needs to be balanced with creativity and a good grasp of

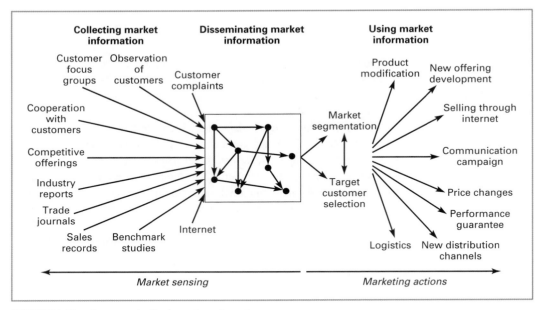

FIGURE 3.1 The elements of a firm's market orientation

the firm's unique capabilities. But it is clear that in order to be successful, firms need intimate knowledge of the markets they want to serve. Numerous studies have shown that market orientation has a positive effect on business performance in terms of profit, customer satisfaction, revenue growth and the success of new products (Kirca et al. 2005; Langerak 2003). Market-oriented firms are also able to charge higher prices and create entry barriers to deter potential competitors. Moreover, a higher market orientation also results in more satisfied and committed employees, which reduces employee turnover and further increases customer satisfaction and profitability.

Unfortunately, it is not easy to transform a product-oriented company into an agile market-oriented player. Instilling a market orientation may require significant changes in an organisation's structure, information systems, compensation systems and procedures (see also Chapter 10). In addition, new employees may be needed who possess the required market-oriented skills. Some firms are convinced that they do not need to invest in improving their market orientation; for instance, because they enjoy a monopoly or because they have only limited capacity and an increased market orientation would only result in increased demand that they cannot fulfil. But this line of reasoning is short-sighted for several reasons:

- Monopolies do not always persist and order books are not always filled to capacity; it is better to change the organisation when business is still doing well.
- Increasing a firm's market orientation is a long-term process that may take several years to deliver results.

- A market-oriented culture reduces employee turnover, which reduces costs and increases profits.
- With a market-oriented approach, the same fixed capacity can be used to target a more profitable mix of customers, which increases the return on investment.

Despite all potential benefits of being market oriented, most B2B firms are characterised by a product or sales orientation and only manage to survive because their competitors fare no better! In such a situation, customers will focus on price and select the cheapest vendor. The way out of this commodity trap starts with collecting detailed market information and building realistic market pictures.

3.2 Collecting information about customers

The most critical market information that firms need is information about customers – both immediate customers and downstream customers. Firms may gather **customer information** at several levels, varying from the individual buying centre member to the total market. This is captured in Figure 3.2, which also shows how one level is embedded in the next and the difference between information about specific customers (the shaded levels) and information at the level of the market or market segments.

Many B2B firms have insufficient knowledge about their customers and what drives their business. A firm's customer knowledge can easily be checked by asking

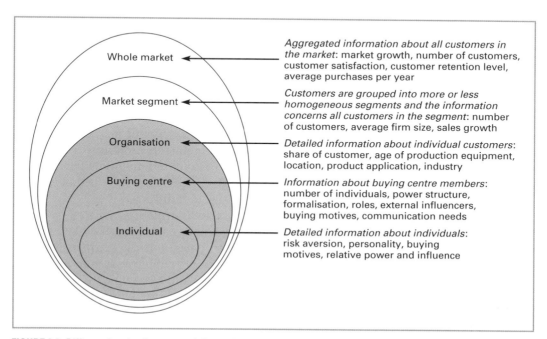

FIGURE 3.2 Different levels of customer information

a few people from top management, middle management and several line functions the following three questions: (1) Who are our customers? (2) Why do they buy from us? (3) How do we contribute to their success? All too often, one will get quite different answers to these very basic questions. At a large global paint manufacturer, managers did not even agree about the answer to the first question: who are our customers? Some managers responded with: 'That's easy: our customer is the wholesaler, because they pay for our paint.' But other managers answered, just as convincingly: 'That's a no-brainer: our customer is the painter, because they use our paint.' In many other firms, marketing and sales only communicate with the customer's purchasing personnel and lack information about the wants and needs of the people actually using their products. Obviously, when such critical information is lacking or people hold varying perceptions of customers, it becomes very difficult to design and implement effective marketing strategies and programmes.

Firms may collect information from current customers, lost customers and potential customers. Managers must decide which specific customers to use as sources of information, taking into account the existing customer relationship and the customer's willingness to cooperate. An obvious start is to look for average customers who are representative of their market segment. But firms should also collect information from trend-setting customers; these so-called **lead users** (von Hippel 1986) are defined as customers who:

- face needs that will be general in the marketplace, but face them months or years before the bulk of the marketplace encounters them
- are positioned to benefit significantly by obtaining a solution to those needs.

For Silicon Graphics, manufacturer of high-performance computers, lead users from the film industry are an important source of new product ideas. Silicon Graphics sends its best R&D people to Hollywood to learn first-hand what the most creative users of its products might want in the future. In addition, it nurtures close relationships with lead users in other industries that require massive computation and high-end graphics. For example, it worked with Genentech to model molecular structures for drug design, and it helped NASA develop systems that support the design of next-generation space vehicles and an internet display of images from a Mars landing. The lead user concept is not limited to high-tech products. Hilti AG, the Liechtenstein manufacturer of components, equipment and materials for the construction industry, conducted a lead user study to develop a new pipe hanger system that is used to fasten pipes to walls or ceilings of buildings.

Firms may use a broad range of sources of customer information, such as customer websites, customer complaints, sales presentations, telemarketing, trade shows, customer days and focus groups. Combining several sources compensates for the weaknesses of individual sources and results in more reliable customer pictures. A common problem is that firms have several databases and systems with customer information, for instance when sales and marketing use their own customer information system. Formulating common definitions and integrating the available customer information across the firm contribute to rich, shared customer pictures that can be accessed by all individuals that need customer information. Such a systematic approach reduces the costs of collecting and reporting customer information by up to 50 per cent. In addition, it increases the quality of customer information, especially when transaction data are combined with detailed information about the customers and individuals behind the transactions. But firms must beware of information overload; customer information sources must be carefully selected and managed to contribute optimally to the construction of useful customer pictures. The five key sources of customer information are public sources, sales records, market research, **customer interaction** and customer feedback.

INSIGHT: Creative collection of customer information

Firms must be creative in collecting customer information, but sometimes a little bit of luck helps as well. An air-conditioning manufacturer offered its installers the opportunity to deposit all empty packaging materials for free at the next delivery. The installers' purchasers really liked this initiative, because it enabled them to optimally comply with environmental regulations, avoiding costs. What they did not realise is that they liked it so much that they gave *all* packaging materials to the vendor, including the packaging of all competing products. The vendor meticulously studied all collected packaging materials for a detailed customer analysis. At a yearly cost of only €50,000, the company gained insight into the buying behaviour and portfolio of all its customers.

Source: Moenaert et al. (2008)

Public sources

Much information about B2B customers can be gleaned from public sources, such as:

- *(Inter)national government organisations*, that publish statistics and background information about industries and countries (Office for National Statistics (UK), Statistisches Bundesambt Deutschland (Germany), European Commission, Organisation for Economic Co-operation and Development).
- *Market research agencies*, that collect and publish information about specific industries (Forrester Research and Gartner provide information about the impact of technology on business through published reports, subscriptions, seminars and consulting).
- *Industry associations*, that publish information about specific industries (European Federation of Biotechnology, European Mortar Industry Organisation, numerous national trade associations).
- *Trade journals and business periodicals* (*Agra Europe, Fabricating & Metalworking, Logistics Management, Rubber World, Waste News, Forbes, Business Week*).
- *National and international newspapers* (*Wall Street Journal, Financial Times, International Herald Tribune*).

- *Online directories* (Google and Yahoo publish global business directories, www.europages.co.uk lists 900,000 European suppliers, manufacturers and distributors).

Much information from public sources is available online. Newspapers and trade journals have online versions, government agencies publish statistics and industry reports online, and market research agencies and consultants offer online subscriptions; for instance, www.internationalbusinessstrategies.com offers market research reports on more than 130 topics from more than 90 countries. B2B vendors may also access public sources of information about consumers and consumer markets to forecast changes in demand.

Most public information is aggregated at the market segment, industry or country level. The European Union introduced the Statistical Classification of Economic Activities (NACE) that groups firms according to their economic activity (such as manufacturing, construction, agriculture or electricity, gas and water supply) to facilitate the compilation of comparable data. NACE has been the official industrial classification in all EU member states as from 2003. A focus on economic activities groups firms with similar needs together, which makes the classification system very suitable for marketing purposes.

Although a wealth of information is available from public sources, this information is not always up to date or in the desired format. But it provides a good starting point for firms looking for general information at the aggregate level. More detailed information about individual firms can be found on corporate websites that frequently offer information about corporate values, strategies, product applications, target markets, technologies, purchasing procedures and expansion plans.

Sales records

A firm's internal records, such as its sales administration and financial records, offer detailed information about customers' transaction histories. Sales records provide information about both current and lost customers. Financial records offer information about various costs and expenditures. Together, these data can be used to calculate several key metrics and identify trends, both at the aggregate market segment level and the level of individual customers. Examples of relevant metrics are sales per market segment, geographic region or customer, average price per customer size or customer, effective margins per market segment or customer, profitability per market segment or customer, number of customers per market segment, customer retention rate per market segment, and average length of customer relationship.

When sales administration registers not only realised sales, but also progress on outstanding tenders and sales presentations, several sales funnel metrics can be calculated, such as funnel value (the potential value of all deals in the funnel), arrival rate (the number of deals being qualified into the funnel), conversion rate (the ratio of deals that are closed to the number of deals that enter the funnel) and flow rate (both the average time that deals spend in the funnel and its spread). When these quantitative metrics are combined with qualitative information from customer visit reports, even more detailed customer pictures emerge.

Market research

Customer information that is not available from public sources or internal records can be collected through market research. B2B **market research** has several characteristics that distinguish it from consumer market research:

- *Most B2B market research is exploratory and uses secondary data and subjective estimates.* Because of the diversity of B2B customers and product applications, most B2B market research is exploratory, aiming to estimate market size and potential. The required information is typically gathered through customer interviews or based on previous experience with similar situations.

- *B2B market research uses relatively small samples.* Many B2B markets have relatively few customers; only a small sample is thus required to obtain the desired information. In-depth interviews provide rich customer information, which is typically difficult to generalise to other customers. In extreme situations, B2B market researchers may research all potential customers in a market segment.

- *B2B market research uses interviews and surveys, rather than observation and experiments.* Experiments are not very suitable for business markets. Observation may be used to discover latent customer needs, but most B2B market research relies on interviews and surveys.

- *B2B market research is plagued by a number of practical problems.* While potential customers are typically easy to identify, identifying and getting access to key decision-makers is much harder; for instance, because they are only accessible during office hours (purchasing officers, in particular, are typically too busy to cooperate). In addition, good interviewers who also understand the vendor's products are hard to find and in many B2B markets customers are unevenly distributed, with just a few large customers and many small ones.

- *Most B2B market research is global.* Due to relatively small national markets, most B2B market research in Europe is global, with problems caused by different languages and cultural differences.

To understand the demand for their products, B2B firms may also need to research consumer markets. When Cargill, a global producer of starch, wanted to expand in southern France it identified potential customers by simply going to supermarkets and looking up the ingredients listed on the packagings of food products.

With the growing role of the internet, B2B market research may also be conducted online. Customer focus group sessions can be conducted online and researchers can analyse clicking patterns to obtain insight into how customers navigate through corporate websites. Digital databases and automated query tools contribute to more professional market research. In addition, sophisticated techniques, such as conjoint measurement and simulation, are increasingly applied by B2B firms and virtual reality software can be used to quickly develop 3D models of new products at low cost and test them with potential customers.

Customer interaction

Much information about individual customers is collected through the regular contacts of marketing and sales staff with customers. Salespeople, maintenance engineers, technical services employees and application managers regularly visit customers, where they can observe and ask questions. It is not just the *amount* of interaction with customers that counts, but also its *content*. In one study, researchers found that the CEOs of the best-performing companies spent more time with customers (18 per cent) than the CEOs of the worst-performing firms (15 per cent), but the difference was not very large. New interviews uncovered the real difference: while the CEOs of the worst-performing firms interacted with customers by taking them to sporting events and the theatre, the CEOs of the best-performing firms interacted with customers by discussing firm performance and how it could be improved (Barwise and Meehan 2004).

Salespeople visit customers on a regular basis and thus appear to be ideal candidates for collecting customer information. Salespeople are often required to fill out customer visit reports or to conduct customer interviews. But there is a big difference between the roles of salesperson and interviewer (Grace and Pointon 1980). Salespeople are trained to persuade customers and deal with subjective arguments, opinions and emotions, which is diametrically opposed to objectively collecting customer information. In addition, their close relationships with customers limit their usefulness for collecting customer information; they tend to be less objective and provide distorted information (for instance, by overestimating customers' focus on price). However, this does not mean that salespeople are useless for collecting customer information, only that firms that want their salespeople to collect customer information must take a number of considerations into account (Grace and Pointon 1980; Liu and Comer 2007). First, the salespeople must be trained in interviewing and observation techniques. Second, customer visits to collect customer information must be separated from regular sales calls. Third, sales managers must communicate clearly what they expect from salespeople, give detailed feedback and use appropriate financial incentives. Fourth, salespeople should only be used to gather objective factual information about customers (organisational characteristics, buying centre structure, names and functions of key decision-makers, product applications, manufacturing facilities, age of plant equipment, expansion plans and product use conditions).

More subjective customer information should be collected through structured customer visits that do not rely on the firm's salespeople. Direct interaction with customers is the best way to gather customer information and should not be left to the firm's salespeople. Top and middle management also need to stay in touch with customers and should not rely on second-hand information. In addition, salespeople typically only interact with immediate customers. Interaction with key players at various levels of the value chain (immediate customers, downstream customers, distributors, end-users) is critical for the construction of complete market pictures that are the cornerstone of effective marketing. Structured customer visits have the following characteristics (McQuarrie 1991):

- Managers visit customers personally to establish direct interaction.
- Customer visits are conducted by teams of representatives from marketing and other relevant departments (R&D, manufacturing). Thus, a vendor's technical designers interact directly with the customer's users about technical issues.
- Customer visits are a continuous activity with carefully formulated objectives, supported by business managers and supervised by a coordinator. The information obtained through customer visits must be translated into actions and both customers and employees must be informed about results and planned actions. Correct feedback to customers is essential for obtaining their cooperation next time!

What makes these customer visits so valuable is that they allow customers to tell their own story in their own words. Customers find this very rewarding and the vendor gets detailed first-hand information. The impact of customer visits can be increased by videotaping them and making the tapes available to other personnel that do not have direct contact with customers. A Dutch marketing manager always shoots some photos during customer visits and shows them to employees at home. This is much appreciated by manufacturing personnel who otherwise never get to see a customer!

 INSIGHT: Customer house calls

A customer visit is more than just having a conversation at a customer site. The customer visit can be used to ask all kinds of questions, but managers should also carefully observe the customer during the visit. Which products are used? Which competitive products are used? How are products used? Which problems can be observed? Such on-site observation provides critical input for product development by offering information about:

- situations in which the product is used
- how the product fits in the customer's business process
- the extent to which the customer has modified the product
- the importance of intangible product characteristics
- new (latent) customer needs.

To broaden its interaction with customers, management at US-based Kennametal (world leader in the metalworking industry) decided to drive buses with Kennametal employees to customers. They were shown around at the customer plant and saw with their own eyes how their product was being used by the customer and the problems the customer experienced in using it. Information from these customer visits was used to modify the firm's manufacturing and sales processes. In addition, the customer visits signalled that to Kennametal the customer comes first!

Sources: Leonard and Rayport (1997) and Wiersema (1996)

Even more intensive interaction with customers occurs through joint strategic cooperation projects. Faced with increasing competition, growing customer demands and the need for shorter time to market, many firms cooperate with suppliers, customers and even competitors (see also Chapter 5). Strategic cooperation with customers usually concerns the development and launch of new products. Customers contribute to the vendor's product development by suggesting new product ideas, testing new product concepts, assisting in the development of prototypes, testing prototypes in real-life user situations, and assisting with product launch.

Customer feedback

In addition to the aforementioned tools employed by firms, customer information may also be initiated by the customers themselves. The most familiar example of **customer feedback** is customer complaints. Many firms do not like to receive customer complaints; management perceives them as annoying and fails to realise that they should really worry when they do not receive any complaints at all! The absence of customer complaints is a sure sign of bad or deteriorating customer relationships. Complaining customers are a source of valuable information and present a vendor with the opportunity to repair the damaged relationship. In business markets, in particular, dissatisfied customers complain to encourage the vendor to solve the problem. Typical reasons why business customers switch to another vendor are inadequate communication with the vendor, the vendor's insufficient knowledge of the customer's organisation or industry, the vendor's aggressive sales approach and products that are delivered too late.

There are three reasons why firms should pay careful attention to customer complaints:

- *Complaints can be used to identify problems.* Systematic complaint analysis uncovers root causes of problems and results in improved communication about product use, product modifications, product elimination, new product development, changed delivery procedures, improved customer service and a changed sales approach.

- *Complaints allow the vendor to repair the relationship.* Complaining customers only want one thing: a fast response that solves the problem.

- *Complaints offer an opportunity to increase the level of customer satisfaction.* Studies show that a complaining customer, whose complaint is dealt with satisfactorily, tends to be more satisfied than a customer who never had a problem at all!

Despite these reasons to pay careful attention to customer complaints and actively stimulate them, many customers have found their vendors to be surprisingly unreceptive to complaints. Vendors who want to improve their complaint handling should start with making it easy for customers to complain; for instance, by posting telephone numbers and email addresses on the corporate website, handing out postage-paid complaint cards and publishing the procedure that explains what happens with a complaint. Next, they should structure the complaint-handling process. The procedure must be clear to both customers and the employees that will handle the complaints. The complaint-handling procedure should include specific and measurable objectives, such as 'call back 90 per cent of complaining customers within one hour' or 'immediately solve 60 per cent of all complaints'. When actually handling customer complaints, the cardinal rule is to take all customer complaints seriously (only the customer knows how important the complaint is!) and to provide a fast and effective response. In specific cases, top management may be involved in complaint handling; for example, to repair a deteriorated relationship with an important customer or to receive direct customer feedback. Finally, all customer complaints must be analysed. Analysis of complaints per market segment, geographic region, sales region, product or industry helps to uncover root causes of problems and to improve the vendor's offering.

Of course, many complaints can be prevented by maintaining a continuous dialogue with customers, which also contributes to customer loyalty. Research has shown that worrying about dissatisfied customers may not be enough. In markets with intense competition, satisfied customers are also potential defectors; in these markets only the really satisfied customer is truly loyal (Jones and Sasser 1995).

All these sources provide pieces of customer information that managers use as building blocks to construct their customer pictures. But it must be emphasised that this involves more than just asking questions of customers and carefully listening to their answers. Many customers are unwilling to provide detailed information or are not even aware of what they really need. This means that customer interviews and surveys must be supplemented by careful observation by all vendor personnel visiting customers to identify latent customer needs. After all, a good company listens to what a customer says it wants, but a great company anticipates what a customer needs!

3.3 Collecting information about other market parties

Customer information is the key ingredient that managers use to construct market pictures. But in itself it is not enough. To construct complete and useful market pictures, managers need information about all relevant market parties. In addition to customers, this includes suppliers, competitors, government agencies, vendors of complementary products and channel partners. The two key market players that every B2B vendor needs information about are suppliers and competitors.

Collecting information about suppliers

Suppliers contribute to the creation of superior value for customers by providing materials and components, developing new technologies and products, lowering costs of materials and assisting with the vendor's product development efforts. Vendors need in-depth information about available suppliers and their capabilities.

Supplier market research is actually very similar to customer market research. There is much secondary information available. Each vendor has internal records about business transactions with suppliers, which provide information about products bought, prices paid, delivery performance and product returns. Interviews and surveys are the most frequently used techniques to collect missing information about suppliers. Purchasing officers (and sometimes product users as well) regularly interact with suppliers, which allows them to ask questions and observe supplier activities. Vendors cooperate with suppliers through joint product development and supplier development programmes. Suppliers provide feedback through supplier evaluations and *supplier councils* (round-table conversations with a few selected suppliers).

MINI CASE: WER LIEFERT WAS

W *er Liefert Was* (WLW) started in 1934/1935 as a German listing for a trade show in Leipzig, but has grown into Europe's premier site about business suppliers. For years, WLW was available as familiar blue books, but with the advent of digital technologies it switched to CD-ROM and the internet. In 1995, WLW went online and the search engine currently provides information about more than 380,000 suppliers and their products and services, classified into more than 42,000 categories. The categories are connected by keywords, facilitating a quick search of the total database. The website only includes business suppliers and provides names and contact information. In 2007, the WLW website was used by more than 1.5 million purchasing decision-makers and registered more than 22 million hits.

Source: www.wlw.de

Firms should systematically conduct supplier market research at three levels: (1) the level of the economic environment (capacity, pricing, employment); (2) the level of the industry (profitability, inventories, number of suppliers, intensity of competition); and (3) the level of the individual supplier (financial situation, product quality, delivery reliability, certified manufacturing processes, pricing structure). Supplier market research may be conducted by purchasing officers or a specialised department, or a firm could create an ad hoc research team consisting of purchasing officers and outside market researchers.

Collecting information about competitors

The primary objective of firms is to create superior value for customers. In this context, 'superior' means 'relative to the value of competitive offerings'. Customers will always compare a vendor's offering with that of its closest competitors to identify the most attractive offering. Therefore, firms need to keep a close watch on their key competitors. A firm's key competitors are those competitors who are considered to be the next-best alternative by customers. These are not always the largest firms active in the market. A small, seemingly insignificant competitor may offer a revolutionary new technology that is seriously considered by customers. In addition, firms must realise that the competitive landscape is continuously changing. Several small competitors may enter a strategic alliance and thus obtain significant economies of scope and scale; or firms from a totally different industry may suddenly decide to enter the market. Even customers and suppliers may become competitors when they expand their capabilities and activities. For all relevant competitors, a firm needs information about objectives, assumptions, strategies, resources and capabilities (Porter 1980). This information is used to predict competitive behaviour.

A competitor's *objectives* directly influence their behaviour; for instance, a competitor that wants to improve its position in a specific market segment will fiercely defend against attacks. Competitor objectives may refer to financial results ('increased profits'), market position ('belong to the top five firms in the market segment') or technological position ('quickly follow new technological developments'). Competitor objectives can often be deduced from a firm's annual report or marketplace signals. A competitor's *assumptions* also influence a competitor's actions. Competitors who think they have a loyal customer base will act accordingly. A competitor's assumptions also refer to the industry and other firms operating in the industry. With every planned action, a competitor will take expected competitive reactions into account. Naturally, these assumptions do not necessarily reflect reality. A competitor's *strategy* concerns the selection of target customers, the firm's selected value proposition and how it uses marketing instruments to implement the value proposition. A competitor's strategy is revealed by what it says (in its annual report, press releases or the business press) and what it does (hiring activity, R&D projects, strategic partnerships). A competitor's *resources and capabilities* are different from the previous three factors. While objectives, assumptions and strategy help to understand how a competitor wants to act or respond, its resources and capabilities determine its ability to act and respond effectively. Resources and capabilities may be analysed in terms of strengths and weaknesses and include a firm's product range, marketing capability, manufacturing scope, patents, R&D capacity, financial position, management skills and speed of response. Firms can use these four factors to construct competitor response profiles, which can be used to predict how competitors will respond to their marketing activities. Information about these four factors can also be used to benchmark the firm's performance with that of their major competitors. Some companies look for inspiration at firms from totally different industries that are considered *best in class* for specific business processes; for instance, Disney is considered the gold standard for customer service, Toyota for lean manufacturing and FedEx for logistics.

> ✍ **INSIGHT: Benchmarking from the customer's perspective**
>
> Identifying the right competitors to benchmark seems like a simple, straightforward task. But many firms fail to address this issue from the customer's perspective. Managers at a four-star hotel will typically benchmark themselves against other four- and five-star hotels, and perhaps even some three-star hotels. But they are using an inside-out product orientation: they define competitors as vendors of more or less the same service. But customers are not limited to such a restricted perspective.
>
> Imagine a European business executive flying from London (UK) to Phoenix (USA). When he has arrived after a long trip he picks up a rental car and then drives to his hotel. At the rental agency everything goes very smoothly: his car is ready and all he needs to do is put his suitcase in the boot and drive off. When he arrives at his hotel, there is a problem with the automated reservation system and all arriving guests are checked in manually, which causes significant delays. After waiting for more than 20 minutes, the business executive wonders: 'How is it possible that I can get my car in just three minutes and need almost half an hour to check in to my hotel?' From his perspective, one service provider delivers a wonderful experience while the other clearly falls short. To him, a rental agency and a hotel are just two service providers and the wonderful experience with the first (the rental agency) has raised his expectations for the second (the hotel).

In addition to analysing the activities of individual competitors, firms also must analyse the relationships between the major players at the industry level. According to Porter (2008), competition in an industry is influenced by five forces:

- *Degree of rivalry* between vendors, which is measured in terms of industry concentration (for example, the percentage of market share held by the four largest firms in the industry) and influenced by the number of firms, industry growth, exit barriers, the amount of fixed costs, product differences and the customers' switching costs.
- *Threat of substitutes*, which refers to products in other industries that customers may use as substitutes and is determined by variables such as the price–performance trade-off of substitutes, the costs of switching to substitutes and the substitutes' functional similarity to the product that is currently used in the industry.
- *Bargaining power of customers*, which is determined by the number of customers, industry product differentiation, the customers' threat of backward integration, the importance of the product to the customers, the customers' sensitivity to price and their switching costs.
- *Bargaining power of suppliers*, which depends on supplier concentration relative to customer concentration, the suppliers' dependence on the industry for revenues, the customers' switching costs, the extent of supplier product differentiation, the availability of substitutes, and the threat of forward integration.

- *Entry barriers*, which determine the ease of entry of new competitors and include supply-side economies of scale, network effects (when the product's attractiveness increases with the number of buyers), capital requirements, advantages of the incumbent firms (such as proprietary technology or access to distribution channels) and government regulation.

〰️ INSIGHT: Predicting how your competitors will react

A key ingredient in a firm's strategic decisions is its predictions about how competitors will react. Nevertheless, a 2005 study uncovered that fewer than one in ten managers actually incorporate expected competitor reactions into their strategic planning. This is because most managers find the task of analysing multiple options for multiple competitors using multiple metrics simply overwhelming. But a recent study shows that it does not have to be so complex. Predicting your competitors' response boils down to answering three basic questions:

1 *Will the competitor react?*

Most companies fail to realise that competitors may simply choose not to respond to a strategic move; for example, because they do not feel threatened, are too busy with their own agenda or fail to notice the strategic action in the first place. If a new product affects several of your competitors' business units, it may not be recognised as significant to any one unit and thus be overlooked. Whereas all competitors will notice a large move, the study's findings suggest that companies overestimate by 20 per cent to 30 per cent the likelihood that a medium to small action will be noticed.

2 *What options will the competitor actively consider?*

The study indicates that, although competitors may discuss many response options, they seriously investigate only two or three. And usually it is not too difficult to work out which options your competitors will consider. A new product introduction, for example, is typically reacted to by introducing a me-too product and price changes are frequently matched.

3 *Which option will the competitor most likely choose?*

The final task is to select the option that your competitor will most likely choose. To discover a competitor's metrics, management must take a look at the competitor's recent actions in the marketplace and ask themselves what measure would have led the competitor to its recent decisions.

Armed with all this information, management is able to mimic the competitor's decision-making process and identify the competitor's most likely reaction.

Source: Coyne and Horn (2009)

To chart and analyse the relationships between the industry's major players, firms must determine the industry they are in (which products; what geographic scope?), identify the major participants (buyers, suppliers, competitors, substitutes, new entrants), assess the underlying drivers of each force, determine overall industry

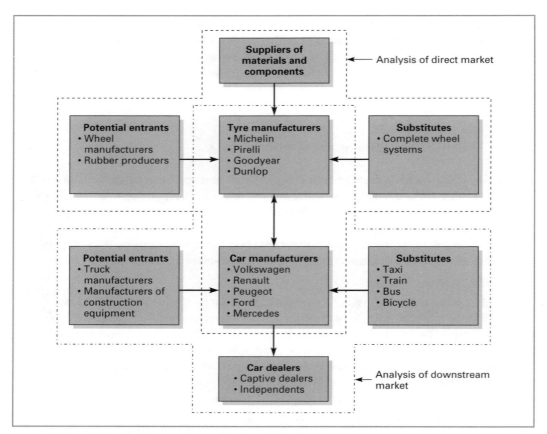

FIGURE 3.3 Competitive analysis for tyre manufacturer Michelin

structure (what determines profitability?), analyse changes and identify the elements of industry structure that might be changed (by others or by the firm itself). Because the demand for B2B products depends on the demand of downstream customers, this five-forces framework should be expanded to include downstream customers. Figure 3.3 shows the major players for a **competitive analysis** for Michelin.

While the five-forces framework is useful to quickly chart the major players and how they relate to each other, it only provides a quick snapshot. A major drawback is that the framework treats each firm as an individual player, while in practice many firms collaborate in value-creating networks (see Chapter 4). In addition, management needs to predict and analyse structural changes that are shaping the industry. Expired patents may lead to new entrants, new substitutes may appear and the relative power of buyers or suppliers may change significantly. This implies that a competitive analysis is not something to be done once every couple of years in the context of a strategic re-orientation. Instead, it must be a part of the manager's toolbox that is used continuously. The information for a competitive analysis can be drawn from many different sources, including the firm's own observations (desk research, market research, salespeople, analysis of competitive products), competitors themselves (annual reports, press releases, advertisements, trade shows, company presentations, websites) and various others (customers, industry associations, financial analysts, business press, distributors, suppliers, discussion groups on the internet, universities, patent offices). Some firms even collect competitor information by having their employees apply for a job at a competitor. After all, you are expected to ask insightful questions during a job interview. This practice, however, could be interpreted as industrial espionage and is not considered to be very ethical.

Firms should use a similar approach to collect information about complementors: their economics, strategies and goals, existing capabilities, incentives for cooperation, and any potential areas of conflict. Many firms that rigorously analyse their suppliers and competitors, however, fail to invest heavily in understanding their complementors (Yoffie and Kwak 2006).

3.4 Constructing market pictures

All collected market information contributes to the firm's understanding of its customers and markets. The newly collected information is sorted, integrated, combined with the firm's existing store of knowledge and interpreted, resulting in **market pictures**. Based on this process of market sensing, appropriate marketing strategies and actions are initiated (Figure 3.4).

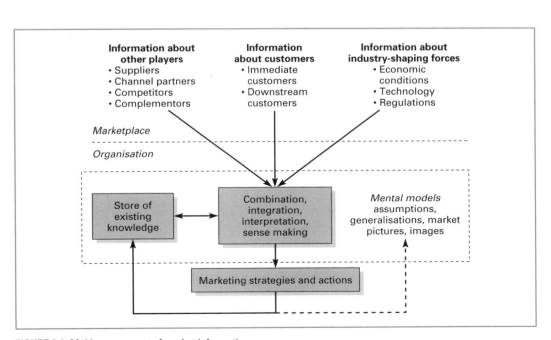

FIGURE 3.4 Making sense out of market information

A firm's competitive advantage increasingly lies in its ability to make sense of market information, rather than in its access to market information. Successful firms are not swamped by data, but make effective use of available market information to create a competitive advantage (Davenport et al. 2001; Mendelson and Ziegler 1999). Every part of their organisation continuously collects market information. They get ideas for new products from customers, but also look at non-customers, compare themselves with their competitors and collect information about best practices in other industries. They use every opportunity to collect useful market information; for instance, when developing a new generation of Word, Microsoft's product developers are forced to use the new prototypes to write their project documentation. Successful firms are also very adept at combining different pieces of market information. They integrate readily available transaction data with rich human-centric insights from customer interviews. They quickly disseminate market information within their organisation, both vertically and horizontally, and learn from their experiences through systematic evaluations. They prevent information overload through a sharp focus; successful firms have fewer product lines, fewer products per product line and focus on their most valuable customers.

The process of sense-making may be facilitated by information technologies. For example, firms use *customer relationship management* (CRM) software to integrate information from personal selling, internet and customer contact centres. And several B2B firms use *datamining* to search for hidden patterns in large amounts of data. Caterpillar used datamining to identify the 10,000 customers who are most likely to purchase a new product in the near future and derive the most value from Caterpillar products.

The benefits from effective information management may be further enhanced by applying it to the firm's entire network of partners. Chrysler used *resident suppliers* who stay on-site at Chrysler while they are engaged in engineering or quality assurance, thus ensuring a natural daily flow of information between the partners. Sun Microsystems initiated a *voice of the supplier* programme by asking suppliers for suggestions to improve the efficiency of the supply chain. Suppliers often provide better demand forecasts because they have a global perspective and deliver products not only to Sun but also to its competitors.

Mindsets and mental models

The process of market sensing, where market information is used to understand business markets, is not an exact science. How an individual perceives, uses and interprets market information depends on their background. This is referred to as a person's *mindset* or **mental model**, which is a series of deeply ingrained assumptions, generalisations, pictures and images that influence how an individual understands the world and how they take action (Senge 1990). An individual's mental model colours the perception of the type of market information that is considered important, the interpretation of market information and the translation of market information into appropriate actions. This can best be illustrated by taking a closer look at two key determinants of an individual's background, and therefore their mental model: functional specialisation and personal job experience. A product development engineer perceives the marketplace in terms of available technologies, technological development, suppliers offering key components and universities working at the cutting edge of science. When looking at customers, an engineer sees product users with a specific level of technological sophistication. In contrast, a marketing manager perceives the marketplace as groups of customers with similar needs and similar response patterns that are served by competing vendors. Looking at customers, a marketing manager sees interacting individuals buying the firm's offering because it offers them superior value. The product development engineer will focus on improving the product's value by developing interesting new features, while the marketing manager focuses on offering value to customers that is superior to the value offered by competitors. In practice, these technical and commercial worlds in B2B firms often clash and result in misunderstandings, miscommunication and even outright hostility (see also Chapter 10). Similarly, a person's job history determines their experiences with other contexts and contributes to the person's mental model. A salesperson who previously worked for a firm selling commodity components will have different ideas about the role of pricing to someone who used to sell capital equipment.

As Figure 3.4 illustrates, mental models influence how people combine, analyse and interpret market information and use this information to develop appropriate marketing strategies and actions. Because of different backgrounds, however, each person's mental model is contextual and subjective. These differences in mental models may be explicit and related to a person's job description; for instance, a marketing manager looks at customers at the level of market segments to design effective value propositions for groups of similar customers. A salesperson, in contrast, is expected to look at individual customers in terms of their decision-making processes and key decision-makers to increase their propensity to buy. In other cases, differences in mental models are much more insidious and people are unaware of how they colour their perceptions and way of thinking. It is senior management's responsibility to bring existing mental models into the open. This reveals the assumptions, knowledge and subjective beliefs that people draw upon to reach conclusions about specific issues. When everybody is aware of the mental models existing in the firm, they can be discussed and modified where necessary. This results in shared mental models that allow individuals to improve communication and coordinated action. These shared models are not set in stone, but modified as new information becomes available. A market's response to the firm's marketing strategies and actions adds to the firm's store of knowledge, but may also be used to modify mental models; for instance, when management expected all key competitors to go along with a price increase, but several of them responded by lowering their price and thus making their own products even more attractive to customers.

3.5 Market segmentation

The most common type of mental model is a firm's **market segmentation** scheme. Market segmentation is used to distinguish between groups of customers having similar needs and similar buying behaviour, allowing management to identify potentially profitable customer groups and develop for each group a distinctive value proposition that offers superior customer value. Identifying the firm's target segments is one of the most important decisions management has to make. It determines where and how the firm is going to compete and who will be the main competitors. Market segmentation and targeting decisions determine the game, the playing field and the key players involved. Management, however, must realise that every market segmentation scheme is a perceptual construct: it is a mental model that helps to make sense of the market and thus to make better decisions. Market segments do not exist in reality; they are just a way of looking at the market.

B2B market segmentation variables

B2B firms can use a large number of variables to partition markets into groups of potential customers with similar needs and/or characteristics who are likely to display similar buying behaviour. These potential segmentation variables can be grouped into three categories:

1 *Characteristics of the buying organisation* (type of organisation, number of employees, sales volume, industry, geographic location, product application, buying situation, degree of source loyalty).

2 *Characteristics of the buying centre* (buying roles, number of decision-makers, degree of formalisation, degree of centralisation, stage in buying process, type of perceived uncertainty, perceived amount of time pressure, decision-making style, purchasing strategy, interaction processes).

3 *Characteristics of the individual decision-makers* (age, education, organisational position, role and influence in buying centre, degree of self-confidence, degree of risk aversion, buying criteria).

Firms selling to large customers consisting of several divisions, plants or business units, may find it useful to treat large customers as markets and use segmentation variables to distinguish between different organisational units with different needs and different buying behaviour. Each type of organisational unit is subsequently targeted with different marketing tools. A vendor of telecommunications gear, for example, may distinguish between the customer's:

- *Headquarters and large business units (separate large accounts)*: personal selling through account managers and telemarketing for follow-up sales.

- *Regional offices and smaller business units (medium-sized accounts)*: personal selling through a regional sales team.

- *Smaller business units (small accounts)*: telemarketing.

〰️ **INSIGHT: Market segmentation in the non-commercial sector**

The literature about market segmentation focuses on how commercial firms may use the process to identify and target profitable customer groups. But market segmentation is also used by not-for-profit organisations and government agencies; for instance, major charities are experiencing increasing competitive pressures in their efforts to secure corporate donors through long-term relationships. To deal with this problem, they have started to apply market segmentation of the corporate sponsorship. Potential corporate donors (their customers) are prioritised given the significant investment costs in scarce managerial time required to develop long-term relationships. This resulted in market segments such as: corporations looking for PR benefits, corporations wanting to increase their brand reputation, corporations wanting to realise tax benefits, and pure altruists.

Source: Mitchell and Wilson (1998)

In practice, firms will often combine variables to identify the most usable market segments. A vendor of ventilation equipment, for example, may first distinguish between customer needs (adding fresh air, removing polluted air), then use the product's technical parameters (high volume/low pressure, low volume/high pressure), and finally distinguish between different buying motives (reputation, reliability, service, ease of use). The idea of combining segmentation variables is also used in two common approaches to segmenting business markets: the two-stage approach of macro-/micro-segmentation and the nested approach.

Macro- and micro-segmentation

Some 35 years ago, Wind and Cardozo (1974) presented a method for the segmentation of business markets that combines general characteristics of customer firms (such as firm size, industry and product application) with behavioural characteristics of the buying centre (the nature of the decision-making process and the individuals involved). Using this method, firms first use **macro-segmentation** to group similar customers together on the basis of their general characteristics (firm size, location, industry). SABIC Innovative Plastics, for example, groups its customers according to their industry and product application, resulting in the following segments: automotive, building and construction, bath and spa, electronics, healthcare, packaging, sign and display, storm protection, textiles, transportation and outdoor, and vehicles. The information required for macro-segmentation can be easily obtained from public secondary sources. Macro-segmentation is a common approach to market segmentation, for instance when vendors distinguish between large corporate accounts, medium-sized customers and small customers.

When macro-segmentation is insufficient to distinguish between differences in buying behaviour, the next step is to use **micro-segmentation** to look for more detailed market segments within a few selected macro-segments by using information about the customers' buying behaviour and buying centres. When Shell Lubricants UK, for example, was dissatisfied with its existing segmentation based on industry codes and geographical data, it went on to segment its markets based on the personal characteristics of the buyers involved. It surveyed 499 lubricant buyers and discovered eight clusters, based on a mix of buyers' personality traits and purchasing styles. The segments were labelled with resounding names such as 'opportunists' (who like to negotiate with small local vendors), 'conservative followers' (who value quality and are loyal to their suppliers), 'competent bureaucrats' (large customers who periodically evaluate their suppliers) and 'urban cowboys' (small firms that select vendors based on price). Using the new segmentation approach, Shell managed to develop a stronger position in the highly fragmented UK lubricant market (Mitchell and Wilson 1998).

This two-stage approach to market segmentation acknowledges that organisational buying behaviour is a complex combination of organisational and individual decision-making processes. The method's disadvantages are that the information required for micro-segmentation is both difficult and costly to collect and that the prescribed order does not always result in usable segments.

 INSIGHT: Segmenting markets based on customer groups, functions and technologies

A straightforward way to segment B2B markets is to use the three dimensions: served customer groups (who), served customer functions (what) and technologies utilised (how). Using these dimensions, a manufacturer of coatings and paint could suggest the following segmentation schemes:

- *Customer groups*: for instance, according to industry (construction, boats, transportation, chemical industry), geographic region (continent, country, province, region), nature of the customer (professional, DIY, government, industry, trade) or customer characteristics (usage, loyalty, buying centre, buying situation).

- *Customer functions*: for instance, decoration, corrosion resistance, wear resistance, making surfaces germ-free, adhesion, low friction, filling, self-healing, fire-proofing and non-wetting.

- *Technologies*: for example, chemical vapour deposition, physical vapour deposition, electroplating, extrusion, mist deposition, plasma spraying and aerosol jet deposition.

The nested approach

Bonoma and Shapiro (1983) proposed a similar, but more detailed approach to segmenting business markets. Their *nested approach* consists of five categories of increasingly detailed information about an organisation's buying behaviour:

1 *Demographics* (industry, size, location), which can be easily obtained from various secondary sources.

2 *Process characteristics* describing the organisation's operations (technology employed, whether or not the organisation uses the vendor's product, financial stability); this information can be found in the customers' annual reports or collected through salespeople, reverse engineering and observation (which names are printed on the trucks delivering products?).

3 *Purchasing approach* (organisation of the buying centre, power structure, purchasing policies, purchasing criteria, relationship with competitors), which can be obtained through salespeople or market research.

4 *Situational factors* defined at the level of the individual order (urgency, order size, product application), which can be collected by the firm's salespeople.

5 *Personal characteristics* describing the individuals participating in the buying decision (motivation, risk perception, relationship with the vendor), which is difficult and expensive to collect.

Bonoma and Shapiro recommend subsequently using all five levels of variable to identify the most useful segmentation variables. Such a systematic, hierarchical approach prevents B2B marketers from missing relevant variables; for instance, many marketers neglect situational factors, while these may be very relevant in specific situations. The required information is more difficult and costly to gather as you work your way down the five levels of variable. Firms are advised to balance the simplicity and low costs of the first levels with the rigour and expense of the later ones.

Whichever method is used, the identification of usable market segments is a process of trial and error that consists of three steps (Day 1990). First, management uses several segmentation variables to identify a number of possible segment groups. Next, they investigate if the chosen variables result in groups of customers with different response profiles. Their buying criteria, geographic location and buying behaviour must be such that they have very different requirements and costs to serve. Sometimes it may be useful to combine segments by collapsing variables that are correlated. Finally, they test the resulting segmentation scheme for relevance. Useful market segments are substantial, durable, distinctive and measurable. After all, markets can be segmented in many different ways and the only criterion to select one segmentation scheme in favour of another is that it helps to make better decisions.

MINI CASE: USING CUSTOMER PROFILES TO IDENTIFY MARKET SEGMENTS

By analysing large numbers of transactions of current customers, firms can identify groups of similar, profitable customers. The resulting profiles of profitable customers can be used to look for potential customers in the marketplace that match these profiles.

US-based Comerica Bank wanted to optimise and leverage the relationships and potential of its small-business segment. The bank collected data from millions of transactions across the enterprise that were previously unconnected and not correlated.

Tens of thousands of small businesses were separated into groupings of firms with similar buying behaviours and transaction volumes. The combinations of products and services consumed were analysed by algorithms, which uncovered patterns of similarity that would otherwise be unnoticeable (*datamining*). The bank then looked at some specific groups that appeared to have the potential for high future value; for instance, two groups had virtually identical characteristics except that one group had highly profitable loans with the bank and the other group had no loans. This information enabled the bank to effectively target the group of customers with no loans. In addition, by identifying small businesses in the marketplace who were not current bank customers but who resembled these profitable customers, the bank could efficiently market to a potentially high-profit set of prospects.

Source: Thompson (2000)

Having identified market segments, firms need to select the segments they want to target. With a differentiation approach, firms target several market segments with different value propositions. An alternative is to focus on just one or a few market segments. The attractiveness of a segment depends on its size, growth, competitive structure, entry barriers, bargaining power of customers, and threat of substitute products. In addition, a selected market segment needs to fit with the firm's competencies and the ease with which these competencies can be further developed. After all, firms want to develop and maintain a sustainable competitive advantage in their selected target markets. The next step is to develop and implement a value proposition for each segment.

Online
Learning Centre

When you have read this chapter, log on to the Online Learning Centre website at **www.mcgraw-hill.co.uk/textbooks/biemans** to explore chapter-by-chapter test questions, further reading and more online study tools.

Summary of Key Concepts

- Effective marketing strategies are based on an intimate understanding of customers and the markets they are a part of. Market sensing is the process of collecting market information and making sense of it.

- A firm's market orientation consists of: (a) collecting market information, (b) disseminating market information within the firm, and (c) using market information as the basis for marketing strategies and activities.

- A firm's market orientation has a positive effect on sales, profits and return on investment (ROI), as well as on employee satisfaction and commitment.

- The key component of market information is information about customers' wants and needs.

- B2B vendors use a wide variety of sources to collect customer information, such as published sources, sales records, market research, interaction with customers and customer feedback.

- Salespeople are a useful source of objective, factual customer information; all other customer information is better collected by specialised market researchers.

- In addition to customer information, B2B vendors need information about other market parties (suppliers, competitors, channel partners) and market-shaping factors (economic conditions, technological developments).

- All market information is combined and integrated to construct market pictures that represent managers' perception of the market.

- Mental models influence the type of market information collected, as well as the interpretation of this information and how it is translated into marketing actions. Managers' mental models are determined by both their background and personality.

- A well-known example of a mental model is the firm's market segmentation scheme. It determines how managers perceive the market by summarising the complexity of the marketplace into a limited number of easily understood market segments.

🔑 Key terms

Discussion questions

1 Effective market sensing requires a firm to be open to a wide variety of market signals and sources. While much of the required information is available through regular channels, firms may identify more hidden opportunities and threats by using their peripheral vision. How can B2B firms develop the peripheral vision of their managers?

2 Suppose that you are a manufacturer of injection moulding machines for the plastics industry. Which information sources would you use to research your markets?

3 Which characteristics should a business market researcher possess? Suppose that you are a marketing manager at a manufacturer of complex medical equipment and are looking for a market researcher. Which requirements would you include in your advertisement?

4 Why do many B2B firms use a sales information system and a separate system for marketing information? Which problems can you expect when these two systems are unable to communicate with each other? How can you solve these problems?

5 Information about customers, suppliers and competitors can be used for various purposes. Describe a number of different ways in which a firm may use information about customers, suppliers and competitors.

6 Efficient and effective dissemination of market information is a prerequisite for effective use of market information. What specific measures can a firm implement to stimulate the effective dissemination of market information?

7 The effective use of market information may be hindered by the existence of different, conflicting mental models in a firm. How can a firm identify existing mental models? How can a firm, faced with several conflicting mental models, develop shared mental models that stimulate more effective decision making?

8 How may firms use the concept of market pictures to improve marketing decision making?

9 Despite the existence of sophisticated methods for market segmentation, most B2B firms use simple classifications based on firm size, industry or geographic location. What are the advantages of such an approach? What are the potential disadvantages of such a simple classification scheme?

10 The implementation of market segmentation is often characterised by all kinds of problems. Describe several problems that may occur when a B2B firm wants to implement market segmentation. In addition, describe for all of these potential problem areas how they may be prevented or solved.

Further reading

Day, George S. (1994) Continuous learning about markets, *California Management Review*, 36(4): 9–31.

Kohli, Ajay K. and Bernard J. Jaworski (1990) Market orientation: the construct, research propositions, and managerial implications, *Journal of Marketing*, 54(2): 1–18.

Mitchell, Vincent-Wayne and Dominic F. Wilson (1998) Balancing theory and practice: a reappraisal of business-to-business segmentation, *Industrial Marketing Management*, 27(5): 429–445.

References

Barwise, Patrick and Sean Meehan (2004) Don't be unique, be better, *MIT Sloan Management Review*, 45(4): 23–26.

Bonoma, Thomas V. and Benson P. Shapiro (1983) *Segmenting the Industrial Market*, Lexington, MA: Lexington Books.

Coyne, Kevin P. and John Horn (2009) Predicting your competitor's reaction, *Harvard Business Review*, 87(4): 90–97.

Davenport, Thomas H., Jeanne C. Harris and Ajay K. Kohli (2001) How do they know their customers so well?, *Sloan Management Review*, 42(2): 63–73.

Day, George S. (1990) *Market Driven Strategy: Processes for Creating Value*, New York: Free Press.

Day, George S. (1994) Continuous learning about markets, *California Management Review*, 36(4): 9–31.

Day, George S. and Paul J. H. Schoemaker (2006) *Peripheral Vision: Detecting the Weak Signals That Will Make or Break Your Company*, Boston, MA: Harvard Business School Press.

Fuld, Leonard (2003) Be prepared, *Harvard Business Review*, 81(11): 20–21.

Grace, David and Tom Pointon (1980) Marketing research through the salesforce, *Industrial Marketing Management*, 9(1): 53–58.

Jones, Thomas O. and W. Earl Sasser, Jr. (1995) Why satisfied customers defect, *Harvard Business Review*, 73(6): 88–99.

Kirca, Ahmet H., Satish Jayachandran and William O. Bearden (2005) Market-orientation: a meta-analytic review and assessment of its antecedents and impact on performance, *Journal of Marketing*, 69(2): 24–41.

Kohli, Ajay K. and Bernard J. Jaworski (1990) Market orientation: the construct, research propositions, and managerial implications, *Journal of Marketing*, 54(2): 1–18.

Langerak, Fred (2003) An appraisal of research on the predictive power of market orientation, *European Management Journal*, 21(4): 447–464.

Leonard, Dorothy and Jeffrey F. Rayport (1997) Spark innovation through empathic design, *Harvard Business Review*, 75(6): 102–113.

Liu, Sandra S. and Lucette B. Comer (2007) Salespeople as information gatherers: associated success factors, *Industrial Marketing Management*, 36(5): 565–574.

McQuarrie, Edward F. (1991) The customer visit: qualitative research for business-to-business marketers, *Marketing Research*, 3(1): 15–28.

Mendelson, Haim and Johannes Ziegler (1999) *Survival of the Smartest: Managing Information for Rapid Action and World-Class Performance*, New York: Wiley.

Mitchell, Vincent-Wayne and Dominic F. Wilson (1998) Balancing theory and practice: a reappraisal of business-to-business segmentation, *Industrial Marketing Management*, 27(5): 429–445.

Moenaert, Rudy, Henry Robben and Peter Gouw (2008) *Visionary Marketing: Building Sustainable Business*, Leuven: LannooCampus.

Porter, Michael E. (1980) *Competitive Strategy: Techniques for Analyzing Industries and Competitors*, New York: Free Press.

Porter, Michael E. (2008) The five competitive forces that shape strategy, *Harvard Business Review*, 86(1): 78–93.

Senge, Peter (1990) *The Fifth Discipline: The Art and Practice of the Learning Organization*, New York: Doubleday.

Thompson, Harvey (2000) *The Customer-Centered Enterprise: How IBM and Other World-Class Companies Achieve Extraordinary Results by Putting Customers First*, New York: McGraw-Hill.

von Hippel, Eric (1986) Lead users: a source of novel product concepts, *Management Science*, 32(7): 791–805.

Wiersema, Fred (1996) *Customer Intimacy: Pick Your Partners, Shape Your Culture, Win Together*, Santa Monica, CA: Knowledge Exchange.

Wind, Yoram and Richard N. Cardozo (1974) Industrial market segmentation, *Industrial Marketing Management*, 3(2): 153–166.

Yoffie, David B. and Mary Kwak (2006) With friends like these: the art of managing complementors, *Harvard Business Review*, 84(9): 89–98.

PART 03
Defining Superior Value for Customers

CHAPTER

04

Creating value for customers

Introduction

Based on their understanding of customers and markets, firms must develop compelling strategies to create a competitive advantage. Developing a strategy involves making two key strategic decisions: (1) Which customers will we target? (2) What value will we offer them? The decisions are closely related and influenced by market conditions and firm competencies. Ultimately, the objective of every B2B firm is to offer superior value to customers, that is, better value than the next-best alternative.

This chapter starts out by describing how B2B firms select target customers and determine the value they will offer these customers. The selection of target customers depends on the value of these customers (expressed in terms of customer lifetime value), the customers' needs, firm competencies and competitive forces. Together, these factors determine where and how a firm may profitably create superior value for customers. Tools such as the customer-activity cycle can be used to identify potentially profitable value gaps. The firm's strategy is translated into a value proposition, which specifies the value offered to a specific group of customers. To implement the value proposition, B2B firms increasingly rely on outside partners who contribute to the creation of value to customers. B2B vendors must be able to explain in detail to prospective customers the value of their products, which requires a detailed understanding of customers and how they derive value from the vendor's product. But this is not a one-time activity; successful vendors continuously monitor and measure the value created for their customers. This information is then used to update their value models, refine their value proposition and substantiate their claims.

4.1 Developing strategy by selecting customers and value

Based on its understanding of customers and markets, a B2B firm creates a long-term competitive advantage by developing and exploiting a unique **strategic position** in its industry. To realise a strategic position, a firm needs to (Markides 2000):

1 Define the business it is in.

2 Decide *who* will be its target customers, *what* value it will offer them and *how* it will achieve this.

3 Implement the appropriate supporting organisational environment.

Armed with knowledge about the market, potential customers and the firm's capabilities, management must first determine the corporate mission by addressing the fundamental question: 'What business are we in?' A firm's **business definition** defines the playing field on which it will compete, provides focus to the organisation and guides decisions about where to invest. As such, a firm's mission captures the firm's identity by describing the superior value it offers to customers. Firms that lack a clear, distinct mission are often plagued by misunderstandings, different and changing priorities and a loss of focus.

Vendors define their business based on their products, the customer needs that they want to fulfil or their unique competences. Kone, a Finnish manufacturer of elevators and escalators, defines its corporate objective as 'to offer the best people flow experience by developing and delivering solutions that enable people to move smoothly, safely, comfortably and without waiting in buildings in an increasingly urbanizing environment' (www.kone.com). In 1980, Kone entered the automatic building door service business, because the skills required were similar to those needed in the elevator business and many of the customers were the same. Based on this reasoning, Kone made several strategic acquisitions and by 2000 it had become the leading company in the field. Dell Computer defines its computer business based on its very successful low-cost capability, which in 2002 was also applied to printers. Whatever method is used, a firm's business definition defines *where* it wants to compete and its strategy describes *how* it plans to compete in that arena.

MINI CASE: UNBRIDLED DIVERSIFICATION BECAUSE OF A VAGUE BUSINESS DEFINITION

Blue Circle Industries PLC, the British company that used to be one of the world's leading producers of cement, decided in the early 1980s to branch out from its core business. Blue Circle diversified into a variety of other businesses: property management, brick production, waste management, industrial minerals, gas cookers, bathroom furnishings and even lawnmowers! The driving logic behind all this diversification was grounded in management's perception of the business they were in. According to one senior executive: 'We started out believing that our business was not just the cement business but the supply of building materials, *one* of which is cement. This led us into the brick business and then soon after that into cooking appliances and central heating boilers – after all, these are all products you need when you build your house with our bricks and cement. The culmination of this strategy was our move into lawnmowers, based on the logic that you need a lawnmower for your garden, which is after all next to the house which our materials built!' This strategy proved to be unsuccessful. In 2001, the company was bought by the French company Lafarge, which thus became the world's largest cement manufacturer.

Source: Markides (2000)

Having defined the firm's business, management needs to decide who will be the target customers, what value they will offer them and how they will achieve this. This chapter focuses on the first two questions (*who* will be targeted with *what*?), which result in the firm's value proposition. How the value proposition is subsequently translated into marketing instruments is presented in Chapters 5–8, and the design and implementation of the appropriate organisational environment is the subject of Chapter 10.

Successful firms create and implement strategies that help them to offer superior value to customers. All too often, strategy development is an annual ritual with the same group of senior managers performing the same analyses, comparing themselves with the same competitors, arriving at more or less the same conclusions and resulting in a strategy that is very similar to that of its major competitors. Firms may stimulate creativity and out-of-the-box thinking by establishing a shadow strategy committee, consisting of employees who are relatively new to the firm and not yet locked into corporate mental models, and by combining the formal process of strategic planning with experiments in the organisation (trial and error). Experiments and spontaneous initiatives contribute ideas to be evaluated by top management during strategy development.

Some firms start their strategy development with the selection of target customers and then determine the value to be offered to them. Others start with the value they want to offer and then identify appropriate customers. Still others start with their core competences and use these to identify both target customers and the value offered to them. No method is inherently superior; successful firms try all of them as thought experiments in the search for the best strategy. The process of strategy development and evaluation should be made explicit to increase its effectiveness. Managers often make the mistake of quickly evaluating a few strategic options, based on their industry experience and intuition. Instead, firms should systematically evaluate strategic options using the following criteria:

- *Usefulness.* Does the strategy solve our strategic problems? Does it capitalise on opportunities in the environment? Does it use our core competences? Will it help us achieve our objectives?
- *Feasibility.* Do we possess the resources, knowledge and skills to implement the strategy? How will our competitors probably react to it?
- *Acceptability.* Does the strategy fit in our organisation? Can we mobilise the individuals who must implement it? What are the financial risks of the strategy? Does implementation of the strategy require organisational changes?

In practice, strategy development is not without problems. The most common mistakes are an emphasis on very ambitious strategies while ignoring their implementation, endless analyses that result in thick reports and vague strategies, too much emphasis on realising operational improvements (how) and insufficient attention to other strategic choices (who and what), a failure to choose because one wants to remain flexible and a failure to revisit the strategy every year (Markides 2000). A key ingredient of successful strategy development is flexibility, especially when faced with rapidly changing environments. In such situations, a biannual planning process is insufficient and firms must continuously monitor important changes in the environment, adapt their strategies and implement the required changes. In this continuous process of renewal, firms should beware of a narrow focus on existing customers, obsolete mental models and past investments in competences that are no longer relevant.

4.2 Selecting customers

Many B2B firms select their target customers by looking at the market and identifying customers that appear to be interesting because of their needs or expected profitability (outside-in). An alternative approach to **customer selection** is to start with the firm's core competences and look for customers who fit with them (inside-out). This approach has the advantage of not using any preconceived ideas about the potential market, which broadens the range of potential customers. Managers are advised to try both approaches in their search for the most promising set of target customers who best match the firm's capabilities to deliver superior customer value. Many B2B firms fail to make conscious decisions about which customers to target. Instead, they embrace the general principle that every paying customer is welcome. Doing so, however, reduces the firm's focus, dilutes its market impact and reduces the ROI on its marketing expenditures. Successful companies carefully select their customers and treat their customer base as a portfolio of **customer relationships**. In making marketing decisions, their central objective is to maximise the value of their customer portfolio.

The value of customers

The value of a company is determined by its current and future profits, which in turn are determined by the firm's revenues and the costs of realising those revenues. In other words: a firm's value is equal to the sum of the value of each customer relationship. This value is called **customer equity** and a firm will make its decisions based on its expected effects on the firm's customer equity (Blattberg et al. 2001).

But how does one calculate the value of an individual customer relationship? The value of a customer relationship refers to all revenues and costs incurred during its lifetime. This **customer lifetime value** or *return on customer* is calculated as the present value of all future cash flows attributed to the customer relationship (Peppers and Rogers 2005). The revenues are determined by future sales and margins, while the costs include acquisition costs (marketing and sales costs to acquire the customer), development costs to expand the relationship (identifying new needs, after-sales service, increasing the share of customer) and retention costs to increase the length of the relationship (reactivating a slumbering account, increasing the value offered). Using these elements, the value of an individual customer relationship can be calculated as follows:

$$V = \sum_{t=1}^{n} S_t m_t d^t - \sum_{t=1}^{n} (D_t + R_t) d^t - A$$

V = value of the customer
S_t = sales to the customer in period t
m_t = margin per product unit in period t
d = discount rate ($d = 1 / (1 + \text{cc})$; cc = cost of capital)
D_t = development costs in period t
R_t = retention costs in period t
A = acquisition costs
n = number of periods that the product is being sold to the customer

In practice, it is not always easy to calculate the various elements of the equation; for instance, how do you allocate the costs of a corporate advertising campaign to individual customers? And how do you estimate the future sales for individual customers? But even rough estimates (for instance, based on information about prior purchases and costs of current customers) are to be preferred over simple intuition and contribute to management's understanding of customers and thus to better marketing decisions. The presented formula is a simplification of reality; for instance, it assumes a constant stream of revenues during a certain time period. But customers sometimes buy from one vendor and at other times from another. Therefore, vendors may improve their customer lifetime value calculations by including the probability of a sale to the customer.

Calculating a customer's lifetime value becomes even more complicated when one takes into account that customers may spread positive word-of-mouth to others, who in turn may also become customers. The value of these new customers acquired through positive word-of-mouth must be added to the value of the customer who spread the word. But some of these new customers would have become customers anyway, even without the recommendation from another customer. That means that the company saves on acquisition costs and these savings should be added to the value of the customer making the recommendation. Kumar et al. (2007) used this line of reasoning to estimate the value of word-of-mouth and found that only a minority of customers actually recommended a firm to others. What's more, very few of these referrals actually generated new customers. Naturally, these numbers will vary per industry. In many business markets, customers will be unwilling to recommend their vendor to others because they do not want to help their competitors.

The results from customer lifetime value calculations can be used to estimate the value of individual customer relationships, of market segments or groups of prospective customers, which can then be used to select target segments. In addition, such calculations help to estimate the effects of marketing strategies on the firm's customer equity, and thus to allocate the marketing budget to the most effective strategies and activities. For example, should one invest in acquiring new customers, developing existing customers, retaining current customers or increasing the likelihood of repeat purchases? Companies that experiment with calculating the value of customer relationships can classify their customers according to their lifetime values and design effective strategies for each group of customers (Figure 4.1). The most valuable customers must be retained and their value further increased. In addition, management may focus on acquiring new customers who match the profiles of these very profitable customers. For the less profitable customers, management must design strategies to increase their profitability; for instance, by eliminating barriers, increasing sales, reducing costs or having them pay for the costs of expensive customer service. As a last resort, management may decide to actively discourage future business with some of these customers (demarketing).

Transactions or relationships?

A key strategic issue in selecting customers is whether to focus on customers looking for transactions or on customers who want long-term relationships. Some customers possess much product knowledge and look for efficient single transactions, while others want a long-term strategic relationship with a vendor that helps to define the problem and identify the appropriate solution. When both vendor and buyer are looking for a transaction, their business is dominated by short-term thinking, focused on the current transaction without any thought about future transactions. In other situations, vendor and buyer cooperate to maximise the added value of their relationship, based on trust, commitment and shared objectives.

Until the 1980s, business markets were generally perceived as collections of independent buyers and sellers, with sellers persuading buyers to buy their products. But a large number of studies by a group of European marketing researchers showed that many B2B markets are characterised by buyer–seller

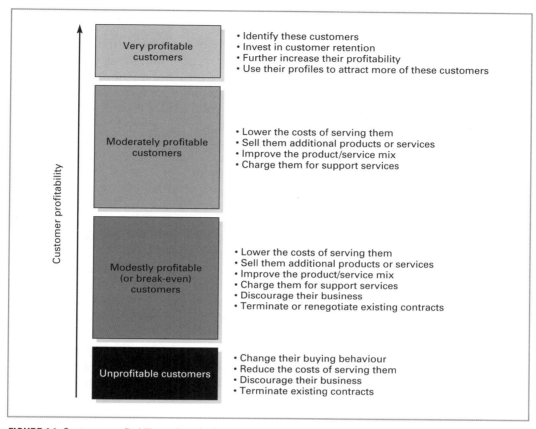

FIGURE 4.1 Customer profitability and marketing strategy

relationships that are stable (frequently lasting ten to 20 years), complex (with contacts between individuals at various levels and from various departments), symmetric (with a balance between resources and capabilities of both parties) and informal (emphasis on personal relationships rather than formal contracts) (Håkansson and Snehota 1995). In such relationships, both parties continuously adapt to each other and cooperation is frequently accompanied by conflict (for instance, about the division of revenues). Personal relationships and social interaction are at the core of the relationship and over time routines and rituals become established. Ford et al. (1998) describe how such B2B relationships develop over time. At first, there is no relationship. Buyers are hesitant to look for a new vendor, but disappointing performance or conflicts may cause them to switch. This *pre-relationship stage* is characterised by much uncertainty, for example about the quality of the new vendor's offering, the exact costs involved and whether the vendor will keep its promises. The buyer's switching costs determine the extent to which the buyer is locked into the current vendor.

During the *exploratory stage*, the relationship starts to take shape, for instance because both parties negotiate regarding a major purchase. The two parties have only marginal experience of each other and, by exchanging information, they create trust and reduce the distance between them. At this stage, establishing commitment is critical to moving the relationship forward. During the subsequent *developing stage*, mutual dependence also increases (for instance, because business between the two companies increases). A growing business volume may also be accompanied by changes in the nature of the relationship, for example because both parties collaborate in product development. Both parties may also increase investment in the relationship by adapting to each other and thus further increasing commitment. As the relationship develops mutual trust also increases.

In the final *stable stage*, both companies have reached a certain stability in their learning about each other and their investments and commitment to the relationship; for instance, when deliveries have become routine and standard operating procedures are established. Such institutionalisation of the relationship may also cause problems down the road; for example, when the routines that allow the relationship to operate at low costs are no longer questioned and no longer match the companies' changed requirements. In practice, B2B relationships may follow this pattern of development, get stuck in one stage or another or be terminated prematurely because of changed conditions or a lack of commitment.

Personal relationships are a key ingredient of successful B2B relationships. Individuals initiate, invest in, expand and even terminate relationships. Personal relationships are used to exchange information and experiences, assess the other organisation's characteristics, capabilities and potential contributions, negotiate about contracts and conditions, solve problems, cement the relationship, exploit new opportunities, obtain useful references, maintain social contacts and search for additional ways to jointly create value. While most of this interaction is task related, social interaction contributes to trust and commitment. But too much social interaction may be detrimental to effective business relationships. Many vendors prevent their salespeople from developing too-close relationships with their buyers' purchasing agents to maintain their objectivity and ensure that they place the vendor's interests above those of the buyer.

Many buyer–seller relationships consist of multiple personal relationships between people from various departments at both organisations. Salespeople have relationships with purchasing managers and end-users, product developers talk with engineers at buyers about their new designs, and marketing managers discuss with their customers' business managers how their products create value. In addition, many employees have personal relationships with people at other organisations. A product developer, for example, may be a member of a professional organisation and meet colleagues at technical conferences and trade shows, or have important contacts with researchers at universities. These personal relationships are developed and maintained through both informal means (lunches, informal visits, golf clinics) and meetings during professional events (conferences, trade shows, workshops, forums).

Trend towards relationship marketing

While close relationships with customers used to be typical for vendors of complex products that require much support, an increasing number of firms have discovered the benefits of relationship marketing. Traditional marketing theory emphasises the acquisition of new customers. But several studies have shown that firms may be better off investing their resources in the retention of existing customers. Existing customers do not require acquisition costs, while marketing and sales costs are also lower (after all, the vendor already knows the customers, their buying behaviour and their key decision-makers). In addition, satisfied customers are more loyal, tend to buy more products and provide positive recommendations to potential customers and thus result in higher profits (Reichheld and Sasser 1990). But there are also potential disadvantages to close, long-term relationships; for instance, when there is no balance in the value brought to the relationship by both partners, one partner may become overdependent on the other. Other potential drawbacks of close relationships are leaking of confidential information to third parties, unexpectedly high costs of coordination and loss of control. In addition, the results from more recent studies question the direct relationship between duration of the customer relationship (loyalty) and profitability (Reinartz and Kumar 2002). Ultimately, while there is a trend towards relationship marketing in B2B marketing, both short- and long-term relationships with customers may be very profitable and managers must carefully estimate customer lifetime values.

4.3 Determining the value offered to customers

The second key component of a firm's strategy is the value offered to customers. Again, firms may use two approaches: (1) start with the value that customers want and determine the value that the firm is able to provide, or (2) start with the firm's capabilities and determine the value that the firm is uniquely equipped to provide. Again, B2B firms are advised to combine both approaches in their search for the superior value to be offered to customers. Based on the customer needs identified, managers should define the **value** offered to customers in terms of (1) the vendor's offering, and (2) the reasons why customers should pay for this offering (*reasons to buy*). The vendor's offering describes the specific products and services offered to customers, but the reasons to buy explain why customers should pay for this offering instead of a competitor's offering. The reasons to buy focus on the superior value that customers are promised to derive from the vendor's offering. On its website, for example, Shell tells B2B customers: 'We aim to make a measurable difference to your business performance', and summarises the reasons to buy in terms of partnership, technology and delivery:

> **Partnership.** We work with you to help you deliver on your promises.
> **Technology.** We have over 100 years' experience as technology pioneers, with a commitment to helping you realise a successful business future.
> **Delivery.** We strive to provide you with what you want, where you want and when you want it.

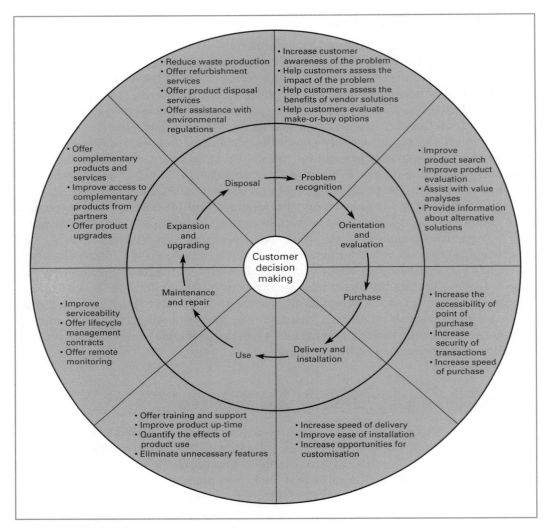

FIGURE 4.2 Identifying opportunities for value creation

The customer-activity cycle presented in Chapter 2 is a useful tool to identify new opportunities to create value for customers. The basic idea is to map the customer-activity cycle and explore opportunities for value creation by analysing a series of critical issues for each stage (Figure 4.2). A vendor of process equipment, for example, might identify and investigate the following opportunities to create customer value: launching a website where customers can virtually evaluate different equipment configurations, offering remote equipment monitoring to lower the costs of maintenance and maximise the product's performance, and assisting customers with product disposal by buying back obsolete equipment and offering new models at attractive prices. All too often, vendors are too much focused on their current products and unaware of customer needs that are not yet addressed.

By mapping the customer-activity cycle vendors can identify such value gaps and translate them into attractive products and services. Most vendors will discover that different types of customer use different customer-activity cycles and that customers differ in the leverage that can be achieved during the stages of the activity cycle. Mapping customer-activity cycles helps a vendor to achieve an outside-in look at its business. In addition, it contributes to corporate alignment by showing people, departments and business units where they contribute to the customer's activities.

4.4 Developing the value proposition

Although the selection of target customers and the definition of the value offered to them were presented as two separate decisions, they are in fact very closely related. Companies select target customers because they are able to provide them with superior customer value. And they develop the value to be offered to customers based on these customers' needs and wants. Both decisions are taken together through an iterative process until management has identified the **value proposition** that offers a sustainable competitive advantage. In practice, we see that firms formulate three types of value proposition (Anderson et al. 2006).

1 The simplest type of value proposition lists *all benefits* that management believes their offering delivers to target customers, usually from the perspective of – the more they can think of, the better. But the problem is that management may claim advantages for features that do not actually provide benefit to target customers. Moreover, competitors may offer the same benefits, thus eliminating their contribution to a distinctive advantage.

2 Firms that recognise that the customer has an alternative, list the *favourable points of difference* between their offering and the next-best alternative. Thus, it answers the question why a customer should buy your offering instead of a competitor's. But this approach may still present points of difference that have no real value to the customer.

3 The best approach is to present a *resonating focus* that describes the one or two points of difference that deliver the greatest value to target customers. It focuses on those features and benefits that are perceived to be most worthwhile by the firm's target customers. While it is the gold standard of value propositions, it also requires the most extensive customer research.

A good value proposition is distinctive (superior to the competition), measurable (the key points of difference identified in the value proposition are quantified in monetary terms) and sustainable (the vendor is able to implement the value proposition for a significant period of time). In addition, many B2B vendors will need to formulate several value propositions; for instance, because customers use the product for different applications or in different situations and therefore value different features and benefits. But even when all customers use the product for the same application, a vendor may need several value propositions to target the different members of the buying centre who all focus on different elements of the vendor's offering. UPS, the world's largest package delivery company and leading provider of specialised transportation and logistics services, presents on its website (www.ups.com) different value propositions for senior directors, small businesses, logistics managers, shipping managers and personal assistants. For senior directors UPS emphasises its global presence and ability to help streamline a complex global supply chain, enhance customer service and improve cash flow. Logistics managers are told that 'UPS can help improve your logistics and distribution operations [and has] the advanced information technology to back it up'. And personal assistants are persuaded that with UPS they can choose when and where to ship worldwide and track their shipments from start to finish.

4.5 Designing the value network

Having developed a value proposition, a firm needs to decide how it will create this value for customers. Each firm's core competencies are necessarily limited and to create superior value for customers most firms rely on contributions from partners. This results in a value-creating network that combines the efforts of vendors, suppliers, channel partners and vendors of complementary products and services to create superior value for customers (Kothandaraman and Wilson 2001; Figure 4.3).

Through cooperation with suppliers, for example, a firm may develop a new jet engine with significantly higher fuel efficiency which reduces costs for airlines and allows them to fly longer direct routes. Cooperation with competitors provides firms with access to missing competencies or allows them to jointly develop an industry standard. Firms may even cooperate with their customers to provide them with

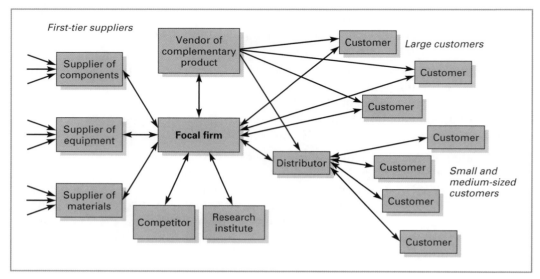

FIGURE 4.3 A value-creating network

better value, for instance through joint product development, online configurators that help customers to design customised solutions, and customised websites that allow customers to efficiently order preselected products at pre-approved prices. Well-known examples are couriers such as DHL, FedEx and UPS, who create value for customers by allowing them to track packages online. On an average day, UPS receives no fewer than 18.5 million online tracking requests.

Within a **value network**, companies that independently provide complementary products or services directly to mutual customers (complementors) are a special type of partner. Firms do business with suppliers and customers and can increase their leverage with them by increasing their purchases from suppliers or by tailoring their products to specific customer wishes. But complementors are independent firms who frequently use very different business models. For instance, a computer manufacturer may make money by selling high-end computers at a premium, while software manufacturers need large volume to recoup their substantial investments in R&D. Firms may use a combination of hard power (inducement or coercion) and soft power (persuasion through indirect means) to manage their complementors (Yoffie and Kwak 2006).

With the rise of value networks, the nature of competition shifts from competition between individual firms to competition between alternative value networks competing for the customer's business. But there is also competition *within* the network. After all, all cooperating partners compete for the customer's margins. In other words, successful value networks manage to balance cooperation and competition. A value network's effectiveness in creating superior value for customers is determined by its design, capabilities and the relationships between the partners. A successful value network is directed by a central firm that creates value for its partners in the network, formulates a strategic vision for the network, selects and motivates suitable partners, coordinates the strategies of the various partners and directs the exchange of information. Strategies, business processes and operational plans are coordinated, which has a positive effect on the effectiveness of product development and production planning and on the efficiency of billing, transportation and inventory management. Information is also shared freely and problems solved jointly (Ashkenas et al. 1995). Internet and e-commerce are key facilitators of many value-creating networks. The internet allows for efficient and fast communication and e-commerce offers firms a larger potential customer base and increases the number of potential partners. Partners can be connected electronically, which reduces inventories and increases the network's responsiveness. In addition, a continuous web presence (24 hours a day, 365 days per year) allows firms to offer new value to customers (for instance, increased availability or customised products) and offers customers the choice of how they want to interact with the firm, either through a salesperson, over the web or a combination of the two.

Supply chain management

To create effective value networks, firms must streamline their interactions both upstream (with suppliers), downstream (with channel partners and customers) and sideways (with competitors and vendors of complementary products), a practice that is also referred to as **supply chain management**. But, in practice, it is not always easy to transform long-held suspicious attitudes into effective cooperation. A purchasing agent who has enjoyed many years of success by squeezing suppliers may find it hard to suddenly treat suppliers as partners in value creation. Sometimes, however, firms discover significant benefits by simply starting a dialogue with their upstream or downstream partners. A producer of aluminium manufactured molten aluminium, then cast it into aluminium bars and shipped these to its customers. But a discussion with a major customer showed that the customer would first melt the aluminium bars again for use in its casting process. Both companies quickly designed a system where the vendor supplies melted aluminium in special containers, thus reducing process steps and costs in both organisations.

Using supply chain management, vendors look beyond their direct suppliers to the second-tier suppliers and so on. Motorola cooperated closely with its first-tier suppliers of critical components and agreed with them that it must approve second-tier suppliers. It also evaluated these supply relationships as part of its quality audit process, and trained its direct suppliers in how to audit their own suppliers. But Motorola went even further – because it wants to have the best suppliers, it also wants to be their best customer. To achieve this objective, the firm annually surveyed its preferred suppliers, asking them to compare its performance on several measures with their other customers (Lewis 1995).

MINI CASE: SUBSTANTIAL IMPROVEMENTS THROUGH SUPPLY CHAIN MANAGEMENT

The results from an effective supply chain strategy can be significant. A major global chemical company substantially increased its return on assets (ROA) by aligning functional activities with supply chain strategy. The benefits from this strategy are captured in the following metrics:

- Sales revenue increased from $2 billion to $2.002 billion.
- Inventory carrying costs decreased by $5 million, production costs by $1 million, transportation costs by $1 million and procurement costs by $1 million.
- The combination of increased sales and reduced costs increased net income from $100 million to $108 million.
- Working capital also improved, because inventory investments decreased by $45 million.
- In addition, fixed capital investments also decreased: a planned distribution centre was no longer necessary, resulting in reduced fixed capital of $3 million.
- These reductions in working capital and fixed capital resulted in a reduction in capital investments from $700 million to $652 million.
- Finally, the increased net income together with the reduced capital investments increased the firm's return on assets from 14.29 to 16.56 per cent.

Source: Slone et al. (2007)

Managing supply chain relationships

In a value network, all relationships with strategic partners must be managed. Successful relationship management encompasses the selection of a suitable partner, designing the partnership and managing the ongoing relationship. A successful relationship begins with selecting an appropriate partner who possesses the required complementary competencies or assets (such as technological know-how or access to specific markets). In addition, the strategies and objectives of both partners should be compatible and both should enter the partnership for positive reasons (creating or exploiting new opportunities) rather than negative ones (compensating a weakness or escaping from a difficult situation). Firms can use a *partner scorecard* to assess the compatibility among potential supply chain partners (Fawcett and Cooper 1998). These scorecards rate the partners' alignment in areas such as information technology, performance measurement, costing systems and organisational capabilities. This type of scorecard helps prevent firms from entering into problematic strategic alliances, but it may also be used to identify shortcomings and opportunities for improvement in existing partner relationships.

After a partner has been selected, the partnership needs to be designed in terms of objectives, contributions, activities to be performed, responsibilities, division of revenues and costs, and time horizon. In addition, both partners need to design mechanisms and procedures to successfully manage the partnership (decision-making processes, procedures to resolve conflicts, stimulation of individuals involved in the partnership, formal and informal communications). Potential partners are advised not to try to regulate the partnership in too much detail but instead to focus on the spirit of the partnership. Relationships are dynamic and change with changing circumstances and partnership contracts should reflect this.

Trust, open communication and flexibility are the key ingredients of a successful relationship. Unexpected situations will always occur and successful relationships are characterised by honest partners who are flexible enough to adapt themselves to changing circumstances. Some firms use relationship managers to coordinate the complex web of personal relationships between partner organisations. But no matter how the relationship is designed and structured, firms should always continuously evaluate the relationship at both the strategic and operational levels, using a *supply chain performance scorecard* (Fawcett and Cooper 1998). Does the partnership still offer the expected benefits? Does the partnership still create enough added value? Is this added value still relevant from the perspective of our strategic plans? A manufacturer of scientific equipment, for example, evaluates its preferred suppliers on metrics about quality, delivery, capacity, quality audits, commitment to continuous improvement, early design participation, technology road maps, cost improvement, service, financial stability, data transfer ability, plant locations and environmental performance (such as recycling and the elimination of chlorofluorocarbons in manufacturing).

4.6 Measuring value

Successful B2B firms are able to explain in great detail the value of their offering. After all, one of the most critical questions every potential customer will raise is: 'Why should we do business with you instead of with one of your competitors?' Only by explaining the value of the firm's offering and substantiating the claims with supporting materials can this question be properly addressed. But this requires in-depth insight into the value of the firm's offering *and* the value of the offering from the next-best alternative, since customers will always compare alternative offerings. The best approach to **measuring value** is to express all benefits and costs associated with the offering in monetary terms. This allows vendors and customers to unambiguously compare an offering's value with its purchase price and to compare its net value (that is, the offering's value minus the purchase price) with that of the next-best alternative. Many seemingly intangible benefits can actually be expressed in monetary terms. For instance, Caterpillar's strong brand name results in a higher resale or trade-in price of Caterpillar equipment versus Komatsu, which reduces the lifecycle costs to customers. In practice, most vendors are unable to articulate the value of their offering to customers and they often suffer the consequences in expensive negotiations about price. But many customers also lack an accurate understanding of what a vendor's offering is really worth to them. For instance, they focus on a product's acquisition costs and fail to realise that the majority of the costs associated with the product are caused by maintenance, repair and operation during the product's total lifetime. B2B vendors can make a real difference by calculating the value of their offering and using this information to educate and persuade their customers. In-depth information about the value of an offering is obtained through a four-stage process: (1) identify the offering's elements that create value for customers, (2) gather data about the firm's offering and the next-best alternative, (3) build a value model, and (4) test, expand and improve the value model (Anderson and Narus 1998; Anderson et al. 2007).

Step 1: Identify the offering's elements that create value

The process starts with identifying the offering's elements that create value for customers in a specified segment. While a typical business offering has many **value elements**, not all of them are considered relevant by customers in making their purchase decision. A team, consisting of individuals from various functional areas who are knowledgeable about the offering and the selected target customers, start by listing all elements that may potentially offer value to customers (including elements on which the vendor is outperformed by the next-best alternative!). The elements should be formulated in very specific terms. It is good for Airbus to know how much an hour of airplane downtime costs a customer, but it is even better to further specify these costs in terms of cost of replacement parts, salary of maintenance workers, waiting time and lost profits. Thus, value elements such as 'the quality of technical service' or 'a personal approach' are too general to be useful.

Next, the selected value elements are tested with a number of customers who are representative of the selected market segment. When the vendor has identified potential sources of value, interviews and focus groups may be used to determine which of these value elements are considered most critical by customers when they are comparing alternative offerings. When a vendor tries to discover completely new sources of value, observation is the preferred approach. A vendor may 'spend a day in the life of the customer' and observe on-site how customers use its products. Ultimately, this procedure trims the list of potential value elements to just a few key elements that customers use in selecting the best offering.

MINI CASE: DELL USES OBSERVATION TO CREATE NEW VALUE

Dell observed how large customers frequently purchase hundreds of computers simultaneously, after which their IT departments spend days installing the required software and distributing them to the desired locations. During this process, the computers are not used, IT employees are full-time installing software and hallways are filled with empty boxes for days. This observation led Dell to introduce a new driver of value for large customers: installing the required software during assembly in the Dell factory and thus streamlining the process of implementing IT for its customers.

Dell Deployment Services (planning, factory integration, delivery and installation) can move approximately 30 per cent of the customer's deployment work into Dell's factory, saving time and reducing costs. For instance, Dell helped Unilever roll out nearly 10,000 pre-imaged Dell OptiPlex™ desktops and Dell Latitude™ laptop computers with Intel® processors running Microsoft Windows® XP across over 100 locations. As concluded by Roger Legendre, Unilever's Director of Technology Solutions Deployment: 'Dell managed the necessary vendors for us and made sure that we had pre-imaged OptiPlex™ desktops and Latitude™ notebooks on site and ready to be installed and tested within the narrow timeframe.'

Source: www.dell.com

Step 2: Gather data about the firm's offering and the next-best alternative

Next, the vendor team determines the customer's next-best alternative. It is important to realise that there is always a next-best alternative and that only the customer's perspective counts. Typically, only one alternative is identified. (In Step 4, when the value model is expanded to other market segments, and the next-best alternative differs across segments, several alternative offerings may be included in the analysis.) Data are gathered for the vendor's offering and all relevant alternative offerings. Data can be gathered through interviews with vendor employees, interviews with customers, focus groups with customers, analysis of customer documents and administrative data, and expert interviews (for instance, with industry experts or trade organisations). Statistical methods such as conjoint analysis may also be used to estimate the value of specific elements to customers. Objective data are always preferred above customer perceptions. Although customers make their decisions based on their perceptions, vendors can use objective data to change customer perceptions. This also means that it is better for the vendor to gather the required data itself than to rely on data gathered by customers.

Step 3: Build a value model

All collected data are combined, integrated, interpreted and summarised into a **value model**, that is, a quantitative representation of the value offered to customers in a specific market segment. A value model lists all value elements and assigns a monetary amount to each element. These monetary amounts are based on an in-depth analysis of all available data. In addition, a value model lists all assumptions that were used to arrive at the numbers. The value of an offering can be expressed using *value word equations* that describe in words and simple mathematical operators how to calculate the monetary value of the performance difference between a vendor's offering and the next-best alternative for a specific value element. Value word equations are constructed for each value element that is included in the value model. The value element, expressed as cost savings or incremental profits, is on the left side of the equal sign, and the components defining the performance differences and what these are worth to the customer are on the right side. For instance, Rockwell Automation claims that its customers enjoy cost savings from reduced power usage when they use a Rockwell pump instead of a competitor's pump. Rockwell constructed the following value word equation for this value element (Anderson et al. 2007):

Cost savings = [kW spent × number of operating hours per year × \$ per kW hour × number of years system solution in operation]$_\text{Competitor solution}$ − [kW spent × number of operating hours per year × \$ per kW hour × number of years system solution in operation]$_\text{Rockwell solution}$

The data for these value word equations are typically collected from the customer's operations by vendor and customer managers working together, but may also come from outside sources (such as industry association studies).

An effective value model demonstrates how the vendor's offering is superior to the next-best alternative. Comparing the vendor's offering with the next-best alternative is not about comparing the different values, but about determining whether the difference in value is larger than the difference in price. This is captured in the following formula:

$$(\text{Value}_V - \text{Value}_A) > (\text{Price}_V - \text{Price}_A)$$

or

$$\Delta\text{Value}_{V,A} > \Delta\text{Price}_{V,A}$$

Value models help vendors to focus on what really matters to customers, but also requires a lot of effort. Vendors may convince customers to cooperate by pointing out the benefits: it helps them to understand their own business, gives them an opportunity to benchmark, gives them earlier access to a new product or service, or provides them with a meaningfully lower price (for example, by sharing the gains of this approach). If customers are unwilling to give detailed access to their operations, vendors may rely on customer perceptions obtained through interviews or focus groups.

Step 4: Test, expand and improve the value model

Constructing a value model is not a one-time effort, but vendors must continuously refine their models to increase their understanding of the value delivered to customers. The first version of the value model is constructed for a limited set of target customers, but this model is then validated using input from a larger number of customers. When the value model is sufficiently rigorous, the vendor further increases its use by developing modified versions of the model for other groups of customers (for instance, customers who use the product for other applications). As the vendor thus continues to test and expand the model's validity, it gains additional insight into how customers perceive its offering compared to competitive offerings.

Vendors must treat their value models as living representations of changing circumstances in the marketplace. Customers' perceptions of what constitutes value and how alternative offerings are evaluated are not constant but change over time (Flint et al. 1997). When a competitor, for example, introduces a product or service with new or significantly improved attributes, this changes a customer's expectations and ideas about acceptable performance. Rolls-Royce, manufacturer of aircraft engines, rocked the market when it launched its TotalCare® programme, under which a customer pays Rolls-Royce a fee for every hour the engine is in flight. In return, Rolls-Royce assumes the risks and costs of downtime and repairs. The programme gives the customer peace of mind by offering lifetime support, from the time the engine is delivered to the customer until the engine goes out of service (Figure 4.4).

To many managers, identifying all relevant value elements and collecting detailed customer information to construct a quantitative, data-based value model appears to be a daunting task. Overwhelmed by all that needs to be done, they continue to do business as usual: that is, based on their current understanding (gut feeling) of the market. Other managers feel that they lack the resources to conduct the comprehensive customer value analysis outlined above; for example, managers in small and medium-sized firms that do not have a marketing department and focus on achieving short-term sales objectives. But all managers must realise that they do not need to follow all the steps of a customer value analysis to improve their decision making. Instead, a marketing or sales manager may use an incremental approach to estimating the value of an offering and conduct only one or more of the following steps:

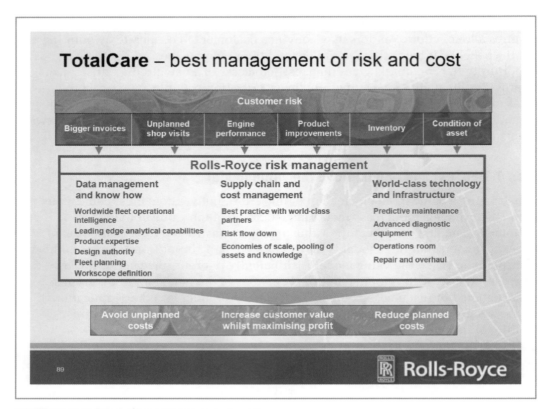

FIGURE 4.4 Rolls-Royce offers total care to customers

Source: Mike Terrett (2005) TotalCare – a dependable way of life, Rolls-Royce. Used with permission.

1 Use one's own insight into the target customers to identify the relevant value elements and estimate the value of the firm's offering and that of the next-best alternative.

2 Collect information from other employees (salespeople, product developers, distribution managers, maintenance workers) to validate and modify the value model.

3 Collect information from target customers to validate and modify the value model.

4 Collect information from additional customers (for instance, in related market segments) to test and expand the model.

Each subsequent activity builds on the knowledge that already exists and improves a manager's understanding of how customers perceive their firm's offering compared to the next-best alternative. Such an iterative cycle of model building, testing and refining allows vendors to flesh out their model. A vendor that begins to build a value model will quickly realise that it cannot express all relevant value elements in monetary terms. But this does not mean that these value elements can simply be ignored (the customer certainly won't do so!). The best way to deal with these elements is to include them as qualifiers in the value model, so that they can be used to qualitatively modify the model's results. As the vendor gains more experience with measuring value, it will discover ways to estimate how much these qualitative value elements are worth to its customers or even find ways to objectively operationalise their value. Thus, a manager may not immediately get the desired complete data-based calculation of customer value, but every improvement increases their understanding and thus allows them to make better decisions. Such an incremental process allows a manager to gradually move their decision making from their gut to their head.

4.7 Demonstrating and documenting value

Just measuring the value of one's offering is not enough. Vendors must put the obtained insight from their value models to use in their marketing and sales efforts. In marketing, value models can be used to select target customers, develop products that offer superior value, determine prices based on the customer's perceived value, communicate value instead of product characteristics and streamline business processes to maximise value to customers. For instance, a vendor may use its insight into what customers value to explore opportunities for improving an offering's value to customers. To generate creative ideas, a vendor team should address the following four strategies/questions: (1) *reduce* (which value elements can be reduced well below the industry standard?), (2) *raise* (which elements can be raised significantly above the industry standard?), (3) *eliminate* (which elements that the industry takes for granted can be eliminated?), and (4) *create* (which new elements can be created that the industry has never offered?) (Kim and Mauborgne 2005).

To increase the effectiveness of their sales efforts vendors must carefully document the value created for customers and use it to demonstrate the value of their offering to prospective customers. This means that they should make a conscious effort to collect data about a customer's operations on an ongoing basis. For some vendors this is easy to realise; for instance, when they can remotely monitor customer equipment performance. For others, this requires detailed agreements when the sale is made. Customers will also benefit from this practice, because detailed information about a product's performance allows vendors to improve their offering and thus to increase the value offered to customers. Below follows a description of some commonly used sales tools for **demonstrating value**:

- *Reference projects* describe successfully completed customer projects. Most B2B vendors compile reference lists that are sent to potential customers to create a positive impression, convince them of the vendor's capabilities and reduce the customer's perceived risk (Salminen and Möller 2006). Reference projects are also mentioned in trade journal articles, press releases, promotional material and during customer visits and seminars. Vendors also post testimonials or webcasts on their website in which satisfied customers explain how they benefited from the vendor's product or service. The effectiveness of reference projects depends on the reference customer's image and visibility in the marketplace.

- *Case histories* provide detailed descriptions of the benefits and costs that specific customers derived from the vendor's offering. Xerox showcases several case histories on its website, including customers from such varied industries as financial services, healthcare, high-tech and communications, manufacturing and energy, public sector and retail and consumer. Each case history summarises the case using three headings: the challenge, the solution and the results. The results are specific and quantified as much as possible (increased fulfilment rate, number of saved workers/year, reduced order cycle, reduced operating cost, increased response rate). GE Infrastructure Water & Process Technologies (GEIW&PT) started documenting the results provided to customers through its value-generation planning (VGP) process and tools in 1992. In 15 years' time, it had documented more than 1,000 case histories, accounting for $1.3 billion in customer cost savings, 24 billion gallons of water conserved, 5.5 million tons of waste eliminated and 4.8 million tons of air emissions removed (Anderson et al. 2006).

- *Value calculators* are spreadsheet software applications used by salespeople as part of a consultative selling approach to demonstrate the value that customers will likely receive from the offering. A sales representative from Rockwell Automation describes how value calculators can give salespeople a competitive edge. Using Rockwell's TCO Toolbox (TCO stands for 'total cost of ownership'), he was able to formulate a very specific value proposition: 'Through this

MINI CASE: SAP DOCUMENTS THE VALUE CREATED FOR CUSTOMERS

SAP is the world's leading provider of business software and dedicated to providing superior value to its customers. Today, more than 46,100 customers in more than 120 countries run SAP applications, from distinct solutions addressing the needs of small businesses and mid-size companies to suite offerings for global organisations. To demonstrate the value offered to customers, SAP published on its website the brochure 'Maximizing value; 100 customer successes' that describes 100 customer projects.

In the words of SAP's CEO, Henning Kagermann: 'We are passionate about the success of our customers and dedicated to maximizing the business value of our world-class technology.' All case histories describe the value drivers (both strategic goals and challenges) and value realisation (in terms of results and SAP solutions). For example, for Henkel it strengthened long-term competitiveness and reduced the total costs of the supply chain. This resulted in lower supply chain costs, smoother production flow, increased service levels and reduced production changeovers. As the accompanying pages from the brochure illustrate, not all value elements have been quantified by SAP. 'Better data transparancy' is clearly of value to customers but cannot easily be expressed as monetary savings.

Source: www.sap.com

Rockwell Automation pump solution, your company will save at least $16,268 per pump (on up to thirty-two pumps) relative to our best competitor's solution through the elimination of most downtime, reduced administrative costs associated with procurement, and lower spending on repair parts' (Anderson et al. 2007). While most value calculators run on the laptops of salespeople, some vendors make them available to prospective customers on CD-rom or via the internet. Bombardier, manufacturer of regional aircraft, business jets and rail transportation systems, developed a program that customers can use to design their own planes. They can even take a virtual tour through the designed plane to better evaluate the consequences of design choices.

- *Service level agreements* (SLAs) are formally negotiated agreements that specify the level of service to be provided by the vendor. An SLA specifies the services to be offered, availability of services, performance to be delivered, criteria to measure performance, priorities to be assigned, guarantees, responsibilities of both parties and billing procedures.

- *Performance guarantees* specify the level of performance promised by the vendor and the penalty to be paid if it does not keep its promise. Mexican cement producer Cemex promises fast delivery: if the product is delivered more than ten minutes late, the customer receives a 20 per cent discount. Effective performance guarantees are unconditional, easy to understand and communicate, easy to implement and believable. An example is the famous unconditional guarantee from 'Bugs' Burger (Figure 4.5).

- *Sales scenarios* are documents and sales presentations created for different sales situations (for instance, different market segments) that are used by salespeople as a standardised starting point to customise their sales presentations.

MINI CASE: BENTLEY SYSTEMS USES SCENARIO-BASED SELLING

US-based Bentley Systems is a provider of software 'for the lifecycle of the world's infrastructure', that is, for the design and management of large construction and engineering projects (roads, buildings, bridges, power plants). Bentley offers the building, plant, civil and geospatial vertical markets a comprehensive portfolio of software and services that spans architecture, engineering, construction and operations. Founded in 1984, it has grown into a company with annual revenues of $450 million and 2,800 employees in 40 countries.

Every one of Bentley's products is mapped to 11 scenarios that have been carefully formulated to match the needs of specific groups of users, such as architectural firms, gas/ electric utilities, manufacturing companies, telecommunications and engineering consultants. For each scenario, Bentley created a three- to five-page document with:

- a brief description of the environment, needs and objectives of the customers in that scenario

> - a detailed overview of decision-makers and the specific challenges facing the customers in that scenario
> - a portfolio of products matching the needs of users within the scenario
> - a list of likely follow-up projects and tasks that are sometimes overlooked by the client, but may require additional software services from Bentley
> - a list of similar accounts that can be used as references and recommendations for the most effective way to present a sales proposal to the client.
>
> Bentley assigned 11 'scenario managers' to be responsible for creating and maintaining the knowledge base associated with each scenario and provide account managers with all the information they need to close deals. The account managers can download richly detailed sales templates from the Bentley intranet, enabling them to generate customised proposals for clients on the spot. Because all the language and prices have been pre-approved, an account manager needs only to customise the document and it is ready to be used. The scenario manager's compensation package includes a commission on sales of products from their scenario.
>
> *Source*: Peppers and Rogers (2001)

Vendors can use in-depth insight about documented value to convince customer managers and provide them with the ammunition needed to persuade other decision-makers in their organisation (*managing evidence*). At the start of the century, Cisco Systems ran a two-page advertisement that communicated two different messages. The left page showed a product with the caption 'I am a Cisco 1200 series dual band Wi-Fi access point'. The right page showed the same product, but this time accompanied by the headline 'I am 70 more minutes of productivity per employee per day'. This ad eloquently illustrates the power of communicating value to the customer instead of product characteristics. GXS, leader of supply chain management solutions, proves to customers that it can cut costs using GXS managed services (Figure 4.6). But vendors must realise that customers use different perspectives to evaluate the value of an offering. Some customers look only at the purchase price, while others calculate all direct costs associated with the offering. More sophisticated customers calculate the offering's total cost of ownership or even the offering's effect on *their* customers. The customer's method of value calculation determines the vendor's sales approach. When a customer uses no preconceived method to evaluate the value of an offering, a vendor should use the method that is most favourable to its offering. When a customer uses a relatively simple method that is unfavourable to the vendor's offering, the vendor should focus on educating the customer and persuade them to use another method. For example, customers who only look at the offering's purchase price can be shown that they should take all lifecycle costs into account. Naturally, this only works in one direction: customers who already use total cost of ownership cannot be persuaded to look only at the

FIGURE 4.5 'Bugs' Burger Bugs Killers' unconditional performance guarantee

Source: Bugs Burger Bugs Killers. Used with permission.

FIGURE 4.6 GXS proves cost savings to customers

Source: GXS. Used with permission.

offering's purchase price. Finally, customers who use a method that is unfavourable to the vendor's offering and who cannot be persuaded to use a different method, should be ignored. In most B2B markets there is a tendency for customers to move from simple value calculation methods to more sophisticated ones (for instance, from purchase price to total cost of ownership). Only in very specific cases is the trend in the other direction; for example, when products and their associated future costs have become so difficult to estimate that customers tend to focus on the product's purchase price or direct costs.

Online Learning Centre

When you have read this chapter, log on to the Online Learning Centre website at **www.mcgraw-hill.co.uk/textbooks/biemans** to explore chapter-by-chapter test questions, further reading and more online study tools.

Summary of Key Concepts

- Based on their understanding of customers and markets, B2B vendors must formulate compelling strategies that help them to create superior value for customers.

- The two key strategic decisions are: (a) which customers will we target? and (b) which value will we offer these customers? These two strategic decisions influence each other and are taken jointly.

- To identify potentially profitable target customers, firms can calculate the value of customers in terms of their customer lifetime value.

- The firm's strategy culminates in a value proposition that describes the value offered to a specific group of customers. This value proposition is used in marketing and sales to communicate to customers the superior value offered by the vendor.

- There are three types of value proposition: (a) one that lists all benefits, (b) one that lists all favourable points of difference between the vendor's product and the next-best alternative, and (c) one that presents a resonating focus that describes the one or two points of difference that deliver the greatest value to customers. The third type of value proposition is the best.

- Having developed a value proposition, a firm needs to decide how it will create this value for customers. Firms increasingly cooperate with outside partners, resulting in a value-creating network.

- With value networks, competition takes place between alternative value networks. In a value network, partners cooperate to create value for customers, but they also compete for the customer's margin.

- Having a compelling value proposition is not enough. Firms need to explicitly measure the value offered to customers. This can be achieved through a structured process based on information from the firm's salespeople and/or information provided by customers. The result is a value model that details the quantified value offered to customers.

- Quantifying the value offered to customers is a continuous process. All new information is used to improve the value model, increase the firm's understanding of its customers and improve the quality of its marketing and sales efforts.

- Successful vendors continuously monitor and measure the value actually created for customers. This information is used to update the value model and communicated to prospects as part of the marketing and sales process. Thus, successful vendors are able to demonstrate that they are able to deliver the value promised in their value proposition.

🔑 Key Terms

Business definition, p. 98
Customer equity, p. 101
Customer lifetime value, p. 101
Customer relationships, p. 100
Customer selection, p. 100
Demonstrating value, p. 117
Measuring value, p. 112

Strategic position, p. 98
Supply chain management, p. 110
Value, p. 105
Value elements, p. 112
Value model, p. 114
Value network, p. 109
Value proposition, p. 107

Discussion questions

1 Strategy development is the process whereby firms design the route to long-term success. Describe a number of methods that firms can use to make sure that the process will be sufficiently flexible and up to date to be competitive in a changing marketplace.

2 Business marketers typically do not maintain relationships with the marketers at their customers. What would be the advantages of developing and maintaining such relationships?

3 Relationships with customers are characterised by a consistent pattern that is referred to as the relationship lifecycle. How may a vendor of B2B products use the concept of a relationship lifecycle in practice?

4 Intensive cooperation between organisations results in blurred boundaries between partners in a value-creating network. What are the dangers of these blurred boundaries? How can firms prevent or deal with these dangers?

5 Trust is a key ingredient in developing and maintaining successful relationships. Which specific measures may managers use to develop trust with their partners?

6 To express the value of an offering in monetary terms is more difficult for services than for physical products. Why is that? What are relevant value elements for an advertising agency?

7 Lately, many firms emphasise the need to be customer oriented or market oriented. Which developments explain this sudden interest?

8 B2B firms are encouraged to be customer oriented. What are the consequences of such a strategy? Think about issues concerning market segmentation, using the marketing instruments and collecting market information.

9 Find examples of B2B value calculators on the internet. What are the differences between the online value calculators? Identify and describe the key elements of a successful online value calculator.

10 To continue offering superior value to customers in the long run, firms must continuously try to increase the value offered to customers. Which specific activities can a firm undertake to implement this process of continuous improvement?

Further reading

Anderson, James C. and James A. Narus (1998) Business marketing: understand what customers value, *Harvard Business Review*, 76(6): 53–65.

Anderson, James C., James A. Narus and Wouter van Rossum (2006) Customer value propositions in business markets, *Harvard Business Review*, 84(3): 91–99.

Peppers, Don and Martha Rogers (2005) *Return on Customer: Creating Maximum Value from Your Scarcest Resource*, New York: Currency/Doubleday.

Reichheld, Frederick F. and W. Earl Sasser, Jr. (1990) Zero defections: quality comes to services, *Harvard Business Review*, 68(5): 105–111.

References

Anderson, James C. and James A. Narus (1998) Business Marketing: understand what customers value, *Harvard Business Review*, 76(6): 53–65.

Anderson, James C., Nirmalya Kumar and James A. Narus (2007) *Value Merchants: Demonstrating and Documenting Superior Value in Business Markets*, Boston, MA: Harvard Business School Press.

Anderson, James C., James A. Narus and Wouter van Rossum (2006) Customer value propositions in business markets, *Harvard Business Review*, 84(3): 91–99.

Ashkenas, Ron, Dave Ulrich, Todd Jick and Steve Kerr (1995) *The Boundaryless Organization: Breaking the Chains of Organizational Structure*, San Francisco, CA: Jossey-Bass.

Blattberg, Robert C., Gary Getz and Jacquelyn S. Thomas (2001) *Customer Equity: Building and Managing Relationships as Valuable Assets*, Boston, MA: Harvard Business School Press.

Fawcett, Stanley E. and M. Bixby Cooper (1998) Logistics performance measurement and customer success, *Industrial Marketing Management*, 27(4): 341–357.

Flint, Daniel J., Robert B. Woodruff and Sarah F. Gardial (1997) Customer value change in industrial marketing relationships: a call for new strategies and research, *Industrial Marketing Management*, 26(2): 163–175.

Ford, David, Lars-Erik Gadde, Håkan Håkansson, Anders Lundgren, Ivan Snehota, Peter Turnbull and David Wilson (1998) *Managing Business Relationships*, Chichester: Wiley.

Håkansson, Håkan and Ivan Snehota (eds) (1995) *Developing Relationships in Business Networks*, London: Routledge.

Kim, W. Chan and Renée Mauborgne (2005) *Blue Ocean Strategy: How to Create Uncontested Market Space and Make the Competition Irrelevant*, Boston, MA: Harvard Business School Press.

Kothandaraman, Prabakar and David T. Wilson (2001) The future of competition: value-creating networks, *Industrial Marketing Management*, 30(4): 379–389.

Kumar, V., J. Andrew Petersen and Robert P. Leone (2007) How valuable is word of mouth?, *Harvard Business Review*, 85(10): 139–146.

Lewis, Jordan D. (1995) *The Connected Corporation: How Leading Companies Win Through Customer–Supplier Alliances*, New York: Free Press.

Markides, Constantinos C. (2000) *All the Right Moves: A Guide to Crafting Breakthrough Strategy*, Boston, MA: Harvard Business School Press.

Peppers, Don and Martha Rogers (2001) *One to One B2B: Customer Development Strategies for the Business-to-Business World*, New York: Doubleday.

Peppers, Don and Martha Rogers (2005) *Return on Customer: Creating Maximum Value from Your Scarcest Resource*, New York: Currency/Doubleday.

Reichheld, Frederick F. and W. Earl Sasser, Jr. (1990) Zero defections: quality comes to services, *Harvard Business Review*, 68(5): 105–111.

Reinartz, Werner and V. Kumar (2002) The mismanagement of customer loyalty, *Harvard Business Review*, 80(7): 86–94.

Salminen, Risto T. and Kristian Möller (2006) Role of references in business marketing: towards a normative theory of referencing, *Journal of Business-to-Business Marketing*, 13(1): 1–51.

Slone, Reuben E., John T. Mentzer and J. Paul Dittmann (2007) Are you the weakest link in your company's supply chain?, *Harvard Business Review*, 85(9): 116–127.

Yoffie, David B. and Mary Kwak (2006) With friends like these: the art of managing complementors, *Harvard Business Review*, 84(9): 89–98.

PART 04
Translating the Value Proposition into Marketing Instruments

Managing products and services

Introduction

The core of a company's value creation are the vendor's products and services that deliver value to customers. B2B customers buy products and services to use the value derived from them for their own business processes. Many vendors of tangible products have come to realise that their products are easily copied and a competitive advantage is more sustainable if it is based on intangible services and business processes. Thus, many B2B vendors employ a customer perspective and present themselves as providers of customer solutions. Vendors must develop and manage a product and service portfolio that allows them to deliver superior value to customers.

This chapter starts by describing the major elements that may be used to create value for customers, but focuses on the management of a firm's products and services. It goes on to explain the link between tangible products and intangible support services and also describes the nature of services and their implications for marketing. To better serve customers, products and services are sometimes combined into packages, solutions or systems. The marketing of systems and projects requires a comprehensive marketing approach that combines the efforts of several companies to create complete solutions for customers. To maintain a competitive advantage, vendors need to continuously update their product portfolio by developing new products, deleting obsolete ones, modifying existing products and replacing old products with new ones. This chapter discusses in detail the management processes involved and also shows how firms can influence the acceptance of new products by customers. Finally, the chapter acknowledges that B2B products and services may also benefit from a branding strategy and it discusses several characteristics of branding in B2B markets.

5.1 Managing the firm's offering

B2B firms create superior value for customers through an **offering** that provides significant advantages over the next-best alternative. The core of a vendor's offering consists of its products or services. Many products require a range of support services (called **product service**), such as advice, installation, maintenance and upgrades. Services are predominantly intangible offerings, which may nevertheless be expressed through tangible manifestations. Management consultants such as McKinsey and Capgemini, for example, offer intangible management audits, but present their findings in very tangible reports. Many B2B vendors offer combinations of products, product service and services and package them as problem solutions, systems or projects. In addition, vendors also create value for customers with other marketing instruments (for instance, a large dealer network, fast and reliable deliveries, knowlegeable salespeople) and by leveraging organisational characteristics (online ordering, technological know-how, cooperation in product development). All these elements of a vendor's offering are displayed in Figure 5.1.

At the core of value creation for customers is the process of planning and managing the firm's range of current and future products and services, including product/service development (designing, developing and launching new products/services), product/service modification (changing existing products/services to boost their performance or to better match changed customer needs), market acceptance management (influencing the speed and nature of customer acceptance of new or modified products/services), product/service deletion (eliminating underperforming products/services) and product/service replacement (replacing an existing product or service with a new one). Thus, it encompasses a large number of decisions and activities related to managing the firm's total range of products and services. Firms may increase efficiency and consistency, for example, by developing product platforms as the foundation of a series of related derivative products (Meyer and Lehnerd 1997; Figure 5.2). The product platforms function as a common structure from which a stream of derivative products are developed and produced for specific market segments. Firms need both to develop derivative products and to periodically renew the underlying **product platform**. Each new product platform is used to develop a new generation of derivative products.

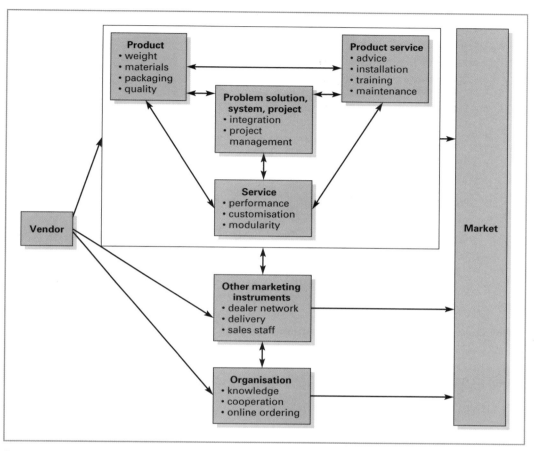

FIGURE 5.1 Elements of a vendor's value-creating offering

This platform strategy is followed by all aircraft manufacturers. Airbus, for example, talks about 'product families', such as the A320 family and the A330/A340 family, consisting of a series of airplanes with a similar range and similar number of seats. The Airbus aircraft families offer a high degree of commonality amongst airframes, on-board systems, cockpits, handling qualities and training. The customer benefits of this strategy are significant: high flexibility for flight crews, highly efficient operations and reduced costs, as pilots, cabin crews and maintenance engineers do not need extensive amounts of training to transfer from one aircraft type to another. All members of the Airbus single-aisle A320 family share the same pilot type rating, enabling crews to fly any of them with a single licence endorsement. The larger A330 and A340 widebodies share the same basic handling qualities and common cockpit layout as the other Airbus fly-by-wire aircraft, so a pilot qualified on any of the A320 family aircraft can easily transition to the A330/A340, and vice versa.

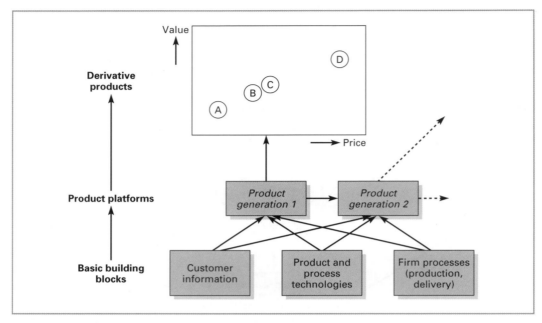

FIGURE 5.2 Using product platforms to develop derivative products

5.2 Products and product service

B^{2B} vendors offer three types of product:

- *Catalogue products*, which are manufactured and inventoried in anticipation of future orders. These are standardised products, produced in large production runs according to predetermined specifications. Critical decisions include adding, deleting and repositioning products, as well as setting optimum inventory levels. Examples of catalogue products are pipes, valves, forklift trucks and machine tools.

- *Modular products*, which are offered as basic products, together with a range of accessories and options. This allows customers to use standard components as building blocks to design the optimal configuration that best fits their needs. This strategy is used by vendors of computer systems and machine tools. Key decisions relate to determining the characteristics of the basic product and designing the proper mix of options and accessories.

- *Custom-built products*, which are created to meet the needs of one or a few customers. Sometimes the resulting product is unique, such as a power plant, while others are produced in larger numbers, such as roller-coasters. With this type of product, the vendor offers a capability that is transformed through a dialogue with the customer into a finished product. UK-based Carbolite, a world-leading manufacturer of furnaces and ovens, presents several examples of custom designed and built products on its website, with the added promise that, 'If you are looking for a similar product, or require a product for a special application, we would be pleased to discuss this with you' (www.carbolite.com).

Different types of product require different marketing approaches. Catalogue products are often distributed indirectly through channel partners at relatively low prices. But custom-built products require extensive personal selling and a range of support services, with the final price being the result of extensive buyer–seller negotiations.

Product service

To support these products, B2B vendors offer a broad range of services, such as advice, installation, maintenance, repair, upgrades, refurbishment of equipment and training of operators. These services can be classified according to their relationship to the sale of the product. *Pre-sales services* are offered before the transaction takes place and aim to persuade the customer to buy the product. Examples are advice about the product configuration that best fits the customer's needs, information about how to use the product, documentation about product specifications, product demonstrations at the site of other customers and calculations about potential cost savings and revenue increases. *Transaction-related services* relate to the delivery of the product and intend to increase the efficiency and effectiveness of the transaction. Examples are easy-to-use ordering procedures, efficient order fulfilment, quick response to questions, short delivery times, reliable delivery, product installation, training of operators, project management and attractive payment conditions. *After-sales services* are performed after the product has been bought and used by the customer and aim to optimise the product's functioning during its total lifetime. Examples are replacements parts, problem solving, refund of damage and lost revenues in case of product malfunctioning, maintenance, repair, complaint handling, help desk, product returns, product upgrades and assistance with product dismantling and disposal.

> ### ᕦ᠊ INSIGHT: Big Brother watches your product
>
> Recent developments in IT allow vendors of medical equipment, elevators, copiers, building control systems and industrial equipment to establish an online connection with their products so that they can monitor product performance from a distance and schedule preventive maintenance. By using specialised chips embedded in the product and *device relationship management* software, maintenance workers collect detailed information about the product's functioning which increases the efficiency of a maintenance visit. Vendors may thus save up to €500 per emergency maintenance visit. Swedish bearings manufacturer SKF helps its customers to extend the service life of their equipment by using a secure electronic monitoring tool to

enable off-site access. For instance, vibration-analysis data provide early warning about potential product failure and allow the company to perform preventive maintenance during routine maintenance visits. Some firms use the data from remote monitoring to ask the customer's personnel to make adjustments on their own, while others connect remotely to a customer's equipment and make changes from their off-site locations, thus saving time and money. The benefits for customers of remote equipment management are numerous and include increased product uptime, reduced costs of ownership, faster diagnosis, faster mean time to repair, early detection of problems, automated software deployment and preventive maintenance based on actual usage.

Source: Reinartz and Ulaga (2008)

Several factors explain management's interest in support services (Cohen et al. 2006). First, products are easily copied by competitors, causing vendors to rely on product services to create a sustainable competitive advantage. It is not unusual for vendors to generate between 30 and 50 per cent of their revenues by servicing products. Second, because product services are intangible and more difficult to copy they allow firms to reap higher margins, create customised problem solutions and increase customer loyalty (Phillips et al. 1999). Third, in many industries vendors have sold so many units over the years that their aftermarkets have become four to five times larger than the original equipment businesses. Fourth, product support generates a low-risk revenue stream over a long period of time; for instance, aircraft manufacturers reap revenues from services for as long as 25 years after a sale. Fifth, aftermarket support provides vendors with a deep understanding of customers' technologies, plans and processes, which they can turn into a competitive advantage.

Improving product service

Although product service is a long-lasting source of revenues requiring only a relatively small investment, many vendors fail to provide product service effectively and thus to turn it into a source of profit (Reinartz and Ulaga 2008). The reason is that product services are notoriously difficult to manage. Customer expectations have increased significantly over the years. In the 1980s, semiconductor manufacturers were content with a two-day response time when equipment failed, but nowadays they expect vendors to respond to requests for help within 15 minutes! In addition, the product service network has to support both current products and products sold in the past, while each product generation has different parts and vendors. This means that delivering effective product services often requires many more parts, people and equipment at more locations than it does to make products. It has been estimated that effective stock-keeping units service networks have to cope with 20 times the number of stock-keeping units (SKUs) that the firm's manufacturing function deals with. Below follows a five-step approach for firms to improve product service quality levels, reduce inventories in service assets and cut operating costs (Cohen et al. 2006; Reinartz and Ulaga 2008).

Step 1: Identify the products to cover

The process starts with the decision about which products to support: all products or a selected few products? Some vendors even support competing products to generate economies of scale for their service operation. For instance, ABB supports all process control equipment in factories that have installed its automation systems, thus providing a one-stop service solution to customers.

Step 2: Select the services to offer

The selection of support services offered depends on both the costs to the vendor and the benefits for the customer. For instance, when a vendor considers providing diagnostic equipment to customers it has to weigh the customer benefits of faster diagnosis and less downtime against the cost of designing and manufacturing such equipment and training customers in its use. Similarly, a longer warranty period reduces the customer's uncertainty but increases the need for spare parts and repair services.

Vendors should not make the mistake of offering a one-size-fits-all service. Different customers want different types and levels of product service and should be segmented according to their willingness to pay for product service. A study of the adoption of catheters by European hospitals found five market segments with different product service preferences. Some hospitals preferred usage-related product services, while others had a strong preference for purchase-related pre-sale product services and services related to the relationship (Frambach et al. 1997). Vendors respond to different customer requirements by designing product services with different performance levels, such as ranging from fast and expensive (platinum) to slow and economic (silver) services.

A common strategy is to use flexible service offerings, with some services being part of the basic product (such as product installation) and others offered as options at a separate price (for instance, training of operators) (Anderson and Narus 1995). The difference between a basic service and an option may be small; for instance, when training of three operators is part of the basic product and customers have to pay extra for every additional operator that needs to be trained. Vendors must continuously monitor changing customer needs and the costs and benefits of providing support services to determine whether new services need to be developed or existing services eliminated or offered differently (for instance, when a much-requested optional service becomes part of the basic product).

Step 3: Design the service pricing structure

Firms may use various pricing structures for their product services. Customers may pay for product service per use, a fixed price (as with a warranty or a lease) or pay per hour that the product is actually used. The strategy of *power by the hour* was introduced by Rolls-Royce and has been copied in many industries. For instance, Liechtenstein-based Hilti promotes an 'all-round, hassle-fee' service package for the power tools it leases to customers in the construction industry. The company's customers do not have to buy a drill for their operations; they pay by the hole and are guaranteed a drill on the construction site. The pricing structure selected depends on the nature of the product (fixed-price models are more suitable for expensive products where the vendor can bear the risk of owning the product) and the stage of the product lifecycle (when the product is new and its performance unpredictable, a cost-plus model, with the customer paying per use of the product service, is the obvious choice).

As part of its service pricing strategy, vendors may start charging for simple services that were always performed for free. When this is successful, more complex services can be added. Switching from *free to fee* clarifies the value of the services to both the vendor and its customers. French gas provider Air Liquide used to purchase gas cylinders to transport small quantities of gas to customers. But it only charged customers for the gas and the cylinders accumulated at customers. In the 1990s, Air Liquide introduced a rental fee of €5 to €7 a month, which generated several hundred million euros in fees and stimulated customers to optimise their inventories.

INSIGHT: Help customers to buy less of your product

Companies typically try to persuade customers to buy more of their products. But recently, several vendors have started to worry about the effects of their products on the environment and begun embracing the vision of *sustainable development*. They changed their business models from selling products to selling a range of services around fewer products. Basically, these vendors try to persuade their customers to buy less of their products!

Coatings manufacturer PPG Industries was confronted by Chrysler wanting to reduce product use because of high costs and environmental regulations. PPG responded by helping Chrysler to reduce paint use. As one PPG manager explained: 'The automotive companies were going to move down a path of trying to decrease usage, whether we participated in that relationship or not. So what PPG decided pretty early in the game was that participating in that transition and helping to manage it was more beneficial than waiting for it to be thrust upon us. We tried to structure a programme that created a win–win scenario.' PPG on-site representatives took over management tasks at the plant such as material ordering, inventory tracking, inventory maintenance and even some regulatory-response duties. With this service, PPG helped Chrysler to reduce material use. The new business model has become the norm for the industry and Chrysler even asked PPG to teach the model to its competitors, such as DuPont Coatings & Color Technologies and BASF.

To help improve the productivity of the office environment, Xerox introduced the Office Document Assessment tool, which analyses the total costs associated with alternative document-making processes. It helps customers to reduce the number of copiers and printers, and thus the amount of toner, paper and other consumables. In the words of Mack McCormick, Vice-President Office Services Practice: 'We've found that companies spend almost $1,000 per year per employee on office document output costs. Reducing that spend by 30 per cent, a company of 3,000 employees can save nearly $1 million per year.' Using Office Document Assessment for customer Honeywell, Xerox made 30,000 documents visible to employees and reduced storage space by 70 per cent, order fulfilment time by 80 per cent and operating costs by 25 per cent.

Even though this shift from products to services reduces product usage by customers, vendors benefit from this strategy because many customers are already focused on reducing the use of materials and would otherwise be lost. In addition, with the new strategy customers are less likely to change vendors, vendors can expand the range of products sold to customers and vendors can use the service to attract new customers.

Sources: Rothenberg (2007) and www.xerox.com

Step 4: Design the product service organisation

Vendors must not forget to design an effective organisational structure for providing product services. Manufacturers accustomed to stable, predictable production processes, must realise that the delivery of services requires high levels of customisation and a focus on customer solutions. Some firms distinguish between product and service salespeople. GE Medical Services uses product salespeople as *hunters* to get orders for new equipment, and service salespeople as *farmers* to grow their relationships with customers and sell services over time. Firms may reduce conflicts between the two sales forces by creating a double credit system, with both product and service salespeople receiving the same commission for each closed deal. Problems are often exacerbated when firms use partners to deliver services; for instance, when vendors use distributors or specialised third-party providers. An example of such a third-party service provider is Maintenance Partners, the market leader in the Benelux countries for the maintenance, repair and reconditioning of all electrical and mechanical rotating machines, such as generators, gas turbines, turbo compressors and expanders.

Step 5: Manage the product services supply chain

Firms need to create a product services supply chain that matches the supply of resources with demand. Materials, components and people must be delivered at the right time, to the right place and at the lowest possible cost. But end products, modules, submodules and piece parts all have different costs and response times. Replacing a failed product with a standby end product is faster but more expensive than replacing a module or providing replacement parts. Similarly, vendors must take into account the different locations from which they will supply parts, ranging from a central distribution centre to stocking parts on customers' premises. The farther stockpiles are from customers, the slower the response times and the lower their costs will be. Several firms discovered the potential of online service delivery. Every year, Boeing used to send an enormous number of technical manuals, part lists and maintenance documents to its 600 customers (representing a 40 kilometre-high pile!). Using the internet, Boeing saved millions in postage and printing costs, while its customers saved additional millions in inventory costs.

5.3 Services

A **service** is an activity, or process, performed by a vendor (the service provider) for a customer. With firms increasingly focusing on their core competencies and outsourcing all other activities to partners, the services sector has grown significantly. Most firms start with outsourcing their catering, security and cleaning, and then outsource other processes such as payroll, maintenance, logistics, market research and even customer service. In addition, many product vendors have packaged their products with services into customer solutions and it could be argued that this has transformed them into service providers.

Characteristics of services

Services have four general characteristics: intangibility, simultaneous production and consumption, heterogeneity and perishability.

Intangibility

All products and services can be positioned on a spectrum from mostly tangible to mostly intangible (Shostack 1977). At the mostly tangible end of the spectrum are products such as industrial gases and lubricants. Customers want a tangible product, but also value timely delivery and delivery reliability. At the mostly intangible end of the spectrum are services such as management consulting. Consultants offer intangible audits and advice but also present their findings in tangible reports. Most vendors offer a mix of tangible products and intangible services. Because services are largely intangible, it is difficult for potential customers to assess their value before actually purchasing and using them. This causes service vendors to build trust in their capabilities through professional sales presentations and a large number of reference projects in the same or similar industries. In addition, they rely on tangible clues to project a professional image. Examples of such tangible clues are the design of offices, appearance of service personnel, trucks, letterheads, company brochures and corporate websites.

Simultaneous production and consumption

Services are produced through interaction with customers; there can be no service without a customer. Thus, customers affect and shape both the performance and quality of the service. The actual level of interaction between service provider and customer varies significantly. With maintenance, repair and other equipment-focused services, interaction with the customer is minimal. Indeed, some equipment can be monitored, diagnosed and corrected from a distance. And cleaning services are largely performed outside regular office hours. With people-focused services such as consulting and training, however, interaction is significant and the customer becomes a co-creator of the service experience.

Heterogeneity

The simultaneous production and consumption of services also means that service quality and performance depend on the employee providing the service and may vary over time. The amount of heterogeneity depends on the labour intensity of the service. The quality of laundry, cleaning and transportation services is fairly constant, while the quality of professional services varies significantly. Service providers reduce service variability through standardisation of the service (for instance, by offering a standard performance level, such as guaranteed delivery within a specified time window), standardisation of the service process (by specifying prescribed steps and sequences) or human resource management (hiring and training). The critical role of service employees implies that internal marketing to service employees is an important prerequisite for successful **services marketing** (see also Figure 5.3).

Perishability

Services cannot be produced for and held in inventory. Service providers have a limited capacity and any unused capacity is lost forever and cannot be reclaimed. Service providers use *yield management* (also called *revenue management*) to understand, anticipate and influence customer behaviour in order to maximise revenues or profits (Chiang et al. 2007). Hotels, rental agencies and airlines, for example, charge different prices for different customers at different times for the same service, improve demand forecasts and hire temporary personnel during peak demand.

In addition, because of the large diversity in customer applications, B2B services are often customised for individual customers. And because most B2B services are focused on the customer's equipment, organisation or processes, they are typically performed at the customer site. Table 5.1 summarises the major characteristics of B2B services and their marketing implications. These characteristics of services have

TABLE 5.1 Characteristics of B2B services and their marketing implications

Characteristic	Problems	Marketing approach
Intangibility	Product characteristics are invisible No protection by patents No inventories Price is difficult to determine	Emphasise intangible elements Translate product characteristics into specific customer benefits Stimulate word-of-mouth Use reference projects
Simultaneous production and consumption	Customer is involved in production of the service Centralised mass production is impossible	Careful selection of employees Emphasis on training of employees Use of mentor system
Heterogeneity	Standardisation of the service is difficult Quality control is problematic	Standardisation of service process Develop systems that minimise human mistakes Automate service delivery Deliver customised services
Perishability	No inventories possible	High quality demand forecasting Plan capacity based on peak demand Use price and communication to smooth demand Overlapping shifts for personnel
Customisation	Service must be adapted to ever-changing circumstances Only limited standardisation possible	Project management Use consultative selling and cross-functional teams Modular service design Develop application knowledge and teams
Performance at customer site	Slow response times in case of problems	Use preventative maintenance Remote diagnostics Use of dense dealer network

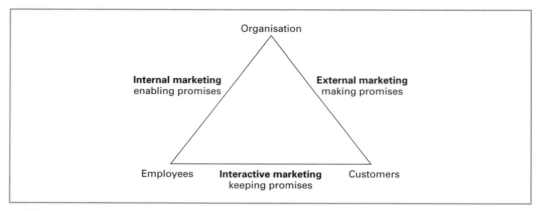

FIGURE 5.3 The services marketing triangle
Source: Zeithaml and Bitner (2000: 16). Reprinted with permission.

led some authors to expand the concept of the four marketing Ps by adding three additional Ps for services: personnel, physical assets and process management (Magrath 1986).

These characteristics of services should not be intepreted as only causing problems. Indeed, some of them may be quite beneficial to service providers (Vargo and Lusch 2004). Heterogeneity, for example, is typically understood as a cause of variable quality, which should be countered by implementing standardised service processes. This will indeed contribute to a firm's efficiency, but it also detracts from the firm's ability to adapt the service to specific customer needs and use situations. Service providers may actually benefit from the factors causing heterogeneity by communicating to customers that they allow them to adapt their services to a broad range of customer situations and address idiosyncratic customer needs through the delivery of customised services.

Marketing of services

Services marketing always involves three parties: the organisation offering the service, the service employees actually performing the service, and the customer buying the service. This results in three types of marketing (Figure 5.3).

External marketing: making promises

A service provider uses external marketing to communicate to customers the nature of the service and the performance level they can expect through advertising, sales presentations, promotional activities and price levels. In addition, numerous tangible elements offer clues about the service provider, such as its offices, parking lot, landscaping, signage, personnel, letterheads, business cards, brochures and website. All these visible clues contribute to the customer's perception of the service provider.

Service providers may formalise their promises by offering a *service-level agreement*, which specifies the agreed service level in a contract (services to be delivered, priorities, responsibilities, guarantees, availability, operations, penalties, performance metrics, problem management). Others make promises by issuing performance guarantees. Such performance guarantees must be based on detailed information about the service delivery process (average performance level, peaks and valleys, probabilities), and its costs and revenues. The corporate website of US-based 'Bugs' Burger Bugs Killers (BBBK), provider of pest elimination services, opens with a very simple and unambiguous performance guarantee: 'You do not pay our initial charges until we Totally Eliminate every roach, rat or mouse nesting on your premises' (Figure 4.5). After being in business for some 50 years, its style of service has not changed. As the son's founder explains: 'We don't send a bill until the problem is completely eliminated' (www.bugsburger.com).

Interactive marketing: keeping promises

By making promises, a service provider creates customer expectations. It is up to the service provider's employees to deliver on these promises. Customers evaluate the quality of service by comparing the perceived service level with the service level they had expected. The service provider's promises may also be kept by third parties performing part of the service (a cleaning firm that cleans the rooms and facilities in a hotel) or technology (order tracking over the internet). Each interaction between service provider and customer is a *moment of truth* where the service provider must live up to the customer's expectations (Carlzon 1987).

The marketing literature frequently suggests that vendors should exceed their promises by *delighting the customer*. Several vendors even promise this on their corporate website. But this is a dangerous strategy, because such explicit promises raise the customers' expectations, which makes it almost impossible to satisfy them. Moreover, service providers that are able to consistently outperform their promises would do better to promise more and thus raise the bar for their competitors.

Internal marketing: enabling promises

The service provider's employees can only keep the promises made to customers when their organisation supports them through training, information systems, procedures, blueprints and incentives. Investment in training, reward systems, personal development and other incentives motivates employees, increases commitment and has an indirect positive impact on customer satisfaction. An important enabling factor is an effective interface between the firm's customer-facing staff (**front office**) and the departments taking care of the firm's operations (**back office**). In the set-up depicted in Figure 5.4, a project manager is responsible for breaking down counterproductive walls between the firm's departments and making sure that the firm projects one single image to the marketplace. While such interdepartmental cooperation is essential, in practice it is quite difficult to realise because of different subcultures, objectives and priorities (Chapter 10). A back office is product centred and focused on control and efficiency. The emphasis is on managing the firm's internal processes, rather than creating value for customers. But marketing and sales want to maximise the value offered to customers, and are tempted to adapt the service delivery to the wishes and needs of individual customers without considering the

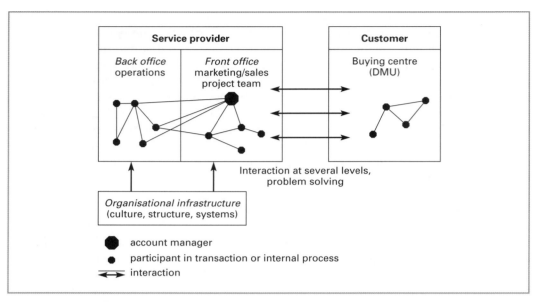

FIGURE 5.4 Relationships in services marketing

consequences for internal processes. Marketing and sales frequently lament that the back office is too far removed from the customer to decide about issues of service delivery and customisation, while the back office only tries to run the organisation's operations as smoothly as possible. In many organisations, this is a source of constant tension. The relationship between front office and back office is also important for the development of new services. Which activities will be put in the back office to increase efficiency and control? Which activities will be part of the front office to increase customer contact, customer involvement and responsiveness?

5.4 Marketing of solutions, systems and projects

B2B customers often use products and/or services in combination. For instance, printing shops buy printing presses together with full service maintenance contracts and other support services. B2B vendors respond by offering product or service bundles: integrated combinations of two or more separate products or services. Global communications provider Alcatel-Lucent, for example, offers optical networks together with comprehensive sets of network management applications, including tools for network engineering and surveillance. Most vendors produce related products and services and make sure that they work well together. By offering a bundled offering, this strategy is reinforced and customers obtain additional value by using a number of related products from the same vendor. This strategy is especially common in the software industry, where different software packages are marketed as a single suite. A bundle of products or services is called a package. Three **bundling** strategies exist (Paun 1993):

- *Pure bundling*: selling two or more products only as a bundled package. Reasons for a pure bundling strategy are: the products complement each other, bundling optimises product performance, customers prefer a bundled offering and one-stop shopping, competitors also sell bundled offerings, the bundle creates entry barriers for potential competitors or bundling results in cost advantages. However, bundling may be illegal when it results in unfair competition.

- *Unbundling*: selling products only individually. This strategy is appropriate when the bundled offering no longer offers superior value, products are standardised, customers can easily assemble the bundle themselves, customer needs are too heterogeneous for a bundled offering, customers are very price sensitive or competitors offer separate products and achieve cost advantages by selling substantial volume.

- *Mixed bundling*: selling products separately as well as in a bundled package, thus offering customers a choice between buying the product bundle or separate products. This strategy is most suitable when the conditions (product characteristics, customer needs, competitors' strategies) do not clearly favour pure bundling or unbundling.

From product to solution

An increasing number of B2B vendors position their bundled offerings as integrated **customer solutions** (Figure 5.5). Bayer CropScience offers 'solutions ranging from general insect and termite control to the maintenance of parks and golf courses and control of insects which transmit diseases' (www.bayercropscience.com). Drent Goebel, a Dutch manufacturer of offset printing presses, offers 'printing solutions for a variety of markets' (www.drent-goebel.com). And communications provider Nortel

FIGURE 5.5 Offering solutions to B2B customers
Source: GXS. Used with permission.

proudly proclaims: 'There's a revolution going on in the workplace and Nortel is leading the charge, with secure, reliable voice, video and data communications solutions that will forever change the way you do business' (www.nortel.com).

Providing customer solutions entails more than coming up with a resounding slogan for the corporate website; it is a change from selling products to providing services (Hanan 1992). This is exactly what many equipment manufacturers have gone through: rather than sell their equipment, they offer customers hassle-free use of the latest equipment for a fixed fee. IT vendors actually run the IT departments of major customers, including all personnel issues. Some equipment vendors even stopped manufacturing their own equipment and use equipment from former competitors to provide their service. The success of this change from product supplier to service provider depends on the number of customers willing to pay for this new offering. And vendors must realise that services marketing is very different from product marketing and requires different skills. Product marketing is all about developing general products that are sold to a large number of customers, but services marketing requires customer-specific information to develop and sell customised services to individual customers.

Systems marketing and project marketing

To increase customer satisfaction, some vendors offer an integrated combination of interlocking products, together with services such as consultancy, implementation and financing. This is called **systems marketing** and vendors frequently cooperate with partners (vendors of complementary products, but also competitors) to create an attractive system. The vendor's sales teams may even include representatives from partner organisations. For example, Airbus includes personnel from engine manufacturers such as Rolls-Royce and Pratt & Whitney in its marketing and sales teams. Systems marketing offers customised product solutions to customers through one-stop shopping, maximises customer value, and increases switching costs and customer loyalty. It is a common strategy in markets where large complex units are purchased and marketed; for instance, major capital equipment such as aircraft and computer systems.

A related strategy is **project marketing**, where a package of tangible products and support services is designed to realise a specific asset for a client. These assets are usually buildings or infrastructure, such as turnkey factories, airports, power plants, harbours or railroads. Typically, one vendor serves as main contractor for the project and hires several specialised firms for specific activities. The client is usually a public organisation which invites several competitors to submit a tender for the project. Candidates present their proposals and a vendor (or consortium) is selected based on the proposals, presentations and one or more rounds of negotiations. Complex infrastructure projects, in particular, are characterised by a large number of parties (client, main contractor, subcontractors, banks, consultants, policy makers, environmental agencies), many evaluation criteria (proposed solution, technologies to be used, estimated costs, feasibility, cycle time, uncertainties, risks) and long and complex decision-making processes. Davies et al. (2009) describe the complex sub-processes involved in the London Heathrow Terminal 5 megaproject.

Because project marketing concerns unique projects, there are no existing long-term relationships between vendors and buyers. Nevertheless, relationships are very important for project marketing. Contractors develop relationships with potential clients so that they are informed about new projects and are included on both the client's shortlist and that of various subcontractors that may be hired to perform specific activities for a project. In addition, relationship marketing is critical during the project to maintain good communications and quickly solve problems. The project marketing process consists of four stages: strategy development, organisation development, tender preparation and tendering (Figure 5.6).

Strategy development concerns the critical decisions about strategic priorities and the value proposition offered to potential clients. *Organisation development*

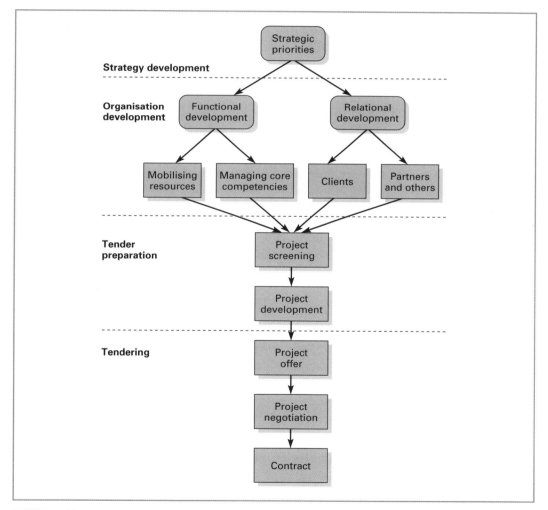

FIGURE 5.6 The project marketing process

Source: Based on Cova and Salle (2007: 140). Used with permission from Elsevier.

encompasses all activities that are not related to a specific project but help to prepare the organisation to effectively acquire and perform projects (such as mobilising resources, managing organisational competencies and maintaining relationships with clients, partners and other relevant parties). For main contractors, the development of a network of external relationships is critical to their ability to form consortia for specific projects. In contrast, the *tender preparation* stage refers to a specific project and encompasses all activities that are required to prepare the tender.

The nature of the activities depends on the role the firm is expected to play: main contractor, subcontractor or supplier. A main contractor must possess both technical knowledge (about products and materials) and application knowledge (about customer situations). Client decision-making processes may take a long time and contractors must invest in several projects without being certain that they will be selected. The main contractor develops a solution based on the customer's broadly formulated functional specifications, divides the total project into sub-projects (which may be awarded to subcontractors) and makes tentative cost calculations per finished stage of the project. Even though projects are unique, a modular design, with key modules recycled across projects, helps to reduce costs. During the *tendering stage* the contractor negotiates with the client about all key elements of the submitted proposal. Final prices and delivery schedules are agreed upon, and for long-term projects the parties also design procedures for price modifications during the project.

A key problem in project marketing is to synchronise the firm's sales efforts (to acquire new projects) with project operations (to perform projects that are won), in such a way that there is a steady flow of work, resources maintain high utilisation and desired deliverables reach customers within the promised lead-time. A useful tool is a sales funnel, with each subsequent stage in the projects pipeline being contingent upon the successful execution of the previous stage, thus allowing only the most advantageous opportunities to move through the funnel. The speed at which new projects are entered into the firm's operations system is determined by the scarce resource (or *critical resource factor – CRF*) in the firm's resource-constrained project scheduling problem (Figure 5.7).

5.5 Developing new products and services

To maintain their competitive advantage, firms must continuously renew their products and services. This section discusses the process of new product development, cooperation with external partners, management of new product development, product modification and new service development.

The process of new product development

New product development (NPD) is the process that results in new products and consists of seven stages: (1) idea generation and evaluation, (2) technical and commercial assessment, (3) concept development, (4) prototype development, (5) testing, (6) trial, and (7) launch.

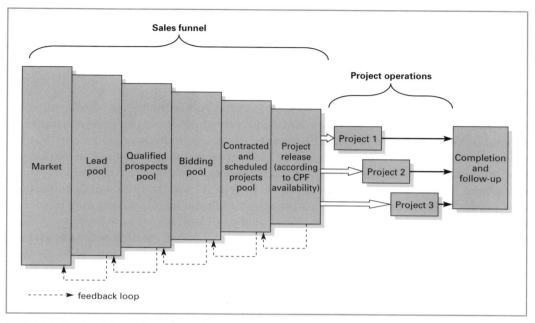

FIGURE 5.7 Synchronising project sales and operations

Source: Cooper and Budd (2007: 174). Reprinted with permission from Elsevier.

Idea generation and evaluation

Ideas may originate in a manufacturer's R&D department as a reaction to new technological developments, a competitor's product or as a new application of an existing technology. Enamel steel, for example, had been used for decades for washing machines and refrigerators before it found a new application as coating for the facades of buildings. Many ideas for new B2B products, however, are suggested by customers (von Hippel 1978). Universities and research centres are other sources of new product ideas. An effective, cheap way to tap into this resource is for vendors to fund several research groups with the stipulation that the vendor has first rights to any promising new product ideas resulting from the research. Vendors scan for new product ideas by maintaining relationships with innovative users (*lead users*), monitoring technological developments, scanning the technical literature and patents issued, and disassembling competitors' products (*reverse engineering*). Every idea is assessed in terms of market potential, required resources, limitations, financial risks, and synergy with existing products, production processes and marketing strategy.

Technical and commercial assessment

After most ideas have been eliminated during the first stage, the remaining ones are examined in more detail. Each remaining idea's technical feasibility is assessed in terms of producability and required technologies and production processes. In addition, they are evaluated on their market potential, which may be assessed by the firm's marketing or sales staff, key customers (information about user requirements and product applications), channel partners (insight into market segments) and industry experts (market trends). The required investments, costs and break-even time are also calculated.

Concept development

Next, the new product concept is developed, tested and refined. A product concept describes the new product's key functions in terms of product specifications and general price level, complete with blueprints, drawings, models or computer animations. Potential customers may test product concepts, but firms must realise that innovative customers may differ from mainstream customers. Medical equipment vendors, for example, cooperate with university hospitals in developing new products, but most potential customers are regional hospitals that may have very different product requirements. Vendors are advised to test new product concepts with a varied group of potential customers, as well as with more objective parties such as channel partners.

 INSIGHT: Beware of innovative customers!

Vendors are sometimes approached by an innovative user who has had an idea for a new product, built an original design, tested it and even used it in practice. Many vendors are persuaded by such innovative users to start redeveloping the user's proven design to make it suitable for large-scale production. But the danger is that the requirements of the average customer are quite different from those of the innovative customer who developed the design. Some vendors discovered to their dismay that the potential market for the new product turned out to be limited to just a few customers.

Vendors that are approached by innovative customers with an original design should go back to the start of the NPD process and carefully assess the product concept and its commercial potential by:

- identifying potential customers
- formulating customer requirements
- determining whether the product meets significant customer needs
- assessing market potential
- analysing the competitive situation
- evaluating the necessary investments and inherent risks
- evaluating the product's fit with the firm's existing products
- testing the product concept with a representative group of potential customers, channel partners and industry experts.

Prototype development

Next, the product concept is developed into a functioning prototype. This is usually done in-house, while partners may develop specific components or modules. Potential customers may also assist in prototype development; for instance, by providing detailed information about their requirements and user situations. In addition, firms start to formulate a marketing plan for the successful product launch and marketing. The marketing plan describes the new product's target customers, key benefits compared to competitive products, timing of market launch, communication media and messages, reasons to buy, price level and pricing strategy, expected reactions from competitors, and training and support of channel partners.

Testing

The developed prototype is tested rigorously. An alpha test (technical test, in-house test) tests whether the prototype conforms to the product's technical and functional specifications and is performed by the vendor. The vendor will mimic the actual user situation as closely as possible; for instance, a manufacturer of conveyor belts uses its own transportation equipment to test the performance of prototypes. As an alternative, vendors may outsource alpha tests to specialised institutes, such as TÜV Product Service, a leading international expert in providing testing, certification and qualification services to industries such as aerospace, defence, medical and health, rail and telecom. Next, the vendor will conduct beta tests (market tests, external tests), which let potential customers test the prototype in their own user situations. After all, no matter how carefully a vendor replicates user conditions in its own test laboratory, customers will always use the product for different applications and under different conditions. In practice, firms use a large variety of tests. Microsoft tests new software with automated quick tests (by individual programmers to test new features), daily build tests (periodic tests of all program components together), usability tests (test of new features by customers in a laboratory), gorilla tests (automated tests of program features under extreme conditions), internal usage and self-hosting (use of the new software by the development group) and beta tests (field tests by customers in real-life situations). The selection of test customers depends on the objectives of the test. Firms use representative customers to test a prototype's overall performance, carefully selected non-representative customers to test specific aspects of the product's performance (such as its performance under extreme conditions) and brand name customers to obtain endorsements that can be used during market launch.

MINI CASE: USING A 'CHICKEN CANNON' TO TEST NEW JET ENGINES

Pratt & Whitney test new jet engines with a series of stress tests, required by the Federal Aviation Administration before a new engine can be certified. Some of these test the engine's performance involving conditions of water and ice. Another test requires dynamite charges to be strapped to the compressor blades and detonated while the

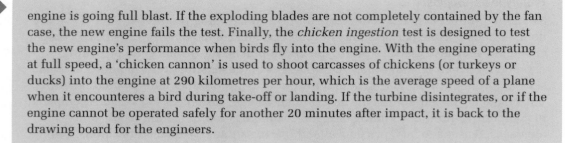

engine is going full blast. If the exploding blades are not completely contained by the fan case, the new engine fails the test. Finally, the *chicken ingestion* test is designed to test the new engine's performance when birds fly into the engine. With the engine operating at full speed, a 'chicken cannon' is used to shoot carcasses of chickens (or turkeys or ducks) into the engine at 290 kilometres per hour, which is the average speed of a plane when it encounteres a bird during take-off or landing. If the turbine disintegrates, or if the engine cannot be operated safely for another 20 minutes after impact, it is back to the drawing board for the engineers.

Trial

During the trial stage, final modifications are made to the prototype and the vendor produces a limited production run. The production process is tested and the marketing plan is finalised. Relatively cheap standardised products may also be tested in a test market (where all elements of the marketing mix are tested by selling the product in a limited geographic region), but for most B2B products this is too expensive and time-consuming. The vendor also finalises its business case for the new product.

Launch

Finally, the production process is scaled up and the new product launched on the market. Brand name customers who tested the prototype are used during market launch. Their names are mentioned in promotional material or during sales presentations, they demonstrate the new product to potential customers (from other industries), they publish scientific papers about the product and its benefits or give presentations during trade shows. In developing the A380 superjumbo, Airbus cooperated with several airlines, but Singapore Airlines conducted the new aircraft's first commercial flight in October 2007 and was used as *launch customer* to stimulate word-of-mouth communication.

New products may be launched globally or rolled out sequentially in one market after another. The latter launch strategy allows a firm to learn from initial customer reactions and modify the launch strategy for later regions. In some markets, customers are strongly influenced by third parties, who are themselves not customers of the new product but strongly influence buying decisions; for instance, a telecom consultant advising companies about purchasing new telephone exchanges. In such industries, it is critical for a vendor to inform these *change agents* about the vendor's strategic vision and the new product's features and benefits.

In practice, the NPD process is not always as neatly linear as this description suggests. Firms frequently go back and forth between stages and several stages may overlap. Indeed, the difference between NPD stages is not always clear-cut. For example, vendors of capital equipment such as printing presses frequently install prototypes at the sites of friendly customers to finalise prototype development. Problems are solved as they occur in an iterative cycle of development and testing.

When these friendly customers are also the first buyers/users of the new product, the distinction between the stages of development, testing and launch is blurred. In addition, many firms design the NPD process as a series of partly overlapping stages, with several activities run in parallel, to reduce time-to-market.

The difference between NPD stages must be carefully communicated to customers. A manufacturer of minor capital equipment enlisted a large customer to test a new prototype. But the firm's sales representative failed to communicate this clearly to the customer, who thought that it was a finished new product. Because the product solved a critical problem, the customer enthusiastically placed a large order. Meanwhile, one of the manufacturer's suppliers was unable to produce a key component with the required tolerances and the NPD process ground to a halt just when the customer's order arrived. It took several meetings at CEO level to explain the situation and repair the damaged relationship.

The NPD stages are separated by go/no go decisions, where management decides whether or not to continue and what will be next. The most obvious decision is to continue with the next stage, but management may also decide to skip a stage or go back to a previous stage. When the project involves only minor changes to a standardised product, several stages can be carried out quickly or skipped altogether. But firms must be careful with skipping stages. Many firms succumbed to competitive pressures and decided to shorten time-to-market by skipping beta tests, only to discover after product launch that the product had some serious design flaws and needed to be redesigned. This results in costly product recalls, increased development costs, repeated launch expenditures and tarnished reputations.

Cooperation in NPD

Firms increasingly cooperate with several partners in developing new products, such as customers, suppliers, complementors and competitors (Figure 5.8). Suppliers and customers, in particular, are frequently used as partners in NPD. **Cooperation in NPD** with suppliers offers several benefits, including:

- improved product quality (by involving suppliers in formulating product specifications)
- reduced costs (by sharing development costs and reducing manufacturing costs through improved product design)
- reduced NPD cycle time (allowing for faster market launch or the use of newer technologies).

Because approximately 80 per cent of product costs are determined in the concept development stage, it is essential to involve key suppliers early in the process (*early supplier involvement*). Based on research in the Japanese automotive industry, Kamath and Liker (1994) distinguished four roles for supplier involvement in NPD: (1) *partner suppliers*, equal partners who are responsible for entire subsystems and participate from the early stages in NPD, (2) *mature suppliers*, who design and deliver complex assemblies, with the customer providing specifications and the supplier developing the system on its own, (3) *child suppliers*, who deliver simple

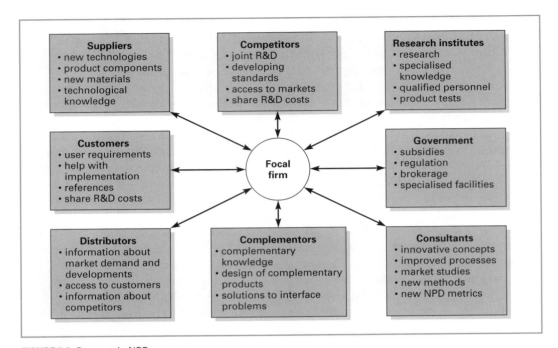

FIGURE 5.8 Partners in NPD

Source: Based on Gemünden et al. (1996: 450). Used with permission from Elsevier.

assemblies based on the customer's design requirements, and (4) *contractual suppliers*, who function as an extension of the customer's manufacturing capability and deliver standard parts.

Firms cooperate with customers to obtain:

- *Information about user situations*: for instance, when a vendor of industrial robots develops a surgical robot that can be used to repair mitral valves, place pacemakers and perform coronory bypass surgery.
- *Access to markets*: customers that cooperate in NPD are frequently also the first buyers of the new product.
- *Shared development costs*: this is only possible when the customer contributes significantly to the development project.
- *Faster time-to-market*: because of continuous feedback from customers during NPD.

Naturally, customers are only willing to contribute to a vendor's NPD project when it offers them clear benefits. Examples of benefits for customers are early access to a new product, which may result in a competitive advantage, the opportunity to influence product specifications, price discounts and temporary exclusive use of the new product. Customers may contribute during all stages of the NPD process (Figure 5.9). The intensity of cooperation varies from asking for customer feedback, to a formulated product concept, to joint development of the whole product.

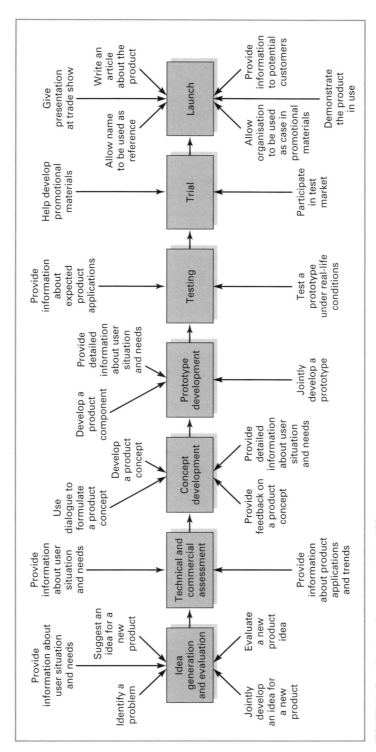

FIGURE 5.9 Contributions of customers during NPD stages

Management of NPD projects

Numerous studies have shown that many new products fail. In addition, most new product ideas do not even make it to the marketplace and are terminated somewhere during the NPD process. Some estimates state that a firm needs no fewer than 3,000 raw ideas for one single profitable product (Stevens and Burley 1997). Firms need a systematic NPD process to weed out all bad ideas; the further an idea progresses in the NPD process, the more expensive it becomes. It is relatively cheap to decide that 20 new product ideas are not viable and should be dropped, but very expensive to translate just one idea into a product concept, build a prototype, have it tested internally and with customers and only then conclude that the project should be terminated. Roughly half of a firm's development costs are spent on products that do not make it to market or fail to become a commercial success.

There are many reasons why products fail in the marketplace; for instance, a product may not offer superior value to customers or the vendor may have neglected to build a reliable supply chain for the new product. Other products fail to get launched because of technical problems during product development, significant changes in customer needs or because a competitor launched a superior product. Most new product failures are caused by a combination of factors; for instance, insufficient attention from top management resulting in inadequate coordination between marketing and R&D, which leads to a product that fails to offer unique benefits to customers. But the good news is that most reasons for new product failure can be influenced by management. After all, the firm's management decides how much to spend on market research, how to manage the NPD process, whether or not to involve customers and suppliers, and the resources to be spent on the project. The NPD literature offers numerous suggestions to improve the management of NPD, such as spend a great deal of time on the initial stages of the NPD process (the so-called *fuzzy front end*) to develop a good product concept, stimulate communication between all people involved in NPD (both inside the firm and with partners), stimulate good cooperation beween marketing and R&D, establish cross-functional teams with representatives from marketing, R&D, purchasing, sales and engineering, assign a *project champion* to promote the project and help it through difficult times, develop new products based on attractive value propositions for customers, remember to develop the required support services, and design the NPD process as a series of overlapping stages to shorten time-to-market.

> ⌒ **INSIGHT: Be creative in encouraging cooperation**
>
> Some firms are very creative in stimulating cooperation between the various business functions involved in new product development. Philips Medical Systems had an extensive user manual drawn up before the actual development of the prototype even began! This required the people involved to consider the product specifications both carefully and in detail, leading to better specifications, reduced problems during actual development, improved internal communication, shorter duration of the development process and therefore early market introduction.
>
> *Source*: Biemans (1990)

NPD processes may involve several parties, both inside (people from several departments) and outside (customers, suppliers, competitors) the organisation. These networks can be quite complex when vendors cooperate, not only with suppliers or customers, but also with universities and research institutes. After all, the academic world is very different from the commercial reality of business firms, frequently resulting in misunderstandings, discussions about patents and time delays (Biemans 1995). These networks of relationships must be carefully managed, with trust, open communication and attention to personal relationships being key ingredients to success.

Management should analyse all NPD projects (successes and failures) after the product has been launched and use the results from these evaluations to improve the management of subsequent NPD projects (Smith 1996). Such new product postmortems can be conducted after each project is finished, once a year or continually. Portmortems should analyse costs, performance and cycle times, but also address questions such as: Why did this happen? How often did this occur? What can we do to prevent this from occurring again? Who will look for a solution to this problem? How do we know if a suggested solution will really work?

Product modification

A relatively cheap alternative to developing new products is to modify existing ones. **Product modification** can also be an alternative to product elimination, when management identifies promising ways to breathe new life into an obsolete product (product rejuvenation). There may be many reasons for product modification, such as changed customer requirements, technological developments, suggestions from suppliers and increasing market saturation. Existing products are modified by changing their tangible characteristics, but also by changing the services that support them. The strategy also allows firms to enter new markets with a modified version of an existing product (for instance, by offering a cheaper, stripped-down version of a product to price-sensitive customers). The advantages of product modification are: less risk than with developing completely new products, lower development, manufacturing and marketing costs, and shorter development cycles, resulting in faster market introduction and higher profits (Berenson and Mohr-Jackson 1994).

A useful strategy for product improvement is *reverse engineering*, especially when firms do not possess the skills and capacity to develop and launch completely new products. Continuous product improvement allows firms to adapt to changing market conditions but can also be dangerous. Research by Christensen (1997) in automotive, computer, pharmaceutical and steel industries, demonstrates how market-leading firms time and again focus only on their current customers and are blindsided by firms using a new technology. Apparently, it is very difficult to build on current success with current customers and still recognise the potential threat of new technologies appearing on the horizon.

Developing new services

The process of **new service development (NSD)** tends to be much less structured than its NPD counterpart because services are predominantly intangible and produced through interaction between service provider and customer. It is relatively easy for service employees to make modifications in the interaction with individual customers, resulting in a proliferation of services. But successful local modifications are not always recognised as promising new services that may be of interest to a larger group of customers. In addition, new services can be developed quickly because a service provider does not have to invest in manufacturing processes. Service providers tend to use a less systematic approach to develop a new service and easily skip stages when the new service appears to be promising and can readily be implemented. For instance, a bank may offer a new service at one of its branch offices to assess customer reactions. Only when the bank decides to add the new service to its regular range of services, and to launch the new service in all its regional offices, are large investments required (training of service employees, development of manuals and procedures, communication to customers). This also illustrates that in NSD the stages of 'testing' and 'launch' overlap: new services can only be tested by offering them to real customers.

On the other hand, NSD is much more complex than this description suggests. After all, innovative service providers must develop not only the new service concept, but also the *service delivery system* that is needed to offer the new service to customers. The service delivery system encompasses all internal processes and procedures, including the coordination between front office and back office and the *customer interface* that defines the interaction with customers (scripts, websites, self-service systems). Roles and responsibilities of both service employees and customers must be made clear. NSD requires extensive training of service employees and may even require hiring of new personnel. When a service provider develops an innovative customer interface, this may significantly impact the firm's operations and internal processes.

Successful service innovators use systematic methods to lower costs and increase the likelihood of success. Because a new service concept's potential can only be assessed by actually delivering the new service to customers, local experiments play a critical role in such structured processes for NSD. A systematic approach to NSD contains the following stages (Thomke 2003):

1 *Idea.* The process starts with the generation of new service ideas from all kinds of internal and external sources. These ideas are evaluated and assigned priorities, after which management selects the most promising ones for further development.

2 *Planning and design.* The selected ideas are further developed into complete designs, including a rollout plan for implementation. Customers do not have to be involved yet; employees can design the new service and practise dry runs without customers to eliminate snags in the delivery process. The objective is to eliminate design errors in the laboratory without confronting real customers with their consequences.

3 *Experimentation.* Experiments are used to test the new service with customers. The service provider may test several versions of the new service in parallel experiments at different locations. Experiments provide maximum information through fast feedback from customers and service employees. Based on the

results, management decides whether the new service design needs to be modified or if it is ready to go live.

4   *Large-scale rollout.* The new service is introduced to all target customers. Significant new services can be brought to the attention of customers through communication campaigns, while minor new services and service modifications can be implemented quietly. But even a silent new service launch still requires training and internal communication.

Successful NSD requires close cooperation with customers. After all, customers are not just buyers of the new service, but also co-producers. New services may change how customers interact with service employees or the service provider's technologies, which changes the customer experience. The service employees providing the new service should also be involved in its development. Because they interact with customers they have a good grasp of customer wants and needs. In addition, their involvement in NSD creates commitment to the new service and prevents them from seeing it as just adding to their workload.

Service providers may also save costs by redesigning existing services, rather than developing new ones. Berry and Lampo (2000) describe several examples of service redesign, such as introducing self-service, direct service at the customer's location or combining multiple services into a package. A useful tool for new service development or service redesign is service blueprinting (Bitner et al. 2008). This technique maps the service process from the customer's perspective as a series of activities and interactions. A service blueprint visualises the service process by describing customer actions, onstage/visible contact employee actions, backstage/invisible contact employee actions, support processes and physical evidence. Blueprinting captures the service in a flowchart that provides a common platform for everybody involved in NSD, generates insight into role and relational interdependencies throughout the organisation, can be printed out or stored electronically to capture innovation knowledge, and defines the customer's moments of truth and the required actions of employees. Service blueprinting can also be used to understand differences between desired, actual and ideal services and thus to identify bottlenecks and opportunities for service innovation.

5.6 Managing market acceptance

When a new product or service is launched on the market a vendor may actively influence **market acceptance**, which occurs at two levels: acceptance by individual customers (adoption) and acceptance by the market (diffusion). Understanding both processes helps vendors to design effective strategies for influencing and shaping market acceptance.

Adoption by individual customers

Market acceptance at the level of individual customers refers to the decision-making process by which a customer evaluates a new product and decides whether or not to incorporate the new product into ongoing practice (Rogers 1995). The **adoption** process consists of five stages:

1 *Knowledge*: the customer becomes aware of the new product and gains some understanding of how it functions. The knowledge is determined by the customer's problem situation (experienced needs), its general characteristics (innovativeness) and its buying centre (communication behaviour of members, individual personalities).

2 *Persuasion*: the customer forms an opinion of the new product, based on the information acquired. Customers look for evaluative information to reduce the uncertainty regarding the new product's expected consequences. The outcome of this stage depends on how the customer ultimately perceives the product's characteristics.

3 *Decision*: the customer chooses to adopt or reject the new product. Small-scale trials help the customer decide. Although the customer decides to adopt the new product, they may reverse this decision at a later stage (*discontinuance*). Indeed, rejection may occur at any stage of the process. Similarly, customers who decide to reject the new product may later decide to adopt; for instance, because an improved version is introduced, key decision-makers have been replaced or the customer's needs or requirements have changed.

4 *Implementation*: the customer uses the new product. Because of potential start-up problems, customers need information about the product's operation, problems that may occur and ways to prevent or solve them. For complex products vendors often provide training and assistance. As a result of using the product, customers may also change or modify it (*re-invention*).

5 *Confirmation*: the customer seeks to reinforce the decision made, but may also reverse it. Discontinuance can be very difficult when considerable investments were made to adopt in the first place. This may result in selective exposure, with the customer only seeking information that supports the original decision.

In practice, adoption is not always a linear process, as decision may precede persuasion. For instance, customers may be 'forced' to follow the competition in adopting innovative production machinery. Customers require information at each stage of the process, which allows vendors to influence their decision making. All in all, the customer's decision to adopt or reject a new product is influenced by the perceived product characteristics, vendor activities, customer characteristics and external factors.

Perceived product characteristics

The most important factors influencing the adoption of a new product or service are its perceived characteristics. The following characteristics are of importance:

- *Relative advantage*: the degree to which the new product is perceived as being better than the next-best alternative. Examples of relative advantage are cost savings, increased productivity and increased prestige.

- *Compatibility*: the extent to which the new product is perceived as consistent with the customers' sociocultural values, past experiences and needs. Does the new product fit with the customer's existing production layout? Can the new product be connected to other related products? A high degree of compatibility means less uncertainty and lower switching costs.
- *Complexity*: the degree to which the new product is perceived as relatively difficult to understand and use. A very complex new product is more difficult to service, experiences more start-up problems, is less hassle-free and requires more support (documentation and training).
- *Trialability*: the degree to which the new product may be experimented with on a limited basis, for instance in a test setting. This is especially important when the product is very new and there are no references yet.
- *Observability*: the degree to which the results of the new product are visible and can be communicated. A vendor may increase the new product's observability by using satisfied customers as references.

Vendor activities

Customers' adoption decisions are also influenced by vendor activities. Vendors stimulate adoption by providing decision-makers with the right information. But it is not only through their marketing communications that vendors influence adoption decisions. Cooperation with competitors during product development, resulting in an industry standard, also has a positive impact on adoption. Similarly, effective organisation of the NPD process (such as a productive marketing–R&D interface) positively influences product quality and time-to-market and thus adoption by individual customers.

Customer characteristics

Adoption decisions are also influenced by customer characteristics, such as size of the organisation, available knowledge and skills, degree of centralisation and contacts with other companies. Firms with many contacts with other companies tend to be more innovative and are more open to new ideas and products. The number of existing customers of the product (*installed base*) may also be relevant. For computer-based communication technologies, in particular, the benefits increase with the number of existing users; collaborative groupware is more attractive when many other firms already use it.

External factors

Finally, adoption is also stimulated by external factors, such as the media (influence the perception of customers), government (issue regulations) and research centres (publish results from comparative product tests). The most important external factor is competition. Competition between customers may cause them to adopt quickly in an attempt to maintain a competitive advantage. Technological competition between vendors may lead customers to postpone their decision until it is clear which technology has emerged victorious.

INSIGHT: Accelerating adoption within oil and gas operating companies

The adoption of new products within oil and gas operating companies is notoriously slow. Nevertheless, these same companies rely on new products to sustain their revenue and growth. In March 2004, Gulf Research asked 500-plus oil and gas professionals about the reasons why new products are not used. The study uncovered that new products must pass three hurdles.

First hurdle: 'Do I need it?'
New products must offer benefits that the customer really needs. Relative to existing alternatives, the new product must save the customer time or money, reduce risk or provide improved performance or functionality. Some illustrative quotes from the survey:

- 'Make sure you develop the right technologies. Do not develop solutions that later are looking for problems.'
- 'Normally suppliers don't offer exactly the technology we need.'
- 'If it saves time or money, we'll try it.'

Second hurdle: 'Does it work?'
Customers require evidence that the product can do what is claimed. Customers want to see published case studies, see performance track records, contact other customers who have used the product, have easy access to all technical information and experience a hands-on demonstration of the product if possible. Some quotes from the survey:

- 'It is easy to say you can do something. But what have you actually done compared with what you said you would do in the past?'
- 'No one wants to be the first to try something new, but once it's been proven, then everyone wants it.'
- 'Get away from development-on-the-run.'

Third hurdle: 'Is it ready?'
The new product and all associated service support must be available in the local area where the application exists. This includes local operations training and support, and contingency plans should the product fail. An illustrative quote from the survey:

- 'Commit to provide quality service with a genuine desire and not just a genuine appearance of desire.'

Source: www.rigzone.com/news/insight/insight.asp?i_id=100

Diffusion in the market

Market acceptance at the level of the market (segment) refers to the adoption of a new offering over time by a group of customers. This illustrates the close link between adoption and diffusion: adoption is an individual decision-making process, while **diffusion** reflects a series of adoption decisions by individual customers in a market. The diffusion of a new product or service is more successful as the speed of individual adoption decisions increases, the number of adopters increases and the time between separate adoption decisions decreases.

Because diffusion is basically a series of subsequent adoption decisions by a group of customers, all factors influencing adoption decisions also influence diffusion. In addition, the variable time can be used to characterise adopters according to their innovativeness, that is, the degree to which a customer is relatively earlier to adopt the new product than other customers. Rogers (1995) distinguishes five adopter categories:

1 *Innovators* (the first 2.5 per cent of all adopters) are the first to adopt and display behaviour that shows that they want to stay ahead of the rest of the market.

2 *Early adopters* (the next 13.5 per cent) look for new products that improve their competitive advantage; they are willing to take risks ahead of the rest of the market.

3 *Early majority* (the next 34 per cent) are more reluctant and wait to see if a new product really works and begins to stand the test of time; they want a finished product that has proven itself and comes complete with supporting services.

4 *Late majority* (the next 34 per cent) are slow to catch on to the popularity of a new product; they are adverse to change and are only willing to adopt a new product when they feel forced by the market to do so.

5 *Laggards* (the final 16 per cent) are more critic than customer and are generally not an interesting market.

This classification is less useful for markets with only a limited number of potential customers. In these markets, vendors usually only distinguish between 'innovators' and 'the rest of the market'. Innovators are willing to take a risk with a new product and frequently function as opinion leader for the rest of the market. Vendors try to persuade the innovators to purchase the new product, hoping that the rest of the market will follow. Vendors of complex medical equipment, for example, offer special discounts to university hospitals, teaching hospitals and specialists who publish a lot.

In practice, this snowball effect, with one group of adopters influencing the next one, does not always happen. For technology products, in particular, there is usually a large difference between innovators and early adopters, on the one hand, and the majority of the market, on the other (Moore 1991). Innovators and early adopters are easily persuaded to try a new product because they are interested in new products (innovators), especially when they can use them to gain a competitive advantage (early adopters). But vendors need the mainstream customers to recoup their development costs and the early majority is much less easily persuaded to try something new. Early majority customers are very pragmatic, avoid risk, look for minor improvements and want a product that has already proven itself and comes with a long list of references and a detailed user manual. Crossing this chasm requires a well thought-out marketing strategy.

The diffusion of a new product typically follows an S-curve, but when there are significant differences between market segments it makes more sense to estimate and analyse the diffusion for each separate market segment. Adoption and diffusion are closely related. Diffusion is a series of subsequent adoption processes and the terms 'speed of adoption' and 'speed of diffusion' are used interchangeably. When the customers are large firms, it may also be useful to analyse the diffusion within organisations. How quickly do organisational units (departments, business units) start using the new product after the organisation has decided to adopt it?

Vendors should analyse adoption and diffusion processes in great detail and use the insights thus obtained to successfully develop, launch and market new products and services. Market acceptance, for example, can be stimulated by involving key users in product development (to improve the new product's relative advantage), involve brand name customers in market launch (to stimulate positive word-of-mouth), announce new products before market launch (to encourage customers to postpone their purchases) and design modular products (to allow customers to adapt the product to their specific needs).

5.7 Deletion and replacement

In most firms, management has the development of a constant stream of new products and services high on their agenda. But all too often they fail to systematically evaluate the current range of products and services and delete underperforming ones. The constant addition of new products results in a large, unwieldy and ineffective range of products, which reduces effectiveness and increases costs. A systematic process of **product deletion** is the antidote to this unchecked growth and consists of four stages (Avlonitis 1984):

1 *Detection of weak products*: management identifies the products that perform weakly (in terms of profit, sales, market share or customer satisfaction). This may be done through a regular portfolio review or by continuously monitoring criteria that function as early warning signals (such as decreasing sales, decreasing margins, launch of effective competitive products and too much attention from product management).

2 *Analysis of the identified products*: the weak products are analysed to determine the nature of the problem and whether or not it can be fixed. There are several revitalisation approaches, varying from minor changes to the product to extensive communication campaigns.

3 *Decision to eliminate the product*: when the weak product cannot or should not be revitalised, management must decide whether to keep the product or eliminate it. Holding on to weak products makes sense when deletion would have a negative impact on sales or profitability of other related products. The decision to eliminate a weak product is based on a systematic analysis of all relevant factors, such as existing contracts with customers,

estimated demand for replacement parts and existing inventories. The availability of a replacement product also influences the elimination decision.

4 *Implementation of the deletion decision*: for effective elimination, management must determine the appropriate timing and method depending on the expected effects on customers, distributors and profits. Immediate deletion is usually not feasible in business markets because of existing contracts with customers. B2B firms use four deletion strategies: (a) phase out the product immediately, (b) phase out the product slowly, by terminating support of the product, maximising revenues and giving customers time to switch to an alternative product, (c) sell the product to another manufacturer (including production machines, existing inventories of finished product and replacement parts), or (d) eliminate the product but offer it as a 'special' on demand (Avlonitis 1983).

The deletion process ends with taking care of the last spare parts, orders from customers and production facilities (for instance, all product codes, blueprints and inventory cards need to be eliminated from the system). Implementation of a deletion decision may take two months to two and a half years, with delays being caused by resistance from customers, changes in expected demand, problems with the replacement product and attempts to coordinate the deletion of the obsolete product and launch of the new one. This illustrates that deletion of an obsolete product often goes hand in hand with the launch of a new one (**product replacement**). But a vendor may also clean up its product range by replacing several obsolete products with just one new one. Product replacement may also be limited to specific market segments or geographic regions. When vendors of copiers replaced obsolete analogue models with new digital ones, the analogue copiers were still very useful to schools. Compared to consumer products, the replacement of B2B products is much more complex. Even when an obsolete product is replaced with a new one, the vendor still needs to offer spare parts and other support services for several years. While this results in double inventories of spare parts, it may also be very profitable. Managers must continuously calculate the costs and revenues of their replacement strategy and orchestrate the product phase-out/replacement accordingly. A vendor, for instance, may gradually decrease the number of years that spare parts are guaranteed to be in stock (by reducing the contract period for new service contracts and not renewing existing ones).

⌒⌒ **INSIGHT: When customers still want the old product**

Existing contracts with customers may force vendors to keep selling the deleted product. A vendor of climate control systems typically needs to deliver discontinued products for six to 12 months after they have been formally deleted from the product range; for instance, because customers have already drilled holes that are incompatible with the holes required for the new product. For truck manufacturers, product replacements require expensive retooling and reconfiguration of production lines, which means that they are unable to manufacture both the obsolete model and the new replacement model. But many customers sign contracts requiring delivery of trucks over an extended period of time. When a truck manufacturer implements a model change, it may offer its customers several options: accept that both old and new models will be delivered, use existing inventories to deliver only the old model for all scheduled deliveries, or reschedule planned deliveries so that the customer only receives the new model.

B2B vendors use two types of replacement strategy (Billington et al. 1998). With a *solo-product replacement*, deletion of the old product coincides with the launch of the new one. With a *dual-product replacement*, both old and new products are offered simultaneously for a period of time. The most appropriate replacement strategy partly depends on the firm's production system. A manufacturer of plastics may easily produce many different products on the same production line; switching from one product to another is just a matter of changing the recipe. But a truck manufacturer must change the whole production line when it switches to a new model. Most B2B firms opt for an overlapping period when both old and new products are offered to customers. They use various tactics to ensure a smooth transition from old to new product, such as offering attractive prices to stimulate customers to switch to the new product (this also reduces the demand for spare parts and other support services), automatically upgrading existing orders for the old product to the new one, and offering product upgrades to customers who recently bought the old product (to reduce the performance gap between both products). In conservative markets, a period of overlap allows customers to get used to the new product and vendors to assess customer reactions. When a significant group of customers keeps demanding the old product, the vendor may even decide to continue the old product (to be produced by the vendor or outsourced to another manufacturer).

Sometimes, vendors do not announce product replacements as such but launch the new product without explicit reference to the old product it is expected to replace. When a vendor has a limited installed base and close customer relationships, for example, such a *silent product replacement* can be implemented through closely targeted direct communication (newsletters, direct mail, online bulletin board). A silent product replacement allows a vendor to let the market decide the old product's fate, whether the old product will be deleted and the speed of deletion. Some new products even end up replacing other products than expected.

5.8 B2B brands

In consumer markets, branding is an accepted and popular way to create a competitive advantage and customer loyalty. But many B2B marketers consider branding too frivolous for their rational products. Nevertheless, there are many examples of successful **B2B branding**. Interbrand's 2008 listing of most valuable global brands starts with Coca-Cola, but then continues with IBM, Microsoft and General Electric, three brands that generate far more B2B revenues than sales to consumers. Other examples of successful B2B brands are Hewlett-Packard, Dell, Oracle, SAP, FedEx, UPS and Siemens. Several venerable B2B brands, like Bosch, Siemens and General Electric, are more than 100 years old. This illustrates the relevance of branding to successful B2B marketing. A recent study of UK tractor buyers showed that brand accounted for almost 40 per cent of the purchase decision, immediately followed by price, and was the most important influencing factor (Walley et al. 2007). Another study of buyers of medium-voltage indoor circuit-breaker panels found that overall brand explained 16 per cent of the decision, but the perceptions across the buying centre members varied a lot. The users of the product and the technical specialists credited the brand name with higher importance (28 and 24 per cent, respectively). At the other extreme, the gatekeeper allocated a very low importance to the brand name. These findings implied that the leading business brand name could command a price premium of 6.8 per cent over the average business brand and 14 per cent over a new, unknown brand (Bendixen et al. 2004). In the context of services, brand has also been shown to be the most important influence on contract renewal (Roberts and Merrilees 2007). These findings illustrate why B2B marketers increasingly turn to branding to create trust, keep customers, focus communication, differentiate the product, reduce purchase uncertainties and stimulate derived demand. The growing use of the internet also contributed to the use of branding. All vendors are just one click away and branding helps customers to make sense of this overload of information.

Like all brands, B2B brands are based on underlying values that define them. But there are also differences with consumer brands. While a consumer brand is essentially a promise to deliver a specific set of product features and benefits, B2B brands need to communicate a much broader range of values. In addition to product performance, B2B brands also must communicate vendor characteristics such as reputation, innovativeness and delivery reliability. When B2B products are installed by distributors, it becomes even more complex to implement a successful and consistent branding strategy.

An effective brand strategy requires communication of the underlying values to employees. When Standard Register, a leading document services provider, introduced a new branding campaign in November 1998, more than 9,000 employees received a booklet entitled *Communicating Our Brand: A Guide for Standard Register Employees*. The booklet informed employees about the objectives of the new campaign and how individual employees could contribute to the campaign's success. B2B marketers must communicate their brand values to all relevant parties, including customers, channel partners, employees, suppliers, consultants, investors and the business press. All communication messages must support the brand and need to be consistent across different media (websites, corporate brochures, advertisements, tradeshow booths and even letterheads). Thus, B2B brands help to identify and distinguish B2B products from the competition, with risk reduction being the most important brand function (Kotler and Pfoertsch 2006).

> ⌒⌒ **INSIGHT: Characteristics of top B2B brands**
>
> In 2007, a Harvard Business School research team conducted a study of top B2B global brands. They identified the following characteristics of such top brands:
>
> - The CEO is a willing brand cheerleader, loves the brand heritage and is a great storyteller. The CMO sees their purpose as helping the CEO achieve this role.
> - The CEO understands that building brand reputation reduces commercial risk, insulates the company in a crisis and provides a common purpose that can bond all stakeholders.
> - Efforts are focused on a single, global corporate brand rather than individual product brands.
> - The payback on marketing expenditures is measured rigorously.
> - Company websites are coordinated worldwide to present a consistent face to shareholders. It also helps to control marketing communications that may have become too decentralised.
>
> *Source*: http://discussionleader.hbsp.com/quelch/2007/11/how_to_build_a_b2b_brand_1.html

The characteristics of B2B markets and B2B marketing have consequences for the use of B2B brands (Hague and Jackson 1994). The small size of most B2B markets does not justify the promotion of different brands. Usually, there is only room for one brand: the name of the firm (Boeing, General Electric, DHL). The emphasis that many B2B customers place on service, continuity and reputation also causes B2B marketers to focus on building the corporate brand. Because of limited communication budgets, corporate logos are effective means to visually support the brand at relatively low cost. Another frequently used strategy is to link the corporate name with product names. This strategy is followed by DuPont, successfully linking product names such as Nylon, Lycra and Kevlar to the DuPont corporate brand.

When downstream markets are important, vendors may use **ingredient branding** to communicate with end-users (Simon and Sebastian 1995). This strategy is especially effective when the logo of the component vendor appears on the final product; examples include: Thinsulate (clothing), Dolby (audio equipment), Intel (computers) and Tetra Pak (juices and dairy products). Ingredient branding is also used in advertising to promote the ingredient's brand with consumers. Microban offers protection against microbes and is used in many different consumer products. Figure 5.10 shows a joint advertisement of Microban and Rubbermaid to increase consumers' awareness of Microban's antimicrobial protection, which is built in during the manufacturing of Rubbermaid sinkware. B2B ingredient branders do not always have to build their brand from scratch with consumers. In 2004, Swarovsky, supplier of crystal components to the fashion, jewellery, interior design and lighting industries, launched its *Brilliant Choice* campaign to offer consumers visible proof of origin and quality.

Ingredient branding is also used in services. In July 2007, Boeing unveiled the 787 to the public. In addition to being built from composite materials rather than

FIGURE 5.10 Microban uses ingredient branding

Source: Microban. Used with permission.

aluminium (thus increasing fuel efficiency), the new aircraft includes many in-cabin innovations, such as superior humidity and climate control and lower cabin pressure that will make air travel more pleasurable. Boeing branded the new plane and called it the Dreamliner, betting that passengers will seek out and pay more for a superior travel experience. Several airlines are already using the name in their advertising and perhaps the Dreamliner brand will feature prominently on 787 fuselages in the future. Successful firms combine ingredient branding with services to support channel partners and end-users, such as in-store demonstrations, advice about product presentations, detailed information packages for end-users, training of salespeople and joint promotions.

Online
Learning Centre

When you have read this chapter, log on to the Online Learning Centre website at ***www.mcgraw-hill.co.uk/textbooks/biemans*** to explore chapter-by-chapter test questions, further reading and more online study tools.

Summary of Key Concepts

- At the core of a company's value creation are the vendor's products and services that offer value to customers.
- Because tangible products are easily copied by competitors, many B2B vendors create a competitive advantage through their services or business processes. Because these are not easily copied, vendors may also charge premium prices for them.
- Services are characterised by a high level of intangibility, simultaneous production and consumption, heterogeneity and perishability. These characteristics complicate the marketing of services, but also offer advantages.
- B2B vendors frequently combine products and services into packages, solutions or systems to create optimum value for their customers.
- Vendors offering systems or projects to customers usually collaborate with several outside firms to create customised solutions for customers. Systems and project marketing require a long-term perspective and careful coordination between the efforts of the various partners.
- To maintain their competitive advantage, vendors must continuously update their portfolio of products and services by developing new products, deleting obsolete ones, modifying existing products and replacing old products with new ones.

- Product development is a systematic process, consisting of a series of activities separated by go/no go decisions. Time to market can be shortened by performing certain activities in parallel, but there are also risks involved in this strategy.

- B2B firms frequently cooperate with other organisations to improve the effectiveness and efficiency of their product development efforts. This strategy of cooperation requires relationship management to effectively manage all communications with and contributions from partners.

- To prevent their product portfolios from becoming bloated with products, vendors must closely monitor product performance and delete underperforming products that cannot be rejuvenated.

- Just like consumer products, B2B products may benefit significantly from a consistent branding campaign. Some B2B vendors use ingredient branding to target their downstream customers and stimulate demand for their ingredients.

🔒 Key Terms

Adoption, p. 158
B2B branding, p. 164
Back office, p. 141
Bundling, p. 142
Cooperation in NPD, p. 151
Customer solutions, p. 143
Diffusion, p. 161
Front office, p. 141
Ingredient branding, p. 166
Market acceptance, p. 157
New product development, p. 146

New service development, p. 155
Offering, p. 130
Product deletion, p. 162
Product modification, p. 155
Product platform, p. 130
Product replacement, p. 163
Product service, p. 130
Project marketing, p. 144
Service, p. 137
Services marketing, p. 139
Systems marketing, p. 144

Discussion questions

1 Vendors that use product platforms to develop a range of derivative products eventually need to develop a new product platform generation. Describe several indicators that a vendor can use to decide that it is time to develop a new product platform generation.

2 An important strategic decision concerning support services is to decide which services will be offered for free (as part of the basic package) and which ones the customer will have to pay for (as options). Which considerations would cause a vendor to offer support services for free, as an additional option or not at all?

3   Some people maintain that all B2B marketing is basically services marketing. Discuss a number of arguments that support this position. Do you agree with this conclusion? Justify your answer.

4   Some vendors implement a full-service concept by offering a performance guarantee. While this allows them to differentiate themselves from competitors and attract new customers, this strategy is not without risks. What are the risks/ disadvantages of offering customers a performance guarantee? What kind of information does a vendor need to make a well-informed decision as to whether or not to offer a performance guarantee?

5   A technology strategy answers several key questions about technology. How may a business marketer contribute to the development of an effective technology strategy?

6   A potential problem in selling technology is price setting. Describe a number of ways to determine the price of a technology. Which one would you prefer?

7   Suppose that your salespeople suggest four new product ideas. Which criteria would you use to rank them?

8   Firms may cooperate with several types of partner in developing new products. Suppose that a manufacturer wants to cooperate with a large customer, a key supplier, a competitor and a university. Describe for each type of partner: the selection criteria that you would recommend for selecting the partners, the problems that might occur during cooperation and strategies to prevent or overcome these problems.

9   Most vendors of B2B products do not use test markets to test market potential and the effectiveness of their marketing strategy. Why not? What other methods can B2B vendors use to assess the market potential of new products?

10   Frequently, external parties influence the market acceptance of a new product. Select a specific product and identify the various external parties that may influence adoption and diffusion processes. Also describe how these external parties influence adoption and diffusion.

Further reading

Biemans, Wim G. (1990) The managerial implications of networking, *European Management Journal*, 8(4): 529–540.

Gemünden, Hans G., Thomas Ritter and Peter Heydebreck (1996) Network configuration and innovation success: an empirical analysis in German high-tech industries, *International Journal of Research in Marketing*, 13(5): 449–462.

Moore, Geoffrey A. (1991) *Crossing the Chasm: Marketing and Selling Technology Products to Mainstream Customers*, New York: HarperBusiness.

Rogers, Everett M. (1995) *Diffusion of Innovations*, fourth edition, New York: Free Press.

Thomke, Stefan (2003) R&D comes to services, *Harvard Business Review*, 81(4): 70–79.

von Hippel, Eric (1978) Successful industrial products from lead users, *Journal of Marketing*, 42(1): 39–49.

References

Anderson, James C. and James A. Narus (1995) Capturing the value of supplementary services, *Harvard Business Review*, 73(1): 75–83.

Avlonitis, George J. (1983) The product-elimination decision and strategies, *Industrial Marketing Management*, 12(1): 31–43.

Avlonitis, George J. (1984) Industrial product elimination: major factors to consider, *Industrial Marketing Management*, 13(2): 77–85.

Bendixen, Mike, Kalala A. Bukasa and Russell Abratt (2004) Brand equity in the business-to-business market, *Industrial Marketing Management*, 33(5): 371–380.

Berenson, Conrad and Iris Mohr-Jackson (1994) Product rejuvenation: a less risky alternative to product innovation, *Business Horizons*, 37(6): 51–57.

Berry, Leonard L. and Sandra K. Lampo (2000) Teaching an old service new tricks: the promise of service redesign, *Journal of Service Research*, 2(3): 265–275.

Biemans, Wim G. (1990) The managerial implications of networking, *European Management Journal*, 8(4): 529–540.

Biemans, Wim G. (1995) Developing a medical equipment innovation within a complex network: the case of applied instruments for respiration, in *Developing Relationships in Business Networks*, Håkan Håkansson and Ivan Snehota (eds), London: Routledge, pp. 332–347.

Billington, Corey, Hau L. Lee and Christopher S. Tang (1998) Successful strategies for product rollovers, *Sloan Management Review*, 39(3): 23–30.

Bitner, Mary Jo, Amy L. Ostrom and Felicia N. Morgan (2008) Service blueprinting: a practical technique for service innovation, *California Management Review*, 50(3): 66–94.

Carlzon, Jan (1987) *Moments of Truth*, Cambridge, MA: Ballinger Publishing Company.

Chiang, Wen-Chyuan, Jason C. H. Chen and Xiaojing Xu (2007) An overview of research on revenue management: current issues and future research, *International Journal of Revenue Management*, 1(1): 97–128.

Christensen, Clayton M. (1997) *The Innovator's Dilemma: When New Technologies Cause Great Firms to Fail*, Boston, MA: Harvard Business School Press.

Cohen, Morris A., Narendra Agrawal and Vipul Agrawal (2006) Winning in the aftermarket, *Harvard Business Review*, 84(5): 129–138.

Cooper, Marjorie J. and Charlene Spoede Budd (2007) Tying the pieces together: a normative framework for integrating sales and project operations, *Industrial Marketing Management*, 36(2): 173–182.

Cova, Bernard and Robert Salle (2007) Introduction to the IMM Special Issue on 'Project Marketing and the Marketing of Solutions': a comprehensive approach to project marketing and the marketing of solutions, *Industrial Marketing Management*, 36(2): 138–146.

Davies, Andrew, David Gann and Tony Douglas (2009) Innovation in megaprojects: systems integration at London Heathrow Terminal 5, *California Management Review*, 51(2): 101–125.

Frambach, Ruud T., Inge Wels-Lips and Arjan Gründlach (1997) Proactive product service strategies: an application in the European health market, *Industrial Marketing Management*, 26(4): 341–352.

Gemünden, Hans G., Thomas Ritter and Peter Heydebreck (1996) Network configuration and innovation success: an empirical analysis in German high-tech industries, *International Journal of Research in Marketing*, 13(5): 449–462.

Hague, Paul and Peter Jackson (1994) *The Power of Industrial Brands: An Effective Route to Competitive Advantage*, London: McGraw-Hill.

Hanan, Mack (1992) *Profits Without Products: How to Transform Your Product Business Into a Service*, New York: AMACOM.

Kamath, Rajan R. and Jeffrey K. Liker (1994) A second look at Japanese product development, *Harvard Business Review*, 72(6): 154–170.

Kotler, Philip and Waldemar Pfoertsch (2006) *B2B Brand Management*, Heidelberg: Springer.

Magrath, A. J. (1986) When marketing services, 4 Ps are not enough, *Business Horizons*, 29(3): 44–50.

Meyer, Marc H. and Alvin P. Lehnerd (1997) *The Power of Product Platforms: Building Value and Cost Leadership*, New York: Free Press.

Moore, Geoffrey A. (1991) *Crossing the Chasm: Marketing and Selling Technology Products to Mainstream Customers*, New York: HarperBusiness.

Paun, Dorothy (1993) When to bundle or unbundle products, *Industrial Marketing Management*, 22(1): 29–34.

Phillips, Fred, Lyle Ochs and Mike Schrok (1999) The product is dead – long live the product-service!, *Research-Technology Management*, 42(4): 51–56.

Reinartz, Werner and Wolfgang Ulaga (2008) How to sell services more profitably, *Harvard Business Review*, 86(5): 90–96.

Roberts, Jane and Bill Merrilees (2007) Multiple roles of brands in business-to-business services, *Journal of Business & Industrial Marketing*, 22(6): 410–417.

Rogers, Everett M. (1995) *Diffusion of Innovations*, fourth edition, New York: Free Press.

Rothenberg, Sandra (2007) Sustainability through servicizing, *MIT Sloan Management Review*, 48(2): 83–91.

Shostack, G. Lynn (1977) Breaking free from product marketing, *Journal of Marketing*, 41(2): 73–80.

Simon, Hermann and Karl-Heinz Sebastian (1995) Ingredient branding: Reift ein Junger Markentypus [Is a new type of branding being used]?, *Absatzwirtschaft*, 38(6): 42–48.

Smith, Preston G. (1996) Your product development process demands ongoing improvement, *Research-Technology Management*, 39(2): 37–44.

Stevens, Greg A. and James Burley (1997) 3,000 raw ideas = 1 commercial success, *Research-Technology Management*, 40(3): 16–27.

Thomke, Stefan (2003) R&D comes to services, *Harvard Business Review*, 81(4): 70–79.

Vargo, Stephen L. and Robert F. Lusch (2004) The four service marketing myths: remnants of a good-based, manufacturing model, *Journal of Service Research*, 6(4): 324–335.

von Hippel, Eric (1978) Successful industrial products from lead users, *Journal of Marketing*, 42(1): 39–49.

Walley, Keith, Paul Custance, Sam Taylor, Adam Lindgreen and Martin Hingley (2007) The importance of brand in the industrial purchase decision: a case study of the UK tractor market, *Journal of Business & Industrial Marketing*, 22(6): 383–393.

Zeithaml, Valarie A. and Mary Jo Bitner (2000) *Services Marketing: Integrating Customer Focus Across the Firm*, second edition, Boston, MA: McGraw-Hill.

CHAPTER 06

Managing sales and delivery channels

Introduction

In order for products and services to deliver value to customers, vendors must get their products and services to these customers. There are basically two major alternative strategies: (1) sell directly through personal selling, a catalogue, the internet or a customer contact centre; or (2) sell indirectly through channel partners. Vendors must design the channel system that best fits the nature of the product, the capabilities of the firm and the needs of customers. In addition to designing and managing effective channel systems, vendors also need to design and implement physical distribution systems that physically move products from the vendor to customers.

This chapter starts with the key strategic decision to use direct or indirect channels for sales and delivery. It describes how this choice involves a trade-off between control and efficiency. Most B2B vendors use direct sales and delivery channels and many combine several channels into a hybrid channel system. The chapter discusses various elements of effective personal selling, including sales tasks, sales approaches, ethical issues, sales organisations and hiring, training, motivation and evaluation of salespeople. Because of the high costs of personal selling, many vendors (also) use other channels, such as a catalogue, the internet or a customer contact centre. Vendors who opt for indirect channels use channel partners to perform specified marketing and sales tasks. The key decisions in this area concern the selection, motivation and evaluation of channel partners. The chapter also shows how vendors can use customer needs to design an effective channel system that delivers superior value to customers at the lowest cost. Despite all efforts to design effective channel systems, conflicts frequently occur and must be carefully managed. The chapter closes with an overview of the elements of effective systems for physically moving products from the vendor's factories to customers.

6.1 Direct and indirect sales and delivery channels

B2B firms have two basic options when it comes to selling and distributing their offerings: direct and indirect channels. With **direct channels**, the vendor targets a set of identifiable customers through direct salesforces, catalogues, the internet and customer contact centres. The vendor owns the channels, makes all strategic channel decisions and controls how the channels are implemented. With **indirect channels**, the vendor relies on channel partners to sell and distribute its offerings to customers. While the vendor still designs the channel, control over implementation is partly relinquished to channel partners. Wholesalers and independent distributors also offer competitors' products and the vendor has little formal control or influence over the channel. Vendors may also use hybrid channels, such as exclusive distributors, dealerships or franchises. These channels are owned and operated by other organisations, but they only carry the vendor's products and their success is largely tied to the vendor's success. Another example of a hybrid channel is the shared channel, where one company uses another's sales or distribution channel to reach customers.

Most B2B vendors use direct channels; some estimates show that 75 per cent of all B2B products are sold and distributed directly, especially products with a high value per unit. The rise of the internet has further increased the use of direct customer contact and allows small vendors to reach out to customers worldwide. Vendors opting for indirect customer contact generally prefer short channels with just a few channel partners, which increases control. But in B2B selling and distribution, one size typically does not fit all. Most vendors realise that they need to combine several channels to effectively and efficiently serve their customers. This requires a channel strategy to achieve an optimal channel mix and avoid conflict among the channels being used; for instance, by having large volume customers being called on by a field salesforce, while small customers have access only to the firm's website and customer contact centre. Even a focused player like Dell discovered that its remote model of mail order, telephone and internet must be supplemented by a salesforce to build relationships with major accounts and resellers.

MINI CASE: DELL LAUNCHES A PARTNERDIRECT CHANNEL SCHEME

Dell Inc. has always been known for its direct-only model that cuts out the reseller channel. However, in February 2008, it launched its PartnerDirect programme: the company was looking for SME and mid-market focused reseller partners to sell its PCs to customers. The resellers may present themselves as 'Dell-authorised partners' and will be visited by Dell's direct salesforce. Dell's Solution Provider Direct programme consists of three sales organisations within the company:

- One group focuses on the commercial sector, including small and mid-sized businesses.
- The Industries Solution Group focuses on customised OEM solutions, such as special product builds, allowing Dell to customise solutions.
- A group that focuses on the 'public' area, including schools and government.

All three of these groups sell both through channel partners and directly. Dell takes this move to the reseller channel seriously: it wants to create channel advocates in its direct salesforce and will use financial rewards to shape staff behaviour. The direct sales teams will only receive their quarterly bonuses when they can demonstrate that resellers have accounted for one-third of their revenues.

On the partner side, Dell distinguishes between five types of partner:

- Dell Registered Partners, who sell Dell products and services and buy from a Dell Distribution Partner.
- Dell Distribution Partners, who sell exclusively to second-tier resellers.
- Dell Certified Commercial Partners, who provide solutions to SMEs.
- Dell Certified Solutions Partners, who provide solutions to corporate and public sector customers.
- Dell Certified Retail Partners, who sell to small office and home office (SOHO) customers.

Each type of partner has access to a wide range of support services from Dell.

Even when firms use multiple channels, they emphasise different channels depending on the stage of market development.[1] In the early stages of market development, direct sales are critical to promote new products and new technologies, either through a sales team that communicates directly with customers or through online sales. As the market matures, most companies turn to solution providers for increased sales, such as value-added resellers, systems integrators, consultants and application service providers. These solution providers recommend or resell the vendor's products to customers, frequently bundled with other products to provide a full solution that addresses a specialised need. When the market reaches maturity and the product becomes mainstream, additional sales are gained through more generic mass-market resellers.

6.2 Selling directly: personal selling

The most commonly used direct channel in B2B markets is **personal selling**. A personal sales presentation is the most effective way to present the offering's value to potential customers. It allows the sales message to be customised to meet a specific customer's needs and the salesperson can directly respond to questions and objections, communicate large amounts of technical information, demonstrate the product and build a long-term relationship. Unfortunately, the costs of a sales visit have increased dramatically; in some industries, it costs well over €250 each time a salesperson contacts a potential customer – and these costs are incurred whether the sale is made or not. The cost of a sales visit includes salary, incentives (commission, bonus), sales support materials, office supplies, telecommunications, car, travel, subsistence and entertainment spending. In addition, personal selling often requires extensive training on product knowledge, industry information and selling skills. Considering that a salesperson can only call on one customer at a time, personal selling is not a cost-effective channel for reaching a large audience. Other potential disadvantages of personal selling are that it may result in inconsistent sales messages and ethical problems. Personal selling is especially suitable for offerings that are complex, critical for the customer, customised to match specialised customer needs, based on new technology, involve major purchase decisions or require personal demonstration and when there are only a few customers and buying centres are large and complex.

Many vendors use specialised salespeople for specific customer groups or sales activities, for instance, vendors may use special salespeople for large accounts, specific product groups or supporting resellers. Another strategy is to use one salesforce to identify and acquire new customers (the *hunters*) and another to build and nurture relationships with existing customers (the *farmers*). But this hunter/farmer sales model assumes that it is easy to hand over customers to other salespeople, which is not always the case. Indeed, the hunter salespeople may leave several loose ends because they do not have to deal with the consequences of ongoing customer relationships. Hit by the financial crisis in 2009, many vendors slowed down their efforts to acquire new business, but in difficult times it is especially important to hunt for new business revenues.

For complex products, vendors may temporarily locate salespeople at the customer's premises to assist with product installation and start-up problems, train operators and develop relationships. Others locate salespeople permanently with major accounts, where they have access to production schedules, inventory data, marketing plans and demand forecasts and use all this information to order the required products. Doing so reduces inventories, improves delivery performance and lowers prices.

Sales tasks

Salespeople perform four **sales tasks**: provide information and sell, manage relationships, collect market information and disseminate it within the firm, and coordinate the sales team.

Provide information and sell

The salesperson's primary task is to persuade customers to purchase their offering. This includes planning and preparing sales activities, giving sales presentations, identifying key decision-makers, submitting bids, educating customers on new offerings, communicating value, expediting orders, providing after-sales support and visiting prospects. While a lot of time used to be spent on travel and waiting, a broad range of products and technologies have increased the effectiveness and efficiency of salespeople on the road. The internet, in particular, has drastically changed the selling process (Long et al. 2007). Salespeople can use business databases, corporate websites and email to collect information about prospects, qualify prospects and prepare for sales visits. Salespeople may even get information from buyer's employee blogs. During the sales visit, the salesperson can tap into the vendor's intranet for online demonstrations, prerecorded product videos and access to the company's online catalogue. LinkedIn, Facebook and Twitter help to maintain relationships with existing customers. Also, prospective buyers no longer need to visit the vendor's plant or other satisfied customers, but can watch online multi-media presentations from their own office. Xerox, for example, provides an online video that details the steps for finding a software solution for an energy utility company, in which satisfied executives from the buying firm explain how digitised engineering drawings and a new digital repository system increased productivity and savings.

INSIGHT: Technology tools for salespeople on the go

The digital revolution has not only flooded consumer markets with new products and high-tech toys, it has also changed how salespeople do their jobs. A broad range of products and technologies contribute to more effective and efficient salespeople on the go. Here are the most commonly used high-tech must-haves for salespeople:

- Ultra-thin and light laptops allow salespeople to give sales presentations and access software applications, while wireless internet (WiFi) connects them to the corporate intranet to enter and retrieve information about inventories and expected order times.
- Salesforce.com, an electronic marketplace, connects buyers and sellers of B2B products.
- Contact management software helps salespeople to effectively manage their customer contacts by remembering key data about customers.
- Smartphones, like the ubiquitous BlackBerry, and personal digital assistants (PDAs) are used to manage the salesperson's day-to-day business; for instance, by accessing the internet just before a sales call and reading the latest press releases or news headlines about the client.
- Sites like LinkedIn, Twitter and Facebook help to create and strengthen networks of contacts, which leads to new opportunities and a larger number of warm calls.
- Navigation systems, like TomTom, allow salespeople to reduce travel times and increase the number of customer visits.
- Software products like Ovation transform lifeless PowerPoint slides into stunning presentations by making the text more readable, adding motion and animation, and building in eye-catching graphical backgrounds.
- Audio/video conferencing tools offer a practical alternative to face-to-face sales meetings through online video conferencing, web/phone conferencing or online text chats.

Manage relationships

An increasingly important task of salespeople is developing and maintaining relationships with customers. B2B customers increasingly want long-term relationships with vendors, built on trust and information sharing. This relationship management task includes identifying key customers, developing relationships with all key decision-makers, developing trust, identifying opportunities to improve product usage, analysing unmet customer needs and problems, and suggesting solutions.

Collect and disseminate market information

Because of their regular contact with customers and prospects, salespeople are an important source of market information (see also Chapter 3). Information about unmet customer needs, experienced problems with products, suggestions for product improvements and activities announced by competitors are important inputs for product development and marketing planning. Salespeople must not only collect this information but also disseminate it within their own organisation.

Coordinate the sales team

Many vendors use sales teams to match the buying centres used by customers. Such a sales team consists of representatives from several departments, such as marketing, sales, R&D and engineering, and is headed by an account manager. The account manager coordinates the activities of the sales team and employs people where and when needed.

The allocation of a salesperson's time across these four sales tasks depends on the situation. With a new customer, the emphasis is on explaining the value of the vendor's offering and persuading the customer to purchase the product, while existing customers are contacted regularly to maintain the ongoing relationship.

Personal selling used to be seen as part of a vendor's communication mix, with salespeople communicating to customers the value offered to them. Communication is still important, but customers no longer depend on salespeople for information about products and services. They have access to the internet and can easily compare different competitive offerings. This means that salespeople must *create* value, rather than just *communicate* value. A vendor's salesforce is part of the vendor's offering and only when customers perceive salespeople as creating significant value will they be willing to pay for sales visits. Figure 6.1 shows how vendors may create value during the various stages of the buying process. For customers who understand the product well and know how it fits their needs, the value is derived from the product itself. These customers see the product as a commodity, get value from efficient purchasing (for instance, through online ordering) and do not want to pay for a sales visit. Other customers are less knowledgeable and need advice and customisation; these customers value salespeople who help them make the right purchase decision.

A salesperson creating value for customers results in a less aggressive sales process that resembles a service. It also changes the requirements that firms will be looking for in their salespeople. Salespeople must identify and analyse customer

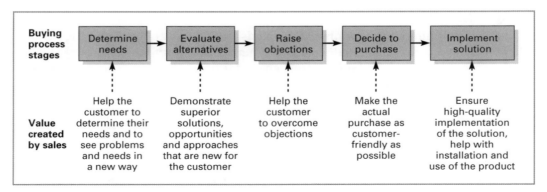

FIGURE 6.1 Creating value in sales

Source: Rackham and DeVincentis (1999: 67). Reprinted with permission.

needs and build relationships with customer decision-makers and with people in the vendor organisation. They must possess customer and industry knowledge, as well as knowledge of the firm's key business processes, be cooperative and analytical, have a good grasp of key success factors, be able to empathise with customers, allow for cultural differences and display ethical behaviour. George Fisher, former CEO of Motorola, acknowledged the strategic role of salespeople as early as 1989, when he stated: 'Members of our salesforce are surrogates for customers. They should be able to reach back into Motorola and pull out technologies and other people that they need to solve problems and anticipate customer needs. We want to put the salesperson at the top of the organisation. The rest of us then serve the salesperson.'[2]

Sales approaches

The effectiveness of personal selling is largely determined by the interaction between salesperson and customer. The quality of this interaction depends on both the *content* of the interaction (product specifications, delivery times, installation procedures, prices) and the *style* of interaction between the salesperson and customer (format, ritual, mannerisms). In the ideal situation both content and style of interaction are compatible; when both are incompatible, there will be no further interaction. When only the content is incompatible, the customer may terminate the interaction or initiate negotiations about the offering's specifications or payment conditions to get a better match. When only the style is incompatible, the customer may end the interaction or get stuck with lingering negative feelings. If the customer informs the vendor about the incompatible interaction styles, the vendor should replace the salesperson with someone who has a more compatible style. Vendors who are repeatedly confronted with incompatible styles in their interaction with prospects should retrain their salesforce, modify their sales approach or change their hiring practices. Vendors who repeatedly have to deal with incompatible content in their interaction with prospects should either change their offering or look for more compatible customers.

⌒⌒ **INSIGHT: Seven types of salespeople**

Salespeople come in different shapes and sizes. Here is a look at seven types of salespeople:

- The *diplomat* is skilled in sales, but afraid to ask for the sale for fear it might offend the prospect. They do well in customer service positions where closing is not necessary.

- The *rejection dreader* takes rejection personally and looks for any excuse to cancel an appointment. They hang out at the office too much and disrupt other salespeople with their constant complaining. They might be better suited for inside sales, where rejection is relatively low.

- The *militant closer* is very aggressive and does anything to close the sale. They do not care whether their product meets the customer's needs; they only care about closing the sale. Because of this short-term focus, they are not suitable for situations where the vendor wants to establish long-term relationships with customers.

- The *sales scholar* studies sales, but is not a professional salesperson. They attend seminars, read books on sales and listen to sales tapes in the car. They always offer clever sales advice to others but do not practise what they preach.

- The *phony* is skilled in many aspects of the selling process but does not care about meeting people's needs. They do not properly address the prospect's concerns and exude insincerity with their slick and glossy ways.

- The *overcooked casualty* is the classic 'burned-out' salesperson. They sell to make a living, not because they enjoy it. They do not take the time to establish rapport, thoroughly handle objections or identify a prospect's needs. On the other hand, they are usually good at qualifying buyers. Often, they are a formerly competent salesperson in a slump.

- The *professional* knows how to close the sale without being perceived as pushy. They ask questions and actually listen to the prospect's answer. They help prospects to discover for themselves the benefits of the product. They are highly ethical, build relationships and aim to establish an extensive list of satisfied customers, who repeat business and are delighted to refer them to friends and business colleagues.

Source: American Salesman, 1 July 2001

Vendors use a variety of **sales approaches**, such as script-based selling, adaptive selling, consultative selling and strategic partner selling (Dwyer and Tanner 2006).

Script-based selling

When all customers and prospects have similar or identical needs, a vendor may use script-based selling. With this sales approach a vendor develops a powerful script, based on its value proposition, success stories and objectives, which is used by salespeople to interact with customers. A sales script instructs salespeople on what to say (opening statements, description of the vendor's offering, appropriate responses to objections) and may also specify what they should do while saying it (for instance, point to the product they are talking about). Script-based selling is especially suitable for relatively simple products of low value, such as office supplies, lubricants and lamps, and is particularly cost-effective in telephone selling.

Adaptive selling

When customers have different needs, adaptive selling is appropriate. With adaptive selling, the salesperson identifies the nature of the selling situation (for instance, the needs of the customer) and selects the appropriate sales presentation and offering. Thus, the salesperson adapts the sales message to the specific needs and beliefs of each customer. Adaptive selling is particularly useful when salespeople encounter a wide variety of customers with different needs and the typical sales situation involves large orders. For instance, one buyer of a copier may make 200 copies at a time, while another rarely makes more than ten copies at the same time. These different customer needs require different offerings and different sales approaches. Adaptive selling allows salespeople to rapidly adjust the message in response to the customer's reactions during the sales process. Effective salespeople are very sensitive to customer signals (both verbal and body language) and quick to adapt their sales approach accordingly. Table 6.1 describes four types of customer and the sales approach that is most effective with each one.

TABLE 6.1 Types of customer and sales approach

Aspect of sales approach	Customer social style			
	Driven	**Expressive**	**Friendly**	**Analytical**
Atmosphere in sales interview	businesslike	open, friendly	open, honest	businesslike
Salesperson's use of time	effective, efficient	leisurely, to develop relationship	leisurely, to develop relationship	thorough, accurate
Pace of interview	quick	quick	deliberate	deliberate
Information provided by salesperson	salesperson's qualifications, value of products	what salesperson thinks, whom they know	evidence that salesperson is trustworthy, friendly	evidence of salesperson's expertise in solving the problem
Salesperson's actions to win customer acceptance	documented evidence, stress on results	recognition and approval	personal attention and interest	evidence salesperson has analysed the situation
Presentation of benefits	what product can do	who has used the product	why product is best to solve problem	how product can solve the problem
Assistance to aid decision making	explanation of options and probabilities	testimonials	guarantees and assurances	evidence and offers of service

Source: Weitz et al. (2007: 115). Reprinted with permission.

Consultative selling

When customers have unique needs, the salesperson should start a dialogue to learn about customer needs before talking about a specific offering. Only when the needs and problem situation are clear does the salesperson look for a suitable solution in terms of products or services. With consultative selling, salespeople create value by helping customers understand their problems, issues and opportunities in a new way, showing customers new or better solutions and acting as customer advocates in the vendor organisation. This sales approach is particularly suitable for complex offerings, offerings that change quickly and first-time customers of the offering. The salesperson functions as a consultant and assists the customer in solving its problem. When the consultative salesperson does not have the best solution to the customer's problem, they may even recommend a competitor's product. After all, this will increase customer satisfaction and cement the long-term relationship, while future revenues will offset the loss of the single sale. Consultative salespeople are often called 'account managers', 'business development managers' or 'client partners'.

Consultative selling requires a salesperson to put a lot of effort into learning the specifics of the customer situation. Several customer visits may be necessary to create the required rapport and understanding. Even when the customer decides to purchase, this may not justify the costs of consultative selling; it may not be until the second or third sale (or the sale of add-on products or services) that the up-front investments in understanding the customer bring a positive return. A long-term perspective is key to successful consultative selling and this must be reflected in the metrics used to evaluate salespeople's performance.

Strategic partner selling

Strategic partnering is appropriate when both parties are willing to invest significantly in the relationship, identify mutual needs and develop customised solutions. In this situation, the vendor organisation becomes the offering. This is too complex to be controlled by a salesperson or even by a sales team. Instead, many people from various departments will be involved to exchange information, design solutions and implement them. Both the vendor and the customer make significant changes to create superior long-term value. Strategic partner selling is characterised by the use of cross-functional teams, adaptations by both partners, significant commitment and open communication.

Ethical dilemmas

Salespeople are often faced with **ethical dilemmas**; for instance, when they are guaranteed a big sale if they offer an illegal payment. Should they make the payment or not? Should they inform their employer or just make their own decision and live with the consequences? These ethical dilemmas concern their relationships with customers, with the vendor organisation and with competitors.

Relationships with customers

Supplying customers with incorrect information (such as unrealistic delivery schedules) is generally considered to be unethical behaviour. But what about withholding relevant information from customers? While this may not be unethical, it has a negative impact on the development of trust and credibility. Another potential problem area is giving presents. Many firms use the general policy that their buyers are not allowed to accept gifts, including invitations to sports events, golf clinics or the theatre. Even the well-established business lunch may cause problems when it takes place in a very luxurious restaurant. Other examples of potentially unethical behaviour in interacting with customers are giving special treatment to specific customers, paying speaking fees to customers and repeating confidential information. Even freely offering useful information about competitors is not appreciated by customers; after all, this proves that you are unreliable and cannot be trusted with confidential information.

Ꮽ INSIGHT: Using sex in selling

Everybody knows that sex sells. So, it is not surprising that some companies use sex as a sales tool. In many industries it is common practice for a sales representative to take a customer to a topless bar to discuss business. *Sales & Marketing Management* conducted a survey on the subject. Nearly 50 per cent of the male sales managers and salespeople said that they have entertained clients in topless bars, sometimes more often than ten times a year. Most said they do not have serious ethical qualms about it: only one-quarter said they would rather lose a customer than go to a topless bar. Many companies lack a clear policy about such visits: 40 per cent of the firms do not allow it, 43 per cent look the other way, 2 per cent stimulate it and 11 per cent have no policy. The predominant corporate attitude is summarised by one sales manager: 'It's part of doing what the customer wants.' According to the survey, the customer initiates visits to topless clubs more than two-thirds of the time. Out-of-town customers lead the pack, since heading to a topless bar is still a sneaky business. The comments provided by sales managers illustrate that they see such visits as a way to build the relationship: 'If you're married, you know you've done something you're not supposed to do. I've done something naughty, you've done something naughty, we've got a secret on each other – and that's good for business.'

But there are also disadvantages to the use of sex. Female sales staffers increasingly speak out against a form of client entertainment from which they are de facto barred and frequent visits to topless bars may wreck a salesperson's health and hurt the vendor's reputation. In addition, there is the risk of problems on the home front. 'I haven't told my girlfriend about this yet,' says a wine distributor who occasionally takes clients to topless bars. 'She appreciates the arts, but I don't think she appreciates this one.' But despite these disadvantages, the practice of using sex in selling will not easily go away. In November 2005, the *New York Times* reported on a strategy used in the pharmaceutical industry to push brand name drugs: hire cheerleaders as sales reps whose 'educational' methods can be relied upon to sell drugs. Pharmaceutical companies deny that sex appeal had any bearing on hiring. According to them, cheerleaders have many qualities the drug industry looks for in its salesforce.

Sources: *Sales & Marketing Management*, July 1995 and *New York Times*, 28 November 2005

Relationship with vendor organisation

Salespeople also experience ethical dilemmas in their relationship with the vendor organisation. Most of these dilemmas concern claims about expenses, hours worked and activities performed. Giving a customer a quick look at a new product is not a product demonstration and the time spent on a business lunch should be accurate. Expense accounts should not be padded with activities that were never carried out or costs that were not actually incurred. Salespeople who intend changing employers should inform their existing employer early and be careful with confidential information.

Relationships with competitors

Making inaccurate statements about competitors and their offerings is clearly unethical. Criticising a competitor's offerings should also be considered unethical behaviour. When a sales director at Northern Telecom was faced with a very sceptical customer, an inquiry showed that a competitor had been very negative about Northern Telecom's products. The sales director used the opportunity to refute all inaccurate claims and put their products' weaknesses in a different light. The customer was very impressed. When it turned out that the competitor had also made inaccurate claims about its own products, Northern Telecom received a €1 million contract.

To prevent problems with unethical behaviour, some vendors issue a code of ethics that specifies unambiguously what kind of behaviour is considered unethical. In 2005, pharmaceutical giant Pfizer published its *Global Policy on Interactions with Healthcare Professionals*, which governs Pfizer pharmaceutical operations around the world. The policy is available in 45 languages and incorporates common legal and ethical standards from many of Pfizer's major markets.

Sales management

The objectives and strategies of personal selling are formulated in the sales plan, which is derived from the marketing plan and provides information about sales objectives, available resources, planned activities, estimated revenues and costs per sales region, salesperson, market segment or individual customer. Companies using account management write account plans that specify for every single account the strategy, objectives, sales activities, revenues and costs. The effectiveness of a sales plan is influenced by how the company organises the sales function and manages the salesforce.

Sales organisation

Most B2B firms structure their sales operation around geographic regions, products or markets, depending on the nature of their products, role of channel partners, diversity in market segments served, nature of the buying behaviour in each segment, available financial resources and activities of competitors. Large firms with several different product groups frequently use a mix of different **sales organisations**.

Geography-based sales organisation

Many B2B vendors organise their sales function around the geographic regions served, with salespeople being responsible for selling all products in their sales region. This allows a salesperson to collect detailed information about customers and local market conditions. A disadvantage is that the salesperson sells all products, which limits the depth of their product expertise, especially when the products have many different applications. Vendors may solve this problem by appointing product experts who support the salespeople. Another disadvantage is that not all territories are equal and this may limit the opportunities and effectiveness of salespeople.

Product-based sales organisation

In a product-based sales organisation each salesperson is responsible for a group of products. This allows a salesperson to specialise in a few related products and increases the quality of information provided to customers. A product-based sales organisation is particularly suitable for vendors with a wide range of products that require much application knowledge. A disadvantage is that a specialised salesforce may be very expensive (costs of training and travel), requiring a certain market size for this organisational sales structure to be cost-effective. Another disadvantage is that customers may be visited by several sales representatives from the same firm. Indeed, one customer got so tired of these multiple sales visits that he made pictures of all sales representatives visiting his firm and sent them all to the vendor with the message: 'I don't care which one it will be, but from now on I only want one of these sales representatives visiting us!'

Market-based sales organisation

From a marketing perspective, a market-based sales organisation seems to be the logical choice. Salespeople are responsible for groups of customers with similar needs, such as hospitals, schools or metalworking firms. This allows them to attend industry association meetings, subscribe to industry trade publications and become industry experts. Many B2B vendors switched from a product-based to a market-based sales organisation in the belief that doing so would bring them closer to customers and increase the chances of offering superior value. A market-based salesforce also allows them to build and nurture relationships with customers. Customer groups, however, need to be sufficiently large to justify such special treatment.

Another way to structure a sales organisation is by skill factor (for instance, by distinguishing between hunters and farmers) or by creating a hybrid structure (such as using separate salesforces for capital sales and MRO items for each geographic region).

MINI CASE: IBM SHAKES UP ITS SALES ORGANISATION TO TARGET SMEs

In the summer of 2007, IBM announced that it would revamp its Systems and Technology Group (STG) to better target small and medium-sized enterprises (SMEs), defined as business customers with no more than 1,000 employees. It will create one sales group to sell to large enterprise customers and another to sell to SMEs. Within each of its 220 geographic sales territories it will create a new level of sales management: the new SME Systems Sales Manager in each territory will focus solely on SME sales efforts. IBM is making the change because its 2006 market share in the SME systems market was just 15 per cent, half of what it was for the overall systems market. It will create positions of SME Systems Sales Managers to offer just one level of IBM sales management to work with partners to sell to SMEs. The partners are usually system integrators or independent software vendors. '[Before], a partner had to go to five different IBM people in a territory. Now they just have one,' according to Bob Samson, IBM vice-president of worldwide systems sales for STG. The sales reorganisation coincides with the introduction of new products designed to appeal to SMEs, including blade servers.

Source: PCWorld, 19 July 2007

A specific type of market-based sales organisation is **account management**, where large and important customers (the *key accounts* or *national accounts*) receive special treatment. Each account is served by a dedicated account manager, who is sometimes supported by a team of sales, customer service and technical employees. The objective of account management is account penetration: maximising the account's opportunities and thus increasing revenues and profits; for instance, by offering additional products and services that fit the customer or by targeting other business units, departments and subsidiaries that might benefit from the vendor's offering.

Account management increases the firm's customer-focused strategy, improves customer relationships, increases revenues and profits, reduces costs and improves the firm's competitive position. Implementation of account management requires a vendor to use unambiguous criteria to identify key accounts, such as revenues, profit, potential revenues or profit, strategic relevance and willingness to cooperate. Vendors using account management typically segment their markets according to firm size, with a different strategy for each size of customer. Each *key account*, for example, is assigned a dedicated account manager, every three to five *large customers* are allocated one account manager, *medium-sized customers* are the responsibility of salespeople covering all medium-sized customers in a geographic region, and *small customers* are targeted with a combination of direct mail, catalogues, telemarketing, the internet and distributors.

In practice, account management takes many forms. Some firms opt for a part-time approach, with employees spending only part of their time in the account management role; others create a separate account division that targets a specific set of customers. Some firms create several account management titles, such as general account manager, account support manager, international account manager, manager new accounts, manager existing accounts and internal account manager (the last job title is common in large multinational firms). But implementation does not always require new job titles; in small firms, account management is done by the CEO or marketing manager.

The key tasks and responsibilities of an account manager are formulating the account strategy, conducting account analysis, internal and external coordination of relationships and building the account relationship. An account manager is a relationship manager and more than an upgraded salesperson. While a salesperson is an individual with specialised product knowledge working within a sales department, an account manager is a teamworker, a generalist with in-depth knowledge of an account and coordinating activities of various departments. An account manager must have a clear picture of the customer organisation, products and services already bought, potential business opportunities and existing and potential contacts.

Implementation of account management is not always without problems. Typical problems are insufficient preparation, lack of top management support, absence of a cooperative culture, absence of a customer-focused organisation, indistinct responsibilities of account managers and a dysfunctional system for measuring results and taking corrective measures.

ᘓᢩ INSIGHT: Key account management in German firms

A recent study of 91 German manufacturers or service providers showed that 70 per cent of the firms used or were planning to use key account management, mostly because of an increasing customer orientation, increasing internationalisation of customers or the wish to improve internal coordination. The majority of the firms located key account management in the marketing and sales functions. Only 12 per cent established it as a separate line organisation and 10 per cent as a staff organisation. In the smaller companies, the managing director took over the responsibilities and coordination of the key account management programme. The prime criteria for selecting key accounts were sales volume (80 per cent of the companies), market share (35 per cent) and customer image (30 per cent). Surprisingly, almost 90 per cent of the companies not using key account management admitted that they already serve their important customers like key accounts, but informally. With respect to the implementation of key account management, only a very small number of firms reported using a formal cost–benefit calculation before implementing key account management.

Source: Wengler et al. (2006)

Salesforce management

Effective management of a firm's salesforce encompasses hiring, training, motivation and rewards, and evaluation and control. It all starts with hiring the right people. Firms may hire experienced, but expensive, salespeople from other firms, or hire young starting salespeople who can be trained internally. As part of an internal traineeship, new hires frequently are assigned an experienced salesperson as mentor. A well-designed training programme includes product and marketing knowledge (products and services, key market segments, key customers, buying processes, buying centres, buying influences, marketing strategy, competitors), firm knowledge (sales, marketing, customer support, R&D, manufacturing, logistics) and skills (interaction with customers, negotiation, presentation, cooperation, communication, countering objections, closing the sale, dealing with complaints). Sales training is not just for newly hired salespeople, but also for established salespeople who need to brush up their knowledge and skills to remain effective. The growing use of digital technologies, such as laptops, PDAs and the internet, in particular, has significantly changed salespeople's interaction with customers. Effective sales training motivates and re-energises salespeople and reduces turnover, which in turn reduces the cost of hiring.

A salesperson's performance is also determined by how the firm motivates and rewards its salespeople. There are two types of motivation. *Intrinsic motivation* refers to salespeople being motivated by inner things such as purpose, passion, mission, a sense of performance and self-image. *Extrinsic motivation* refers to salespeople being motivated by external things like money, recognition and rewards. Bonuses are often based on the realisation of predetermined objectives, such as a specific sales volume. Recognition can come from either the vendor organisation (a reward or plaque) or from customers.

Firms also need a system to constantly monitor, evaluate and control sales performance. It is important that companies measure and evaluate sales performance (results) rather than sales activities (input). Many firms only measure sales activities, such as the number of customers visited or the number of bids submitted. But this encourages unfocused customer visits and submission of as many bids as possible. A better alternative is to define a number of milestones in the sales process, based on the customer's buying process, and assign specified commissions to each of these milestones. An instrument manufacturer supplying control instrumentation and software to the petrochemical industry, for example, had a selling cycle that took experienced salespeople between six and nine months to complete. The firm's management created the following four milestones: (1) *joint study team*, where the customer's instrument engineers agree to spend a day with the manufacturer's technical people to go through a carefully designed meeting agenda to review current instrument performance and the technical issues involved in instrumentation changes (10 per cent of commission), (2) *technical test*, where both parties set up a test of one of the manufacturer's products within the customer plant (25 per cent of commission), (3) *customer contract*, where the customer signs the order (35 per cent of commission), and (4) *successful installation*, where the installation meets certain defined performance standards, including customer satisfaction measures (30 per cent of commission) (Rackham and DeVincentis 1999).

6.3 Selling directly: catalogues, the internet and customer contact centres

A part from personal selling, firms also interact directly with customers through catalogues, the internet and customer contact centres.

Catalogues

A catalogue contains detailed information about the products and services offered by a firm, and their applications. **Catalogues** are used as a stand-alone sales channel or to support personal selling. Salespeople leave the catalogue with customers, so that they can look up and order products later. That is why the catalogue is also called the *silent salesperson*. Catalogues are especially useful for vendors (both manufacturers and distributors) with a large range of products of relatively limited value, such as computer products, office supplies, pipes and fasteners. Because of the increasing cost of personal selling, catalogues are an interesting alternative for many firms. A manufacturer's catalogue may also support distributors when they are unable to stock all the manufacturer's products. Then, distributors stock only the fastest-selling items, while all other items can be ordered from the manufacturer's catalogue. Interactive technologies, such as CD-rom and the internet, significantly boost the value of a catalogue. An online catalogue has much lower production and distribution costs, contains more up-to-date information, presents all products and applications in an accessible format and simplifies the ordering process. In addition, online catalogues may contain a streaming video of products and can be used to display products in 3D, which is important for product developers who can download the 3D images to their own computer for virtual testing or to use in product design.

MINI CASE: SABIC POSTS A WEALTH OF INFORMATION ONLINE

Sabic, the Saudi Basic Industries Corporation, is one of the world's leading manufacturers of chemicals, fertilisers, plastics and metals. Its website contains a tremendous amount of information about a large number of products, including product descriptions, product data sheets, case studies, design guides, industry brochures, marketing brochures, supplier material selectors, specwizards, product selection guides, processing guides, technical papers, web seminars and white papers. For some products, the site even offers comprehensive products, markets and processing guides. For resins, for example, these guides describe all relevant properties (thermal properties, flammability, mechanical properties, electrical properties, environmental resistance, haze temperature) and how they may be used by designers who want to take full advantage of the resins' physical properties and the design freedom offered by the injection moulding process. The website also contains a section entitled *Build My Application*, which offers a wide range of tools that can be used by customers to develop or enhance applications, from conceptual design to prototype testing to a commercialised product.

Source: www.sabic-ip.com

The internet

The increasing use of the **internet** allows small and medium-sized firms to establish a global presence and extend their reach by participating in global electronic marketplaces. Use of the internet has three major effects on sales and delivery (Pitt et al. 1999); it:

- *Eliminates distance.* With the internet, location becomes irrelevant. No matter where a vendor is located, it can target customers all over the world. Buying and selling no longer take place in the marketplace, but in market*space.* This increases the options for both buyers and sellers. Vendors starting to sell through the internet find that they receive orders from customers in countries where they have never sold before. Thailand-based Silvermover offers marketing services to property and real estate customers. Using the internet, the firm has clients in Thailand, but also in Sweden, Australia, the UK and Canada. Naturally, when physical products must be delivered, the distance between buyer and seller does influence delivery times and distribution costs.

- *Homogenises time.* In the real world, manufacturers and distributors are only open during business hours. But websites have a 24/7/365 presence and allow vendors to serve their customers without needing to be present. Often, the customer does not need to be present either to be served by the vendor.

- *Eliminates transportation costs.* For digital products, transportation costs are eliminated. Software, financial services, teaching materials and manuals are efficiently distributed to worldwide customers at very low cost. Customers of Oracle and McAfee download the latest software from their websites. SAP offers online training and tutorials to its customers.

As a result of the internet customers are better informed about vendors and their offerings, which makes it more difficult for vendors to maintain a competitive advantage and creates a downward pressure on prices. Some vendors are forced out of business, while others flourish because of the internet (such as numerous electronic marketplaces that broker contacts between buyers and sellers).

MINI CASE: TOSHIBA CANADA USES THE INTERNET TO SUPPORT DEALERS

Toshiba Canada's Office Product Group created an online partner community that enables its channel partners to use the internet to enter and manage orders more effectively and improve customer satisfaction. It replaced the traditional ordering process, which required phone calls, faxes, manual look-ups and credit checks that was cumbersome and labour-intensive for dealers. By using web-based technology, Toshiba has automated partner business processes to improve delivery cycles and enhance dealer satisfaction. Dealers received greater visibility into product availability and order status, enhanced technical support and training, sales support and marketing collateral, marketing communications management and a dealer discussion forum. For Toshiba, it reduced channel management costs through reduced paperwork, training costs and other delays. In addition, it reduced order processing time, improved order status, offered complete access to dealer account information and enhanced dealer loyalty. In 2001, the online partner community won the eCustomer World Golden Award for the category of Collaborative Partnering Solution Excellence.

Source: Business Wire, 15 October 2001

It must be emphasised that the internet improves the exchange of information and money but cannot be used to exchange tangible goods. Thus, for most industries and products the internet helps to improve and support existing channels, rather than replaces them. Use of the internet may cause business to shift from one channel to another. When a vendor uses the internet to obtain orders which are then transferred to local distributors, for example, it moves business from the direct sales channel to the indirect distributor channel. This may cause conflict between channels and between the people responsible for them, such as a company's salesforce and distribution group. Vendors who want to integrate e-commerce with their traditional distribution system must develop strategies to avoid conflicts, such as never pricing products on their website below the prices of channel partners, diverting fulfilment of orders placed on their websites to their channel partners, providing product information on their websites without taking orders, promoting their channel partners on their websites, offering only a limited set of products on their websites, and communicating their overall channel strategy both internally and externally (Webb 2002).

In B2B markets, e-commerce took off with a flying start. Many initiatives were launched and promised stellar returns. Electronic markets would revolutionise business, searchbots would automate purchasing processes, and both buyers and sellers would benefit from increased access. Covisint, for example, connects over 300,000 users in almost 50,000 firms in approximately 100 countries in the global automotive and healthcare industries and was projected to handle some $750 billion in goods annually. In many industries, however, the promise of e-commerce has not been fulfilled. Over 75 per cent of SMEs are not making a living wage on the internet, SMEs are still paying too much (often on the wrong sites), many e-concepts do not work, a lot of online information is out-of-date and many dotcom marketplaces have closed up shop. The internet may not have revolutionised all firms and industries, but it has earned its place as a useful tool to increase market presence and lower costs in specific situations.

Customer contact centres

'Did you know that 80 per cent of your customers enter your business via the phone? And still organizations spend more budget on the physical entrance and the red carpet. Treat your customers as the VIPs they really are....' These words can be found on the website of NEC Philips Unified Solutions, a leading provider of enterprise networking and communications solutions to organisations of all types and sizes (Figure 6.2). It offers advanced IP-based solutions that unify products, applications and services, enabling organisations to communicate and collaborate more effectively, efficiently and reliably. As it states on its website, many companies implement customer contact centres (CCCs) to generate new sources of revenue, maximise customer loyalty and optimise customer service.

A **customer contact centre** uses the telephone for both inbound and outbound calls. *Inbound calls* include answering questions, registering orders, answering

FIGURE 6.2 NEC Philips offers customer contact centre solutions
Source: NEC Philips. Used with permission.

complaints, setting up meetings with salespeople and providing product support. *Outbound calls* encompass sales promotions, introducing new products, generating and qualifying sales leads and making appointments. A CCC may either support personal selling or be the sole customer touchpoint (for instance, for small customers). The key functions of a CCC are generating sales leads, qualifying sales leads, supporting salespeople, dealing with small customers and building relationships. Some firms outsourced their CCC to specialised service providers such as Electronic Data Systems.

CCCs may be used for all kinds of products, from office supplies to aircraft. The costs of a CCC are significantly lower than those of personal selling. A disadvantage of contacting customers by telephone is that the customer is disturbed in their daily activities. That is why many firms combine direct mail with inbound telemarketing, by mentioning a toll-free number in their mailing that customers can call when it suits them.

6.4 Selling indirectly through channel partners

When direct customer contact is too expensive or unnecessary, vendors may use a **channel partner** to reach their customers and carry out specified marketing and sales activities. In B2B markets, the most commonly used channel partners are distributors and dealers, value-added resellers (VARs), agents, jobbers and brokers.

Distributors and dealers

A **distributor** buys products from a manufacturer or another distributor and resells them to B2B customers. Distributors have their own salesforce and perform a wide range of channel tasks, such as keeping stock, offering a range of related products, building relationships with customers, offering credit, acquiring new customers, delivering products, installing products and performing after-sales activities. Selling through distributors offers several advantages to a supplier, including reduced overhead (buildings, equipment, personnel, marketing, market research), information about local market conditions, economies of scale (larger orders, reduced administration costs), increased sales because of distributor-related synergies (customers who prefer one-stop shopping result in additional sales), specialisation (distributors are specialised in selling to specific markets and possess effective local networks of relationships) and various additional services (market research, demand forecasts, trade show support, production of sales collateral, technical support, sales trend analysis).

B2B vendors use three types of distributor:

- *General distributors* offer a broad range of products to a large number of markets. These distributors are the B2B counterparts of supermarkets.

- *Specialised distributors* focus on one or a limited number of product lines, such as welding equipment, or on products for one market, such as the automotive or pharmaceutical industry. Because of their knowledge of local markets and extensive networks of relationships, specialised distributors may be essential for vendors that want to enter new markets. Their largest disadvantage is that they also carry products from competitors, which dilutes the attention they give to the vendor's products.

- *Hybrid distributors* sell to both business customers and consumers. Examples are found in the computer industry and in telecommunications, where products attract both consumers and small business owners. The sales to B2B customers may have a positive effect on the sales to consumers, who are attracted by the image of high-quality professional products.

The terms *distributor* and *dealer* are closely related. While a **dealer** focuses on reselling the product, a distributor creates additional value for customers by performing a range of distribution tasks, such as installing the product and offering technical support. Dealers focus on standardised products that can be installed by the customer, and distributors sell more complex products that require technical support. Nevertheless, many vendors use the terms distributor and dealer interchangeably.

MINI CASE: EUROPEAN PHARMACEUTICAL COMPANIES SWITCH
TO DIRECT DISTRIBUTION

Beginning March 2007, Pfizer introduced a direct distribution model for its products in the United Kingdom, making them available only from the company's sole appointed distributor, UniChem, rather than from a choice of 18 wholesalers. This move reflects an industry-wide change, with two-thirds of European pharmaceutical companies considering changes to their distribution model, thus threatening the European pharmaceutical wholesale market. In this new distribution model, throughout the process the stock is owned by the manufacturer, who pays a fee to the distributor for its service. The new distribution model gives big pharma companies end-to-end control of the distribution process and control of price at the point of sale. A Pfizer spokeswoman said: 'It has been estimated that a medicine can pass through 20–30 pairs of hands before it reaches the patient. When we sell to wholesalers we lose sight of where our medicines go. There is no visibility in the supply chain.' The new distribution strategy allows pharmaceutical companies to reduce the threat of counterfeit drugs, improve their comparative advantage relative to parallel imports and realise efficiency improvements in the distribution process; for instance, by using radio frequency identification (RFID), manufacturers can track products from the manufacturing line all the way through to the pharmacists' dispensing. Because this technology is still relatively expensive as opposed to 2D barcodes, it is currently only used for the most valuable and heavily counterfeited drugs, such as Viagra. End-to-end ownership of the distribution process also makes it easier for manufacturers to implement process improvements and redesign. Through the implementation of integrated processes and systems, manufacturers and distributors can streamline data accessibility and analysis. The ability to act on this analysis is made easier by the single point of contact between the manufacturer and distributor, which is further strengthened by the partnership approach.

Source: *The Times*, 28 September 2007

Value-added resellers

A **value-added reseller (VAR)** is a company that adds value to one or a set of related products and then resells them as an integrated product or turn-key solution to business customers. The added value comes from professional services, such as integration, customisation, consulting, training, implementation, strategic planning and system design. VARs are common in the electronics industry, where software is added to hardware and sold as a customised solution.

For a vendor, it may be difficult to select the right VARs. While some are hardware centred, other are more focused on the services offered to customers. Problems may arise when VARs start to operate outside their assigned territories or markets. Another potential problem is that VARs are independent and use products from several vendors to build solutions. When a vendor's salesperson refers a prospect to a VAR partner, the VAR may go on to build a customer solution with products from other vendors.

INSIGHT: VARs want to be called solution providers

A 2007 study by Crimson Consulting and Ziff Davis concludes that 'the term VAR is now officially passé.' A whopping 75 per cent of the firms responding to the survey want to be called and think of themselves as solution providers, because services account for an increasingly significant portion of their business. Their main objective is to increase their revenues from new customers and they are less focused on improving their business through cost or margin control. However, most agree that their own marketing capabilities are weak, which suggests an opportunity for vendors to help bridge this gap.

Although the solution providers typically work with 100–200 vendors on a monthly basis, they average only three to four primary vendors. Almost two-thirds sell to business decision-makers first, rather than technical decision-makers. Half of the solution providers aim at broad solutions that appeal to a wide range of clients, and the other half focus on niche solutions. Some 60 per cent of the solution providers have fewer than 150 customers and two-thirds of the firms generate more than 50 per cent of their revenues from their top three customers.

The solution providers are not impressed with vendor channel programmes. Trust is a major issue and pre- and post-sales support and service are key areas that need to be improved by vendors.

Source: www.crimson-consulting.com

Agents

 An **agent** acts on behalf of a vendor to customers. An agent is similar to a salesperson, but is independent and works on a contractual basis for several vendors. Agents typically operate in a geographical region and sell a range of related products. However, in contrast to a distributor, agents do not assume any financial risk in transactions. They represent vendors, but do not buy products from them and do not keep stock, except for some spare parts. They get orders from customers, transmit these orders to vendors and receive commission on the sales made (around 7 to 15 per cent, depending on the product and sector). In addition, vendors may pay agents a fee for stocking spare parts, advising and training customers and acquiring new customers. The power of agents is based on their market expertise, technical expertise and relationships with customers. Because agents are only paid after the customer has paid the vendor for the products and services received, selling costs are known in advance and can be built into the vendor's pricing.

Agents also have disadvantages, however. The vendor bears the cost of all deliveries and no stock is held in the market, which complicates the distribution process. Also, agents do not take responsibility for after-hours client service and are unlikely to fund promotional activities and undertake marketing and promotion of the vendor's products. The commission structure will also encourage agents to focus on the products with the highest commission.

Agents are especially useful for small companies who cannot afford their own salesforce. The use of agents allows these firms to cover large geographical regions, while the selling costs are directly related to revenues. Large firms use agents for regions with many small customers or to export their products to foreign markets.

Jobbers and brokers

A **jobber** buys small lots of goods (also called *jobs*) and sells them to merchants rather than ultimate customers. Jobbers are frequently used for bulk products such as iron ore, coal, wood and chemicals. Because of the bulky volume of these products, the vendor takes care of the physical distribution to customers, but the jobbers do own the products that they sell. The relationship with a jobber is mostly for the short run.

A **broker** connects buyers and sellers and thus facilitates commercial transactions. Brokers represent either the buyer or the seller and the relationship is usually limited to one specific transaction. Brokers do not own or handle the products and are paid a commission by the party that hires them.

Most B2B vendors sell their products in several countries and have to deal with regional differences, national legislation, different trading practices and cultural differences. This increases the complexity of distribution systems. Vendors that want to operate internationally have three options. One option is to use distribution partners in the home country, such as agents, trade organisations and export organisations, who export the products to the target countries. Another is to use local partners in the target countries, such as importers, international trade organisations and local distributors and dealers. A third option is to establish a local presence in the target countries (for instance, by establishing local sales offices or acquiring local distributors).

6.5 Designing a customer-focused channel system

A vendor's cooperation with channel partners will only be successful when the vendor designs the distribution system from the customer's perspective and carefully manages all partners, channels and relationships. In designing a **channel system**, a B2B vendor has three basic options:

- In a *single-channel system* all products are distributed through one channel; for instance, all products are sold and delivered directly or through a distributor. This is appropriate when the vendor wants to target only a few market segments or customers, when customer needs are stable and when the vendor has only limited resources.

- With a *multiple-channel system* a vendor uses more than one channel to sell and distribute its products to different customers; for instance, when a vendor uses distributors to sell to small and medium-sized customers, but sells directly to large accounts. This is appropriate when customers have different needs and supply preferences.

● In a *hybrid channel system* a vendor uses multiple channels to reach the same customers; for instance, when a vendor sells directly to customers, but uses local distributors to install the product and provide maintenance and technical support. This requires careful coordination of all activities because customers do not care about this distinction and perceive distributors as being part of the vendor organisation. They want a seamless customer experience across all touchpoints.

Most B2B firms use multiple channels to reach their customers. Different customers have different needs, customers demand more than one channel to choose from and new channel options cause firms to experiment with different channels in an attempt to reduce costs and increase customer satisfaction. Many firms, for example, combine a salesforce with distributors, a customer contact centre and the internet. But firms must realise that the addition of channels increases the problems and costs of coordination and may result in conflicts and cannibalisation between channels (Sharma and Mehrota 2007). To manage the relationships between multiple channels companies can use a *coverage map*, which lists customer groups along the vertical axis of the chart, with highest-value customers at the top, and product groups along the horizontal axis in increasing order of product sales complexity (Wilson and Daniel 2007). Figure 6.3 shows a coverage map for IBM, with seven

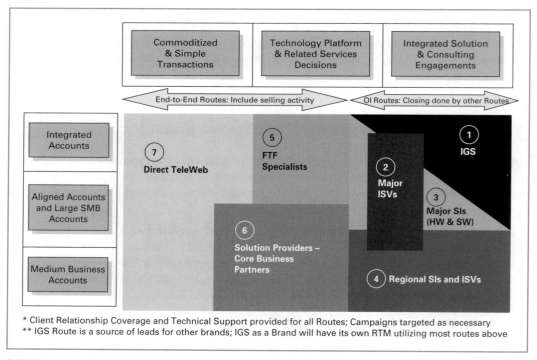

FIGURE 6.3 A distribution coverage map

Source: Wilson and Daniel (2007:15). Reprinted with permission from Elsevier.

main routes to customers. These include the IBM Global Services channel for major outsourcing projects (route 1), the direct salesforce for large system implementations (route 5), and a range of distributor types (routes 2, 3, 4 and 6), as well as a direct telephone/web operation (route 7). This standardised focus on seven routes to market for the entire global organisation reduced IBM's costs of channel management, because everybody had a clearer idea of their role, by an estimated 50 per cent.

Vendors only rarely find themselves in a position where they can design a channel system from scratch. More typically, they already have a channel system that they want to improve. Because the design and implementation of a channel system requires substantial time and resources, especially when the firm wants to employ multiple channels, most vendors will hesitate to redefine their channel systems. But the need for growth, new customers and changing channel options and dynamics causes vendors to reappraise their distribution systems. Given that a new channel system is likely to experience resistance from both existing channel partners and employees (especially from sales), successful implementation requires buy-in across the organisation and a champion to manage the change process. Figure 6.4 presents a seven-step process for a customer-focused channel design (Stern et al. 1993).

Step 1: Customer analysis

The process starts with the vendor listing various distribution elements (such as delivery of small lots, after-sales technical support and product returns) and assessing how much value customers attach to each of these elements. This will vary across products and across customers and allows the vendor to select the channels

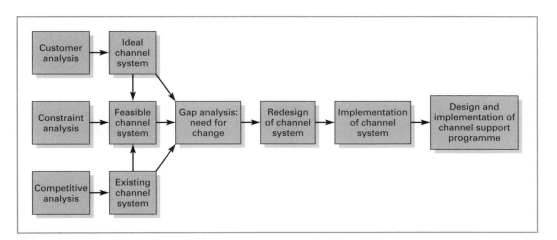

FIGURE 6.4 Designing a customer-focused channel system

Source: Stern et al. (1993:2). Reprinted with permission.

that are most appropriate to target the customers selected. This step results in the design of an 'ideal' channel system.

Step 2: Evaluation of current channel system

Next, the vendor must analyse the current distribution system in the context of corporate strategy and competitive situation. Interviews with key customers provide information about the perceived performance of the current channel system. The vendor must analyse the channels used, the distribution and sales functions performed within each channel, the cost of these functions and the effectiveness of the channel system in meeting customer needs.

Step 3: Constraint analysis

A constraint analysis defines the boundaries to the set of solutions that are deemed acceptable to management; for instance, management may want to remain loyal to a certain type of channel partner. Constraints may force a channel design that is different from what was considered to be the ideal channel system. Examples of constraints are the availability of channel partners, existence of traditional channel patterns, product characteristics, financial resources and customer dispersion across regions or industries. The constrained design is combined with both the ideal and the current channel system to formulate a feasible channel system. This represents the best compromise between what the firm currently has, what customers consider ideal and what limits the design options.

MINI CASE: CUSTOMERS FORCE XEROX TO SWITCH CHANNELS

Xerox used to sell directly to large corporate customers. But when the market changed and large corporations started to purchase mid-range and low-range printers from distributors and dealers, Xerox found it was losing business. As a result, Xerox had to rethink not only what kind of products its customers wanted but also *how* they wanted to buy them. When it became clear that some customers simply would not purchase the complete range of Xerox products through a direct salesforce, Xerox realised it was time to cultivate a variety of indirect sales channels, such as distributors, dealers, value-added resellers and e-commerce. But the transition from a purely direct sales model to a model that mixes direct sales and channel sales proved to be difficult. In the words of Nina Smith, Xerox's vice-president of integrated corporate marketing: 'The direct salesforce felt extremely threatened by the introduction of new channels.' Initially, Xerox sales reps were asked to turn orders for low-range products over to a distributor in return for a small 'finder's fee'. But since these fees did not compensate for the lost sales, sales reps were not enthusiastic. Only when sales reps were stimulated to partner with distributors and received actual revenue credit for the transactions, did the programme gain acceptance.

Source: Peppers and Rogers (1999)

Step 4: Gap analysis

Management considers the current, ideal and feasible channel systems and makes a decision on the need for redesign. Which distribution elements should be kept, modified, eliminated or added? Which channels should be maintained, strengthened, eliminated or added? When the desired distribution elements cannot be provided by the firm, cooperation with partners may offer a solution.

Step 5: Redesign of the channel system

The redesigned channel system must offer superior value to customers relative to competitors' distribution systems. Channel system redesign requires detailed insight into how channels create value for customers; for instance, by facilitating transactions, providing access to products or providing product service. Channel system redesign involves the number and nature of channels, length of channels, types of channel partners, number of channel partners per supply chain level, and division of tasks and responsibilities. The resulting channel design depends on the nature of the product, market characteristics, customers' buying behaviour, distribution costs and distribution objectives.

Step 6: Implementation of the channel system

Successful implementation of the new channel system requires buy-in across the company and a champion to manage the implementation process. In addition, it must be made clear who or which groups will be responsible for the channels. A significant part of the implementation process is the selection, training and motivation of channel partners. Effective channel relationships are based on open two-way communication, a genuine liking for each other and high levels of trust. Candidates should be evaluated on issues such as knowledge of the local market, confidence in the vendor's company, product and chances for success, financial health, membership of trade associations, years of experience in the market sector, network of representatives and contacts, number of employees in sales, product range represented (amount of overlap with the vendor's products), market coverage and understanding of competitive products. Formal channel partner agreements should address a broad range of issues, such as territories involved, customers to be served, products involved, period of agreement, prices, minimum orders, training and technical support, advertising and promotion, and inventory policies.

Step 7: Design and implementation of a channel support programme

Vendors will significantly improve the quality of a channel system with a support programme for channel partners; for instance, through assistance in advertising, frequent deliveries of small lots, technical support, training, newsletters, joint trade shows, 24-hour delivery and joint sales calls (Magrath and Hardy 1992).

6.6 Managing channel systems

To maintain their competitive advantage and continue offering superior value to customers, vendors must carefully manage their channel systems. This **channel management** includes managing channel conflicts, encouraging cooperation and improving the channel system's performance.

Managing channel conflicts

Because a channel system consists of independent organisations, who cooperate but also have their own objectives and interests, interorganisational conflicts frequently occur. Vendors may reduce the chance of **channel conflict** through a customer orientation, careful selection of partners and an effective channel support programme. There are *horizontal channel conflicts* (between two organisations at the same level; for instance, two distributors) and *vertical channel conflicts* (between two organisations at different levels; for instance, a vendor and a reseller). Serious conflicts upset harmonious relationships and result in inefficient use of resources, damaged relationships, reduced channel performance and therefore reduced value for customers. The most common channel conflicts occur between the following partners:

- *Between vendor and channel partner*, for instance when large customers demand lower prices than charged by a distributor or want to buy direct from the vendor. A common strategy is for vendors to sell directly to large customers and to refer all other customers to their distributors, but not all distributors appreciate this. Vendors may resolve such conflicts by compensating distributors for sales to large customers in their territory, letting resellers compete head to head with the vendor's direct salesforce or by selling only through resellers. Other conflicts revolve around inventory policies, exclusivity and the attention paid to the vendor's products.

- *Between company-owned channel partners and independents* about the prices charged and support provided. They can be managed by implementing a clear policy that defines the ground rules about sales territories, products sold, prices, promotion and support activities.

- *Between discounters and service-oriented resellers*, for instance small resellers who cannot compete with discounters often respond by dropping the vendor's products. Vendors may resolve these conflicts by refusing to sell through large chains or by offering them different products or brands. Naturally, this only works when there are real differences between the products or brands.

- *Between resellers*, for instance intense competition between resellers hurts profits and may cause them to discontinue the products. Vendors must limit the number of resellers per geographic area, so that each reseller can make a decent profit on the vendor's brands. In addition, vendors may refuse to sell to resellers offering giveaway prices or direct certain resellers to different markets where they will not collide so much with other resellers.

Channel conflicts are likely to occur when vendors employ complex systems with multiple channels. When vendors start to experiment with direct selling through the internet they are particularly likely to experience conflicts with their traditional channel partners. Webb and Lambe (2007) emphasise that multiple channels may also result in *internal channel conflict*, that is, conflict between the various channel entities within the supplier organisation. These internal conflicts can be resolved through the use of superordinate goals, effective internal communication and effective internal coordination between the vendor's channel entities.

Encouraging cooperation

An effective channel system is based on cooperation between all partners involved in getting the vendor's offerings to customers. Vendors invest substantial resources in turning their resellers into partners. This is reflected in clear channel policies and agreements. But not everything can be regulated through formal policies; personal relationships are important as well. Sometimes, problems arise because personnel changes affect the relationships with resellers. Vendors should develop relationships with resellers that do not depend on one or two individuals.

Ultimately, the proof of the pudding is in the eating and the quality of the relationship is determined by the day-to-day interactions between vendor and resellers. Does the vendor keep its promises? Do the vendor's deliveries match the reseller's orders? A resounding channel vision is not sufficient; reseller commitment is based on actions such as referring all customers to resellers and limiting the number of resellers per region. It is through actions such as these that a vendor contributes to the success of its resellers. Vendors may improve their channel relationships by organising dealer councils, where the vendor demonstrates new products, builds and renews personal relationships, shows commitment, discusses problems, analyses market trends and obtains market information.

Improving channel systems

To keep their competitive advantage, vendors must continuously improve their channel systems. All resellers' performances must be regularly assessed using objective variables (sales growth, market share) and subjective evaluations provided by sales managers (attention paid to the vendor's products, level of customer service, market coverage, quality of management). Consistently underperforming resellers should be subjected to additional training and support or replaced. When it is impossible to improve reseller performance, a vendor may improve its distribution performance by interacting directly with customers; for instance, by selling directly to customers or creating a helpdesk or web interface for customers.

Another, more drastic, way to improve channel performance is to create new channels. The increased costs of personal selling have led many vendors to look into e-commerce. But vendors should be careful when replacing resellers with the internet. Many vendors are blinded by the potential cost savings and forget that resellers are also an important source of market information and create value through close relationships with customers. Vendors may also switch to more expensive channels; for instance, when product complexity has increased to such an extent that the vendor decides to replace the current resellers with more specialised resellers. Whenever a vendor considers moving to a new channel, management should address the following questions: Can we reach new customers with the new channel? Will the new channel result in additional sales or only in a redistribution of sales over the various channels? Does the new channel create new value for customers? Can use of the new channel be postponed until there is more information available about its opportunities and limitations?

6.7 Physical distribution

Creating and managing effective channel systems is just one part of the firm's sales and delivery system. Vendors also need to physically move products from the vendor, through the channels, to customers. **Physical distribution** is the physical connection between vendor and customers that ensures that the right products are delivered in the right quantities at the right time through the right channels. According to some estimates, physical distribution costs amount to approximately 20 per cent of a country's total gross national product (GNP). At the level of individual firms, physical distribution activities account for some 7 per cent of total revenues, often representing almost half of the total marketing costs of a product. For couriers like FedEx and DHL, physical distribution is at the core of their marketing strategy. These numbers have led many firms to shift their cost-cutting efforts from production to physical distribution. Physical distribution has also increased in importance because customers demand faster deliveries of smaller quantities, which puts a strain on the whole supply chain. Advances in ICT continue to allow firms to significantly improve the efficient flow of goods through the supply chain.

Physical distribution management encompasses transportation, warehousing, inventory control, order processing, location of production facilities and protective packaging. How each of these elements is managed depends on the level of customer service the firm wants to offer its customers. A vendor might, for example, define the following standard of customer service: 60 per cent of all products reach the customer within 48 hours of ordering, 85 per cent of all products reach the customer within 72 hours and 100 per cent of all products reach the customer within 96 hours. Next, the firm needs to set up a physical distribution system to achieve these goals at the lowest possible cost. Naturally, the vendor may use market segmentation to distinguish between customers with different needs and formulate different customer service levels for each group of customers. Vendors need to use a systems approach to design the physical distribution system that achieves the desired levels of customer service at the lowest cost. For example, using a high speed of transportation reduces the need for large local inventories. Of course, outsourcing to specialised firms is also an option. Such contract distribution lowers costs and increases quality, but also causes the vendor to lose know-how, short communication lines and control over operations. UK-based S&S Distribution performs distribution and warehousing services for more than 300 customers.

Transportation

Vendors can choose from several modes of transportation to ship their products to the customer. *Trucking* is the most-favoured transportation mode, especially by small and medium-sized firms. Trucks are particularly useful for short-distance shipments of small batches of manufactured products. *Air freight* is faster but more expensive, and is only used for valuable and highly-perishable products. *Water carriers* are slow but inexpensive. Barge lines are efficient for bulky goods of low value (grain, gravel, lumber, sand). Ocean-going ships are used in international commerce for all kinds of products. *Railroads* are used for long-distance shipping of bulky products. *Pipelines* are used to transport natural gas and oil from mining sites to refineries and harbours. Slurry pipelines transport products such as coal, which is ground to a powder, mixed with water, and moved as a suspension through the pipes. *Digital networks* deliver digital products to customers instantaneously at very low costs. Vendors evaluate transportation modes on their costs, speed, reach, reliability, usability and availability. They may also combine modes of transportation; petrochemical products are transported in steel drums, which are loaded in containers and shipped by trucks, trains and ships.

Warehousing

Vendors must decide whether they will maintain their own strategically located depots or stock their products in public warehouses. Vendors that use distributors do not need local warehouses, but vendors that rely on agents need their own network of warehouses. If a vendor decides to create its own network of warehouses, it needs to choose between storage warehouses (hold products for moderate to long-term periods, for instance when supply and demand are seasonal) and distribution warehouses (assemble and redistribute products quickly to get them to customers). In addition, vendors need to decide on appropriate locations for their warehouses, based on the location of customers, desired level of customer service, nature of the product, available infrastructure and costs of transportation, handling and storage. A second set of warehousing decisions concerns their internal layout, storage methods, vehicles, terminals, printers and handheld devices and how they interact to create an efficient system. The order-picking process typically consumes as much as 60 per cent of all labour activities in the warehouse.

Inventory control

Inventory costs include the funds invested in inventory (cost of capital, cost of services such as insurance, cost of keeping stock), depreciation and cost of obsolescence of the goods. Inventory control has obvious implications for marketing. Vendors offer just-in-time delivery to lock in customers and charge higher prices. Vendors use ABC analysis to manage their inventories, which classifies products according to their value: A class inventory contains the highest-ranking products that account for 70 per cent of total value, B class inventory accounts for the next 20 per cent of total value, and C class inventory accounts for the remaining 10 per cent of total value. Each category requires its own approach. A class items are critically important and require close monitoring and tight control. For B class items standard controls and periodic reviews of usage suffice. C class items require the least controls. In addition, firms use economic order quantity (EOQ) ordering to trade-off between inventory-carrying costs and order-processing costs and determine the optimal warehouse inventory quantity for each product. The EOQ point is the quantity at which total costs are minimised.

Order processing

Order processing directly impacts customer satisfaction; each time that an order is kept on hold, the customer is kept waiting. Order processing encompasses order planning, order generation, cost estimation and pricing, order receipt and entry, order selection and prioritisation, scheduling, fulfilment, billing, returns and claims, and after-sales service (Shapiro et al. 1992). In practice, many problems occur because of insufficient internal coordination (with an order falling between the cracks as it moves from one department to another), inadequate order selection and prioritisation and a lack of insight into the value and costs of individual orders (resulting in sub-optimal pricing). Vendors should chart the total order management cycle, identify gaps and align activities and departments into a unified, harmonious process that is geared to creating optimal value for customers. Technological innovations, such as barcodes, EDI and the internet, have greatly increased the efficiency and accuracy of order processing.

Location of production facilities

The location of a firm's production facilities influences transportation costs and how fast materials can be brought into the firm or finished goods delivered to customers. Location decisions are determined by manufacturing costs, costs of logistics and the desired level of customer service. Common strategies are to locate near raw materials (when raw materials are geographically concentrated or perishable and when transportation costs are high), near customers (when finished products are perishable and transportation costs are high) or near transport facilities (for instance, location near harbours or river mouths). Some manufacturers even produce on the premises of major customers.

Protective packaging

Packaging influences physical distribution performance by protecting goods and facilitating the efficient transportation of goods; for instance, by combining packages into a single load on a pallet, using steel bands and shrink wrapping. The advantages are reduced labour, rapid movement and reduced pilferage and damage. Another way to combine products is containerisation, which greatly increases the speed of loading and unloading and reduces in-transit damage to products. In selecting packaging it is important to see which type of packaging is preferred by customers and best fits their handling of the product. Taking a supply chain perspective in looking at packaging may result in significant cost savings.

Online
Learning **Centre**

When you have read this chapter, log on to the Online Learning Centre website at
www.mcgraw-hill.co.uk/textbooks/biemans to explore chapter-by-chapter test
questions, further reading and more online study tools.

Summary of Key Concepts

- In order for products and services to deliver value to customers, vendors must get their products and services to these customers. Doing so involves two sets of decisions: (a) designing and managing the channels to sell products to customers (*channel management*), and (b) designing and managing systems to physically move products from the vendor's factories to customers (*physical distribution*).

- Channel management starts with the strategic choice between selling directly to customers (through a salesforce, catalogue, the internet or a customer contact centre) and selling indirectly to customers (through channel partners). This decision involves a trade-off between control and efficiency.

- Most B2B vendors sell directly to customers through personal selling. But many vendors use several channels in combination to optimally serve their customers. This requires careful coordination between all channels involved.

- Effective sales management includes decisions about sales tasks, sales approaches, ethical issues, the sales organisation and hiring, training, motivation and evaluation of salespeople.

- Because of the high costs of personal selling, many firms use other channels to sell directly to customers (catalogue, internet, customer contact centre).

- In B2B markets, the most commonly used channel partners are distributors and dealers, VARs, agents, jobbers and brokers.

- The design of an effective channel system starts with customers' needs and also takes the competitive situation and availability of channel partners into account.

- The management of channel systems includes managing channel conflicts, encouraging cooperation and improving the channel system's performance.

- There are two types of channel conflict: horizontal channel conflicts between two organisations at the same level (for instance, two distributors) and vertical channel conflicts between two organisations at different levels (for instance, a vendor and a reseller).

- To physically move products from the vendor's factory to customers, vendors need to design physical distribution systems by making decisions about transportation, warehousing, inventory control, order processing, location of production facilities and protective packaging.

🔑 Key terms

Account management, p. 187
Agent, p. 196
Broker, p. 197
Catalogues, p. 190
Channel conflict, p. 202
Channel management, p. 202
Channel partner, p. 193
Channel system, p. 197
Customer contact centre, p. 192
Dealer, p. 194
Direct channels, p. 175

Distributor, p. 194
Ethical dilemmas, p. 183
Indirect channels, p. 175
Internet, p. 190
Jobber, p. 197
Personal selling, p. 177
Physical distribution, p. 204
Sales approaches, p. 181
Sales organisations, p. 186
Sales tasks, p. 177
Value-added resellers (VARs), p. 195

Discussion questions

1   In a multiple-channel system a vendor employs several channels to reach its customers. Under which circumstances is this a good strategy? What problems might occur when a vendor uses a multiple-channel system?

2   Many firms use the hunter–farmer sales model. What are the advantages of this sales model? What are its disadvantages?

3   What are the differences between a sales visit and a meeting with a salesperson at a trade show? Can these interactions with a salesperson be considered substitutes?

4   One way to prevent unethical behaviour from salespeople is to publish a code of ethics. But for many small and medium-sized firms this may not be feasible. How can such firms encourage ethical behaviour from their salespeople?

5   Part of redesigning a channel system is evaluating the firm's current channel system. Design a method to evaluate the performance of an existing channel system. Explain also where management can find the required information.

6   By supporting channel partners vendors can contribute to a consistent brand strategy. Describe several specific support initiatives that contribute to a consistent brand strategy.

7   Various conflicts may occur within channel systems, which can be classified as either horizontal or vertical channel conflicts. Are horizontal channel conflicts beneficial from the channel partner's perspective? And from the vendor's perspective?

8   Adding the internet to the firm's customer contact strategy has several major consequences. Describe the key consequences of adding the internet to the firm's channel system. Also describe the implications for the firm's marketing strategy.

9   Which specific costs impact a firm's decision to outsource its physical distribution?

10   What is the relationship between a firm's physical distribution system and its communication strategy?

Further reading

Long, Mary M., Thomas Tellefsen and J. David Lichtenthal (2007) Internet integration into the industrial selling process: a step-by-step approach, *Industrial Marketing Management*, 36(5): 676–689.

Pitt, Leyland, Pierre Berthon and Jean-Paul Berthon (1999) Changing channels: the impact of the internet on distribution strategy, *Business Horizons*, 42(2): 19–28.

Stern, Louis W., Frederick D. Sturdivant and Gary A. Getz (1993) Accomplishing marketing channel change: paths and pitfalls, *European Management Journal*, 11(1): 1–8.

Wilson, Hugh and Elizabeth Daniel (2007) The multi-channel challenge: a dynamic capability approach, *Industrial Marketing Management*, 36(1): 10–20.

References

Dwyer, F. Robert and John F. Tanner (2006) *Business Marketing: Connecting Strategy, Relationships, and Learning*, third edition, New York: McGraw-Hill.

Long, Mary M., Thomas Tellefsen and J. David Lichtenthal (2007) Internet integration into the industrial selling process: a step-by-step approach, *Industrial Marketing Management*, 36(5): 676–689.

Magrath, Allan J. and Kenneth G. Hardy (1992) Manufacturer services for distributors, *Industrial Marketing Management*, 21(2): 119–124.

Peppers, Don and Martha Rogers (1999) *The One to One Manager: Real-World Lessons in Customer Relationship Management*, New York: Currency/Doubleday.

Pitt, Leyland, Pierre Berthon and Jean-Paul Berthon (1999) Changing channels: the impact of the internet on distribution strategy, *Business Horizons*, 42(2): 19–28.

Rackham, Neil and John R. DeVincentis (1999) *Rethinking the Sales Force: Redefining Selling to Create and Capture Customer Value*, New York: McGraw-Hill.

Shapiro, Benson P., V. Kasturi Rangan and John J. Sviokla (1992) Staple yourself to an order, *Harvard Business Review*, 70(4): 113–122.

Sharma, Arun and Anuj Mehrota (2007) Choosing an optimal channel mix in multichannel environments, *Industrial Marketing Management*, 36(1): 21–28.

Stern, Louis W., Frederick D. Sturdivant and Gary A. Getz (1993) Accomplishing marketing channel change: paths and pitfalls, *European Management Journal*, 11(1): 1–8.

Webb, Kevin L. (2002) Managing channels of distribution in the age of electronic commerce, *Industrial Marketing Management*, 31(2): 95–102.

Webb, Kevin L. and C. Jay Lambe (2007) Internal multi-channel conflict: an exploratory investigation and conceptual framework, *Industrial Marketing Management*, 36(1): 29–43.

Weitz, Barton A., Stephen B. Castleberry and John F. Tanner, Jr. (2007) *Selling: Building Partnerships*, sixth edition, New York: McGraw-Hill.

Wengler, Stefan, Michael Ehret and Samy Saab (2006) Implementation of key account management: who, why, and how? An exploratory study on the current implementation of key account management programs, *Industrial Marketing Management*, 35(1): 103–112.

Wilson, Hugh and Elizabeth Daniel (2007) The multi-channel challenge: a dynamic capability approach, *Industrial Marketing Management*, 36(1): 10–20.

Notes

[1] Krakora, Diana, A practical introduction to multi-channel strategies, Amazon Consulting, http://secure.amazonconsulting.com/resources/docs/MultiChannelStrategies.pdf (accessed 14 October 2008).

[2] Avishai, Bernard and William Taylor (1989) Customers drive a technology-driven company: an interview with George Fisher, *Harvard Business Review*, 67(6): 106–114.

Managing communication

Chapter contents

Introduction

All B2B communications ultimately contribute to selling the firm's products or services. B2B communication serves to communicate the value that customers may derive from the vendor's products. But B2B communication also creates value for customers; for instance, salespeople help customers to define problems and identify appropriate solutions. To achieve their communication objectives, B2B vendors may use a large number of communication tools, including advertising, personal selling, the internet and more recently YouTube, blogs and Twitter. All these communication messages must be coordinated to achieve consistent communication to customers.

This chapter begins by introducing the wide variety of communication tools available to B2B vendors and the many different communication objectives used in practice. It explains that each communication tool has specific characteristics that make it ideal for some objectives and less appropriate for others. Next, B2B communication is categorised into one-to-one communication and mass communication. One-to-one communication allows a vendor to communicate with individual customers; for instance, through personal selling and direct marketing instruments such as direct mail, telemarketing and internet marketing. Mass communication focuses on efficiency in communicating with a group of customers; the most commonly used tools in B2B markets are advertising, trade shows and public relations. The growing use of the internet has greatly changed the nature of B2B communication. B2B vendors use websites to communicate with customers, identify prospects with Facebook and maintain relationships with YouTube. Finally, the chapter explains how all communication efforts must be integrated at three different levels to communicate one consistent message to all relevant stakeholders and achieve integration between communication and the other marketing instruments.

7.1 Communication strategy and planning

Communication strategy and planning are vital. Ultimately, all B2B communications have the same objective: to help sell a vendor's offering. B2B marketers achieve this goal with a large number of communication instruments, such as personal selling, advertisements in trade journals, trade shows, direct mail, websites, billboards, TV and radio advertising, infomercials, catalogues, webcasts, product brochures, email, customer contact centres, publicity, public relations, product demonstrations, showrooms, blogs and web communities. The communication media most frequently used by B2B firms are personal selling and advertising. Personal selling is the most effective way to communicate a brand or company, but very expensive. Firms using personal selling typically rely on advertising to support their salesforce. Advertisements in trade journals are the most common type of B2B advertising. But B2B marketers increasingly turn to the internet to communicate with business customers through websites, webinars and even Twitter, LinkedIn and YouTube. A 2009 survey showed a dramatic growth in the use of social media by B2B marketers.[1] An overwhelming 81 per cent of B2B marketers use LinkedIn, 70 per cent use Twitter and 60 per cent use Facebook. These social media are used primarily for brand building and demand generation.

INSIGHT: B2B buyers use YouTube

B2B buyers looking for information about products, services and vendors use many different sources to guide their purchasing decisions, such as trade journals, product brochures and the internet. But on the internet, they go beyond Google and company websites and use LinkedIn, Facebook and YouTube to communicate with customers. YouTube is home to an increasing amount of business content; according to a survey from MRI in 2007, nearly one-third of IT managers visit YouTube each month. A 2009 study by Google and Forbes found that there are 1.5 million business searchers daily on YouTube, making it the second-most visited destination for business searchers, behind Google.

B2B vendors can reach potential customers through a YouTube channel, which is a customisable place where users can access the vendor's videos, post comments and talk about the vendor's brands and products. According to some estimates, some 90 per cent of internet users will be watching online video in 2012. Video captures users' attention and makes a message stick. MarketingSherpa reported that over 98 per cent of business technology decision-makers found viral videos more memorable than other forms of marketing. Vendors interested in reaching business buyers using these new online channels can use them to upload videos that display the vendor's products and company, such as recorded webcasts, product demonstrations, video case studies, TV or video advertisements and company presence at industry events. An example of such a YouTube channel is the Google Channel.

Source: *Social Media*, 19 September 2008 and *BtoB Online*, 12 June 2009

Although the final objective of all B2B communication is to help sell the firm's offering, vendors formulate more specific communication objectives, such as informing customers about the full range of products, announcing the launch of a new product and supporting customers after they have purchased a product. Each communication medium has specific attributes that make it best suited for particular communication tasks (Table 7.1). Advertising in trade journals, on TV and billboards is particularly effective at informing potential customers about the company and its offerings, while

TABLE 7.1 Communication media linked to objectives

Communication media	Communication objectives					
	Awareness	**Knowledge**	**Liking**	**Preference**	**Conviction**	**Purchase**
Publicity	X					
Advertising	X	X	X			
Fax	X	X				
Email	X	X	X			
Direct mail		X	X	X		
Catalogues			X	X	X	
Internet	X	X	X	X	X	X
Trade shows				X	X	
Promotions				X	X	X
Telemarketing					X	X
Face to face					X	X

Source: Lichtenthal and Eliaz (2003: 10). Reprinted with permission from Elsevier.

telemarketing is most effective at persuading prospects and customers to buy. The internet, on the other hand, may be used for a wide range of communication objectives.

The multitude of communication objectives is also illustrated by the practice of new product announcements. A vendor's communications to announce the launch of a new product may serve to: (1) inform potential customers about the imminent launch to persuade them to postpone their purchase and give them time to prepare their organisation for the new product; (2) discourage competitors and persuade them to terminate their own development efforts; (3) identify cooperation partners, such as suppliers, competitors or suppliers of complementary products; (4) encourage investments by suppliers to ensure supply of critical components or materials; (5) encourage investments by complementors to enhance the product's value to customers; (6) stimulate market acceptance by creating a positive attitude with potential customers and market influencers and promote positive word-of-mouth; (7) develop a supportive channel system by enlisting and developing channel partners; and (8) motivate employees by making the new product highly visible and something to be proud of (Biemans and Setz 1995).

In effective B2B communication, all messages communicated across all customer touchpoints are consistent and reinforce each other. This requires careful **communication planning**, consisting of the following steps:

1 *Formulate communication objectives.* This includes selecting target customers and formulating the central message to be communicated. Is the objective to attract new customers or to nurture relationships with existing customers? To create awareness for a new product or to urge customers to place an order? Communication objectives must be specific, useful and measurable. To attract 300 people with a trade show booth is not a very useful objective. It is relatively easy to attract a large number of people, but the key question is how many of those visitors belong to a buying centre for your product (the so-called useful contacts).

2 *Select appropriate media.* Each communication medium has specific strengths and weaknesses, which determine its effectiveness in achieving specific communication objectives. Advertisements in trade journals are very useful to create awareness and interest in a large audience and to build a B2B brand (Figure 7.1). The internet is particularly useful for establishing an interactive dialogue with customers and prospects. A trade show or sales visit are appropriate for communicating a wealth of detailed information and to build relationships. Thus, B2B vendors must select media that fit both the offering and its target customers.

3 *Create messages.* Communication messages must support communication objectives and match the characteristics of the target audience and the media selected. In addition, they must be effective within the flood of communication messages that are sent to target customers by competitors. To be effective, vendors often need to formulate several messages to target different members of the buying centre. A user requires detailed product specifications, but a business manager wants information about the product's impact on the customer's processes or performance.

4 *Place the messages in the selected media.* Some media require long-term planning. Many trade shows, for example, are organised only once a year and popular

FIGURE 7.1 Creating B2B brand personality

Source: Nokia. Used with permission.

televised events are frequently much-sought by advertisers. Other media, such as newspapers, require only a short lead-time.

5 *Measure results*. Many B2B vendors neglect to carefully measure the results from their communication efforts; for instance, they cheerfully conclude that this year's trade show was a success because lots of potential customers visited their booth. But how many of them were subsequently visited by a salesperson? And in how many cases did this result in an order? Unambiguous, measurable objectives, together with systematic measurement of results, are key to effective evaluation.

6 *Adapt messages and/or media.* Based on the evaluation, both communication messages and media may be changed. Management, for example, may decide to no longer participate in a specific trade show because an analysis of trade show visitors shows that the trade show is no longer visited by key decision-makers for the firm's products.

MINI CASE: B2B FIRMS SPONSOR RACING TEAMS

In selecting their media, vendors choose media that most effectively and/or efficiently reach their target audience. Several B2B vendors of frequently purchased products of low value have discovered that the demographics of the people buying their products are very similar to the demographics of racing enthusiasts. This led a number of B2B firms to sponsor individual racers or even racing teams. W.W. Grainger, one of the largest distributors of MRO products, sponsors a NASCAR driver. Office Depot linked up with NASCAR in 2005, when it served as Official Office Products Partner of the racing circuit and the primary sponsor of driver Carl Edwards. In February 2007, it launched its 'Official Small Business of NASCAR' promotion. The company announced that it will pick one small business owner to become the Official Small Business of NASCAR. The winning company will receive a $10,000 small business makeover package and have its logo displayed on the car of NASCAR driver Carl Edwards. In 2008, Office Depot became one of the primary sponsors of Tony Stewart. In the words of Stewart: 'Office Depot focuses on small business owners, and with my role as a driver and owner next year, I'm both their spokesman and their customer.'

Sources: www.btobonline.com and www.officedepotracing.com

All communication instruments can be classified as either one-to-one media (personal selling, direct marketing) or mass media (websites, advertising, trade shows), but the difference between them is not always clear. Sponsoring of sports events allows firms to communicate their brand to a large number of customers and prospects. But they can also be used to build individual relationships with selected key customers in an informal setting. Similarly, the internet is a very efficient medium to communicate to a large group of customers, but also allows firms to interact one-to-one with individual customers.

One-to-one communication is directed at individual customers or even individual members of the buying centre, which allows a firm to tailor its message to the specific needs of individual customers and decision-makers. The most frequently used one-to-one communication media are personal selling and direct marketing. Personal selling is discussed in Chapter 6.

7.2 One-to-one communication: direct marketing

With **direct marketing** the vendor sends its messages directly to customers and prospects to stimulate a measurable response, mostly in terms of sales. Direct marketing is also referred to as *one-to-one marketing*. It delivers the marketing message directly to individual customers, using addressable media such as mail (direct mail), telephone (telemarketing), humans (personal selling), email (email marketing), the internet or even mobile phones. Because direct marketing requires extensive customer data and lists, usually in databases, it is also called *database marketing*. Direct marketing is a very cost-effective method that creates direct contact with customers, allows the vendor to tailor the message to the profile of individual customers and results in a measurable response. This used to be achieved primarily through mailings aimed at clearly defined groups of customers, but advances in ICT allow vendors to create customised direct mail packages for individual customers, send personalised catalogues and create tailor-made websites. While direct marketing may create several responses from customers, such as improving a firm's image, the objective is to create a measurable response (sales leads, orders, hits on a website). This measured response is compared with the costs of the direct marketing campaign to calculate its cost-effectiveness. The major disadvantage of direct marketing is that it also generates unwanted solicitations (junk mail, spam).

Direct marketing activities are based on information about current, potential and lost customers. Databases or mailing lists can be bought from suppliers or built from scratch. A vendor may use its website to offer prospects and customers access to special content (such as a product guide or white paper) in exchange for their email address to build the company's email marketing list, for example. This list can then be used to send newsletters and direct marketing messages. While it is expensive to create or buy a list of email addresses, sending direct marketing messages using email is much cheaper than sending them through regular mail. It is of critical importance to regularly check and update email lists since their information becomes obsolete very quickly.

MINI CASE: THE LIST GUYS

EDMA (www.list-search.net) started, in 1965, to collect datacard information from reputable list providers and compiled a database of up to date datacards. Since the advent of the internet, the service has become 100 per cent free for users, with the list companies paying them a fee for making their lists available through their search engines. EDMA's list search engines allow their users to search, using one or more keywords, over 75,000 different direct mail, telemarketing and email lists through a single search box. Every year, EDMA sends out its annual list survey, named ListShopper, to the 12,500 most influential buyers of lists and data, including the world's major advertising agencies, direct marketing consultancies and large volume end-users. The objective of ListShopper is to determine which company provides the best lists. Some 3,058 different list companies were mentioned in the 2008 survey and Clear Blue was named the top list company, which is why Clear Blue opens its website with the words: 'We are the list guys...'.

> Clear Blue offers a large number of lists for the UK, Europe and the US, which can be purchased online. For the UK, for example, Clear Blue offers lists with application development managers, business systems analysts, call centre managers, charity donors, exporters, facility managers, financial controllers, health product buyers, IT security managers, Lotus Notes users, new business start-ups, office equipment buyers, UNIX users, users of executive coaching services and many more. The number of records per list varies from 500 to 1,500,000. Users can find the desired lists using a user-friendly search engine.
>
> *Sources*: www.list-search.net and www.clearbluegroup.net

Direct mail

Direct mail is the delivery of advertising material to customers, prospects, suppliers, distributors and other parties through postal mail. The advertising material could be product or company brochures, circulars, catalogues, CDs, DVDs and all kinds of commercial merchandising materials. The most common formats of direct mail include:

- *Catalogues*: multi-page, bound promotions, usually featuring a selection of products for sale.
- *Self-mailers*: pieces usually created from a single sheet that has been printed and folded; for instance, a page-length advertisement or promotion on one side of a sheet of paper, which is then folded in half with the promotional message on the inside. The two outside surfaces are then used for the address of the recipient and some teaser message designed to persuade the recipient to open the piece.
- *Postcards*: simple, two-sided pieces, with a promotional message on one side and the recipient's address on the other.
- *Envelope mailers*: mailings in which the marketing material is placed inside an envelope, which permits the marketer to include more than one insert.
- *Clear bag packages*: large, full-colour packages sealed in a clear, plastic outer wrap. The contents are visible through the clear bag for maximum initial impact.
- *Dimensional mailers*: mailers that have some dimension to them, like a small box.

The advantages of direct mail are its ability to precisely target customers and prospects, to address the customer personally and to tailor the message to the customer's needs based on previous transactions and gathered data, and optimise the approach used (message, timing, offer, list). In addition, the responses can be analysed to determine the effectiveness of the direct mail activity and to improve the quality of the database to allow for better targeting in the future. Direct mail allows the vendor to tell a detailed story at relatively low cost. Naturally, the costs of direct mail depend on the chosen format: sending a cover letter with a small product leaflet is much cheaper than sending a teaser package with a promotional gimmick.

The disadvantages of direct mail are the large amounts of waste (packages that are thrown away) and irritation with customers who perceive the mailing to be junk

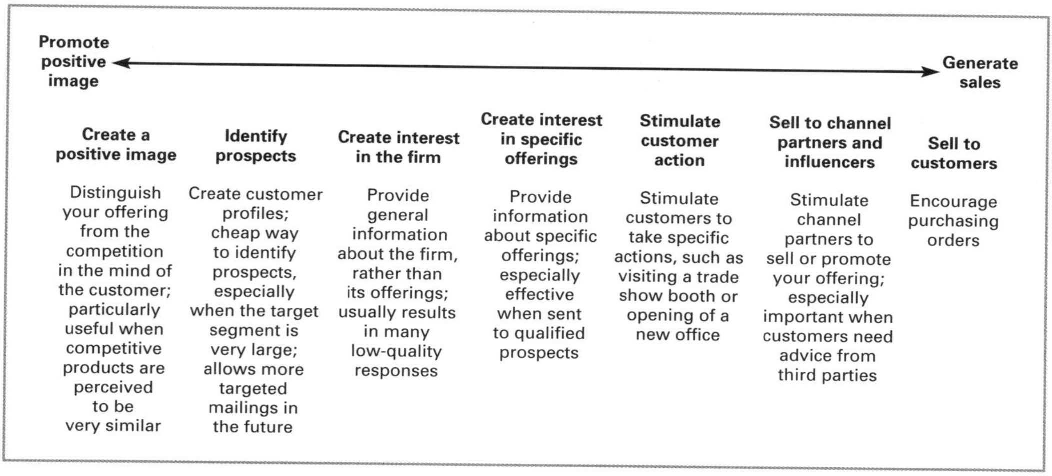

Promote positive image ←						→ Generate sales
Create a positive image	**Identify prospects**	**Create interest in the firm**	**Create interest in specific offerings**	**Stimulate customer action**	**Sell to channel partners and influencers**	**Sell to customers**
Distinguish your offering from the competition in the mind of the customer; particularly useful when competitive products are perceived to be very similar	Create customer profiles; cheap way to identify prospects, especially when the target segment is very large; allows more targeted mailings in the future	Provide general information about the firm, rather than its offerings; usually results in many low-quality responses	Provide information about specific offerings; especially effective when sent to qualified prospects	Stimulate customers to take specific actions, such as visiting a trade show booth or opening of a new office	Stimulate channel partners to sell or promote your offering; especially important when customers need advice from third parties	Encourage purchasing orders

FIGURE 7.2 Range of direct mail activities

mail. The problem of junk mail can be partly solved through the use of more powerful computers and larger databases, which allow for more in-depth processing of mailing lists and better targeting. Another option is to ask customers' permission to send them direct mail pieces (*opt in*). The objectives of direct mail range from creating a positive image to generating sales (Figure 7.2). For more complex and expensive products, in particular, the objective of direct mail is to move the prospect to the next stage in the buying cycle, rather than asking for the order.

Because there may be many reasons why a customer did not respond to a direct mail piece (it got lost in the postroom, the secretary threw it out, the customer was on holiday), resending a direct mail piece may significantly increase, often double, the response rate. Another option to increase response is to design a series of follow-up mailings, with each mailing building on the interest created by the previous one.

INSIGHT: Seven tips for more direct mail sales leads

Business marketing consultant Mac McIntosh offers seven tips for increasing direct mail sales leads and response:

1 Be sure to include a covering letter whenever you send printed literature to prospects or customers. Use the covering letter to acknowledge the request, give a few bullets about features or benefits and specifically ask the reader to take the next action.

2 Always include 'where to buy' information in your direct mail packages (email too) if you sell through field salespeople, independent representatives, resellers or distributors; for instance, by including a list or map or by mentioning the information in the covering letter. Be sure to include the sales contact's name, title, company, address, phone and fax numbers, and email and website addresses.

3 If you are mailing multi-product brochures or catalogues to inquirers who asked about a specific product, mention the appropriate page numbers in the covering letter, or use a sticky note or paper clip to mark the pages.

4 If your company's sales are influenced by more than one contact at a prospect company, consider including a question on all reply forms asking for the names of others at their company who would like to receive information about your products or services. Add these people to your mailing list or database for future mailings.

5 If you mail a free newsletter or catalogue to prospects or customers, include a built-in reply card or coupon that can be used by pass-along readers to request their own subscription.

6 Re-qualify your newsletter or catalogue subscription list by periodically including a reply card or form requesting that readers confirm their interest in continuing to receive the newsletter. Be sure to ask readers to update their title, address, phone and fax numbers, and email address. Also include a few qualifying questions about their product interest, application, buying role and timeframe.

7 Consider asking the people on your mailing list how they would prefer to receive future information and updates: by mail, fax or email? If you are prepared to deliver information by email or fax, you can shorten the delivery time and save a bundle on printing and postage.

Source: M.H. (Mac) McIntosh at www.sales-lead-experts.com

Email marketing

A cheaper and faster alternative to direct mail is email. **Email marketing** uses electronic mail to send a message to an audience, usually prospects or customers. The objectives of email marketing are just as varied as the objectives of direct mail and include building relationships, encouraging customer loyalty, obtaining trial orders, stimulating repeat purchases and acquiring new customers. The advantages of email marketing are its low costs, fast execution, ability to push the message to the audience (in contrast to a website where the customer needs to be persuaded to visit the website to read the message), the opportunity to include graphics and other rich content, and the fact that most B2B customers check their email daily. The major disadvantage is the problem of spam, with many customers becoming increasingly irritated with the large volume of unsolicited email messages. Most customers use sophisticated spam filters to reduce the number of unwanted email messages and anti-virus programs to flag infected files. But these programs may result in false positives: files that are mistakenly identified as infected or legitimate emails that are misidentified as spam.

To deal with the problem of unwanted emails, some vendors use *opt-in email* (or *permission marketing*), where the potential recipient grants permission to send email. Thus, the email messages (for instance, a company newsletter) are anticipated and more relevant. Some vendors even use a *double opt-in* method, where the potential recipient needs to manually confirm its request for information (such as a company newsletter) by clicking a unique link and entering a unique code identifier. It is better, although definitely more expensive, to build your own opt-in list than to buy or rent an opt-in list from an outside source. Commercial opt-in lists have usually been resold many times and have what is known as 'list fatigue' (containing many inactive addresses).

The success of email marketing depends on the quality of the mailing list and the right mix of words and message that appeals to the target audience. A 2008 study by the Aberdeen Group found that 96 per cent of organisations believe that email personalisation can improve email marketing performance.[2] Break through the perceived spam barrier created by filtering software by using an appropriate subject line. Identify your own company in the message's front line. And create a compelling message, incorporating customer profile information, that fits the electronic medium and uses its creative possibilities. To be effective, the email message should be combined with offline communications, such as a phone call from a sales representative or an information package sent by postal mail.

Telemarketing

An older but still very common form of direct marketing is **telemarketing**, with the vendor contacting prospects by phone to make a sale, direct the prospect to a website or schedule a sales visit or web conference call. Telemarketing can also be used for a series of phone calls to nurture customer relationships, penetrate target accounts and create a dialogue between seller and buyer. Usually the first call (or series of calls) is to determine the customer's needs and the final call (or series of calls) is to encourage the customer to purchase the vendor's offering. Telemarketing is frequently used to generate sales leads, qualify sales leads and speed up the sales cycle. Effective telemarketing requires a high-quality targeted list and a carefully prepared script. The telemarketer must be able to quickly gain the customer's interest with a credible pitch, handle objections, answer direct questions, make an appointment and use qualifying questions to obtain useful background information. Of course, telemarketing may also be outsourced to specialised providers. Numerous companies offer telemarketing services to customers, providing services such as lead generation, appointment setting, customer surveys, event invitation and follow-up, direct mail follow-up and database development and cleansing.

Internet marketing

Internet marketing, web marketing, online marketing or e-marketing is the marketing of products and services over the internet. It has the advantages of low costs, global reach and interactivity. Internet marketing can be used to offer product information, obtain orders, acquire new customers, support channel partners and nurture relationships. A key characteristic of internet marketing is that customers take the initiative by clicking on an online ad or accessing a website and determining whether or not to click through. The explosive growth in internet sites makes it critically important for vendors to effectively communicate their web address to prospects and customers. Every organisation mentions its website on its stationery, business cards, brochures and trucks, but more creative firms weave the web address in carpets or put it in fortune cookies that are handed out during trade shows. *Search engine marketing* is a form of internet marketing that seeks to promote websites by increasing their visibility in search engine result pages (such as used by Google and Yahoo). Search engine marketing offers precise targeting because the customer is actively looking for the subject of interest. The objective of search engine marketing is to make the website appear as high as possible on a search engine's listings for relevant keywords. Since different search engines use different ranking criteria it requires an in-depth understanding of how the major search engines work and strategies to increase visibility. Optimising a website primarily involves editing its content and HTML coding to increase its relevance to specific keywords and to remove barriers to the indexing activities of search engines.

MINI CASE: TEN GREAT WEBSITES

Each year *BtoB* magazine invites five industry experts to select ten great B2B websites that are particularly good examples of how companies can use the web to communicate with their customers. The selected sites do an exceptionally good job with the basics year after year, allowing visitors to find product and company information quickly and easily, providing a brand experience consistent with other marketing channels and offering a way to take the relationship to the next level. In the words of William Rice, president of the Web Marketing Association and one of the experts invited in 2008, '[Business] sites are all about effectiveness. You need to find the quickest way to get potential customers to understand not just about your products but what the real issues are in their industry and how those products can solve their problems and challenges. It's also crucial to build a long-term relationship rather than simply hawk your wares.' Another industry expert emphasises that, although business customers make purchasing decisions for a business entity, they are also consumers and used to being in control and they will no longer settle for a substandard customer experience. But many B2B vendors find it hard to look at their business from the customer's perspective. Menus should be easily visible and make sense. Categories and subcategories should reflect what the customer calls your products and services – not what you do. In addition, the experts suggest using video, blogs and widget-generated microsites to give customers and prospects more information about what they are looking for. And because most customers arrive at a site through a search engine, they will generally not arrive at the front page. This suggests that every page should function like a home page and include a search box at the top so that customers can easily find whatever they need within that site.

One of the 2008 winners is Formway, a New Zealand-based designer of high performance office furniture. Its new site was considered edgy and interactive, using Flash-driven drop-down menus to draw visitors deeper into the site. Customers can browse products by product category and by product use. Visitors already familiar with the entire product line can browse by product name. The site offers a lot of product data and customers can download more detailed information via brochures, component guides and high-resolution images.

Sources: www.btobonline.com, 15 September 2008 and www.formway.com

The simplest form of internet marketing is *pay-per-click advertising* (for instance, banner ads), where the advertiser pays for each time someone clicks on the ad. The effectiveness of pay-per-click advertising depends on the quality of the online ad, which can be measured by its click-through rate (calculated as the number of clicks on an ad divided by the number of times the ad appeared). In addition, firms should optimise the landing page (the web page on which the customer arrives after having clicked on the online ad). But the internet also allows vendors to combine text, images and streaming video into a compelling experience; for instance, to demonstrate new products or new applications. By analysing how much time visitors spend on each page and how visitors navigate through the site, a firm obtains a wealth of information about its customers' search behaviour. The interactive nature of the internet even allows a firm to use *dynamic profiling* to adapt the website's content to the visitor's search behaviour. Electronic forms can be used to gather additional information about customers.

With *webcasting,* firms can broadcast live events, such as conferences, shareholder meetings or messages from the CEO. Webcasting is also used for seminars and training. A webcast or **webinar** transmits a sales message to a large audience, at relatively low cost, and allows for interactive feedback from the audience.[3] RealNetworks (the company that offers consumers the familiar RealPlayer) offers firms the technology to record webinars and make them available to prospective buyers when and where they want to view them, sometimes for 12 months after the event or more. Webinars are an attractive alternative to email marketing, which is plagued by the spectre of spam, and are an important source of information for prospective buyers. A recent study from online media leader TechTarget found that 73 per cent of its audience had viewed at least one webinar in the past three months and 84 per cent of those viewers contacted the sponsoring vendor via email or phone. The ROI of a webinar is calculated as follows:

$$\text{ROI}_{\text{webinar}} = \frac{\text{Number of leads} \times \text{Lead conversion percentage} \times \text{Deal size}}{\text{costs}}$$

The costs include both the marketing costs and the costs of delivering the webinar. Using live session monitoring, a vendor can track the effectiveness of a presentation at any time by monitoring the attentiveness of the audience.

A *podcast* is an audio or video file that can be downloaded from the internet. When customers subscribe to podcasts, new content is downloaded automatically as soon as it becomes available. Podcasts must be relevant and to the point, interesting to listen to, avoid advertising and selling and not exceed 20 to 40 minutes. Oracle posted several online audio interviews with technical experts about new tools, technologies and trends in application development.

Vendors may also create online communities, where customers meet in cyberspace to discuss the company's offerings and market trends (Hagel and Armstrong 1997). Such communities offer a common forum where customers share information and solve problems. Vendors can access these communities to collect information about customer concerns and market trends.

Because of its almost limitless possibilities, the internet is more than a direct marketing medium. Customers may also use it to determine their needs, configure appropriate solutions or place orders. An online digital library offers customers a wealth of up-to-date information, such as sales brochures, product specification sheets, repair manuals, application guides, product design modules and ordering instructions. Vendors create *virtual private networks* (VPNs) for effective communication with customers, channel partners, suppliers and other stakeholders.

Vendors may also combine several one-to-one communication media for increased effectiveness. Personalised URLs (called PURLs), for example, are personalised websites used in combination with direct mail that are designed to gather information about the person visiting the website. The PURLs are printed on the direct mail piece (for instance, JohnBuyer.domain.com or domain.com/JohnBuyer). When recipients of the direct mail piece log in using their PURL, the information from the vendor database is used to tailor the web page's content to that specific individual; for instance, by welcoming the customer by name and tailoring the text, offers and graphics to the specific customer.

7.3 Mass communication: advertising

In contrast to one-to-one media, **mass communication** media are directed at groups of customers or other stakeholders, such as a selected market segment or even the whole market. Companies such as UPS, FedEx, KLM Cargo, British Telecom and local energy companies target all businesses. Mass communication media are used to send the same message to a large number of recipients. In B2B markets, the most frequently used mass communication media are advertising, trade shows, catalogues and other sales collatoral and public relations.

After personal selling, **advertising** is the most frequently used communication medium in business markets. Because of its low cost per thousand and large reach, advertising allows vendors to cost-effectively communicate with a large number of decision-makers and buying influencers. Firms may use several **advertising objectives**:

- *Create awareness.* Prospects can only purchase a vendor's offering when they are aware of its existence. Advertising creates or increases awareness of the vendor's organisation, offerings, prices, experience with specific industries, flexibility or location. When entering a new market, in particular, this type of advertising is critical to inform potential buyers of the company's capabilities. Frequent and consistent advertising contributes to a strong corporate or brand image.

- *Create a positive attitude.* Advertising increases the effectiveness of personal selling by informing prospects about the firm and its offerings before they are visited by a sales representative. This is illustrated by McGraw-Hill's famous 'man in the chair' ad (Figure 7.3). The original ad is from 1958 and has only been updated a couple of times. The original black-and-white version was named one of the ten best ads by *Advertising* and in 1999 *Business Marketing* pronounced it the best business marketing advertising campaign of the century. The ad emphasises advertising's role in supporting personal selling. Because salespeople usually talk with only one or two people at a customer firm, advertising is an effective medium to reach other unknown influencers. Advertising also helps decision-makers to justify their purchase decision.

FIGURE 7.3 The famous McGraw-Hill ad
Source: The McGraw-Hill Companies. Used with permission.

- *Stimulate sales.* Much B2B advertising aims to move the prospect or customer to the next stage in the buying process; for instance, by generating sales leads. These sales leads need to be qualified and the most promising ones are followed up with a phone call or sales visit. Companies like Intel, W. L. Gore & Associates and Shimano successfully stimulate sales by promoting their ingredient brand with customers. Caterpillar boosts its brand equity by offering a wide range of merchandise. Naturally, advertising may also directly remind customers to place an order.

B2B advertising is generally more rational than advertising in consumer markets. The emphasis is on moving decision-makers and influencers towards a purchase by providing them with information about the vendor's offering. But with B2B products becoming increasingly similar and B2B marketing becoming increasingly professional, B2B advertising has started to embrace emotions and image-related themes.

Using advertising media

B2B vendors use a wide range of **advertising media** to promote their companies and offerings:

- *Business publications.* The primary outlet for B2B advertising are a large number of trade journals and business magazines. Some of them focus on a subject (computers), while others focus on an industry (agriculture, construction), which allows for highly targeted advertising. High reader involvement means that they will pay more attention to ads and the high quality of most magazines permits good quality reproduction and full-colour ads. When magazines are published monthly or quarterly, readers can go back to the message during a relatively long period of time. The disadvantages of business publications are their generally long lead-times, relatively high costs and limited flexibility. Business publications frequently publish the results of reader polls to assist firms in selecting the appropriate journals and magazines.

- *Consumer magazines.* Many B2B firms advertise in consumer magazines to support their corporate brand or promote specific products. Decision-makers and influencers are also consumers and can be reached effectively through popular consumer magazines.

- *Newspapers.* Both national and regional newspapers are used extensively to advertise B2B offerings. Large firms communicate their corporate brand in national newspapers, while small and medium-sized businesses rely on regional newspapers to promote their products and services. Newspapers reach a large audience in a given geographic region, have short lead-times and allow firms to place large ads telling a complicated story. The disadvantages are the poor quality of the paper, the clutter of ads aimed at consumers, a short shelf life and a declining readership (because people increasingly get their news from the internet).

- *Television and radio.* Vendors of B2B products and services that may be used by all businesses, such as office supplies, insurance and consultancy services, frequently advertise on television and radio. Both television and radio offer a large audience. Television has the added advantage of being a visual medium, while radio is a universal medium enjoyed by people at home, at work and in the car. The disadvantages are that the audience cannot go back and revisit the message, the limited length of the message and the long planning required for television ads. In addition, the production of television ads is relatively expensive.

- *Internet.* While a growing number of firms advertise on the internet, most companies still overlook the power of internet advertising. The most frequently used forms of internet advertising are display ads (such as banner ads), pay-per-click search and online classifieds. The largest advantage of internet advertising is that the viewer has actually chosen to see the commercial. The largest disadvantage is that it is increasingly difficult to stand out among the clutter. Online advertisers pay a cost per impression (paying for exposure of the message to a specific audience), cost per visitor (paying for the delivery of a targeted visitor to the advertiser's website), cost per click (paying for the number of times that users click on the ad and are directed to the advertiser's website) or cost per action (paying for the number of users completing a transaction). Online ads include the floating ad (moves across the screen or floats above the content), expanding ad (changes size), wallpaper ad (changes the background of the page being viewed), pop-up (new window which opens in front of the current one), pop-under (only becomes visible when the user closes one or more active windows) and video ad (moving video clip). Because the effectiveness of the more traditional internet ads has decreased, firms increasingly use pay-per-click ads coupled with keywords on search engines, such as Google.

- *Outdoor advertising.* This includes all forms of advertising that reaches prospects and customers while they are outdoors. Examples are billboards, neon signage, digital signage, bus advertising, street furniture, posters, streetcar/trolley/taxi advertising, displays, stadium signs, bench advertising, wallscapes and skywriting. The advantages of outdoor advertising are that it can be experienced 24 hours a day, seven days a week, without being surrounded by a lot of clutter, its relatively low costs and the fact that it catches the audience at a time when they are relatively bored and looking for a distraction. Outdoor advertising is particularly effective when buyers are geographically concentrated and may even be used to target single buying firms cost effectively (Lichtenthal et al. 2006). The major disadvantage of outdoor advertising is that it only catches the viewer's eye for two or three seconds, which requires a very concise and resonating advertising message.

MINI CASE: BRITISH TELECOM SPLURGES ON CORPORATE ADS

British Telecom (BT) demonstrates how its biggest corporate ad campaign, including ads placed in a range of business and professional titles, helped generate £8 billion worth of IT network orders and led to plans for further investment of £18.5 million in a second phase to enhance its credibility as a global provider of networked IT services. BT's biggest corporate advertising campaign used a range of media, including professional magazines such as *The Economist, Finance Week, Time, Financial Director, Public Finance, Government Computing, Computing Weekly* and *Information Age.* The campaign positioned BT as the ideal partner to help transform organisations around their communications networks, enabling employees to communicate and exchange information using different technologies, no matter where they are.

Launched in August 2004, the first, awareness-building, phase of the campaign helped improve BT's sales. BT signed up an average of two new business or government customers each working day and generated more than £8.2 billion worth of orders with these customers over 12 months. In its best-ever period, it signed up £22 million in new orders each day; examples include significant contract wins for BT with Reuters, Bristol-Myers Squibb, the Ministry of Defence and Visa. The campaign ran in multiple languages in international and local media across Europe, the Americas and Asia Pacific. In the UK, campaign activities spanned press, TV, outdoor and online advertising. Outside of the UK, there was a similar mix of advertising, with the outdoor ads focused on international airports, complemented with below-the-line activities such as direct mailings and network security masterclasses for customers. Tim Evans, BT's group marketing and brand director, said: 'This campaign has really made its mark with the business community, and has shifted perceptions of us from being simply the UK's telco: our growth certainly reflects that. We will continue to play to our strengths with our new business, building on our networking heritage and expertise.'

Source: www.businessmediauk.co.uk

Evaluating B2B advertising

Like any other business activity, advertising also needs to be evaluated in terms of how effectively and efficiently it contributes to realising the advertiser's objectives. It is not a matter of liking or not liking an ad, but whether it does the job that it was designed to do. For products with extensive buying processes, however, it is particularly difficult to determine the effect of a specific ad on moving the prospect to a purchase decision. **Advertising effectiveness** depends on variables such as the key concept presented in the message (product features, benefits), how the concept is presented (design, slogan, text, visuals), the advertiser's corporate image (values and norms) and the focus on the target customer (extent to which the ad's language matches the customer's jargon and interests).

INSIGHT: Ten criteria for a successful ad

More than 50 years ago, *Business Marketing* (now *BtoB*) formulated the *Copy Chasers' Criteria*: ten criteria to evaluate business ads. Half a century later these guidelines are still useful for creating successful business ads. The Copy Chasers' Criteria state that a successful ad:

1 has a high degree of visual magnetism

2 selects the right audience

3 invites the reader into the scene

4 promises a reward

5 backs up the promise

6 presents the selling proposition in a logical sequence

7 talks 'person-to-person'

8 is easy to read

9 emphasises the service, not the source

10 reflects the company's character.

Source: BtoB

TABLE 7.2 Measures to evaluate B2B advertising

Measure	How it is calculated	How it is used
Recall	Surveys of magazine readers (or television viewers) asking which ads they remember seeing	Did the ad attract attention? Was it remembered? Assumption is that if the ad is remembered, it was effective
Inquiries	Number of response cards, faxbacks or calls to toll-free number in an ad	Did the ad cause readers to take action? Were the people who responded really interested in buying the product?
Position	Pre-advertisement and post-advertisement surveys of attitudes towards a product	Did the ad change the market's attitudes towards the product? Is the attitude now as desired relative to attitudes towards competitors' products?
Reach	Using circulation or readership audits, the number of readers among the target market is calculated	Does the magazine reach the desired audience? Used to assess media choices, rather than the effectiveness of a particular ad
Cost per thousand (CPM)	Divide cost by readership, expressed in thousands	How does the reach of a magazine compare to the reach of a similar magazine, relative to how much each charges? Again, used to assess media choice

Source: Dwyer and Tanner (2006: 322). Reprinted with permission.

B2B marketers use several measures to evaluate the effects of advertising. Table 7.2 presents the most frequently used measures. An ad's cost per thousand (CPM) is calculated by dividing the costs of the ad by the number of target customers reached (that is, the number of useful contacts). Trade journals tend to have relatively many useful contacts, because they are often distributed through controlled circulation, which means that they are only sent to qualified readers. This improves the match between the advertiser's target customers and the readers of the journal. When they are distributed for free, however, one may wonder to what extent their readers actually read them.

In addition, B2B firms evaluate the effectiveness of their advertising by asking their customers how they found out about them. This enables them to assess the relative effectiveness of the various media employed (such as a newspaper ad or the internet) and other communication mechanisms (such as referrals and networking). Vendors can evaluate the effectiveness of online advertising with a website statistic package, such as the free *Google Analytics*. Such packages allow firms to calculate cost per click, cost per action metrics (such as cost per sale) or even cost per revenue (which calculates how much it costs to generate a euro of revenue from a particular site or online ad). Google Analytics calculates various metrics, creates custom reports and custom dashboards, and can be used to learn which keywords are most profitable, how visitors navigate through the site, how key metrics compare to aggregate performance metrics in the same industry, identify pages that result in lost conversions and identify the most lucrative geographic markets.

Using advertising agencies

In contrast to their consumer marketing colleagues, B2B vendors do not make much use of advertising agencies. This can partly be explained by the technical product orientation of many B2B firms, which clashes with the highly commercial approach of advertising agencies. Many B2B firms feel that an advertising agency lacks the required in-depth knowledge of both their products and their industry applications. But B2B firms may benefit significantly from a more commercial approach to their communication efforts, especially when the involvement of communication consultants goes beyond traditional advertising. An example is Cicero, a UK-based business marketing communications agency that opened its doors in Manchester in 1914. Cicero has worked with customers in a wide range of industries and offers clients a wide range of communication services.

Successful cooperation between a B2B firm and a marketing communication agency requires from both partners that they understand each other's perspective and contribution. This means that small and medium-sized business firms must be educated about the role of communication in effective B2B marketing and how a specialised agency can help them to achieve their objectives. For advertising agencies, this means that they should transform themselves into B2B communication specialists. Such a transformation requires that they need to possess marketing communication expertise and be knowledgeable about the needs of specific industries. Some of their employees should have a technical background and be able to think in terms of total communication rather than just advertising.

7.4 Mass communication: trade shows

Trade shows are the second most important medium for mass communication in B2B markets. Together, trade shows and personal selling account for over 60 per cent of the marketing budget of B2B firms. Trade shows date back to the trade fairs from the Middle Ages and are still all about displaying your wares to the public. In the twenty-first century an increasing number of trade shows moved online (*virtual tradeshows*; Figure 7.4), featuring online booths, webinars and online chats. Virtual trade shows greatly reduce the costs to both vendors and customers, often result in more targeted leads and allow vendors to track attendees' behaviour.

MINI CASE: GATES CORP. USES ONLINE SHOW TO CAPTURE LEADS

Gates Corp., a Denver-based manufacturer of automotive and industrial products, was looking to generate leads and engage prospects for its power transmission division in a way that was difficult to achieve with traditional marketing campaigns. To this end, it participated in the 2008 Online Manufacturing WebExpo and Conference. Visitors to Gates' virtual booth were greeted with an introductory Flash video, which positioned Gates as a provider of solutions, not simply products. Visitors could then browse various pieces of Gates content, such as white papers, case studies and brochures and participate in an online chat with Gates employees. Gates also sponsored a webinar, *Designing Belt Power Transmission Systems for Energy Savings*, during the online show. This presentation featured one of Gates' product application engineers and was followed by a live Q&A session in which participants could raise specific questions or concerns. Gates found that the online show and webinar was a great opportunity to target prospects in varying stages of the buying cycle. 'It was great for informing people about the possibilities in energy savings but also provided more details if they were ready to take the next step,' says Mary Ann Amari, advertising specialist for Industrial Power Transmission Marketing, Gates Corp. Gates generated 123 qualified leads and the average visitor spent between 20 and 60 minutes in the online booth. Amari is especially pleased with how long visitors stayed in the webinar. 'That really tells you very clearly that the content you're providing is what they thought they would get and what they wanted to hear and needed to hear,' she said. 'It was nice to see people really stick in there, and pay attention and ask a lot of questions at the end. It was great feedback.'

Source: www.btobonline.com, 13 October 2008

Trade shows can be classified according to the characteristics of the participating vendors and their visitors (Figure 7.5).

Customers are attracted by a concentration of vendors, which makes it efficient for developing a good overview of what the market has to offer. Trade shows offer vendors the opportunity to efficiently present their products to a large number of prospects and customers. In addition, they allow for face-to-face interaction where the offering can be explained and demonstrated in detail. At some trade shows, products are actually sold to customers, while at others the sales cycle is initiated, which reduces the costs of personal selling at a later date. Several studies have demonstrated the benefits of trade shows:[4]

FIGURE 7.4 A virtual trade show

Source: ON24. Used with permission.

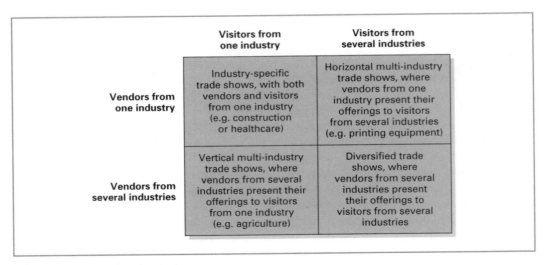

FIGURE 7.5 Classification of trade shows

- 91 per cent of business decision-makers consider trade shows very useful sources of purchasing information.
- 85 per cent of trade show attendees are buyers of one or more of the products exhibited.
- Vendors get up to 40 per cent of their sales from trade shows.
- Trade shows reach hidden prospects.
- 39 per cent of trade show attendees have final say in a purchasing decision.
- 50 per cent of trade show attendees place an order because of their visit to a trade show.
- It only takes 1.6 personal sales calls to close a sale with a trade show lead, while without a trade show lead 3.7 sales calls are required.

Smith et al. (2004) demonstrated the complementary relationship between trade shows and personal selling by showing that follow-up sales efforts generate higher sales productivity when customers have already been exposed to the firm's product at a trade show. Overall profits were also found to be greater when the trade show is used together with optimal levels of sales effort. Blythe (2002) shows that trade shows can be very effective tools to build relationships with customers as part of a key account management strategy.

The major disadvantage of trade shows is their cost, which can be quite substantial. The cost of trade shows includes rental of the trade show booth, design and construction of the booth and accompanying displays, telecommunications and networking, travel, accommodation, promotional literature and give-away items, as well as the marketing costs of communicating the trade show to the target audience. In addition, trade shows are organised by third parties, which requires firms to coordinate their planning with the timing of a trade show; for instance, many firms want to launch important new products at a large annual trade show for maximum impact.

Customers often send cross-functional purchasing teams to trade shows, consisting of representatives from various departments (such as marketing, finance, IT); top management may also be part of the team. This requires that the vendor's booth staffers must be able to identify purchasing team members and address their specific concerns. It may not be sufficient to have only marketing and salespeople staffing the booth; technical specialists may be required as well. Some vendors establish a direct connection between the trade show booth and the corporate head office to let important prospects communicate directly with the vendor's top management.

Management of trade shows

Vendors must carefully manage their participation in trade shows. **Trade show management** includes formulating trade show objectives, selecting trade shows, designing the booth, pre-show marketing, participating in the trade show and follow-up and post-show evaluation.

Formulating trade show objectives

Firms participate in trade shows to generate sales leads, launch new products, demonstrate complex products, reach hidden decision-makers, observe the competition, educate customers, build relationships, support local distributors and expand the mailing list. Trade show objectives should be derived from the firm's marketing strategy. When the firm has just launched an important new product, for example, generating sales leads for the new product will be an obvious goal of trade show participation. There is an important difference between the large (bi-)annual trade shows (where visibility and relationship building are the primary objectives) and the many smaller local trade shows (that are more suitable for generating sales). Trade show objectives must be carefully communicated to all employees involved and used to select the best staffers for the trade show booth.

Selecting trade shows

In selecting trade shows, vendors need to ask themselves questions such as: How many people will attend, who are they and what do they buy? Does the nature of the visitors match our target market? Do key decision-makers visit the trade show? When and where will the show take place? How much will participation in the trade show cost? (Berne and García-Uceda 2008). Most industries have one or two major shows that all major players attend. Management is often afraid that absence will send negative signals to customers and competitors. But trade show participation should not become automatic. By experimenting with different combinations of trade shows and carefully evaluating their results vendors will increase their insight into trade show effectiveness. The key to selecting the right trade shows lies in identifying the shows that attract the most decision-makers for the vendor's offerings. Show organisers provide demographic profiles of past attendees and non-competing exhibitors who participated last year may also provide useful information. Another option is to get an exhibit-only pass and check out the show in person before deciding to participate.

Designing the booth

Depending on the floor plan and the rented space (for instance, near the centre of the hall or on aisles leading to meeting rooms), the vendor needs to design an effective trade show booth. The type of booth selected depends on the functional needs of the booth (seating to talk with customers, shelves to display products, easy to assemble), aesthetic needs (backlighting, corporate image necessitating specific colours), marketing needs (message to be communicated, start-up versus established firm) and the booth budget (prices vary greatly depending on size and format).[5] Trade show booths come in many different shapes and sizes but can be classified as portable displays (easy to assemble structures that can be shipped by DHL or UPS), modular displays (structures that are easily assembled and look like custom displays) or custom displays (high-end displays that are designed from scratch).[6] Whatever the design, a trade show booth must communicate clearly to visitors who you are, what you have to offer and why a customer should do business with you.

Undertaking pre-show marketing

All pre-show promotional activities must be designed to increase the trade show's effectiveness in bringing qualified buyers to the booth. Examples are personal invitations from the salesforce, advertising, announcements in catalogues and emails and on websites, telemarketing, billboards, press releases, tag lines on all outgoing faxes, invoices and emails, posters, video presentations and on-hold phone messages.

Participating in the trade show

During the trade show it is up to the booth staffers to convey the appropriate message and move prospects to the next stage in the buying process. The ideal booth staffer is both people-oriented and very knowledgeable about your company and offerings. There should be enough product literature available to hand out to visitors, but it should not be too easy for visitors to grab brochures, because most of them will be thrown away. Games, give-aways and gimmicks help to attract attention, but also attract many non-buyers who clutter up the booth space. Booth staffers must be dressed correctly, always introduce themselves to visitors, look fresh and alert, be good listeners, refrain from smoking, eating, drinking and making phonecalls, smile at visitors and should never ask 'May I help you?', because that only results in the predictable answer 'No, I'm just looking' and another lost customer.

Carrying out follow-up and post-show evaluation

The first priorities after the trade show are order fulfilment and lead follow-up. All orders must be handled and products delivered according to agreed-on schedules. Leads must be followed up according to the 48–10–30 rule: follow-up with the customer within 48 hours after the initial contact via email or a phone call, talk with the contact within ten days to investigate opportunities that have not been addressed yet, and establish a third contact within 30 days. In addition, booth staffers and other employees involved in the trade show must be debriefed to identify what worked and what did not work, in order to learn and improve future trade shows. Table 7.3 offers several measures for trade show evaluation. Lee and Kim (2008) stress that companies should use multiple criteria to measure trade show performance, such as criteria related to sales, image building, information gathering and relationship improvement. Their study also found that pre-show activities had a much greater effect on trade show performance than at-show activities.

In addition, one may ask questions such as: Was there enough literature, product, demos and give-aways available? What did we learn about our target audience and our competition? What worked at the show? What did not? Was there something we saw that might work for our company? What could we have done differently to make our show a bigger success?[7] Vendors should also calculate the value of trade shows by estimating the value of a new customer, of a face-to-face meeting with an existing customer, of evaluating the competition and of meeting with suppliers. It may not be easy to generate those numbers, but even a rough estimate is better than just a gut feeling. Too many B2B firms only evaluate their trade shows by counting the number of business cards received from booth visitors.

TABLE 7.3 Measures to evaluate trade shows

Measure	How it is calculated	How it is used
Traffic counts	Number of visitors per hour, multiplied by the number of hours; number of brochures given out; number of business cards collected	Did the trade show programme bring people into the booth? When the number of people in the aisle was also counted, it may also be used to determine the percentage of aisle traffic that actually entered the booth
Direct mail redemption	Number of direct mail pieces redeemed at the booth	The redemption rate indicates how effective pre-show promotions were
Attraction efficiency	Number of qualified prospects divided by the total number of attendees with the same profile (available from show management)	Shows how effective the trade show programme was in attracting the right audience
Total press coverage	Number of interviews; number of attendees at press conferences; number of press visitors to the booth	Indicates the extent to which the press was attracted (of course, they still need to write about it in order for it to be effective)
Anecdotes	Stories about buyers that came to the booth and what happened during their visit	Tangible evidence of success; supplements other quantitative measures
Recall	Post-show surveys by independent auditors asking attendees which booths they remember visiting	Indicates how memorable the booth experience was

Source: Dwyer and Tanner (2006: 332). Reprinted with permission.

Showrooms

Vendors may also create a showroom to display products to customers, channel partners, suppliers and the press. A showroom can be used to demonstrate large products to prospective buyers, support the corporate image, stimulate sales or provide training to customers. Showrooms may also be created by channel partners. In that case, vendors should provide the channel partners with displays, advertising materials and product videos to send a consistent and uniform message and brand image to customers. Another option to show products to customers is a *roadshow*: a travelling exhibit that is a cross between a trade show and a showroom. For many years, 3M used a mobile Integrated Solutions show that visited some 300 customers per year. The 3M roadshow varied from one sales representative visiting customers with a three-metre-wide booth, to 12 employees from ten different 3M divisions organising a local show for several hundred people and offering product training.

7.5 Mass communication: public relations

Public relations (PR) is the management of beneficial relationships between an organisation and its publics, such as customers, suppliers, employees, competitors, shareholders, investors, politicians and the press. Because PR encourages exposure in third-party outlets (such as the business press), it offers a third-party legitimacy and credibility that paid advertising does not have. Publicity is the spreading of information to gain public awareness for a company or its offerings and can be seen as the result of effective PR. B2B vendors use PR to: create a positive corporate image, for instance the popular CEO biographies about Bill Gates (Microsoft), Jack Welch (General Electric) and Michael Dell (Dell Computer); build product awareness for products that have just been introduced; (re)position a product; reinforce the brand by maintaining positive relationships with key audiences; offer general information (annual report, strategic vision, changes in the firm's top management team); and manage crises that threaten company or product image. Examples of well-published crises are Intel's flawed Pentium chip and Shell's sinking of the Brent Spar oil storage buoy. Product recalls are very costly but may also be used to the firm's advantage when they are implemented quickly and unconditionally. After an Alaska Airlines crash on 31 January 2000, Boeing's investigation quickly focused on the horizontal stabiliser assembly and on 9 February Boeing urged all airlines to perform a series of inspections on their MD-80 series jets and three similar models.

The advantages of PR are a high level of credibility by capitalising on the influence and reputation of a third party, the opportunity to tell a detailed story, possible multiplication effects because other media pick up the story, and relatively low costs. Technical articles published by reputable journals are especially effective. The primary disadvantage of PR is the firm's lack of control over what the media will publish. Firms try to influence what is being published by issuing press releases and press kits, but ultimately the media write the story and sometimes the firm's name or product will not even be mentioned. In other cases, the carefully prepared and distributed information gets distorted by a journalist. Also, other breaking news may bump the firm's carefully prepared and planned event to the background.

Although vendors do not pay for the editorials published by independent media, PR is not without costs. Firms must develop press kits, containing background information, product brochures and videos, that are distributed to journalists to assist them in writing the story. And large firms usually have a PR department that coordinates all PR activities. Since the media are inundated with press releases, vendors should carefully select the media targeted and adapt the press release to the medium's editorial policy.

B2B vendors use a variety of PR tools, including media relations (stimulating media coverage by providing the press with press kits, videos and press releases), newsletters (distributed by regular mail or electronically), e-zines (electronic corporate magazines), special events (receptions, dinners, plant openings), speaking engagements (at industry conventions, trade shows, universities), sponsorships (sports events, art centres, university chairs), employee communications (through virtual private network, email, newsletters) and community relations (product donations, guided tours, financial support to public parks).

ᦌᦌᦌ **INSIGHT: The changed face of PR**

As with most communication instruments, the internet also changed the face of PR. Many firms and managers have, for example, discovered the power of creating and stimulating vibrant online discussions. Some top managers even write their own blogs to discuss recent corporate developments. These blogs may be combined with podcasting to create more engaging content. Management must realise that a one-time blog or podcast is not sufficient to engage an audience; they must be refreshed periodically to keep the attention of the audience.

Just repeating the same happy PR message in a new medium is also not enough to engage the customer. Forrester Research reported in July 2008 that the number of blogs started by B2B firms fell by nearly half from 2006 to 2007. Rather than discarding corporate blogs, Forrester advises to try again, adopting the best practices used by successful individual bloggers. '[B]uild conversations and engage community members in sharing their experiences with their online peers' – in other words, treat social media as a conference call rather than a billboard. Indeed, some large companies like Hewlett-Packard, General Motors and Marriott have figured out how to use corporate blogs to their best potential and redoubled their commitment. Their philosophy is embedded in the STRAIGHT principle: blogs must be succinct, transparent, responsive, accepting, insightful, genuine, humorous and timely. One way to do this is to speak in the first person and let real employees do the talking. After all, customers and other audiences relate better to people than to institutions.

Source: www.btobonline.com, 14 July 2008

7.6 Integrated communication

B2B marketers use an ever-growing number of instruments and media to communicate with their audiences. The internet introduced opportunities for real-time online communication, while mobile phones allow B2B vendors to communicate with buyers on the go; for instance, in 2008 Visa set up the Visa Business Network on Facebook to communicate with small business owners. At the same time, customers are faced with an increasing number of commercial messages clamouring for their attention and use sophisticated tools to find the messages that offer real value. **Integrated communication** means that business marketers must carefully select their communication messages and media depending on their marketing strategy, the communication objectives and the cost per useful contact. Is the goal to communicate reinforcing brand messages to a large number of customers? Or to initiate a dialogue with a selected group of individual customers? Whatever combination of messages and media is selected, business marketers need to ensure that the message is consistent. *Integrated marketing communication* (IMC) attempts to combine, integrate and synergise elements of the communications mix, with the strengths of one offsetting the weaknesses of others (Kitchen et al. 2004). It embodies the central idea of *one sight, one voice* marketing communication and implies communication consistency and integration across media and messages, across communication instruments and across marketing instruments.

Integration across media and messages

A communication campaign uses several media to get the message across to the targeted audiences, requiring integration across messages and media. A B2B firm, for example, may repeat the central theme or a key image from a TV commercial on a billboard, in an ad in trade journals or in a direct mail piece, thus creating a similar look across all communication messages. Customers seeing the image on a billboard will combine this with the message they have seen in the TV ad or read in a trade journal ad, thus reinforcing the message. In addition, by using several media B2B firms reach a larger number of decision-makers and influencers. Vendors may stimulate synergistic effects between media and messages by mentioning their web address in an ad. While this is a relatively simple strategy, many vendors neglect to think strategically about their communication messages and media. When communication messages and images are available in digital form, it is particularly easy and inexpensive to recycle messages, create synergy and enhance impact.

Integration across communication instruments

Vendors must also integrate the various communication instruments. A vendor may, for example, use direct mail to identify prospects, telemarketing to qualify these prospects, personal selling to visit the most interesting prospects and telemarketing or the internet to maintain relationships with existing customers. In addition, vendors need to integrate corporate communication with communication about individual products.

Integration across marketing instruments

B2B vendors must also integrate their communication activities with how they employ other marketing instruments. This all depends on the selected positioning for both the firm and its offerings. Does one want to be perceived as a vendor of innovative, high-quality products or as a provider of value for money? Another example relates to price changes. When a vendor raises its prices, it will communicate the high quality of the products to limit the loss of customers. But when a vendor lowers its prices, it will communicate these lower prices to attract new customers and stimulate orders.

In addition, integrated marketing communication also requires coordination between external communication (to customers, channel partners, suppliers, investors) and internal communication to the firm's employees (*internal marketing*). Successful integrated marketing communication requires outside-in, customer-oriented planning rather than the product-focused, inside-out approach that is so common in many B2B firms (see also Chapter 10). In 2004, Siemens launched its *One Siemens* strategy to enhance cooperation across the entire organisation. As part of this programme, Siemens developed a message hierarchy based on the key requirements of clarity, consistency and continuity. This hierarchy distinguished between communication messages at four levels: (1) corporate statements communicated to all stakeholders describing Siemens' reasons for being, (2) Siemens' value proposition communicated to customers, (3) market-specific sales stories communicated to all customers, and (4) specific internal and external messages (Kotler and Pfoertsch 2006).

When you have read this chapter, log on to the Online Learning Centre website at ***www.mcgraw-hill.co.uk/textbooks/biemans*** to explore chapter-by-chapter test questions, further reading and more online study tools.

Summary of Key Concepts

- Despite the variety of communication objectives used in practice, all communication ultimately serves to help sell the vendor's products and services.

- One-to-one communication allows B2B vendors to communicate with individual customers. In B2B markets, the most commonly used one-to-one communication tools are personal selling and direct marketing instruments such as direct mail, telemarketing and internet marketing.

- Mass communication allows B2B vendors to efficiently communicate with groups of customers. In B2B markets, the most commonly used mass communication tools are advertising, trade shows and public relations.

- In B2B markets, the most important communication tool is personal selling. The second most important communication tool is advertising. Personal selling and advertising are often used in combination, with advertising supporting and increasing the effectiveness and efficiency of personal selling.

- Direct marketing is a form of one-to-one communication where the vendor sends its messages directly to customers and prospects to stimulate a measurable response, mostly in terms of sales.

- The growing use of the internet has changed the nature of B2B communications. Vendors use websites to communicate with customers, identify prospects with Facebook and maintain relationships with YouTube and email.

- Email is increasingly used by B2B vendors to communicate with customers and other stakeholders. But the ever-growing volume of emails makes it increasingly difficult for vendors to cut through the clutter and communicate effectively.

- Trade shows are an important tool to communicate with a large group of customers, but may also be used to communicate one-to-one with individual customers visiting the trade show booth.

- Public relations (PR) is the management of beneficial relationships between a vendor and its publics, such as customers, suppliers, employees, competitors, shareholders, investors, politicians and the press. PR is relatively cheap, but allows the vendor only limited control.

- All communication efforts must be (a) coordinated across messages to communicate one consistent message to all relevant stakeholders, (b) coordinated across communication tools, and (c) coordinated with the use of the other marketing instruments.

🔑 Key Terms

Advertising, p. 224	Integrated communication, p. 238
Advertising effectiveness, p. 228	Internet marketing, p. 221
Advertising media, p. 226	Mass communication, p. 224
Advertising objectives, p. 224	One-to-one communication, p. 216
Communication planning, p. 214	Public relations (PR), p. 236
Communication strategy, p. 212	Telemarketing, p. 221
Direct mail, p. 218	Trade show management, p. 233
Direct marketing, p. 216	Trade shows, p. 230
Email marketing, p. 220	Webinar, p. 223

Discussion questions

1 The effectiveness of one-to-one communication strongly depends on the quality of the firm's database of customer information. As many firms have experienced, customer contact data quickly deteriorates. What specific measures can B2B vendors use to keep their customer contact information up to date?

2   Lately, several new media have emerged that may also be used by B2B firms; for instance, YouTube, Facebook and Twitter. What are the advantages of using such media for B2B marketing communications? What are their disadvantages? Describe the effectiveness of YouTube, Facebook and Twitter for achieving the communication objectives of creating awareness, increasing knowledge, maintaining relationships and encouraging orders.

3   Compare the advertising media most commonly used by business marketers. How are they different from each other? What are the advantages and disadvantages of each advertising medium?

4   To what extent are television and radio suitable for advertising business products? Which type of products are most likely to be advertised on television and radio?

5   Discuss a number of criteria that a firm can use to evaluate the effectiveness and efficiency of an in-house advertising department.

6   What are the advantages of direct mail, the internet, trade shows and catalogues compared with advertising? What are the most important disadvantages? Is it possible to rank the communication instruments in order of preference?

7   Telemarketing is sometimes considered to be the precursor of internet marketing. To what extent are these two media substitutes? In which situations or for what type of firms would telemarketing be preferable? When would internet marketing make more sense?

8   An effective channel policy requires that channel partners are treated as partners, which may result in joint advertising by the manufacturer and a reseller. What are the advantages and disadvantages of such a strategy? Is this strategy suitable for all B2B products?

9   In contrast to many other communication media, public relations is often criticised for its lack of control. How can B2B vendors increase their control over the content and effect of their public relations activities?

10 Integrated communication is often an elusive goal for B2B vendors. Why is it so difficult to achieve consistent integrated communication in B2B markets? What kind of circumstances make integrated communication easier to achieve?

Further reading

Berne, Carmen and M. E. García-Uceda (2008) Criteria involved in evaluation of trade shows to visit, *Industrial Marketing Management*, 37(5): 565–579.

Kitchen, Philip J., Joanne Brignell, Tao Li and Graham Spickett-Jones (2004) The emergence of IMC: a theoretical perspective, *Journal of Advertising Research*, 44(1): 19–30.

Lichtenthal, J. David and Shay Eliaz (2003) Internet integration in business marketing tactics, *Industrial Marketing Management*, 32(1): 3–13.

References

Berne, Carmen and M. E. García-Uceda (2008) Criteria involved in evaluation of trade shows to visit, *Industrial Marketing Management*, 37(5): 565–579.

Biemans, Wim G. and Henriëtte Setz (1995) Managing new product announcements in the Dutch telecommunications industry, in *Product Development: Meeting the Challenges of the Design–Marketing Interface*, Margaret Bruce and Wim G. Biemans (eds), Chichester: Wiley, pp. 207–229.

Blythe, Jim (2002) Using trade fairs in key account management, *Industrial Marketing Management*, 31(7): 627–635.

Dwyer, F. Robert and John F. Tanner (2006) *Business Marketing: Connecting Strategy, Relationships, and Learning*, third edition, New York: McGraw-Hill.

Hagel, John, III and Arthur C. Armstrong (1997) *Net Gain: Expanding Markets Through Virtual Communities*, Boston, MA: Harvard Business School Press.

Kitchen, Philip J., Joanne Brignell, Tao Li and Graham Spickett-Jones (2004) The emergence of IMC: a theoretical perspective, *Journal of Advertising Research*, 44(1): 19–30.

Kotler, Philip and Waldemar Pfoertsch (2006) *B2B Brand Management*, Heidelberg: Springer.

Lee, Chang Hyun and Sang Yong Kim (2008) Differential effects of determinants on multi-dimensions of trade show performance: by three stages of pre-show, at-show, and post-show activities, *Industrial Marketing Management*, 37(7): 784–796.

Lichtenthal, J. David and Shay Eliaz (2003) Internet integration in business marketing tactics, *Industrial Marketing Management*, 32(1): 3–13.

Lichtenthal, J. David, Vivek Yadav and Naveen Donthu (2006) Outdoor advertising for business markets, *Industrial Marketing Management*, 35(2): 236–247.

Smith, Timothy M., Srinath Gopalakrishna and Paul M. Smith (2004) The complementary effect of trade shows on personal selling, *International Journal of Research in Marketing*, 21(1): 61–76.

Notes

1 Booker, Ellis (2009) Social media use soars among b-to-b marketers, *BtoBonline.com*, 20 July, www.btobonline.com/apps/pbcs.dll/article?AID=/20090720/FREE/307159994/1445/FREE (accessed 6 September 2009).

2 Michiels, Ian (2008) Email marketing: get personal with your customers, Aberdeen Group, June.

3 Hanson, Bob (2007) Generating more sales at a lower cost: the Return-On-Investment (ROI) case for Webinars, Quantum Leap Marketing White Paper, August.

[4] For instance, research conducted by the Center for Exhibition Industry Research (CEIR), www.ceir.org.

[5] Lee Ann Obringer (2003) How trade shows work, www.howstuffworks.com, 1 January, http://money.howstuffworks.com/trade-show.htm (accessed 4 November 2008).

[6] *ExpoDisplays Trade Show Manual*, www.envisio.net/resources/expoideas.pdf (accessed 4 November 2008).

[7] See note 4.

Managing price

08

Chapter contents

Introduction

B2B vendors use products and services, sales and delivery channels and communication to create value for customers. Customers pay prices to enjoy the value offered by vendors. In other words, vendors use price to extract value from customers in return for the value offered to them. Price is a very important marketing instrument. Every firm's basic profit equation (profit = (sales × price) – cost) illustrates that effective pricing has a direct effect on the firm's bottom line. Nevertheless, the potential of price is often ignored and prices are all too often simply based on costs and bear no relationship to the value created for customers.

This chapter first discusses price from the perspective of both the customer and the vendor. Customers use price to assess the relative value of a vendor's offerings, while vendors use price to recoup their costs and investments. This perspective on price emphasises that prices should be based on the value offered to customers. But in practice this is not always the case. The chapter goes on to discuss the most commonly used methods for price setting, which are classified into (a) prices based on costs, (b) prices based on value, and (c) prices based on competition. It also explains that costs represent the lower limit on price, value the upper limit and competition further moderates the prices that can be charged. Next, the chapter discusses how different products and/or services may be related, which affects their pricing decisions. The chapter also discusses such common aspects of B2B pricing as negotiations, bidding and guaranteed pricing. From a management perspective, the chapter argues that successful B2B pricers understand the relationship between price, value, costs and competition, base their prices on detailed information about both the marketplace and the firm's operations, and use pricing as a tool to improve profits. The chapter concludes with a discussion of leasing and barter, which are sometimes used as alternatives to pricing.

8.1 The role of price

In most B2B firms, pricing does not receive the attention it deserves. Managers emphasise product benefits, quality and delivery times, and perceive price as something they have only limited control over. Managers are quick to point out that their product is a commodity or that in their industry pricing levels are set by a major competitor. As stated by Garda (1991: 17): 'Pricing is a bit like the weather. People complain about it; they worry about it; and in the end, they feel there is nothing much they can do about it.' But they are wrong! As Garda continues: 'But unlike the weather, pricing can in fact be controlled. It can be managed. And it can be a powerful profit tool for business.' Nevertheless, most B2B firms fail to investigate the effects of price. This limited interest in price is very surprising, considering the significant effects of effective price management on the firm's bottom line: on average, a 5 per cent price increase leads to a 22 per cent improvement in operating profits (Hinterhuber 2004).

Price from the customer's perspective

A customer compares the value of a vendor's offering with the price they have to pay for that offering (see also Chapter 2). A customer calculates the offering's net value by deducting the offering's costs from its benefits, and compares the net value from several alternative offerings from competing vendors. As illustrated in Figure 8.1, vendor B offers more benefits (expressed as monetary value) than vendor A, while its price is also lower. Nevertheless, customers will select vendor A because its much lower costs result in a higher net value.

In the situation depicted in Figure 8.1, the customer prefers vendor A's offering above the alternative offering from vendor B. While this illustrates the **role of price** from the customer's perspective, it assumes that customers are able to express all benefits and costs associated with a vendor's offering in monetary terms. In practice, this is not always the case; for instance, the value of a firm's technological reputation or a salesperson's willingness to go the extra mile may be difficult to capture in monetary terms.

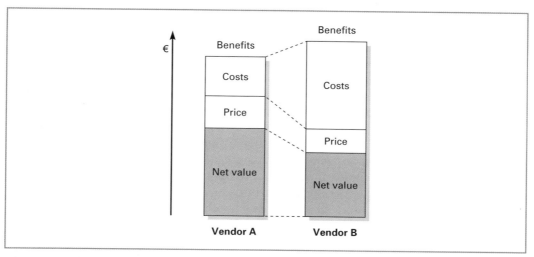

FIGURE 8.1 Price in the context of value

Successful vendors analyse not only the benefits and costs of their offerings, but also understand how their offerings contribute to their customers' value-creating processes. They know their customers' key success factors and how they can help to make them more successful.

Price from the vendor's perspective

From the vendor's perspective, price is conceptually different from all other marketing instruments. All other marketing instruments are employed to deliver value to customers; by developing products with useful features, offering support services that enhance the product's performance, using channels that match buying processes and communication needs, and communicating how customers can increase the benefits from the vendor's offering (*value creation*). Price, on the other hand, is used by a vendor to recoup investments and costs (*value extraction*). The basic equation for any business states that:

Profit = (Volume × Price) − Costs

Managers put a lot of effort into strategies and tactics to increase volume; for example, by developing new products, identifying new market segments, acquiring new customers, increasing customer retention, finding new product applications, employing interactive media, establishing new channels, improving channel partner performance and training salespeople. In addition, they look for methods and approaches to reduce costs; for instance, by selling products directly to customers, improving the firm's supplier base, cooperating with suppliers, redesigning the firm's business processes, reducing the number of employees and improving cross-functional coordination.

But strangely enough the third element of the equation, price, is typically neglected. Prices are accepted as a given, or as determined by large competitors or powerful customers. But a firm's profits are extremely sensitive to price. A 1 per cent price improvement, with stable volume, increases net income of the average S&P 1500 company by 8 per cent – an impact nearly 50 per cent greater than that of a 1 per cent fall in variable costs such as materials and direct labour, and more than three times greater than the impact of a 1 per cent increase in volume (Marn et al. 2003). A price improvement does not necessarily imply a price increase; when the price is too high, a price reduction will have a positive influence on profits.

But lately, this situation appears to be changing. Results from the 2007 Global B2B Pricing Benchmark Survey, in which more than 500 pricing professionals participated, shows that business pricing groups have become larger and more influential, have taken on more strategic responsibility and are investing in better processes, tools and capabilities.[1] Most respondents (72 per cent) cited 'improved profits/margins' as the principal driver of their pricing strategy, and 82 per cent cited a 'high' or 'very high' level of executive attention to the pricing function. In addition, the recent global credit crisis has further illustrated the need for careful price management. Being able to charge the right prices for the right customers may be a company's greatest source of value.

⟨⟩ INSIGHT: Pricing software for better pricing decisions

Most firms respond to economic crises, such as the 2009–2010 global credit crisis, by cutting costs in an effort to improve their bottom line. But leading companies realise that this may erode their capabilities and competitive advantage. Instead, they use the hidden opportunities of price optimisation. Price optimisation technology leverages a company's transactional data and combines it with statistical techniques and business application software to improve pricing decisions. Price optimisation measures opportunities to differentiate prices for individual deals, customers or geographic regions. Prices are delivered to the salesforce as a band of price points (start, target and ceiling), to be used during negotiations with customers. While the underlying mathematics may be quite complex, the output of price optimisation software is intuitive and simple for business users to understand and act upon. Price optimisation is especially relevant during economic downturns, when growth begins to stall and inferior pricing practices (intuition, rule of thumb) further decrease profits. During an economic upturn, too, price optimisation is also a useful tool to get rid of rudimentary pricing practices and increase profits.

Because price improvements have an immediate effect on the bottom line, the impact can be significant. After deploying price optimisation software, one Fortune 500 industrial manufacturer watched its operating margins grow by 12.8 per cent in one year. For another Global 1000 manufacturer, price optimisation technology generated $40 million of incremental margin and was recognised as the company's 'most impactful growth initiative of the year'.

Several software firms offer software solutions to improve pricing decisions. Zilliant, for example, offers a broad range of pricing software solutions that help business firms 'to adopt quantitative, data-driven pricing practices across all facets of pricing – segmentation, analysis, setting, and execution – to increase their revenue and profit'. In addition to its software, which is designed specifically for large manufacturing, distribution and industrial service companies, Zilliant also offers deep pricing domain expertise, standardised methodologies and a wide range of best practices. According to Zilliant, it has been proven to increase its customers' margins by 10–15 per cent and more.

Sources: www.zilliant.com and Peters (2008)

8.2 Drivers of price

There are three major factors that influence pricing decisions: costs, value and competition. Each of these three factors can be used as a driver for price setting in business markets.

These **drivers of price** are described below.

Cost-based pricing

The most frequently used methods to determine prices of B2B products are based on costs. Technology-oriented firms, in particular, use costs as the main driver of prices. The logic of basing prices on costs makes intuitive sense: costs are real and visible and prices need to be higher than the costs incurred to generate profits. In addition, **cost-based pricing** methods are easy to understand and apply, with prices based on costs according to a fixed formula. Small firms especially base their prices on costs incurred; prices below cost are detrimental to the firm's financial health and the resulting problems may threaten the firm's viability. The three most commonly used cost-based pricing methods are cost-plus pricing, target-rate-of-return pricing and geographical pricing.

Cost-plus pricing

With *cost-plus pricing* a vendor determines the price by calculating the costs of the offering and adding an amount to represent profit. The costs may be calculated using the offering's direct costs and indirect costs, as well as part of the fixed costs that are allocated to the offering, resulting in a per unit cost of the offering. Next, a predetermined percentage of these costs or a fixed amount is added to provide a profit margin. Ideally, the price is such that it recovers both the offering's variable costs and the allocated part of the fixed costs and contributes to the firm's profit. *Variable costs* are expenses that change in proportion to the firm's level of production or sales. They may be directly associated with an offering (*direct costs*, such as the costs of labour and materials) or indirectly associated with an offering (*indirect costs*, such as manufacturing overhead costs). Variable costs are expressed as costs per unit. In contrast, *fixed costs* do not vary in proportion with the activity level of the business; examples are salaries, rent, depreciation, property tax and insurance. To calculate an offering's total costs, the fixed costs must be allocated across all offerings. The appropriate allocation key is not always easy to determine. Activity-based costing links every activity to the resources it uses and thus avoids rather arbitrary cost allocations.

The cost-plus pricing formula is as follows:

$$P = (VC + aFC) \times (1 + MK)$$

P = price
VC = unit variable costs
FC = fixed costs
a = percentage of fixed costs allocated to the offering
MK = mark-up percentage

The mark-up percentage may be either a fixed percentage or vary per product, product group or situation; for instance, when different market segments are characterised by different intensities of competition. Some firms ignore the fixed costs and just increase the offering's variable costs with a predetermined percentage; for instance, many resellers add a percentage to the product's purchase price paid to their suppliers. In these cases, the fixed costs allocation is incorporated in the mark-up percentage. When it is not possible to recover an offering's total costs, vendors may base their prices on the variable costs and only part of the allocated fixed costs. This strategy is used by hotels and airlines when they are stuck with unsold rooms or seats. Naturally, price should at least recover the variable costs. Extreme pricing, with the price set at or below variable costs, is sometimes used to acquire an important customer or large order.

Some customers demand information about the vendor's cost structure to assess whether the prices are fair. Others make detailed cost estimates to evaluate prices. With target cost analysis, customers use the price of their own offering to calculate the prices they are willing to pay for materials and components. This may result in price negotiations or even in product redesign to arrive at a better cost structure for the product. Vendors also use target costing to establish price objectives and pricing ranges during product development.

Target rate of return pricing
With *target rate of return pricing* a vendor uses a predetermined return objective (x% of invested capital, y% of sales revenue) to calculate the price using the following formula:

$$P = VC + (FC + RR)/S$$

RR = target rate of return
S = sales volume

In practice, firms may use more complex formulas that also allow for interest rates, tax rates and inflation percentages. The major advantage of this price-setting method is that it achieves the desired rate of return on investments in production and distribution. The most important disadvantage is that the target rate of return is typically set as a rule of thumb instead of based on solid reasoning. Use of target rate of return pricing may also result in increasing prices: a price increase leads to reduced sales, which increases the variable costs per unit and therefore further increases the price of the product. A related pricing method is *break-even pricing*, which calculates the price where total revenues equal total costs. Because the rate of return is 0 at the break-even point, the break-even price is calculated as:

$$P = VC + FC/S$$

Geographical pricing

A vendor selling to several geographical regions may use *geographical pricing* to modify a basic list price based on the customer's geographical location. This pricing method reflects the shipping costs to different locations. Commonly used geographical pricing methods are:

- *Free on Board (FoB) origin*: the shipping costs are paid by the customer; ownership of the goods is transferred to the customer as soon as the product leaves the point of origin.
- *Zone pricing*: prices increase as the shipping distance from the manufacturing plant or warehouse to the customer increases. Different price zones represent different shipping costs. Sometimes, this is simplified and price zones are established as concentric circles around the manufacturing plant or warehouse.
- *Basing point pricing*: all goods shipped from a specified basing point (usually a city) are charged the same amount.
- *Freight-absorption pricing*: the vendor pays for all or part of the shipping costs (which is essentially a price discount).

When all customers are charged the same price, it is called *uniform delivery pricing* (or postage stamp pricing). There are obvious advantages to using cost-based pricing methods: they are easy to use, require only minimal information and insure sellers against unpredictable later costs. But there are also disadvantages: they kill the incentive for efficiency improvements and ignore market opportunities, market demand and competitors.

The popularity of cost-based pricing is a sign of naivety. Prices should reflect the value offered to customers, which has nothing to do with the costs incurred. Generally, a vendor's costs represent the bottom of the acceptable price range.

Value-based pricing

While the vendor's costs determine the lowest price to be charged, the value offered to customers sets an upper limit on price. When different customers perceive different levels of value, vendors can use **value-based pricing** to charge different prices. Sealed Air Corporation is a manufacturer of packaging materials, including the well-known Bubble Wrap packaging and Jiffy Mailers (protective padded envelopes). Sealed Air discovered that some customers could also use alternative packagings, while other customers enjoyed significant benefits from using Sealed Air's products (such as reduced product damage and increased speed and reliability of the packaging process). By using price differentiation the company managed to become one of the world's leading packaging firms. There are several methods to estimate customers' price sensitivity (Dolan and Simon 1996):

- *Expert judgement.* Several experts (at least ten) are interviewed to provide information about the lowest realistic price, the highest realistic price, the medium price, and expected sales volumes at these three prices. Experts should have different functional backgrounds (sales, marketing, general management) and discuss divergent results to obtain consensus. This low-cost method works well in B2B markets with few customers, where experts have in-depth knowledge about individual customers.

- *Customer surveys.* Customers are asked how they would respond to certain price changes, using questions such as: What is the likelihood you would purchase this product at price X? At what price would you definitely buy this product? How much would you be willing to pay for this product? How much of this product would you purchase at price Y? At which price difference would you switch from product A to product B? Customer preferences can also be obtained through a conjoint measurement experiment, where customers are shown a series of two alternative product descriptions and asked each time which one they prefer. The resulting data can be analysed statistically to determine the perceived importance of price.

- *Price experiments.* Particularly for frequently purchased B2B products, prices can be varied and their effect on sales and market shares observed. The advantage is that actual customer behaviour is observed, but the method is relatively expensive and time-consuming.

- *Analysis of historical market data.* Similarly, analysis of historical data also offers information about the effect of price on sales and market share. This method is especially useful for markets with frequent price fluctuations. Statistical methods can be used to estimate price response and price elasticity.

Most B2B vendors have only limited insight into the price sensitivity of their customers and simply do not know how customers will react to price changes.

Perceived-value pricing

With *perceived-value pricing* a vendor bases its prices on the perceptions of customers regarding the value of the offering. Both benefits and costs are calculated and the highest price that a customer is willing to pay equals the offering's perceived benefits minus costs. The use of perceived-value pricing requires detailed insight into the offering's attributes, customer perceptions and the customer's circumstances (Cross and Dixit 2005). In the chemical industry, prices of materials used to seal pipes are based on the costs of cleaning up leaked products and the avoidance of customers' potential liability. And when an airline purchases an aircraft with new jet engines that offer 1 per cent increase in fuel efficiency, this saves millions of euros per year, but also allows the airline to fly longer routes non-stop.

Using information about customers' price sensitivity, vendors can charge premium prices when customer value is high. A vendor of gas escaped the commodity trap by segmenting buyers on the basis of their risk. Low-risk customers (with predictable and stable energy requirements) were offered standard capacity at a standard price. But high-risk customers (who face extreme peaks in their energy requirements) received a guaranteed additional capacity at a relatively high price.

While perceived-value pricing makes perfect sense from a theoretical perspective, it is not always easy to implement in practice. A customer's perception of a product's value, for example, depends on subjective factors related to the product itself or to the customer's particular circumstances in relation to the product. In urgent situations customers are willing to pay premium prices. In addition, vendors may find it hard to estimate the costs associated with their product, which requires detailed information about the product's expected economic life, resale value, tax advantages, investment subsidies, interest rates and inflation. Sometimes, customers make investments that benefit more than one specific product; for instance, when production workers must be trained in a new manufacturing technology. Allocating these costs to different products, some of which will be purchased in the future, is often problematic. Finally, cost elements like the risk of product failure (resulting in downtime) and fear of incorrect deliveries are difficult to express in monetary terms.

 INSIGHT: Performance-based pricing in the capital goods industry

Some vendors in the capital goods industry base their prices on the performance of their equipment. A well-known example is General Electric selling power by the hour. There are three types of performance-based pricing:

- *Input-based prices relating to the intensity of use*: number of times used, time of use (number of operating hours), number of end-products produced, number of users.

- *Output-based prices relating to performance levels of the capital goods*: performance (maximum output/hour), availability (up-time of capital goods, necessary maintenance periods), quality (manufacturing tolerances, number of rejects).

- *Output-based prices relating to the customer's economic results from using the capital goods*: cost savings realised, revenues generated, contribution margin or profit generated.

Price per user and prices based on quantity or quality of output are particularly frequently used. Performance-based pricing transfers part of the buyer's risk to the vendor and requires the buyer to pay a higher price. Buyers should consider performance-based prices in high-risk situations, such as when their demand is highly specific and innovative, when there are numerous and heterogeneous fields of applicability, when the procurement market is complex, and when single decisions constitute a rather high financial burden. Performance-based prices can help reduce potential negative effects and also let the buyer profit from better performance. Vendors should only use performance-based pricing when this allows them to create a competitive advantage without substantial risks. This means that the parameter measuring performance should be within the vendor's sphere of influence (for instance, cost savings or production tolerances). If the performance parameter is not completely under the vendor's control (for instance, output, contribution to profit), it needs higher prices to compensate for the risk.

Vendors implementing performance-based pricing must decide which parameters to use and how to measure them, which proportion of the price to make variable and which amount to ask for more or less immediately and whether to combine the concept with other price instruments (such as finance offers for the fixed portion of the price). Performance-based pricing can be used to attract new customers and realise a price premium, but this requires additional marketing efforts, such as carefully explaining the potential advantages to customers.

Source: Hünerberg and Hüttmann (2003)

Competition-based pricing

Customers will always compare a vendor's offering with the next-best alternative. Therefore, it is better to say that the highest price that can be charged is determined by the offering's relative value as perceived by the customer. The importance of competition depends on the number of buyers and sellers and the extent to which sellers are able to differentiate their offerings in a way that matters to customers. European state-owned telecommunication and energy firms used to enjoy monopolies and high margins, but this changed drastically when these markets were deregulated and competition arrived in full force.

When pricing new business offerings, the expected reactions from major competitors are also important. Competitors are not always able to react adequately. When a vendor launches a new product at a low price, or reduces the prices of existing offerings, competitors may be unable to respond quickly because they are locked into long-term contracts with customers or are unable to replicate patented process improvements. When a low price is expected to be followed immediately by competitors' price reductions, vendors may prefer to reduce prices indirectly and only communicate this directly to customers. Examples of indirect price reductions are more beneficial terms of payment, lower prices for supplementary services and higher discounts. B2B vendors who want to temporarily reduce prices, but prevent a price war, should carefully inform their competitors of the temporary nature of the price changes (for instance, through a press release). However, they should be careful of not breaking the law and being accused of collusion. Examples of **competition-based pricing** are going-rate pricing and following the price leader.

MINI CASE: PRICE FIXING BY LCD MAKERS

In 2008, coordinated efforts of enforcement officials in Europe, Asia and the US uncovered an international price-fixing cartel. Three leading flatscreen producers, located in South Korea, Japan and Taiwan, pled guilty and agreed to pay a total of $585 million in criminal fines for their role in fixing the price of liquid crystal display panels. The price-fixing conspiracy affected screens sold to American companies, such as Dell, Motorola and Apple. The price-fixing cartel was an effort to slow the speed of price declines. In the second half of 2008, the price of a 15.4-inch panel for a notebook PC dropped from $97 to $63, and a 32-inch LCD for a television went from $321 to $223. But without the price-fixing scheme, LCD screens would be even cheaper, and because the screen represents 10 to 20 per cent of the total cost of a notebook, millions of customers were harmed by this illegal practice.

Source: *International Herald Tribune*, 13 November 2008.

Going-rate pricing

With *going-rate pricing* a vendor sets the price at the level of the average price charged by other firms in the industry (that is, the market price). This practice is typically used when products from different vendors are nearly identical. For many products it is easy to establish the market price by using online markets such as MachineTools.com and eSpotMarket.com.

Follow the price leader

When one vendor enjoys such a powerful market position that other vendors match its price changes (both price increases and price reductions), such a vendor is called a *price leader*. The price leader serves as the pricing benchmark for the rest of the market. This pricing policy leads to a stable market, but may also result in cartels and price collusion. One firm with a dominant market share may act as price leader, but price leadership may also be assumed by a small group of dominant competitors. Price leaders are usually also market leaders, but this is not always the case. Price leadership is also context dependent: a firm may be price leader for one group of products but a price follower for other products. When the price leader enjoys a very dominant market position, the strategy of following the price leader is identical to using going-rate pricing.

The largest disadvantage of *competition-based pricing* is that it assumes that the firm's offerings, cost structure, market position and image are identical to those of its competitors. Often, this is not the case and competition-based pricing is a sign of weakness. But competitors' prices must be taken into account because customers will also use them as a point of reference in assessing a vendor's net value. The offering's perceived value to customers indicates the maximum price that can be charged and the variable costs per unit represent the minimum price. Competitors' prices distort this picture; for instance, when a major competitor charges a price

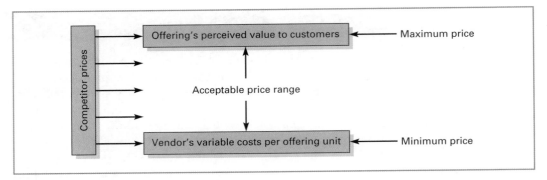

FIGURE 8.2 Key determinants of price

below the offering's perceived value, this reduces the attractiveness of the vendor's offering and further limits the vendor's acceptable price range (Figure 8.2).

Price setting

The offering's perceived value, its costs per unit and the prices of competitors serve as the basic building blocks for price setting. Depending on the nature of the situation (new or existing product, single product or a number of related products, one-time project or long-term relationship) and the firm's pricing objectives (profit maximisation, market share maximisation, acquiring new customers, retaining existing customers) the optimal price is established; for instance, when launching a new product a vendor may use skimming or penetration pricing (Table 8.1). With *skimming*, the product is launched at a relatively high price to quickly recoup development costs and investments. This strategy is directed at innovative customers, who are less price sensitive, while subsequent price reductions are used to attract other more price-sensitive customers. *Penetration pricing*, on the other hand, means that the product is introduced at a relatively low price to maximise sales and market share in the short term.

In addition, the purchase situation influences the price as well. In many B2B markets, a distinction can be made between initial demand and replacement demand. When a buyer purchases a product for the first time, there is less time pressure and buyers can use the available time to identify alternative vendors, evaluate their offerings and negotiate on price. But in replacement markets, buyers are in a hurry to replace the product and fast delivery of components or a replacement product is more important than price; for instance, because every hour of downtime is very expensive. The cost of downtime includes not only the costs of unproductive labour and equipment, but also the costs of supervising repairs, rescheduling employees, setting up equipment, having a quality control inspection at start-up, having a plant manager on the scene to set priorities and get the facts first-hand, downtime-related scrap and bringing in consultants. In addition, prolonged downtime may also result in lost transactions or lost

TABLE 8.1 Circumstances that favour skimming and penetration pricing

Skimming	Penetration pricing
• The product is protected by a patent or other entry barrier, such as close relationships with key customers • It is a really innovative product that offers significant value to customers, such as cost reductions or the opportunity to develop new products • Customers are willing to pay a higher price for the product's benefits; for instance, because early adoption of the new product creates a competitive advantage and an innovative image • The firm's primary objective is to maximise profit or to realise a specified payback period (rather than to develop long-term relationships with customers) • The product has a relatively short lifetime, which means that investments must be recouped quickly • There are many weak potential competitors or competitors that are expected to react slowly • There is uncertainty concerning the appropriate price level; when the price is wrong it can always be reduced (for instance, by offering discounts or changing the terms of payment), while price increases are often impossible • There are distinct market segments with different levels of price sensitivity	• Customers seem to be very price sensitive; for instance, because of large similarities between products, budget restrictions or purchasing procedures • Manufacturing and distribution costs reduce significantly when the sales volume increases • There are strong potential competitors looking for opportunities to grow; this is particularly important when there are established vendors with close relationships with key customers • The firm's primary objective is to grow market share by creating close relationships with key customers (rather than short-term profits) • The product has benefits that only become visible after it is used; diffusion is encouraged by communication between customers • Launch of the product will also increase sales of complementary products • The market is characterised by very close relationships between vendors and customers; a low introductory price may be the only way to achieve sales

customers. The estimated downtime costs per hour vary from €40,000 for a computer network to several million euros for companies that rely entirely on technology, such as online brokerages, trading platforms and e-commerce sites.

8.3 Pricing a product line

Many pricing decisions do not involve a single product, but a number of related products – **product line pricing**. In B2B markets, two common relationships between products are:

- An increase in demand for product A leads to a higher demand for product B (A and B are *complements*).
- An increase in demand for product A leads to a lower demand for product B (A and B are *substitutes*).

Pricing complementary products

When an increase in demand for product A results in a higher demand for complementary product B, this product B brings the firm additional margins and profit that can be attributed to the sales of product A. This reduces the variable unit cost of A, which impacts the optimal price for A: the optimal product-line price for A is lower than the optimal isolated price. Some profit from A is sacrificed in order to get an overall higher profit from the whole line. An example of complementary B2B products is a vendor charging separate prices for both a tangible product (for example, an elevator) and the accompanying support services (for example, maintenance and repair). In such situations, vendors often modify prices over the life cycle. If the initial service price is too high, customers applying life-cycle costing will not buy the product. This suggests a relatively low service price at the beginning to encourage product sales and build a service base. Later on, when product sales start to decline, increased service prices offset reduced product sales. This increases profits, but may also encourage customers to switch to a follow-up product. Frequently, the service life cycle is much longer than the product life cycle (in the case of elevators, the service cycle can be ten times longer).

Another example of complementary products is when a vendor unbundles elements of a product and starts charging separate prices for them; for instance, an engineering firm makes detailed blueprints as part of its tendering process. When it does not win the construction project, the costs of these blueprints are charged to the firm's overhead and need to be covered by the prices of other projects that are awarded to the firm. Because the blueprints require a significant investment, the engineering firm may split its offering into making blueprints and implementing building projects. Both the blueprints and building projects are offered and priced separately, which means that customers will always pay for the blueprints, even when they award the building project to another firm. The feasibility of such an unbundling strategy depends on the firm's relative power position and on what is customary in the industry. The unbundling strategy might even result in the engineering firm specialising in blueprints and leaving the implementation of the building projects to others. Unbundling also occurs for business services, where accountants may offer fraud detection and auditing a customer's financial statements as two separate services.

Pricing substitute products

The pricing of substitutes can be illustrated with an example from the chemical industry, where a firm introduced a new special-use chemical, NEW (Dolan and Simon 1996). The product was expected to substitute partially for the firm's current product, OLD, which had a market share of 39 per cent and was the market leader. Because the firm did not want to upset the current market situation of stable prices, it imposed the constraint that the price of OLD should not be reduced, because this could have triggered competitive reactions. The firm's management requested that the price for NEW be set to maximise product-line profit. A conjoint measurement study was used to estimate market share curves. If NEW were priced at €27.50 per kilogram, rather than €32.80 per kilogram, its market share would go up from 12 to 21 per cent. But this 9 per cent market share gain comes largely from OLD, which loses six market share points or 17.6 per cent (6/34) of its original business. Because of this strong cannibalisation between the two products, management decided to launch NEW at the relatively high price of €32.80. This sacrifices some profit from NEW, but maximises total profits from both products. Because the price of OLD was only €18.50 per kilogram, the large price difference allowed the firm to position the two products very differently, which would minimise cannibalisation.

8.4 Pricing tactics: negotiations, competitive bidding and guaranteed prices

Pricing decisions involve more than formulating pricing objectives and pricing strategies. Various pricing tactics may play a key role in setting prices for B2B offerings, such as negotiations, competitive bidding and guaranteed prices.

Negotiations

While some B2B products are sold at fixed prices, most prices for B2B products are the result of **negotiations** between buyer and seller. Table 8.2 displays the characteristics of three negotiation strategies: competition, collaboration and adaptation. The negotiation strategy used depends on the buyer's relative power, the frequency of negotiations between both parties, the number of issues that are the subject of the negotiations (just price, or also quality and delivery times?) and time pressure. Most buyers prefer a collaborative strategy.

Usually, price is just one of the issues negotiated on. In addition to price, buyers and sellers also negotiate on inventory levels, product designs, production methods, advertising efforts, delivery schedules, packagings, after-sales service, complaint handling, order procedures, communication lines and product guarantees. The first lesson for vendors is that they should try to make the sale based on the added value of their offering. Only when the added value has been made clear and the value claims substantiated, does price enter the discussion. For each sale, the vendor needs to make a value-added analysis, comparing the value of its offering with that of the next-best alternative.

Discounts

A key topic in most price negotiations is the **discounts** provided by the vendor. Although most vendors use list prices, which are quoted to potential buyers, it is a common practice to offer discounts. Because of the widespread use of discounts, actual prices are typically much lower than the published list prices and it is sometimes difficult for a vendor to determine the actual prices paid by customers. In contrast to direct price reductions, price discounts are less visible and more difficult to identify and copy by competitors. Discounts have also become an essential part of the game: in some industries, purchasers are more focused on the discount negotiated than the actual price to be paid! They perceive high discounts as a sign of their superior negotiation skills.

A well-designed discount system is an important tool to create competitive advantage. The most commonly used discount is the *quantity discount*, which

TABLE 8.2 Characteristics of different negotiation strategies

Aspect	Competition	Collaboration	Adaptation
Key attitude	'I win, you lose'	'What's the best way to address the needs of all parties?'	'You win, I lose'
Pay-off structure	Usually a fixed amount of resources to be divided	Usually a variable amount of resources to be divided	Usually a fixed amount of resources to be divided
Goal pursuit	Pursuit of own goals at the expense of those of others	Pursuit of goals held jointly with others	Subordination of own goals in favour of those of others
Relationships	Short-term focus; parties do not expect to work together in the future	Long-term focus; parties expect to work together in the future	May be short term (let the other win to keep them happy) or long term (let the other win to encourage reciprocity in the future)
Primary motivation	Maximise own outcome	Maximise joint outcome	Maximise other's outcome or let them gain to enhance the relationship
Trust and openness	Secrecy and defensiveness; high trust in self, low trust in others	Trust and openness, active listening, joint exploration of alternatives	One party relatively open, exposing own vulnerability to the other
Knowledge of needs	Parties know own needs, but conceal or misrepresent them; neither party lets the other know real needs	Parties know and convey real needs while seeking and responding to the needs of the other	One party is over-responsive to the other's needs so as to repress own needs
Predictability	Parties use unpredictability and surprise to confuse the other side	Parties are predictable and flexible when appropriate, trying not to surprise	One party's actions are totally predictable, always catering to the other side
Aggressiveness	Parties use threats and bluffs, trying to keep the upper hand	Parties share information honestly, treat each other with understanding and respect	One party gives up on own position to mollify the other
Solution search behaviour	Parties make effort to appear committed to position, using argumentation and manipulation of the other	Parties make effort to find mutually satisfying solutions, using logic, creativity and constructiveness	One party makes effort to find ways to accommodate the other
Success measures	Success enhanced by creating bad image of the other; increased levels of hostility and strong in-group loyalty	Success demands abandonment of bad images and consideration of ideas on their merit	Success determined by minimising or avoiding conflict and soothing all hostility; own feeling ignored in favour of harmony
Evidence of unhealthy extreme	One party assumes total-zero-sum game; defeating the other becomes a goal in itself	One subsumes all self-interest in the common good, losing self-identity and self-responsibility	Abdication to the other is complete, at expense of personal and/or constituent goals
Remedy for breakdown	If impasse occurs, mediator or arbitrator may be needed	If difficulties occur, a group dynamics facilitator may be needed	If behaviour becomes chronic, party becomes bankrupt in regard to the negotiation

Source: Dwyer and Tanner (2006: 423). Reprinted with permission.

reduces prices for large purchases, passing on economies of scale from large orders to the customer. Cumulative quantity discounts are based on the quantity purchased over a set period of time, thus increasing switching costs and stimulating loyalty. Non-cumulative quantity discounts are based on the quantity of a single order, thus encouraging larger orders, reducing billing, order filling, shipping and sales personnel expenses. *Cash discounts for prompt payment* encourage timely payments and improve the firm's liquidity. Examples are 2/10 net 30 (buyers must pay within 30 days of the invoice date, but receive a 2 per cent discount if they pay within ten days), 3/7 EOM (buyers receive a cash discount of 3 per cent if they pay within seven days after the end of the month indicated on the invoice date) and 2/15 net 40 ROG (buyers must pay within 40 days of receipt of goods, but receive a 2 per cent discount if they pay within 15 days of the receipt of goods). Large customers sometimes pay too late, but deduct the cash discount anyway. *Functional* or *trade discounts* are offered to channel members for performing a specified function, such as warehousing, shipping or product installation. Trade discounts are common in industries where channel members hold powerful positions. Other examples of discount are cash discounts for preferred payment method (for instance, cash payment to avoid credit card transaction fees), seasonal discounts (given during slack periods), forward dating (moving forward the date on the invoice), promotional allowances (for promotional activities performed by the buyer) and trade-ins (to encourage replacement sales).

In designing a price discount structure, vendors must address the following questions (Day and Ryans 1988):

1 *Who are the target customers?* Discounts can be offered to all customers or a few customers can be selectively targeted. Universities receive discounts on computers and teaching hospitals on medical equipment. Most discounts are paid to the buying organisation, but some of them are given to individual employees (such as frequent flyer miles). Another form of selectivity is based on the customer's willingness to make prior commitments to purchase according to a mutually agreed schedule (such as negotiated blanket orders).

2 *What is included?* Most discounts are based on an order for a single product, while others apply to purchases of all products from a product line (especially effective for full-line vendors). Cumulative quantity discounts apply to all purchases of a product over a specified period of time.

3 *What is the discount schedule?* This involves decisions about break points, flat portions and the size of the discounts. A complex discount schedule capitalises on differences between customers, but also increases the costs of administering and communicating the schedule.

4 *What form does the discount take?* The most common form of discount is a direct price discount, either a reduction in the invoiced price or a rebate at the end of an agreed time period. Discounts can also take a non-price form, such as more favourable terms of payment, free goods and reduced charges for delivery.

Customers will demand higher discounts when there are fewer customers, they represent a large proportion of the vendor's sales, the purchase involves a high euro amount, the product is standardised, the product is not important to the value of the customer's product, switching costs are low and customers are well informed about demand, costs and prices. Thanks to the internet and online e-markets, customers are better informed about real market prices.

Price discount programmes run the risk of customers becoming used to them, which makes them difficult to change or remove. Vendors must carefully assess how the price discount programme impacts customers and salespeople. A complex discount schedule hides the benefits to customers and may result in misunderstandings with salespeople. Sometimes, evaluation and compensation systems need to be changed to encourage the salesforce to use the discount programme. Finally, an implemented discount programme must be administered by the vendor's order handling, billing and accounting systems and be continuously modified to reflect changed market conditions.

Online negotiations

Internet technology has significantly changed many aspects of B2B marketing and selling, including pricing. E-marketplaces allow networks of buyers and sellers to conduct business online and exchange information about trading conditions and prices. Online auctions are used to negotiate prices for a wide range of products, varying from MRO supplies, chemicals, metals and coal to computers, components, programming services and even cattle. Perishable products, in particular, such as advertising space, are auctioned online. The product or service is offered by the seller and customers offer increasing incremental bids. The bidder with the most advantageous bid for the seller wins.

Alternatively, *reverse auctions* are initiated by the buyer, inviting potential vendors to bid on announced requests for quotations (RFQs), featuring decreasing incremental bidding. The price offered by vendors continues to decrease until a theoretical market price is achieved (Smeltzer and Carr 2002). Using an electronic format, vendors observe the price changing in real time, allowing them to note the prices offered by competitors, as well as the price required to obtain the sale. Reverse auctions offer buyers the advantages of reduced purchase prices, administrative costs and inventory levels, access to new vendors and information about market prices. Vendors participate in reverse auctions to obtain additional sales, penetrate new markets, understand competitors' pricing, reduce administrative costs and reduce cycle time between bid and actual sale.

But reverse auctions also have potential disadvantages. The largest disadvantage for vendors is that the purchase decision may be based entirely on the lowest price. Thus, vendors that offer better value at a higher price will lose to low-cost competitors. Buyers may include non-price aspects in reverse auctions through extensive pre-qualification of potential bidders, weights based on a vendor's expected performance on non-price aspects, and post-bid negotiations that focus on non-price characteristics (Schoenherr and Mabert 2007). Other disadvantages are that buyers only use online auctions to negotiate better prices from existing or preferred vendors, or that vendors get caught up in the emotions of the race and offer unreasonably low prices. A disadvantage to buyers is that the practice may destroy vendors' trust and discourage them from investing in the relationship. Some infuriated vendors refuse to bid on a customer's business for years. Another potential disadvantage to buyers is that only a few vendors respond and a competitive price does not develop. A rule of thumb states that four or five competitive bidders are required for an effective reverse auction. In addition, one must realise that a reverse auction only automates a part of the buying process. The auction may be very efficient, but some 97 per cent of the purchasing effort is still conducted offline (such as preparing the request for proposals and screening potential vendors). The spectacular cost savings mentioned in the business press are not always achieved. Finally, frequent vendor changes increase the buyer's switching costs. Some firms give their incumbent vendors an advantage by not requiring them to be the lowest bidder to retain the business; for instance, they may allow the incumbent bid to be 20 per cent higher than the lowest bid. To conclude, it has been suggested that reverse auctions should only be used in situations with easily defined products, many qualified bidders, excess capacity in the supply base, low switching costs and no contract barriers (Mabert and Skeels 2002).

Competitive bidding

Government contracts, in particular, are often awarded through a process of competitive bidding, where potential vendors are invited to submit a bid for a project. In the European Union, the process of **competitive bidding** is regulated through extensive rules and procedures. Before 1 January 2006, for example, EU member states had to adopt the 'competitive dialogue', a new procurement procedure for public sector contracts, aimed at opening up national markets for government procurement to greater competition.

With *closed bidding*, pre-qualified potential vendors are invited to submit written, sealed proposals (bids) for a particular business opportunity. The request for proposals contains detailed specifications, but also information about delivery schedules, structure of the proposal, payments, guarantees, installation, training and certification. The contract is generally awarded to the lowest bidder who meets the formulated specifications. Some vendors are known to submit very low bids, followed by price hikes when the project has been awarded. Experienced firms take this kind of opportunistic behaviour into account. When a buyer uses closed bidding, it is critical for vendors to be invited to the bidding process (relationship marketing). *Open bidding*, on the other hand, is a more informal process, where any vendor can bid for the business up to a certain date. This allows the buyer to deliberate with several vendors during the bidding process. Open bidding is used when specifications are defined rigidly and when customer needs are only vaguely defined. In the latter case, the buyer is likely to publish functional specifications. The buyer negotiates a price with the vendor with the best proposal.

INSIGHT: Eight hidden costs of bidding

1 *There are better uses of your time*: making a bid takes much more time and effort than just looking up a price. That time and effort could also be used to serve current customers.

2 *When you win the business, you lose money*: a customer who is won on price alone is telling you that they have no loyalty. You can only make money on the project when you have a lower cost structure than the incumbent vendor.

3 *The incumbent can retaliate*: if you win a good customer, your win is someone else's loss and the incumbent vendor is likely to respond.

4 *Your existing customers will want a better deal*: the price that won the deal is unlikely to stay secret and will encourage current customers to ask for a similarly attractive deal.

5 *New customers will use the low price as a benchmark*: new customers will also focus on the low price.

6 *Competitors will also use the low price as a benchmark*: even if the low price was an exception, competitors will expect the low price in the future and thus create a downward pressure on price.

7 *It gives your customers' competitors a better cost position*: giving your customer's competitor to get a better cost position will hurt your own customers.

8 *Do not destroy your competitors' glass houses*: if you make things too difficult for the competition, they are more likely to go after your customers.

Source: Brandenburger and Nalebuff (1996)

Before submitting a bid a vendor should analyse the results from previous bid situations. Two common mistakes are: (1) only analysing the firm's own bids, without comparing them to competing bids, and (2) comparing the firm's own prices (for both won and lost projects) with the competitive prices that won projects. Both mistakes lead to a downward pressure on prices. The only relevant comparison is the one between real market prices, that is, both the vendor's prices and the prices of competitors that won the customer's business. Next, a vendor must decide whether to focus on the short or long term. In many industries, initially won business from a new customer may be just the first of several lucrative follow-up contracts. In other situations (particularly with some government projects) it is not permitted to award a follow-up contract to the initial vendor.

MINI CASE: MASSIVE BUILDING FRAUD IN THE NETHERLANDS

Unfortunately, competitive bidding is no guarantee of realising real market prices. In many industries there are examples of price cartels: agreements between competing firms to keep prices at an artificially high level. For instance, in 2001 it became obvious that Dutch building companies had massively cheated on their customers. The former director of building firm Koop Tjuchem revealed a widespread fraud in the building industry by handing over to the Dutch authorities so-called 'shadow accounts'. It was subsequently revealed that Dutch construction companies had defrauded the government of millions of euros by illegally entering into price agreements on large-scale infrastructure projects. This resulted in a parliamentary inquiry in 2002 and extensive criminal investigations. According to the final report of the parliamentary inquiry committee, the illegal price agreements increased the costs of infrastructure projects by an average 8.8 per cent. The profits from these inflated prices were recorded on the shadow accounts.

The Netherlands Mergers and Monopolies Authority (NMA), the government watchdog responsible for fair trade, issued fines to more than 300 companies, ranging from several thousand euros to millions of euros (to a total of some 75 million euros). After the building fraud, the Dutch government and the NMA set up new rules and started to work on a major culture change in the building industry.

Guaranteed prices

Long-term business contracts frequently include provisions for price adjustments, such as cost-based pricing, escalator clauses and prices tied to a published index (**guaranteed pricing**). Two common clauses to guarantee prices are (Brandenburger and Nalebuff 1996; Levy 1994):

- *Most-favoured-customer clause* (MFC), which assures that each buyer may insist on the lowest price paid by any of the vendor's other buyers (either retroactive or contemporaneous).
- *Meet-the-competition clause* (MCC), which gives the vendor an option to retain the customer's business by meeting any rival bids.

Sometimes, MFCs and MCCs are not included in the contract but are informally approved and part of the vendor's reputation. MFCs and MCCs are particularly useful for markets with frequent and unpredictable price changes. When price changes are predictable, buyer and seller usually opt for indexed pricing. Guaranteed prices assure against significant deviations from prevailing market prices and provide a means for modifying contracts when price deviations become clear. The advantages to vendors are reduced costs of negotiating price modifications, while customers do not need information about the vendor's costs, which avoids discussions about the allocation of a vendor's fixed costs. In addition, price quotes presented by buyers provide the vendor with useful information about buying habits and competitors' prices. Guaranteed prices increase trust, encourage long-term relationships, increase sales, prevent pricing wars and increase entry barriers. Low prices from new vendors are immediately matched, which forces them to compete on reputation and product range where incumbent vendors have an advantage.

MFCs sound like a good deal for buyers because they are guaranteed never to be at a cost disadvantage versus competitors who buy from the same vendor. Therefore,

MFCs are particularly attractive to buyers who consider themselves to be poor negotiators. But an MFC may also reduce the customer's incentive to bargain, because they are no longer worried about their competitive position, while it increases the vendor's drive to negotiate favourable prices. This results in relatively high prices that favour the vendor. But there are also disadvantages to vendors. An MFC makes it harder to keep customers. When a competitor tries to steal a customer with a low price, a low price is often the only way to hold on to the customer. But reducing the price sets a precedent among other customers, who will expect the same break. Thus, holding on to the customer may prove to be too expensive. In addition, it will be too expensive to target a competitor's customers with a low price because this low price will also have to be offered to other existing customers. Even price reductions to clear surplus inventory become unattractive, which further reduces the vendor's control over its pricing policy.

An MCC is beneficial to vendors because it discourages competitors from offering low prices to the vendor's customers. Customers usually go along with an MCC because it is the accepted norm in the industry or because it assures long-term relationships with vendors, which cause them to invest in serving their customers better.

Guaranteed pricing clauses only work for standardised products that can easily be compared to each other. When this is not the case and products are modified to individual customer requirements, guaranteed pricing results in complex discussions. A second precondition for the use of guaranteed pricing is that price information is readily available. When the prices charged to customers are not generally known, there is still room for price differentiation.

8.5 Price management

Pricing involves much more than setting prices for specific offerings. Effective **price management** is a systematic approach to decisions in five key areas (Schindehutte and Morris 2001):

1 *Price objectives*: measurable performance levels that a firm tries to accomplish with the prices it charges customers, such as maximising profit, obtaining access to specific markets, discouraging specific customers, eliminating small competitors and using one product to stimulate sales of another.

2 *Price strategy*: the general direction of a firm's pricing efforts, such as skimming, penetration pricing and price leadership.

3 *Price structure*: the architecture around which a firm's price mix is designed, which specifies how prices will vary based on the offering (bundling, unbundling), customers (different prices for different market segments) and time and form of payment (discount structure).

4 *Price levels*: the actual prices for individual offerings, including price gaps among related offerings.

5 *Price promotions*: situational use of price promotions and discounts.

Management must use a systematic approach towards these pricing decision areas, reflecting the company's overall marketing strategy, competitive positioning and target markets. The pricing decisions should be made in logical order (starting with the price objectives, followed by the price strategy and so forth) and there must be internal consistency among the five decision areas. The overall approach to these pricing decision areas can be considered the firm's pricing orientation, the guiding philosophy about pricing behaviour that underlies all pricing decisions. A vendor's pricing orientation can be characterised as cost-based or market-based (focus on covering costs versus offering value to customers), risk-averse or risk-assumptive (conservative versus innovative), reactive or proactive (reacting to competition, customer or legislation versus taking a leadership role) and focused on standardisation or flexibility (one universal price versus different prices for different circumstances). Successful vendors make pricing decisions that are market-based, risk-assumptive, proactive and flexible. They recognise price as a key driver of profits, use detailed data to support their pricing decisions, use tools to analyse their data and are focused on implementation of pricing decisions (Dolan and Simon 1996).

Recognition of price as a key profit driver

The first characteristic of successful pricers is that management recognises price as a key driver of profits. Price is high on management's agenda and not determined by the competition. Price is perceived as a marketing instrument that can be managed to increase profits. The vendor's offering creates value for customers and pricing is used for value extraction. Figure 8.3 illustrates this value and pricing process.

Facts support pricing decisions

Successful pricers use accurate, timely, relevant and disaggregated data to support their pricing decisions. They understand how competitive offerings influence the value that customers derive from their offerings, and how and why this perceived value varies by customer. They also understand their competitors' cost structures, capabilities and business model and have detailed information about the costs of manufacturing, marketing and sales. Many vendors do not know the true costs of serving an individual customer, but even rough estimates may help improve pricing decisions.

Tools of analysis

All information is systematically analysed to assess the outcomes of alternative pricing scenarios. For given prices, sales volumes and profits are estimated, using break-even analysis and market simulations. These analyses include both customer reactions and competitor responses to price changes and chart the impact on sales, market share and profitability.

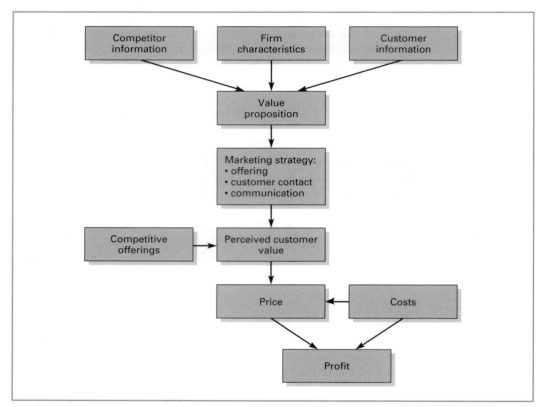

FIGURE 8.3 Value and pricing process

Focus on implementation

The effective implementation of pricing goes beyond the marketing and sales department. Several departments may cause difficulties in developing effective pricing strategies (Lancioni et al. 2005). Finance, for example, frequently resists pricing decisions because they want all products to make a profit, emphasising cost-plus pricing and full cost recovery. In addition, they generally resist price reductions and limit overall flexibility in the implementation of pricing strategies. Similarly, manufacturing also wants to recover all direct and fixed costs and desires large quantity purchases and increased production runs to lower manufacturing costs. Even the sales department may prove to be a hindrance because of its tendency to cut prices in response to competitive pressures, not adhere to existing pricing policies and make individual deals with customers without considering their ramifications. Successful pricers overcome these implementation barriers by emphasising the strategic nature of pricing. Thus, traditional departmental silo thinking is replaced by an overall pricing plan that is supported by all departments.

In many companies it is not clear who has the final say in pricing decisions. Successful pricing requires input from both the marketing/sales side and the finance/accounting/controlling side of the organisation. The hierarchical level where these two sides flow together and the final pricing decision is made depends on several factors. Pricing decision-making authority, for example, should be placed higher the more important the product is for the firm, the more homogeneous the markets are, the more critical consistency of pricing across segments is and the better higher management is informed about products and markets.

8.6 Leasing and barter

In return for their offering vendors receive a purchase price from their customers. But there are other ways for a vendor to extract value from its customers. Two alternative approaches are leasing and barter.

Leasing

B2B customers buy products to run their business operations; they need the value offered by these products rather than the products themselves. Many B2B customers realise that it sometimes makes more sense to lease products instead of outright buying and owning them. With **leasing**, the customer (the lessee) obtains the use of a business product from a vendor (the lessor) for which it pays a series of contractual payments. The major benefits of leasing are that it avoids upfront investments, protects against equipment obsolescence and increases flexibility and control. Firms can quickly expand production capacity by leasing equipment, thus shortening the cycle from equipment acquisition to increased revenues. Other important benefits are that leasing improves cash flow forecasting, allows firms to focus on their core activities and the monthly lease payments are fixed and tax deductible (Table 8.3). The major disadvantage of leasing is that the lessee pays the lessor for using the equipment, but also for the lessor's retained risk of ownership. Basically, the lessee ends up paying more than the cost of the equipment, which results in higher fixed costs per month. In addition, the lessee has no equity at the end of the lease term and is unable to sell the equipment in case of an economic downturn.

The basic type of lease is the *operating lease*, where the leasing company retains ownership during the term of the lease and the leased product does not appear on the lessee's balance sheet. At the end of the lease term, the lessee has three choices: (1) return the equipment to the leasing company, (2) purchase the equipment at its fair market value or option amount, or (3) extend the lease term. This type of lease is particularly used for equipment that rapidly depreciates. The costs for the lessee are relatively high because the leasing company also assumes the risk of obsolescence. An alternative is the *finance lease*, which is basically a method of raising finance to pay for an asset, with the lessee taking on the risks of ownership of the leased asset. The leased asset is shown on the lessee's balance sheet, with the amounts due on the lease also shown as liabilities. The full purchase price and

TABLE 8.3 Advantages and disadvantages of leasing

Advantages	Disadvantages
• Fast access to cutting-edge technology, avoiding equipment obsolescence and easy upgrading to newest technology when the lease ends • Avoids large upfront investments, which can be used for other purposes • Fast cycle time from acquisition to utilisation, which improves business agility and flexibility • Allows firms to focus on core activities • Better utilisation of equipment, which is only leased when necessary • Removes the burden of equipment disposal • Lease payments are fixed monthly fees, which improves cash flow forecasting • Lease payments are tax deductable as business expenses • Simplified cost calculations, because costs are fixed and directly attributable to a specific product • Finances 100 per cent of the costs, including service, shipping, installation and maintenance, which spreads the cost out evenly over the term of the lease • Lease contracts can be tailored to specific business needs (length and amount of payments) • Does not dilute ownership by bringing in investors to finance capital expenditures	• Lease contracts have a minimum length, which makes them less suitable in some situations • Lease contracts can typically not be terminated before the lease term is completed, which is disadvantageous in an economic downturn • The long-term expenses are more than the actual cost of the equipment • Leasing results in higher fixed costs per month • Although the equipment is not owned, the lessee is still responsible for maintenance, which can prove to be very costly • Leasing does not result in equity unless the lessee decides to purchase the equipment at the end of the lease term, when the equipment has depreciated significantly

interest charges are spread over the length of the lease and the lessee will own the equipment at the end of the lease period.

Leasing is used for a variety of products, such as aircraft, power plants, buildings, ships, roller-coasters, helicopters, trucks, cars, printing presses, containers, computers, software, telecommunication equipment, copiers, printers, fitness equipment, wheel loaders, cranes, bulldozers, cement mixers, medical equipment, dryers, point of sale terminals, wheelchairs and bed linen. In the UK, NTS Catering Equipment sells and leases a wide range of products to restaurants, hotels, bars and coffee shops, such as food slicers, dough mixers, bar blenders, commercial cookers, ovens, fryers, heated food displays and freezers. Engine Lease Finance (ELF), headquartered in Shannon, Ireland, is the world's leading independent spare engine financing and leasing company. ELF offers a comprehensive range of individually tailored services, including operating leases, short-term leases, engine acquisitions and disposals, sales and leasebacks, and engine and portfolio management services (Figure 8.4). In many countries, leasing represents a major part of the national investment volume. For instance, in Germany, leasing companies handle an investment volume of over €50 billion each year; more than 20 per cent of investments in equipment are financed on a lease basis.

Leasing is attractive to vendors because it attracts new customers who are unable to purchase the equipment and it encourages fast market acceptance of new products. Because potential customers are not always familiar with all the ins and

FIGURE 8.4 Leasing aircraft engines

Source: Engine Lease Finance Corporation. Used with permission.

outs of leasing, some vendors have invested in a financial specialist who can calculate all financial consequences of leasing, as well as explain all non-financial aspects. Vendors that want to offer customers both options of purchase and leasing must set prices for each alternative. The difference between each type of price depends on the firm's objectives: to what extent does one want to stimulate sales or leasing?

Barter

While leasing is an alternative approach to financing business purchases, sometimes trade takes place without money changing hands. With **barter**, goods or services are exchanged for other goods or services instead of money. In international trade with countries whose currencies are not readily convertible, such as communist countries during the Cold War and countries in present-day Africa and Asia, in particular, goods are frequently accepted as payment, sometimes in addition to money. Barter exists to a limited extent parallel to monetary systems in most developed countries. There are several reasons why companies would engage in barter; for instance, barter allows for transactions that would otherwise never take place and thus creates additional revenues. Sometimes, barter is the only way to acquire a new customer who might be able to pay in accepted currency in the future. Barter may also be used to sell excess inventory and to ensure a steady supply of raw materials. Barter is not only useful for international trading with developing countries; it also plays a significant role in business transactions between small and medium-sized local companies in developed countries.

The two types of barter that are easiest to use are direct trade and barter exchange. With *direct trade*, one business owner trades a product or service with a product or service from another business owner; for example, a restaurant owner might offer a number of meals to a printer in exchange for having their menus or flyers printed. A *barter exchange* is a network of business owners and professions who have agreed to offer their products and services on a trade basis to other clients of the exchange. The barter exchange is a fully accountable third-party record-keeper similar to a credit card company. Barter exchanges use an industry standardised 'banking system', using 'barter dollars' and send monthly 'bank statements' to all members. Being in the network's listings increases the visibility of a company and its offerings and expands the company's customer base. A member can, for example, sell office furniture to an advertising agency and use their credit to hire a law firm, have a website built or pay an accountant. This is particularly interesting for start-up businesses, which can conserve operating cash by making purchases with products rather than profits. Commissions are paid by the buyers as a fixed percentage of purchases, while some barter exchanges charge both buyers and sellers to encourage equal buying and selling activity. Nordic Barter, in Reykjavik, offers services to clients wanting to engage in barter in the Nordic and Baltic countries, and Monas Group provides barter opportunities to clients in Belgium. U-exchange offers a guide with helpful suggestions on how to barter (www.u-exchange.com/barter101).

Online
Learning Centre

When you have read this chapter, log on to the Online Learning Centre website at ***www.mcgraw-hill.co.uk/textbooks/biemans*** to explore chapter-by-chapter test questions, further reading and more online study tools.

Summary of Key Concepts

- B2B vendors use products and services, sales and delivery channels and communication to create value for customers. In return, they extract value from customers through pricing.

- Although effective pricing has a direct positive effect on the firm's bottom line, most managers ignore the potential of pricing. They consider pricing to be a marketing tool that lacks glamour and has only limited possibilities.

- An increasing number of firms use pricing software to improve their pricing decisions and increase profits.

- The major drivers of B2B prices are costs, value and competition. Most B2B vendors determine their prices by calculating the costs and adding a mark-up. Costs function as the lower limit of prices; value as the upper limit. This results in many different methods for price setting, some of which may be used in combination.

- The demand for different products and services may be related (as in complementary products and substitutes). This implies that their prices should be related as well.

- B2B pricing is often characterised by negotiations, with vendors using formal list prices and actual prices being the result of extensive negotiations. Such negotiations focus on prices and discounts, but may also concern other relevant issues such as delivery schedules, inventory levels and after-sales service. Price negotiations are sometimes conducted online.

- Government projects are often awarded as the result of a competitive bidding process. With closed bidding pre-qualified potential vendors are invited to submit written, sealed proposals (bids) for a particular business opportunity. Open bidding is a more informal process, where any vendor can bid for the business up to a certain date.

- Long-term contracts frequently include clauses to guarantee prices, such as most-favoured-customer clauses, which assure that each buyer may insist on the lowest price paid by any of the vendor's other buyers, and meet-the-competition clauses, which give the vendor an option to retain the customer's business by meeting any rival bids.

- Successful B2B pricers understand the relationship between price, value, costs and competition, base their prices on detailed information about both the marketplace and the firm's operations, and use pricing as a tool to improve profits.

- In some situations, leasing or barter are used as an alternative for pricing. Leasing is often preferred by customers because they do not want to own the product but just to enjoy its value.

🔓 Key Terms

Discussion questions

1 Explain why the concept of 'perceived value' is so important for pricing business products. In which situations should a vendor not set the price for the product at the level of the value of the product, as perceived by the customer?

2 Which type of B2B products usually face elastic demand? Which type of B2B products are usually confronted with inelastic demand? Provide clear examples and justify your answer.

3 What is the influence of a buying centre, consisting of several different individuals involved in the buying decision, on establishing and communicating prices for B2B products?

4 Suppose that, as a marketing manager, you consider raising the price for one of your products. How could you use market research to justify your decision? What kind of information do you need to justify your decision? What are the disadvantages of this approach?

5 It is sometimes stated that 'competing on price is a sign of incompetence'. Explain the reasoning behind this statement. Does this statement always hold true? Justify your answer.

6 Which characteristics of the firm and its environment influence the firm's price-setting method?

7 Many vendors use separate prices for the core product and for the product's various support services. What are the advantages of this approach for a vendor of printing presses? What are its disadvantages?

8 What are the advantages and disadvantages of competitive bidding for the customer? And for the vendor?

9 How do online auctions impact a vendor's pricing policy?

10 Customers will always demand lower prices. How should salespeople deal with this situation? What kind of information or tools do salespeople need to effectively counter customers' focus on a lower price?

Further reading

Cross, Robert G. and Ashutosh Dixit (2005) Customer-centric pricing: the surprising secret for profitability, *Business Horizons*, 48(6): 483–491.

Day, George S. and Adrian B. Ryans (1988) Using price discounts for a competitive advantage, *Industrial Marketing Management*, 17(1): 1–14.

Dolan, Robert J. and Hermann Simon (1996) *Power Pricing: How Managing Price Transforms the Bottom Line*, New York: Free Press.

Hinterhuber, Andreas (2004) Towards value-based pricing – an integrative framework for decision making, *Industrial Marketing Management*, 33(8): 765–778.

Schoenherr, Tobias and Vincent A. Mabert (2007) Online reverse auctions: common myths versus evolving reality, *Business Horizons*, 50(5): 373–384.

References

Brandenburger, Adam M. and Barry J. Nalebuff (1996) *Co-opetition*, New York: Doubleday.

Cross, Robert G. and Ashutosh Dixit (2005) Customer-centric pricing: the surprising secret for profitability, *Business Horizons*, 48(6): 483–491.

Day, George S. and Adrian B. Ryans (1988) Using price discounts for a competitive advantage, *Industrial Marketing Management*, 17(1): 1–14.

Dolan, Robert J. and Hermann Simon (1996) *Power Pricing: How Managing Price Transforms the Bottom Line*, New York: Free Press.

Dwyer, F. Robert and John F. Tanner (2006) *Business Marketing: Connecting Strategy, Relationships, and Learning*, third edition, New York: McGraw-Hill.

Garda, Robert A. (1991) Use tactical pricing to uncover hidden profits, *Journal of Business Strategy*, 12(5): 17–23.

Hinterhuber, Andreas (2004) Towards value-based pricing – an integrative framework for decision making, *Industrial Marketing Management*, 33(8): 765–778.

Hünerberg, Reinhard and Axel Hüttmann (2003) Performance as a basis for price-setting in the capital goods industry: concepts and empirical evidence, *European Management Journal*, 21(6): 717–730.

Lancioni, Richard, Hope J. Schau and Michael F. Smith (2005) Intraorganizational influences on business-to-business pricing strategies: a political economy perspective, *Industrial Marketing Management*, 34(2): 123–131.

Levy, David T. (1994) Guaranteed pricing in industrial purchases: making use of markets in contractual relations, *Industrial Marketing Management*, 23(4): 307–313.

Mabert, Vincent A. and Jack A. Skeels (2002) Internet reverse auctions: valuable tools in experienced hands, *Business Horizons*, 45(4): 70–76.

Marn, Michael V., Eric V. Roegner and Craig C. Zawada (2003) The power of pricing, *McKinsey Quarterly*, 37(1): 27–36.

Peters, Greg (2008) Banish the bottom-line blues, *Sales & Marketing Management*, 3 November.

Schindehutte, Minet and Michael H. Morris (2001) Pricing as entrepreneurial behavior, *Business Horizons*, 44(4): 41–48.

Schoenherr, Tobias and Vincent A. Mabert (2007) Online reverse auctions: common myths versus evolving reality, *Business Horizons*, 50(5): 373–384.

Smeltzer, Larry R. and Amelia Carr (2002) Reverse auctions in industrial marketing and buying, *Business Horizons*, 45(2): 47–52.

Note

[1] Zilliant (2008) Survey reveals that B2B companies are turning to pricing professionals and enterprise software to increase profitability, www.zilliant.com/downloads/pr2008/news_pr_zilliant_global_benchmark_survey.pdf (accessed 27 November 2008).

PART 05
Marketing Evaluation and Control

CHAPTER 09

Marketing implementation, evaluation and control

Introduction

Firms need creative strategies and compelling value propositions to persuade customers to do business with them. But a large part of a firm's success is determined by its quality of execution: how capable is the firm of executing its strategy and planned marketing activities? Vendors need a comprehensive control system to monitor their performance, compare performance with objectives and take corrective measures. Such a system for marketing evaluation and control must include all levels of marketing in the firm, from its quarterly marketing activities to its overall marketing function.

This chapter first discusses marketing strategy formulation and implementation and emphasises that they are interrelated and that disappointing performance may be due to an inappropriate strategy or to poor execution. It then goes on to explain the concept of marketing evaluation and control and shows how monitoring, evaluation and correction are all part of an iterative cycle to improve firm performance. The rest of the chapter is devoted to the four major areas of marketing control. The most common type of marketing control concerns the firm's ongoing annual marketing activities. This continuous tracking of performance may relate to overall firm performance or to the underlying customer relationships. The second type of marketing control analyses the profitability of marketing entities such as products, sales territories, customers and channels. A third type of marketing control looks at the efficiency of marketing activities. The fourth type of marketing control uses a much broader perspective and examines all aspects of the firm's marketing function. All together, the process of marketing evaluation and control concerns a large number of relevant metrics that are carefully scrutinised to measure performance and identify areas for improvement.

9.1 Formulating and implementing marketing strategy

Successful B2B marketing starts with the formulation of an effective **marketing strategy**, which requires input from various business functions. Firms can easily chart the involvement of various departments and individuals in marketing strategy decisions by constructing a table, with each row representing a type of marketing strategy decision (such as designing product performance and selecting channels) and each column representing a department or individual (such as marketing, sales and the SBU manager). Next, the cells are used to describe the role of each department or individual (such as responsible for the decision or consulting on the decision). The SBU manager, for example, approves offering support decisions, marketing is responsible for them, sales provides input to these decisions and implements them through customer visits, and customer service implements offering support through telemarketing. Several studies have shown that improved collaboration between business functions has a positive effect on business performance (Kahn and Mentzer 1998); for instance, more involvement of other departments in marketing decisions increases the firm's effectiveness, efficiency and adaptability (Krohmer et al. 2002). But involvement of other departments in decision making complicates the process and is not always desirable. While it makes sense, for example, to involve other departments in product development and pricing decisions, the development of advertising messages is usually left to marketing.

Most managers have experienced first-hand that a good marketing strategy does not automatically result in successful implementation of the strategy. Implementation decisions and problems occur at different levels (Bonoma and Crittenden 1988). In large B2B firms, for example, many implementation problems occur at the level of specific marketing actions because specialists in the areas of product planning, pricing, distribution and advertising must coordinate their activities. But implementation problems may also occur at the level of marketing systems because of unproductive habits and ineffective collaboration between organisational units.

Marketing strategy formulation and implementation are not independent from each other. Management may select a strategy that is easy to implement because a required corporate ROI causes them to focus on short-term results. And a strategy is doomed to fail if management neglects the strategy's consequences for employees. The close relationship between strategy development and implementation is also illustrated by the evolutionary perspective on strategy. According to this perspective, new strategies may be based on successful local practices, which effectively means that strategy formulation follows implementation.

Strategy implementation is a complex process that encompasses much more than simply communicating the new strategy to the organisation's employees and other stakeholders. Critical success factors are a detailed planning approach, employee involvement in strategic planning, anticipation of surprises, an early warning system to identify potential problem areas and the use of appropriate rewards. A study of strategy implementation uncovered three levels of *strategy killer* (Beer and Eisenstat 2000):

- *Inadequate quality of strategic direction*: caused by an ineffective senior management team, an inappropriate senior management style (for example, top-down or laissez-faire) or unclear strategies and conflicting priorities.

- *Inadequate organisational learning*: because management does not explain why the organisation needs to change, does not listen to lower-level employees or does not stimulate honest feedback.

- *Inadequate implementation*: caused by poor coordination across functions or departments, or inadequate leadership skills.

Strategy implementation ends with a systematic evaluation of results and modification of the strategy and/or the implementation approach. The results from the implementation approach are not always easy to assess. When both the strategy and implementation are of high quality there is no problem. But, when the results are disappointing and there have been problems with the strategy's implementation, it may be hard to decide whether the disappointing results were caused by an inappropriate implementation or a poor strategy. Good strategy implementation is essential to success; a five-year study of 160 companies found that success is strongly associated with the ability to execute flawlessly (Joyce et al. 2003). Good implementation of marketing strategy requires effective evaluation of marketing activities.

9.2 Marketing control

Effective marketing implementation is not achieved by simply implementing marketing strategies and measuring their results afterwards. Instead, firms must continuously measure the results from marketing activities, compare them against formulated performance standards and take corrective actions when performance is unacceptable (**marketing control**). To control a product development project, for example, a firm compares actual progress with planned progress to see whether the

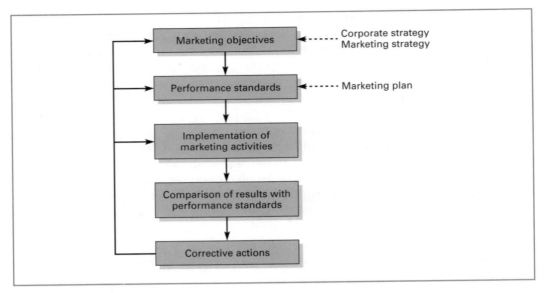

FIGURE 9.1 Marketing control

project is still on schedule. When the NPD team faces unexpected delays, management may decide to conduct some of the remaining activities in parallel or otherwise speed up the process to make sure that the product can be launched according to schedule (for instance, during an important bi-annual trade show). When results are above performance standards, the evaluation uncovers valuable lessons that can be used to replicate the success in future situations. When results are below standards, evaluation focuses on identifying root causes of failure so that they can be avoided in the future. The evaluation of results may also lead to modification of objectives or performance standards; for instance, when an NPD team uses its experience to plan a somewhat longer, but more realistic, time to market for a future development project. This iterative cycle of setting objectives, formulating performance standards, implementing marketing activities, evaluating results and taking corrective actions contributes to a learning organisation (Figure 9.1).

Many B2B firms fail to systematically evaluate and control their marketing activities. They participate in expensive trade shows in the absence of measurable performance objectives, launch new products without a clear idea of who the first target customers should be and do not measure the results from advertising and PR activities. Many managers in B2B firms argue that it is simply not possible to measure the effect on profits of every single marketing activity. But while that is definitely true, managers can typically measure and evaluate much more than they currently do. A more systematic approach to marketing evaluation and control, for instance by using intermediate metrics (such as brand awareness) instead of profits, improves the quality of the firm's marketing function. There are four types of marketing control (Kotler and Keller 2006): control of ongoing annual marketing activities, control of profitability, control of efficiency and control of the marketing function (Figure 9.2).

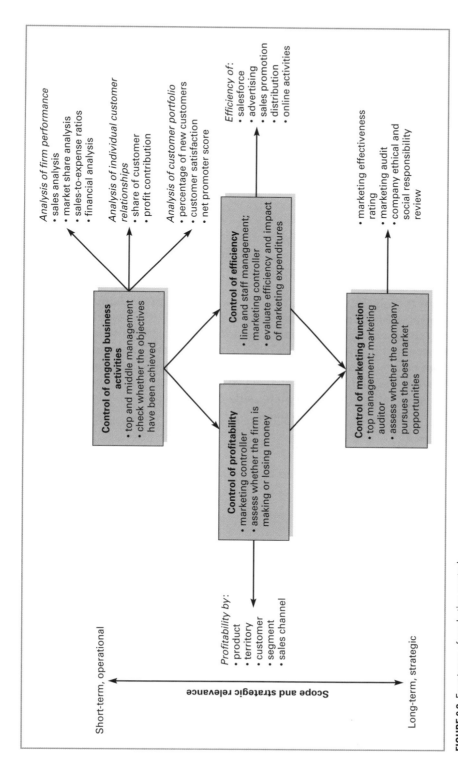

FIGURE 9.2 Four types of marketing control

Source: Based on Kotler and Keller (2006)

9.3 Control of ongoing annual marketing activities

Firms formulate their objectives and planned marketing activities in annual plans, with the activities usually specified per quarter or month. During the year, firms measure results, compare them with planned progress and take corrective actions when necessary – **control of ongoing marketing activities**. This continuous tracking of performance concerns two types of variable: overall firm performance, usually measured in terms of revenues and market share, and the underlying customer relationships that determine firm performance, measured as customer retention and customer satisfaction.

Analysis of firm performance

Annual plans contain information about planned revenues, sales, market share and profits, which allows firms to track these metrics and compare actual firm performance with objectives. An example of an **analysis of firm performance** is presented in Table 9.1.

In the example from Table 9.1, actual sales were more than planned, but this was caused by salespeople giving high discounts to customers. This resulted in an actual price that was significantly lower than the planned €250. At the same time, total market size increased by almost 50 per cent, which resulted in a market share loss of five percentage points. Using both the planned (p) and realised (r) values of the variables sales (S), margin (m), market size (M) and market share (ms), management can analyse the deviations from the plan using the following formulas.

The *total deviation* can be calculated as:

$$S_r m_r - S_p m_p = (18 \times 52) - (16 \times 80) = -\text{€}344$$

This deviation can be partly attributed to a difference in margin:

Table 9.1 Analysis of firm performance

Metric	Plan	Result	Deviation from plan
Sales	16 million	18 million	2 million
Price per unit	€250	€222	−€28
Revenues	€3,750 million	€4,200 million	€450 million
Market size (in units)	64 million	90 million	26 million
Market share (%)	25	20	−5
Variable cost per unit	€170	€170	–
Contribution:			
Margin per unit	€80	€52	−€28
Total contribution	€1,280 million	€936 million	−€344 million

$$S_r m_r - S_r m_p = S_r (m_r - m_p) = 18 \times (52 - 80) = -€504 \text{ million}$$

The rest of the deviation from plan is caused by a difference in sales:

$$S_r m_p - S_p m_p = m_p (S_r - S_p) = 80 \times (18 - 16) = €160 \text{ million}$$

Because the firm's sales are calculated as the firm's market share multiplied by the size of the total market, the deviation caused by a difference in sales is partly caused by a difference in market size:

$$m_p (M_r ms_p - M_p ms_p) = m_p ms_p (M_r - M_p) = 80 \times 0.25 \, (90 - 64) = €520 \text{ million}$$

The rest of the deviation caused by sales is due to a difference in market share:

$$m_p (M_r ms_r - M_r ms_p) = m_p M_r (ms_r - ms_p) = 80 \times 90 \, (0.20 - 0.25) = -€360 \text{ million}$$

Thus, the calculated deviation from planned profits (€936 – €1,280 = –€344 million) can be attributed to a lower price (–€504 million), increased total market size (€520 million) and a reduced market share (–€360 million). But these calculated differences only offer information about the results. To initiate the appropriate corrective measures, management needs insight into the underlying causes of these results. This insight can be obtained by taking a closer look at the firm's relationships with customers.

Analysis of customer relationships

Analysis of customer relationships can be carried out by firms at the level of individual customers (for example, individual key accounts) and at the level of the total customer portfolio (for example, all relationships with customers in a specific market segment). At the individual customer level, management can assess the quality of the relationship using metrics such as:

- *Share of customer*: ratio between revenues from customer X and total purchases by customer X in this product category (also called *share of wallet*).
- *Relationship size*: ratio between revenues from customer X and the average revenues per customer in the market segment that customer X belongs to.
- *Share of order*: ratio between the number of orders from customer X and the total number of orders.
- *Share of revenues*: ratio between the revenues from customer X and total revenues.
- *Share of contribution*: ratio between contribution generated by customer X and the firm's total contribution to profits.

At the level of the customer portfolio (a market segment or the whole market), firms can measure and track metrics related to customer satisfaction, loyalty and retention. Examples of such metrics are the percentage of new customers to average number of customers, percentage of lost customers to average number of customers, percentage of win-back customers to average number of customers, percentage of customers falling into very dissatisfied/dissatisfied/neutral/satisfied/very satisfied categories, percentage of customers who say they would repurchase the product, percentage of customers who say they would recommend the product to others, percentage of customers who say that the company's product is the most preferred in its category, percentage of customers who correctly identify the positioning and differentiation of the company and its offering, and average perception of the company's offering quality relative to the next-best alternative (Kotler and Keller 2006).

One way to measure customer satisfaction is to compare customer expectations with customer experiences. The *gap model*, formulated by Parasuraman et al. (1985), postulates that a customer's perception of the quality of a vendor's offering is equal to their expected perception of the quality of the offering minus the offering's experienced quality. In other words: customer satisfaction equals experiences minus expectations. A customer's experiences and expectations may relate to several elements of a vendor's offering, such as product quality, availability of support services, access to the vendor organisation, reliability and expertise of contact personnel and the number and quality of commercial references. In practice, most customers use only a few variables to assess their vendors' performance (see also the discussion in Chapter 4 about the characteristics of a good value proposition). Next, the gap model analyses the difference between experiences and expectations and breaks it down into a number of variables and gaps that firms can use to identify the causes of customer (dis)satisfaction and design appropriate actions (Figure 9.3):

- *Gap 1: Not knowing what customers expect*. Management's perception of customer expectations may deviate from actual customer expectations. Management of a large maintenance and repair firm, for example, may think that customers prefer to deal with large vendors because size is an indicator of quality, while many customers actually prefer to do business with small firms because of their greater flexibility, faster response and higher customer orientation. Management may reduce this gap through research into customer expectations, direct contact between management and customers, improved communications between management and contact personnel and reduction in the number of management levels.

- *Gap 2: Not selecting the right offering specifications*. Management translates its perceptions of customer expectations into offering specifications. A customer's desire for 'fast response times', for example, may be operationalised as 'all emergency repairs must be carried out within 36 hours'. In translating expectations into specifications, all kinds of trade-offs are made, which may result in a new gap. Management can reduce this gap with analytic tools such as Quality Function Deployment, and by involving representative customers in the process.

- *Gap 3: Not delivering to specifications*. Despite all carefully formulated specifications and quality control procedures, the actual offering does not always conform to specifications. With services, in particular, the human

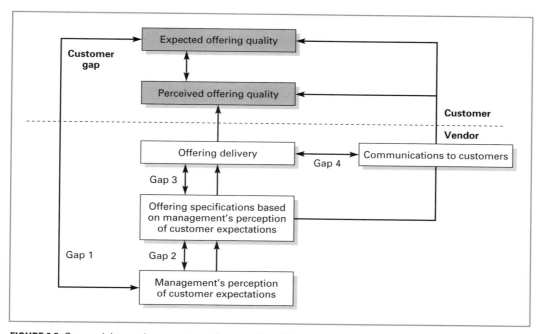

FIGURE 9.3 Gap model to analyse a customer's perception of the quality of an offering

Source: Parasuraman et al. (1985: 44). Reprinted with permission from the *Journal of Marketing*, published by the American Marketing Association.

factor may cause deviations from specifications. Careful selection and training of contact personnel, unambiguous job descriptions and customer-focused incentives and reward systems help to reduce the impact of this gap.

- *Gap 4: Not matching performance to promises.* A customer's expectations are based on a myriad of factors, including the customer's past experiences and word-of-mouth from other customers, but also on the vendor's communications. Careless communication may raise customer expectations to unrealistic levels and result in dissatisfaction when the vendor fails to live up to these expectations. Training of contact personnel and coordination of communication efforts go a long way to preventing these problems.

Zeithaml et al. (1990) developed the measuring instrument SERVQUAL, which companies can use to measure the gap between customer experience and expectations.

Customer satisfaction, however, is often not enough; many firms have discovered to their dismay that even satisfied customers switch vendors. What really counts is the extent to which customers are loyal to the firm. Customer loyalty is often measured in terms of customers' purchasing behaviour. Several metrics can be used to conduct **customer retention analysis**; Table 9.2 provides an example.

Table 9.2 Customer retention analysis

Metric	Customers in 2010	Retained customers in 2011	Deviation
Total number of customers	65,763 (100%)	41,117 (63%)	−24,646 (−37%)
Average number of orders	11.6	14.3	2.7 (23%)
Average revenues per customer	€15,236	€21,538	€6,302 (41%)
Total revenues	€1,001,965,068	€885,577,946	−€116,387,122 (−12%)

Table 9.2 can be used to analyse the firm's relationships with all customers that have been retained from the previous year. Based on this analysis, management can draw several conclusions: (1) customer retention was 63%, (2) the retained customers ordered 23% more orders that were on average 41% higher, and (3) the lost customers represent lost revenues of more than €116 million (12%).

But real loyalty implies not just repeat purchase behaviour, but also a positive attitude to the firm. Growth depends on customers being so loyal that they act as the firm's advocates in the marketplace. This led Reichheld (2003) to suggest that firms need to ask their customers only one question: 'How likely is it that you would recommend us to a colleague?' Customers are asked to provide a score on a scale from 0 to 10, which allows the firm to calculate its *net promoter score* as the percentage of promoters (customers scoring a 9 or 10) minus the percentage of detractors (customers scoring 0 to 6). To be successful, firms should not treat net promoter score (NPS) as just another metric, but make it part of a comprehensive programme that includes a customer focus, the collection of trustworthy NPS data, root cause analysis, actions towards customers and accountability of employees, and transformation of products and business processes (Owen and Brooks 2008).

9.4 Control of profitability

More detailed insight into a firm's financial performance can be gained by analysing the profitability of products, sales territories, customers, segments, order sizes and channels – **control of profitability**. Many B2B firms analyse contribution to profits (sales less direct costs) of products, order sizes, customers, salespersons and geographic areas. But the number of firms analysing net profit (sales less direct costs less indirect costs allocated) of products, order sizes and so on is much lower. Firms can only analyse profitability if they possess the required information and are able to allocate all relevant costs. In practice, this is often not the case and many firms unknowingly sell products at a loss to large customers. This happens easily, because management believes that the most important customers are the largest customers, so these get pampered (more sales visits, more favourable payment conditions, more frequent deliveries). But all this extra attention costs money and reduces profitability. After conducting a detailed profitability analysis, one marketing manager discovered that his firm had been losing money on a large customer for 20 years!

The basic idea behind profitability analysis is straightforward: one calculates all costs, allocates them to the marketing entities to be analysed (products, market segments, sales channels) and calculates profits or losses per entity. In practice, this is often problematic because of discussions about the costs to be included and their allocation to specific marketing entities. There are three types of cost:

- *Direct costs* can be assigned directly to marketing entities; for instance, sales commissions can be directly assigned to specific customers, orders or geographic regions.
- *Traceable common costs* can be assigned only indirectly, but according to a plausible reasoning, to marketing entities. The costs of a marketing information system, for example, can be allocated to the customers included in the system.
- *Non-traceable common costs* are costs that can be only arbitrarily assigned to marketing entities; examples are the costs of a corporate image campaign and top management salaries. Proponents of *full costing* assign these common costs to marketing entities by using arbitrary allocation rules.

The complexity of cost allocations can be illustrated by an example about product mix decisions. These decisions should be made using information about marginal product cost (the additional cost incurred when product output is increased by one unit, assuming all other cost and output levels are held constant), total costs and plant capacity utilisation. Table 9.3 presents information about price, material cost and production data for three products. Plant capacity is 400 units per week and all other costs (all costs except material costs) are €8,000 per week. In addition, the table shows profits for eight different product mixes, each of which requires exactly 400 capacity units (which means that the plant is fully utilised for each product mix).

The first three product mixes use all capacity for production of just one of the three products. The data show that product B is most profitable. Product C does not generate enough revenue to cover all costs and is therefore 'unprofitable'. But product C is 'marginally profitable'. If the firm in question can only produce and sell products A and B (both of which are fully profitable), there is no problem. But market conditions do not always allow this and the addition of a product that is only marginally profitable causes a drag on profits. If the firm produces too much of the marginally profitable product, negative profits may result. Assume that the firm produces mix 5 (20 of A, 32 of B and 8 of C), because that is the maximum of products A and B that the market will absorb and the rest of the plant's capacity is used for product C. The addition of product C caused a drop in profits from €1,425 to €980. But if product C were dropped from the mix, the plant would only operate at 80 per cent of capacity and the €8,000 other costs would have to be reallocated. Assuming that 50 per cent of these other costs will be fixed, the weekly costs will be reduced by $0.20 \times 4,000 = €800$ to €7,200 and the new profits become €340. Thus,

Table 9.3 Selecting a product mix

	Product A	Product B	Product C	Profit
Price per unit	€225	€145	€230	
Material cost per unit	€40	€25	€50	
Units of production capacity per unit	8	5	10	
Mix 1: only product A	50	0	0	€1,250
Mix 2: only product B	0	80	0	€1,600
Mix 3: only product C	0	0	40	−€800
Mix 4: only products A and B	25	40	0	€1,425
Mix 5: especially products A and B	20	32	8	€980
Mix 6: especially product B	15	24	16	€535
Mix 7: especially product C	10	16	24	€90
Mix 8: almost only product C	5	8	32	−€355

Source: South and Oliver (1998: 191). Reprinted with permission from Elsevier.

elimination of the 'unprofitable' product C from the product mix causes a 65 per cent reduction in total profits.

An increasing number of firms use *activity-based costing* to calculate the profitability of marketing entities. This focuses management's attention on the allocation of all costs to the marketing entities that enjoy their benefits, increases the quality of market information and helps to make better marketing decisions. It allows management, for example, to base their marketing strategy on information about customer profitability and customer loyalty. Activity-based costing also allows firms to calculate customer lifetime values. This goes beyond a customer's current profitability and accounts for all future revenues and costs associated with an individual customer. In practice, many B2B firms find it hard to operationalise customer lifetime value and answer key questions such as: At which level should you define a customer? How do you establish whether a customer is still active? Which products and services should be included in the calculations? How do you determine the length of a customer relationship? How do you allocate the costs of a corporate image campaign to individual customers?

Alignment of marketing and sales is a prerequisite for successful demand generation. Marketing can help make sales more productive and meet quotas. But how can managers demonstrate that marketing improves sales productivity? Useful metrics concern the firm's lead-generation process (number of qualified leads, cost per qualified lead, leads to appointments), lead management process (number of requests for proposals, time spent with prospects/customers, number of valuable sales calls/meetings), sales closing process (number of meetings to close, time to close, marketing spend per sales amount) and customer retention efforts (breadth and depth of customer relationships, net promoter score, customer share of wallet).

It should be noted that it is not always possible to determine the profitability of all marketing activities. In that case, one may assess the effectiveness of marketing activities by estimating their effect on intermediate variables. The profitability of a corporate advertising campaign, for instance, may be difficult to estimate, but instead management can calculate the effect on intermediate variables such as awareness and attitude.

9.5 Control of efficiency

When profitability is low, management may analyse whether they can improve the firm's efficiency, that is, reduce the costs that are required to achieve a certain result. Management may use a large number of variables to assess the efficiency of marketing activities, such as average number of sales calls per salesperson per day, average call time per contact, average revenue per sales call, average costs per sales call, advertising cost per thousand target buyers reached by a media vehicle, before and after measures of attitude towards the offering, number of inquiries generated by a direct mailing, logistics costs as a percentage of sales, percentage of order filled correctly, percentage of on-time deliveries, number of billing orders, sales cost per acquired customer, cost per qualified sales lead and cost of trade show participation.

Management frequently pays more attention to costs (efficiency) than to effects (effectiveness), because costs are far more readily measurable. Naturally, it is the combination of costs and results (**marketing productivity**) that counts: delivering greater value to customers at lower cost (Sheth and Sisodia 2002). Firms must first establish the desired effectiveness (doing the right things) and then select the most efficient way to achieve that effectiveness (doing things right) – **control of efficiency**. But, in practice, firms always have a limited budget and management must make trade-off decisions between marketing effectiveness and efficiency. Because of a limited budget, for example, management may lower their effectiveness aspirations before they determine the most efficient way to achieve them. What is needed is a marketing system that delivers both effectiveness (greater customer satisfaction) and efficiency (low costs). But many firms create satisfied customers at unacceptably high costs or alienate customers in their search for efficiencies. Firms can improve their marketing productivity by: (1) changing their focus from markets to market segments and customers, which allows them to focus on the most profitable segments or customers and identify unprofitable ones, (2) treating marketing as an investment rather than an expense and estimating the effects of marketing decisions on the total customer portfolio, and (3) making marketing responsible for all activities that influence customer acquisition, retention and win-back.

MINI CASE: B2B FIRMS DISCOVER MARKETING ACCOUNTABILITY

In most B2B firms, marketing expenditures are still justified by the conviction that marketing contributes to the firm's strategic position and brand image. But in several B2B firms this is no longer sufficient and marketing is required to demonstrate its contribution to the bottom line. Like all other business functions, marketing is held accountable and needs to prove its value to the firm. This is the result of two separate developments: increasing marketing costs and increasing availability of marketing data and technologies to analyse them. Salespeople are armed with laptops to input customer information during sales visits, central databases record all customer transactions, websites track online customer interactions, and datamining is used to identify patterns in large amounts of customer data.

But the new technologies also raise new questions; for instance, how do you measure the ROI of online marketing activities? Click-through percentage, cost per registered customer, conversion percentage, bounce rate, visitor path, length of visit and the number of downloads have all been suggested as online marketing metrics. An increasing number of vendors offer software and consultancy services to improve the effectiveness and profitability of online marketing activities. An example is Dutch-based Nedstat, which presents itself as the European leader in website analytics. Despite these advances, many B2B firms still use simple rules of thumb to improve their online marketing presence, such as:

- 'A navigation page must take no longer than eight seconds to download.'
- 'A page with content must take no longer than 25 seconds to download.'
- 'The number of clicks required to download a document must be no more than two.'

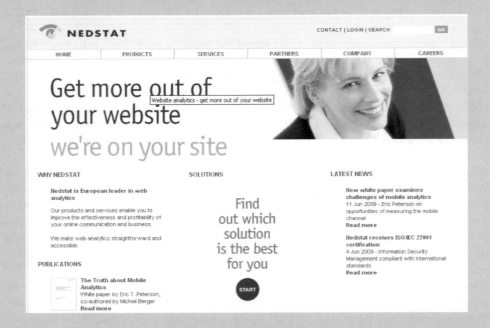

Source: Nedstat. Used with permission.

9.6 Control of the marketing function

A key task of marketing is to develop and improve the marketing function. A **marketing audit** provides a detailed examination of the firm's marketing function. A good marketing audit will allow for **control of the marketing function** and has the following four characteristics (Kotler and Keller 2006):

- *Comprehensive*: a marketing audit covers all major marketing activities and the relationships between them. Excessive salesforce turnover, for example, can be caused by poor salesforce training or compensation, but also by weak products.

- *Systematic*: a marketing audit looks at the firm's marketing environment, marketing objectives, marketing strategies, marketing systems and marketing activities. Weak elements are identified and improvements are incorporated in a corrective action plan.

- *Independent*: while management may conduct their own marketing audit by rating their own operations, this lacks objectivity and independence. It is better to hire an outside firm with broad experience in several industries, some familiarity with the industry being audited and the required objectivity, time and attention to conduct a high-quality audit.

- *Periodic*: a marketing audit is frequently initiated in times of crisis (for instance, when sales have fallen), but it is advisable to periodically conduct a marketing audit that allows the firm to track performance over time and measure the effects of implemented improvements.

While the other three types of marketing control evaluate the effects of marketing actions, a marketing audit looks at the marketing strategies, systems and activities that cause these effects. A marketing audit is quite complex and includes the marketing environment (markets, customers, competitors, sales channels, suppliers, economy, technological developments, regulation), marketing strategy (business definition, marketing objectives, value propositions), organisation (structure, departments involved in marketing activities, quality of cooperation between marketing and other departments), marketing systems (marketing information system, marketing planning system, procedures for marketing control, new offering development process), marketing productivity (effectiveness, efficiency) and marketing instruments (sales and delivery channels, product and service management, communication, pricing, integration between marketing instruments).

A study of the use of marketing metrics by firms in the US, Japan, Germany, the UK and France found that market share and the perceived product/service quality are the most popular metrics (Barwise and Farley 2004). In addition, the study showed that most firms use multiple measures. Seggie et al. (2007) discuss several metrics to measure the return on marketing investments and develop guidelines for the formulation of better metrics. In their opinion, marketing metrics should offer financial information, be forward-looking, be focused on long-term performance, provide information about individual customers, describe causal relationships between marketing actions and metrics, measure performance relative to competitors

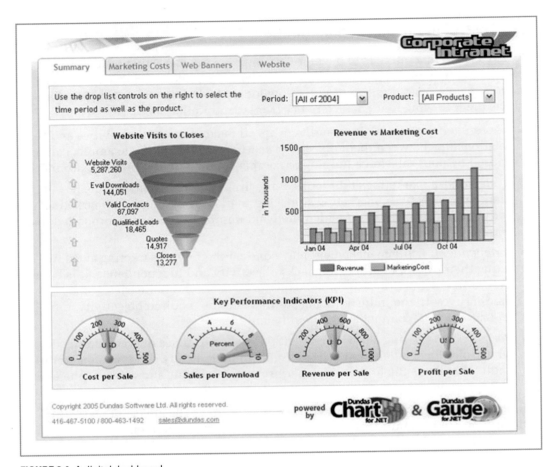

FIGURE 9.4 A digital dashboard

Source: Dundas Data Visualization. Used with permission.

and be objective. They conclude that no single existing measure satisfies all these criteria. Customer equity looks at the long term, provides information about individual customers and links marketing efforts with results, but a comparison with competitors is difficult and there are limitations as to how objective calculations of customer equity are. The balanced scorecard incorporates forward-looking metrics and measures long-term performance (including financial performance), but does not allow causal interpretations about the effect of marketing actions on long-term financial performance, fails to provide information about individual customers and does not allow for comparison with competitors. Therefore, firms should use a combination of metrics that together encompass all of the dimensions. Thus, the weak aspects of one metric can be compensated by the strong points of another.

Business intelligence software can be used to combine data from various sources and present them in a customised **digital dashboard** (Figure 9.4). Management can

FIGURE 9.5 Relationships between firm actions, outcomes and metrics

Source: Gupta and Zeithaml (2006: 719). © 2006 Institute for Operations Research and the Management Sciences. Reprinted with permission.

specify the key performance indicators (KPIs) they want to track and design digital dashboards to their own specifications to graphically display them. Using a digital dashboard, management can quickly identify high-performing products and retained customers. Because the dashboard uses real-time data (for instance, about customer transactions), management can easily analyse the root causes of performance and take quick corrective action when necessary.

Systematically measuring marketing metrics is necessary to improve a firm's marketing decisions. It helps firms to understand the relationships between what they do, what customers think, what customers do and what firms get (Figure 9.5). Indeed, recent empirical studies have shown that measuring marketing performance has a positive impact on firm performance (O'Sullivan and Abela 2007; O'Sullivan et al. 2009).

Online
Learning **Centre**

When you have read this chapter, log on to the Online Learning Centre website at ***www.mcgraw-hill.co.uk/textbooks/biemans*** to explore chapter-by-chapter test questions, further reading and more online study tools.

Summary of Key Concepts

- Firms need creative strategies and compelling value propositions. But firm performance is largely determined by the quality of execution.

- Strategy formulation and implementation are closely related. In the case of disappointing performance, it is often very difficult to determine whether this is caused by an inappropriate strategy or poor execution.

- Firms use comprehensive evaluation and control systems to systematically compare their performance with objectives and take corrective actions when necessary. In such a system, monitoring, evaluation and correction are all part of an iterative cycle to improve firm performance.

- Marketing control must include all levels of marketing in the firm, from its quarterly marketing activities to its overall marketing function.

- The most commonly used type of marketing control concerns the firm's ongoing annual marketing activities, measured annually or quarterly. This level of marketing control looks at both firm performance and its underlying causes in terms of customer relationships.

- Another type of marketing control analyses the profitability of several marketing entities, such as products, sales territories, customers and channels.

- A third type of marketing control looks at the efficiency of marketing activities. Sophisticated firms combine effectiveness metrics with efficiency metrics to evaluate the firm's marketing productivity.

- A final and broader type of marketing control examines all aspects of the firm's marketing function. Such a comprehensive marketing audit is typically performed by an outside firm.

- There is no single perfect metric to measure a firm's marketing performance. B2B firms use several metrics in combination to gain insight into their marketing performance and identify areas for improvement.

- The most sophisticated B2B firms use software to design customised digital dashboards that provide their managers with real-time information that allows for quick corrective action.

> ### 🔑 Key Terms
>
> Analysis of customer
>   relationships, p. 285
> Analysis of firm performance, p. 284
> Control of efficiency, p. 291
> Control of ongoing marketing
>   activities, p. 284
> Control of profitability, p. 288
>
> Control of the marketing function, p. 293
> Customer retention analysis, p. 287
> Digital dashboard, p. 294
> Marketing audit, p. 293
> Marketing control, p. 281
> Marketing productivity, p. 291
> Marketing strategy, p. 280

Discussion questions

1 Explain the relationship between formulating marketing strategy and marketing evaluation.

2 Many different departments or business functions may be involved in setting marketing strategy. Describe the role of several key departments that are involved in product decisions. Next, describe the role of several key departments that are involved in pricing decisions. Which tools can a B2B firm use to encourage communication and cooperation between these departments?

3 Why is it useful to evaluate marketing activities from different perspectives (annual activities, profitability, efficiency and the marketing function)? Would it make sense to combine all these perspectives into one overall marketing evaluation process?

4 Companies that start to assess the profitability of individual customers frequently discover that some of their largest customers are unprofitable. What should a marketing manager do to remedy such a situation?

5 Describe how marketing evaluation and control for a B2B firm is different from marketing evaluation and control for a manufacturer of consumer goods.

6 The specifics of a marketing evaluation and control system depend on the size of the organisation. What would be the key characteristics of a marketing evaluation and control system for a small manufacturer of machine parts? Design such a system.

7 Assessment of a firm's marketing function is often done by outside organisations. What are the reasons for using an outside organisation for such audits? Are there also disadvantages to using an outside organisation for a marketing audit?

8 Explain the relationship between customer satisfaction, customer loyalty and profits. Do you know products or industries that are characterised by a direct relationship between customer satisfaction and customer loyalty? How would you measure customer satisfaction? How would you measure customer loyalty?

9 An important characteristic of marketing metrics is whether they are forward- or backward-looking. Explain the difference between these two concepts and provide examples of both types of marketing metric.

10 Several firms use digital dashboards to access all kinds of information. List the benefits of using such digital dashboards. In addition to the numerous benefits, the use of digital dashboards also has potential disadvantages. What are the major disadvantages of using them?

Further reading

Bonoma, Thomas V. and Victoria L. Crittenden (1988) Managing marketing implementation, *Sloan Management Review*, 29(2): 7–14.

Kahn, Kenneth B. and John T. Mentzer (1998) Marketing's integration with other departments, *Journal of Business Research*, 42(1): 53–62.

Parasuraman, A., Valarie A. Zeithaml and Leonard L. Berry (1985) A conceptual model of service quality and its implications for future research, *Journal of marketing*, 49(3): 41–50.

Seggie, Steven H., Erin Cavusgil and Steven E. Phelan (2007) Measurement of return on marketing investment: a conceptual framework and the future of marketing metrics, *Industrial Marketing Management*, 36(6): 834–841.

Sheth, Jagdish N. and Rajendra S. Sisodia (2002) Marketing productivity: issues and analysis, *Journal of Business Research*, 55(5): 349–362.

References

Barwise, Patrick and John U. Farley (2004) Marketing metrics: status of six metrics in five countries, *European Management Journal*, 22(3): 257–262.

Beer, Michael and Russell A. Eisenstat (2000) The silent killers of strategy implementation and learning, *Sloan Management Review*, 41(4): 29–40.

Bonoma, Thomas V. and Victoria L. Crittenden (1988) Managing marketing implementation, *Sloan Management Review*, 29(2): 7–14.

Gupta, Sunil and Valarie Zeithaml (2006) Customer metrics and their impact on financial performance, *Marketing Science*, 25(6): 718–739.

Joyce, William, Nitin Nohria and Bruce Roberson (2003) *What (Really) Works*, New York: HarperBusiness.

Kahn, Kenneth B. and John T. Mentzer (1998) Marketing's integration with other departments, *Journal of Business Research*, 42(1): 53–62.

Kotler, Philip and Kevin L. Keller (2006) *Marketing Management*, twelfth edition, Upper Saddle River, NJ: Pearson Education.

Krohmer, Harley, Christian Homburg and John P. Workman (2002) Should marketing be cross-functional? Conceptual development and international empirical evidence, *Journal of Business Research*, 55(6): 451–465.

O'Sullivan, Don and Andrew V. Abela (2007) Marketing performance measurement ability and firm performance, *Journal of Marketing*, 71(2): 79–93.

O'Sullivan, Don, Andrew V. Abela and Mark Hutchinson (2009) Marketing performance measurement and firm performance, *European Journal of Marketing*, 43(5): 843–862.

Owen, Richard and Laura L. Brooks (2008) *Answering the Ultimate Question: How Net Promoter Can Transform Your Business*, San Francisco, CA: Jossey-Bass.

Parasuraman, A., Valarie A. Zeithaml and Leonard L. Berry (1985) A conceptual model of service quality and its implications for future research, *Journal of Marketing*, 49(3): 41–50.

Reichheld, Frederick F. (2003) The one number you need to grow, *Harvard Business Review*, 81(12): 46–54.

Seggie, Steven H., Erin Cavusgil and Steven E. Phelan (2007) Measurement of return on marketing investment: a conceptual framework and the future of marketing metrics, *Industrial Marketing Management*, 36(6): 834–841.

Sheth, Jagdish N. and Rajendra S. Sisodia (2002) Marketing productivity: issues and analysis, *Journal of Business Research*, 55(5): 349–362.

South, John B. and John E. Oliver (1998) What is a profitable product?, *Industrial Marketing Management*, 27(3): 187–195.

Zeithaml, Valarie A., A. Parasuraman and Leonard L. Berry (1990) *Delivering Quality Service: Balancing Customer Perceptions and Expectations*, New York: Free Press.

PART 06
Implementing a Value-creating Organisation

Designing and implementing a value-creating organisation

Chapter contents

Introduction

Successful B2B firms create superior value for their customers and are strongly focused on customers. Unfortunately, most B2B firms are plagued by a short-term product or sales orientation. They focus on products and their characteristics and do not look beyond the immediate sale. In contrast, a **value-creating organisation** has a customer focus programmed into its DNA and uses the customer's perspective to guide its decision making. While most B2B managers agree with the necessity of a customer focus, they are at a loss as to how to achieve such a consistent focus on their customers' success.

This chapter emphasises the need for a customer-centric organisation and contrasts it with the more traditional product or sales orientation. It explains that organisations should be designed outside-in (starting with the customer's needs), but at the same time notices that most B2B firms are designed inside-out (focusing on what is good for the organisation). An outside-in organisation is designed to create superior value for customers. To design their organisation outside in, management must start with the customer's needs and use these to design the appropriate business processes and supporting infrastructure. The chapter goes on to discuss the role of marketing in such a value-creating organisation at the corporate, SBU and tactical levels. One of the primary tasks of marketing is to instil a customer-oriented culture and make sure that all decisions ultimately serve the customer. Next, the chapter discusses the relationship between marketing and other departments in the organisation. Effective marketing requires effective cooperation between all elements of an organisation, but all too often firms struggle to make their departments work together. The chapter concludes by bringing all these themes together and developing a blueprint for firms that want to transform their product- or sales-driven organisations into a market-oriented one geared towards the creation of superior value for customers.

10.1 Characteristics of a value-creating organisation

Successful B2B firms create superior value for their customers. But most B2B firms are focused on products and technology, rather than customers. Enraptured by the technical challenges of developing new products, which are seen as the key to success, they are focused on products and their distinguishing features. Unfortunately, all too often this results in great new products that face only lacklustre demand from customers. Other B2B firms are sales-driven and primarily focused on getting the next sale. They do not care who will buy from them, as long as they can sell a product to a paying customer. Marketing is usually not a very popular term in these firms. It is associated with advertising and tricking customers into buying products that they do not really need and is only considered useful for fast-moving consumer products. In these firms, marketing is perceived as expensive overhead, while its contribution to firm performance is unclear. Therefore, many B2B firms avoid the term 'marketing': their organisation chart does not mention a marketing department. But that does not mean that these firms do not conduct marketing activities. Typically, many marketing activities are carried out by sales engineers, business development managers, sales managers and technical sales support employees. A sales manager, for instance, must prioritise market segments or individual customers and a business development manager might conduct a focus group with key customers to discuss new product ideas and concepts. Usually, these employees have a technical background and lack formal marketing training. Marketing is not located in a separate marketing department, but dispersed through the organisation and carried out by various employees as part of their job description (Workman 1993). This is partly caused by the strategic nature of B2B marketing, but also by the numerous employees that have direct contact with customers (not only salespeople, but also product developers, maintenance engineers, sales support employees and customer service employees).

Those B2B firms that do apply marketing, typically only do so sparingly; for instance, they carry out market studies and define market segments. But most of them fail to systematically investigate and analyse their customers, develop market segments based on different customer requirements, identify key segments to focus on and develop marketing approaches that are tailored to the characteristics of selected target segments. Indeed, most B2B firms do not realise that identifying target customers also implies a decision about which customers are better left to their competitors. They lack a clear focus in their activities and do not set priorities; every paying customer is welcome and it is very much against their business nature to 'refuse' or ignore certain customers. But this lack of focus results in widely dispersed marketing activities and customers in many different market segments, which limits the return on marketing expenditures. In addition, customer knowledge is often limited to information about the primary contact person(s), without detailed insight into the underlying reasons to buy and the value created for their customers. Moreover, most B2B firms do not know the key drivers of their customers' success and the requirements of downstream customers.

Table 10.1 summarises the differences between a product-centric and a **customer-centric** approach. Truly market-oriented firms that create value for their customers are characterised by an externally oriented culture focused on creating superior value for customers and retaining customers (Day 2003). They treat different customers differently and give their employees authority and responsibility to improve the customer's experience. This external orientation is used by everyone

TABLE 10.1 Product-centric versus customer-centric approach

	Product-centric	**Customer-centric**
Basic philosophy	Sell products to every customer that wants to buy	Serve customers; all decisions start with the customer and aim to create customer value
Business focus	Transaction-oriented; managing a portfolio of products	Relationship-oriented; managing a portfolio of customers
Organisational design	Based on what is good for the company	Based on what works best for customers
Organisational structure	Vertically structured around products or business functions	Horizontally structured around customer segments or value-creating processes
Customer information	Diffused throughout the organisation in separate databases, using separate customer definitions; focus on transaction data	Centralised database containing detailed customer pictures; accessible to all relevant departments and individuals; focus on rich customer information
Marketing/sales approach	Selling the product to as many customers as possible	Creating as much value as possible for customers
Communication	Communicate offering characteristics	Communicate value to the customer
Metrics	Number of new products, market share per product, profitability per product	Share of customer, customer satisfaction, customer lifetime value, customer retention, customer equity

in the organisation and information is shared freely. In addition, the organisation has a supporting infrastructure that keeps the organisation focused on customers and other relevant market parties. At Siebel Systems, 50 per cent of a manager's salary and 25 per cent of salespeople's sales commission is based on measured customer satisfaction. To determine salespeople's commission, Siebel measures customer satisfaction one year after the customer signed the contract, to make sure that they measure real customer satisfaction. Finally, a value-creating organisation focuses on collecting, sharing and using market information. IT systems and software (such as relationship management software) help, but only play a supporting role.

Such a value-creating organisation excels at the three core processes of defining value (based on its understanding of the market and captured in a competitive value proposition), developing value (through product development and input from partners) and delivering value (through marketing, sales and activities of channel partners). To maintain their competitive advantage, vendors must continuously re-evaluate their choices and decisions. Is the value offered to customers still superior to that of alternative offerings? Do we still collaborate with the best partners available? Can we identify new sources of value that are of interest to our customers? Can we find new customers for our offering? Market-oriented value-creating firms are learning organisations that continuously adapt to changing circumstances and learn from their experiences. They evaluate what went wrong to learn from their mistakes. But they also evaluate their successes to identify the underlying root causes and repeat what worked in new settings.

10.2 Designing a value-creating organisation

The underlying problem in many B2B firms is that they are designed *inside out*; they are designed the way they are because that is most practical for the organisation, but this means that the customer is expected to adapt! Products, for example, can only be purchased in specific order sizes, through certain channels or in specific configurations. The focus is on the efficiency of the firm's business processes rather than on what is best for the customer. This frequently results in an organisation structured around business functions, such as manufacturing, R&D, purchasing and sales, and a strong focus on the firm's products, manufacturing processes and other internal competencies (such as R&D). Marketing plans emphasise products and brochures describe in detail the characteristics of technologies and the range of products offered to customers. But ultimately it all revolves around the customer: it is the customer who pays the bills and the primary objective of every business firm should be to create superior value for the customer. To achieve this, firms must be designed *outside in*, with customer needs as the key principle in guiding all decisions that impact customers (Bund 2006).This means that the customer is central to all the firm's activities and decisions and that the organisation is designed to optimally serve the customer; for instance, with an organisation structured around customer groups, prices based on the value offered to

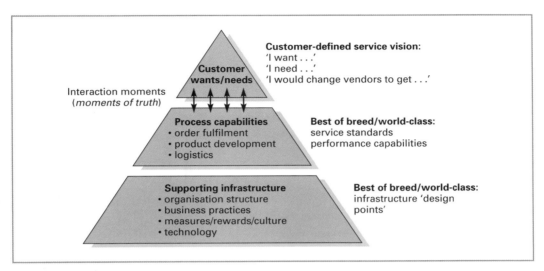

FIGURE 10.1 Designing a value-creating organisation
Source: Thompson (2000: 36). Reprinted with permission.

customers, brochures describing how customers benefit from the organisation's
products and sales channels that match the customers' preferred buying behaviour.

A market-oriented organisation that is geared towards creating superior value for
customers consists of three sets of building blocks: perceived **customer value** as the
key driver of organisation design, several process capabilities that are required to
realise this customer value and a supporting firm infrastructure (Thompson 2000).
See Figure 10.1.

Perceived customer value as the key driver of organisation design

The key to designing a value-creating organisation is taking a relentless outside-in
view of the business by putting the customer first. This is illustrated by BASF, the
world's leading chemical company, which proclaims on its website: 'We help our
customers to be more successful.' But, while the concept of putting the customer first
sounds easy and logical, it is very hard to achieve. Even firms that take the
customers' interests to heart find themselves falling into the trap of talking about
selling the firm's products instead of creating superior value for customers. This is
illustrated by numerous corporate websites that start by proudly presenting the
vendor's product range. But truly market-oriented companies focus on the value
offered to customers and design their organisation to optimally serve the customer.
They start with a clear, highly actionable customer-defined vision of themselves as
the ideal provider of products and services. This customer view becomes the focal
point for their business strategy and operations. Customer wants and needs are
translated into interaction moments or **customer touchpoints**, such as sales visits,
corporate websites, channel partners and corporate brochures. Each of these
customer touchpoints serves as a moment of truth, where the vendor has to prove

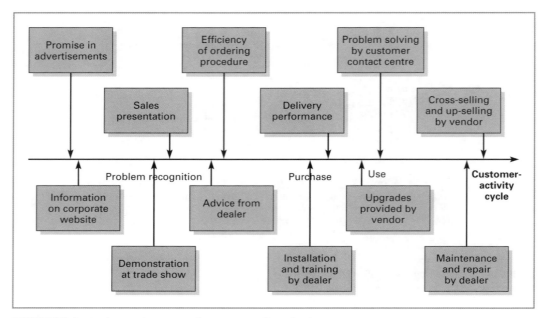

FIGURE 10.2 A seamless customer experience across all touchpoints

itself and contribute to an effective, seamless customer experience (Meyer and Schwager 2007). Fast and hassle-free product installation, for example, is promised on a corporate website, explained during a sales visit and implemented by a channel partner. B2B firms must craft a seamless **customer experience** across all touchpoints (Figure 10.2).

In B2B markets it is not always easy to determine which customer's view should be used to formulate the guiding vision. Is it the purchaser who negotiates with the salesperson about buying the product? Or is it the engineer who actually uses the product? Or maybe the channel partner who buys the product and sells it to numerous customers in many different markets? Or should the vendor focus on the perspective of downstream customers? All these customers may be relevant. The direct interaction with a customer's purchasing agents is a valuable starting point, but a vendor must determine the impact these individuals have on the ultimate buying decision and the role they play in repeat buying behaviour. By improving customer interactions with these parties, for example, a vendor may create value and become a preferred vendor. In addition, several non-direct-contact influencers may be critical in persuading a customer. These may be the actual users of the product and strongly influence the buying decision. But also non-users may influence the buying decision by reviewing alternatives, selecting vendors, approving or funding purchases. Vendors must chart all buying influences and develop value propositions for each key buying influence.

Channel partners are often treated as customers, especially when they own the relationships with end customers. But vendors should focus on both end customers and channel partners. They must create a vision of what the end customer wants and then design their company processes to enable their channel partners to be ideal for the end customer. Thus, vendors help their channel partners to be successful in creating value for end customers and create synergy between their own marketing efforts and those of their sales partners. A similar reasoning applies to the role of other downstream customers.

Before vendors start to formulate their customer vision they must decide which customers really count. By using market segmentation and selecting key target segments, vendors can develop effective, focused value propositions and increase the return on their marketing efforts. In some business markets, it may even make sense to focus on individual customers (segments of one). In these markets, vendors must prioritise their customers based on their estimated lifetime values. Armed with information about customers' profitability vendors may vary the level of service and attain a balance between the value received from and the value provided to customers.

Process capabilities

The firm's value proposition is the starting point for designing the **process capabilities** and supporting infrastructure that align the organisation with the needs of the customer. The vendor must analyse each key customer need to determine the implications for the required process capabilities and infrastructure. The vendor's organisation is a collection of value-creating core processes, such as product development, sales fulfilment and customer service (Barabba 1995). Firms that want to design effective core processes need to (Ashkenas et al. 1995; Hammer and Stanton 1999):

1 *Define the core processes.* Each core process creates value for customers and requires input from several business functions; for instance, sales fulfilment requires input from sales (order generation), manufacturing (production scheduling) and logistics (inventory management and delivery). Supporting processes that enable a smoothly functioning organisation are not core processes and may be outsourced.

2 *Formulate customer-based metrics for each process.* Examples are 'percentage of products delivered on time to customers', 'average up-time percentage' and 'order cycle time'.

3 *Assign process owners.* An effective process requires a process owner. Process owners are responsible for designing the process, implementing the process, measuring and evaluating process results and implementing process improvements.

4 *Eliminate barriers and streamline processes.* With *business process re-engineering* firms use the customer view to totally redesign their existing processes (Hammer and Champy 1993). Hammer (2007) provides a framework that allows firms to evaluate the maturity of their business processes and opportunities for process-based change.

A firm that changes from a functional organisation structure to a process-based structure changes its orientation from vertical to horizontal. The creation of a horizontal, process-based organisation does not mean that the vertical structure of geographic regions or product divisions disappears. Frequently a matrix organisation

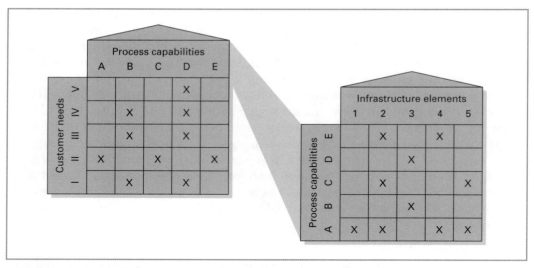

FIGURE 10.3 Translating customer needs into process capabilities and infrastructure
Source: Thompson (2000: 161). Reprinted with permission.

results, with division managers closely cooperating with process owners. Nevertheless, the primary emphasis is on the firm's key processes and the process owners direct the rest of the organisation.

Supporting infrastructure

The firm's enabling **infrastructure** encompasses all organisational elements that support the process capabilities. By systematically converting customer needs into business requirements, firms can design the required infrastructure that is needed to enable the essential process capabilities. However, most firms fail to conduct such a systematic analysis or to monitor the alignment between infrastructure and customer interactions, resulting in an organisation that slowly drifts away from the customer. An organisation's enabling infrastructure includes its organisation structure (alignment around customers, specialised sales groups, focus on core value-creating processes), management and measurement system (measuring and tracking customer value, identifying root causes of missed objectives), employee reward system (encouraging teamwork, focus on customer satisfaction and loyalty), skills and training (formalised programmes that continuously educate employees about customer value and value-creating processes), information and communication technology (centralised information that offers a holistic view of customers, efficient and effective information dissemination) and organisation memory (effective system for storing information and learning from experience).

There is no one-to-one relationship between process capabilities and infrastructure elements. Tools such as *Quality Function Deployment* can be used to systematically translate customer needs into process capabilities and infrastructure elements (Figure 10.3). The design of a value-creating organisation is further complicated when the firm cooperates with partners in creating value for customers. When this is the case, core processes and capabilities extend beyond the organisation and must be coordinated with processes and capabilities of partner organisations. Firms must develop a viable network position that allows them to contribute to a successful value network and extract significant value from customers.

10.3 The role of marketing in a value-creating organisation

B2B marketing is all about creating superior value for customers, which helps them to be more successful. B2B marketing concerns a large number of strategic decisions that impact firm performance. This begs the central question: what exactly is the **role of marketing** in a value-creating organisation? The central role of marketing is to keep all business units, departments and outside partners focused on customers and their changing definition of value in the competitive marketplace. Marketing must be the 'expert on the customer' and help decision-makers to make market-oriented decisions by providing them with the appropriate customer and market information. A more detailed discussion of the role of marketing in a value-creating network organisation makes a distinction between marketing at the corporate level, at the business (SBU) level and at the tactical level (Webster 1994).

Marketing at the corporate level

At corporate level, the key strategic decision is to define what business the company is in and to determine the firm's mission, position in the value network and its distinctive competences. The key responsibilities of marketing are:

- *Customer advocacy*: marketing represents the customer in the firm by making sure that all business decisions take the customer's point of view as the starting point.
- *Market structure analysis*: as a key input to the firm's strategic planning process, marketing provides information about market segments, competitors' positions and strategies and how customers define superior value.
- *Positioning in the value network*: marketing translates the customer's definition of value into specific organisational capabilities and activities.
- *Professional development of the marketing function*: marketing ensures that there are programmes for hiring, developing and deploying capable marketing employees; in larger organisations marketing also develops and delivers training programmes to nurture an understanding of marketing and the marketplace throughout the organisation.
- *Strategic partnering*: marketing initiates, develops and manages strategic partnerships with key customers, resellers, suppliers and other partners (such as complementors and universities).

These strategic activities do not require a large corporate infrastructure. But they do require staff with experience, expertise and sophistication in understanding customer needs and customer value and communicating this understanding throughout the organisation.

Marketing at the business (SBU) level

At the corporate level, the key strategic decision is to define the business the firm is in. Accordingly, at the level of the individual business unit the key strategic decision concerns how to compete in that business. The essential marketing tasks at this level are:

- *Market segmentation, targeting and positioning*: marketing understands each market segment in detail, selects the segments that the firm will focus on and develops a viable market positioning.

- *Developing the value proposition*: the firm's value proposition captures the firm's strategy at the business level and it is marketing's task to focus all departments and outside partners on the customer's definition of value and coordinate their efforts in delivering superior value.

- *Developing partnering strategies*: since virtually every activity can be outsourced to partners, marketing analyses whether marketing activities (such as advertising, personal selling, distribution and package design) should be outsourced or performed in-house.

Marketing at the tactical level

At the tactical level, marketing is responsible for all traditional marketing decisions required to implement the business strategy and create superior value for customers. This includes all decisions about the firm's offering, customer contact, communication and pricing. These decisions are made by functional specialists, such as product managers, sales managers, channel managers, sales promotion experts, advertising managers, application engineers and customer service employees.

   The foregoing discussion focuses on the role of marketing as a business function, that is, a series of activities to be performed. But where in the organisation should these activities be carried out? One might argue that a truly market-oriented firm, where all employees base their actions on the firm's vision of superior customer value, does not need a marketing department. After all, everybody in the organisation is focused on the customer and contributes to the creation of superior value. While it is true that such an organisation requires a smaller marketing department, it cannot do without a formal marketing function because someone must direct the firm's key marketing decisions and develop the firm's marketing capability. In B2B firms such a marketing function may also be located in a strategic business development group, while in small firms it is usually the responsibility of the firm's CEO or management team.

10.4 Coordination between marketing and other business functions

A defining characteristic of a value-creating organisation is the existence of effective interfaces between organisational units (business functions, departments, business units). The creation of superior value for customers requires effective internal communication and collaboration. In a value-creating organisation, everybody is focused on the customer's perspective and core processes are carried out by cross-functional teams with representatives from several functional areas. But, in practice, **interfunctional coordination** is often far removed from this ideal situation. Business functions and departments operate as isolated silos and focus on their own objectives that only rarely involve the customer. An 'us versus them' attitude prevails, resulting in a lack of communication and misunderstandings at best, and distrust, resentment and conflict at worst. Many B2B firms experienced first-hand that one of the toughest parts of implementing a value-creating organisation is to align all functional areas towards the same objective: creating superior value for customers.

Marketing and R&D

The largest differences between functional areas are found between marketing and R&D, representing the commercial and technical sides of a firm. The differences between marketing and R&D are rooted in different personalities and backgrounds. Marketing people tend to be externally oriented, dominant, assertive, enthusiastic and enterpreneurial, while R&D people are more internally oriented, quiet, reactive and analytical. Marketing people look at customers and competitors, judge new product ideas on their competitive merits, use a short-term perspective and communicate primarily with other managers in the organisation. R&D people are focused on technical opportunities, judge new product ideas on their technical challenges, feasibility and opportunities for patents and scientific publications, use a long-term perspective and communicate primarily with colleagues at other organisations. These differences often result in very stereotypical perceptions of each other (Griffin and Hauser 1996; see Table 10.2). Marketing considers R&D people to

TABLE 10.2 Stereotypical perceptions of marketing and R&D

Marketing about R&D	R&D about marketing
• They are not interested in costs • They hide in the laboratory • They must be kept away from customers • They want customers to adapt • They do not look at competitors and do not know what a competitive advantage is • They are inflexible and conservative • They do not stick to planning • They are only interested in technology • They are never ready with developing a new product	• They want everything as soon as possible • They are not realistic and make promises they cannot keep • They only look at customers, who do not know what they want anyway • They constantly change specifications • They make bad predictions • They are impatient and always in a hurry • They do not understand technology • They want to introduce a new product as quickly as possible

be technical nerds, who are out of touch with the real world. They do not understand customers or the realities of the competitive marketplace. Instead, they are only focused on technology and never finished with developing a new product. R&D, on the other hand, perceives marketing as being too much focused on the customer, making all sorts of promises that they cannot keep. If a customer asks for changes to a product, marketing is all too ready to agree, even though they do not realise the consequences of these customer requests for R&D or manufacturing.

These stereotypical perceptions limit the organisation's effectiveness. Because marketing feels that R&D people do not understand customers, they will keep them away from customers, which only increases their lack of understanding of customer needs and their focus on technology. On the other hand, because R&D people think that their marketing colleagues do not understand technology, they are unlikely to inform them of new development projects, which will reinforce marketing's lack of knowledge about technology. Thus, the existence of stereotypical perceptions only reinforces the differences between marketing and R&D. These differences cause numerous problems in the marketing–R&D interface. In many firms, marketing and R&D do not appreciate each other's unique contribution and are therefore less likely to cooperate and coordinate activities. In other firms, the actual or perceived distance between the two functions limits communication and the use of different languages results in misunderstandings and conflict. Sometimes, there is even deep resentment and distrust between the two functions; for instance, when R&D feels that marketing has taken too much credit for the success of new products. But not all problems between marketing and R&D can be attributed to different personalities and backgrounds. Problems may also occur because top management fails to encourage and reward cooperative behaviour.

In many firms, the differences between marketing and R&D are pronounced and seemingly insurmountable. Suggested measures to improve communication and cooperation between marketing and R&D include joint activities (such as joint customer visits), co-location, job rotation, appropriate incentives and rewards, project teams, informal interaction, open communication, formal management tools (such as Quality Function Deployment) and training about each other's discipline (Griffin and Hauser 1996). A study of integration between marketing and R&D in the context of new product development found that co-location, a cross-functional new product development review board, equal remuneration and career opportunities, and cross-functional teams were most effective in fostering integration (Leenders and Wierenga 2002).

Marketing and other functions

The relationships between marketing and other business functions display many similar problems. An example is the interface between marketing and manufacturing. Marketing aims at stimulating demand and wants to comply with every individual customer wish by offering a large number of different products.

TABLE 10.3 Conflict areas between marketing and manufacturing

Area of conflict	Marketing objective	Manufacturing objective
Managing diversity ● Product line length/breadth ● Product customisation ● Product line changes	Many and complex models Customer specifications Product changes immediately; high risk	Few and simple models 'Stock' products Planned, only necessary changes; low risk
Managing conformity ● Product scheduling ● Capacity/facility planning	Constant change Accept all orders	Inflexible Critically evaluate 'fit' of orders
Managing dependability ● Delivery ● Quality control	Immediate; large inventory High standards	As soon as possible; no inventory Reasonable control

Source: Crittenden et al. (1993: 301). Reprinted with permission from Elsevier.

Manufacturing, on the other hand, tries to control the firm's manufacturing process and prefers to produce a limited number of products in large quantities (thus minimising set-up costs). In addition, marketing likes an extensive inventory of products so that they can meet the expected and unexpected needs of customers, while manufacturing wants to minimise inventories to reduce costs (De Ruyter and Wetzels 2000a).

Key decisions that must be taken by marketing and manufacturing concern the length and breadth of product lines, product customisation and product line changes (Crittenden et al. 1993; see Table 10.3). Another key joint decision involves the allocation of available manufacturing capacity, especially when the existing capacity is insufficient for the current level of demand. Should the firm's loyal customers be served first or that one large customer that was recently acquired with a lot of effort? Typical marketing decisions such as the selection of target customers also significantly impact the mix of products that must be manufactured and should therefore be a joint marketing and manufacturing decision.

Some firms, for example in the aircraft industry, realise a harmonious marketing–manufacturing interface by using a built-to-order strategy. Others manufacture standardised products and only add customer-specific modifications relatively late in the manufacturing process. This strategy achieves a compromise between offering customised products (marketing) and minimising inventory costs (manufacturing). De Ruyter and Wetzels (2000a) found that measures such as co-location, movement of personnel between marketing and manufacturing, informal networks, joint responsibility for projects and compensation based on marketing–manufacturing team performance also contribute to an improved marketing–manufacturing interface.

While marketing's relationships with R&D and manufacturing are plagued by cultural differences, marketing and purchasing are very similar. Both are focused on transactions and relationships with other organisations and develop close relationships with these organisations to maximise customer value. Basically, marketing and purchasing are mirror images and thus closely related. But there are also differences. Marketing tries to increase revenues through a large number of product modifications and customised products to meet a large range of customer needs. Purchasing, on the other hand, aims to minimise costs and prefers to buy standardised products in large quantities.

The relationship between marketing and finance is important because all marketing decisions and activities are based on financial information (budgets, prices, margins, revenues) and have financial consequences. Because marketing is more dependent on information from finance than vice versa, the relationship between the two functions is not always harmonious (De Ruyter and Wetzels 2000b). Marketing, for example, wants to offer more favourable terms of payment to expand business with an important customer, while finance does not want to approve a new order before the last one is paid for. The key decision-making areas where marketing and finance must cooperate are investment decisions, brand valuation, inventory management and pricing. Firms that measure and evaluate marketing's performance (*accountability*) are more likely to create an effective interface between marketing and finance.

An increasingly important interface is the one between marketing and information systems (IS). This interface is especially important in firms using CRM systems, customer databases, data-mining and a large amount of market information. Both marketing and IS people acknowledge the relevance of an effective marketing–IS interface, but in practice this interface is not always without problems. Many IS managers think that marketing people fail to capitalise on the opportunities offered by information technology. Historically, IS personnel have been hired principally for their technical expertise and intellectual capacity to design systems, but they are increasingly involved in projects requiring interpersonal communication skills.

Marketing and sales

The two business functions that are most similar are marketing and sales. They both serve customers in complementary roles, with marketing entrusted with strategic tasks such as providing support to salespeople and building a consistent brand image in the marketplace, and sales traditionally performing tactical tasks like contacting customers, executing marketing strategies and closing the sale in the field. Ideally, marketing and sales activities are closely coordinated, with salespeople collecting valuable customer-related information and passing it to their marketing colleagues, and marketing using the information to create customised products and programmes, and thus increasing value for customers. Unfortunately, in practice the marketing–sales interface is not always harmonious and constructive (Beverland et al. 2006). One study found that 'in many companies as much as 80 per cent of marketing expenditures on lead generation and sales collateral are wasted – ignored as irrelevant and unhelpful by sales'.[1] Another recent study concluded that 'senior managers often describe the working relationship between Sales and Marketing as unsatisfactory. The two functions, they say, undercommunicate, underperform, and overcomplain' (Kotler et al. 2006: 78).

The problems between marketing and sales are attributed to different goals, different perspectives, different thought worlds, physical separation and poor communication. Problems also arise because the sales organisation feels that it owns the customer relationships and resists all efforts from other departments to contact its customers. Or they question the value and costs of marketing; salespeople see themselves as generating revenues, while marketing is only expensive overhead. In B2B firms, fundamental job differences also contribute to the divide between marketing and sales: marketing people talk to end-users, while salespeople typically spend their time with purchasing agents. Marketers deal with market segments and product groups; sales looks at individual accounts. Many B2B firms also exacerbate the problem by creating separate marketing and sales functions, with the sales vice-president often outranking the senior marketing manager.

Biemans et al. (forthcoming) found several distinct marketing–sales configurations in B2B firms. In small firms, in particular, there is often no separate marketing department and marketing activities are performed by the firm's CEO or sales manager. As a firm grows, it establishes a formal marketing department to support short-term sales activities. Eventually, this marketing department evolves into a fully-fledged marketing department, with a strategic focus and a distinct identity separate from sales. The marketing–sales interface can be improved by focusing both functions on the creation of superior value to customers, stimulating open communication and formulating joint objectives and activities. In addition, both functions should be involved in each other's activities and planning. Sales, for example, should be involved in the selection of target segments and the formulation of marketing strategies. This encourages the free flow of information and increases mutual appreciation and understanding.

Cross-functional teams

Marketing's effectiveness depends on its collaboration with other departments. Similarly, marketing activities and decisions also impact other business functions. Many business processes require inputs from several functional areas, all of which need to collaborate to achieve joint objectives. Successful product development, for example, requires close cooperation between marketing (providing information about customer needs, segmenting the market, testing product concepts with customers and channel partners, testing prototypes with customers), R&D (translating customer needs into product specifications, developing prototypes), design (designing modules and product interfaces, translating product performance into product characteristics and user interfaces), manufacturing (information about manufacturing limitations and possibilities, trial production run) and purchasing (potential cost savings, involvement of suppliers, make-or-buy decision).

✍ **INSIGHT: Advantages of cross-functional teams**

Although **cross-functional teams** must be carefully managed to deal with the inherent differences between functions, the potential benefits are significant. In product development, in particular, the use of cross-functional teams is much preferred over the traditional approach of throwing the new product 'over the wall' to the next department. The major benefits of using cross-functional teams are:

- Increased speed, for instance faster time to market in product development.
- Ability to solve complex problems, by bringing together people with different skills and perspectives.
- Faster decision making, through interaction between all relevant people.
- Creative solutions, for instance radical new products or services result from the confrontation of different perspectives.
- Customer focus, by breaking down barriers between business functions and other organisational units.
- Organisational learning, which is stimulated by the interaction between people with different backgrounds, communication styles and skills.

Firms should only expect these benefits to materialise when all relevant team members are included in the team, team members are open-minded and motivated, the team has authority to accomplish its task and is headed by a strong team leader, and management provide adequate resources and support for the team. But there are also potential disadvantages of cross-functional teams. For instance, team members may become too narrowly focused on just a few clients or products handled by the team.

10.5 Transforming the organisation

Organisations are only rarely designed from scratch. Instead, firms already exist and possess a history, culture, market position and a host of other characteristics that were shaped by business decisions and market forces. A firm, for example, may have started out as a spin-off from a university to commercialise a newly developed technology, resulting in a strong focus on technology where customer projects were selected because of their technical challenges rather than their commercial potential. When such a firm wants to transform itself from an inside-out, technology-focused business into a nimble outside-in, value-creating firm, it must develop a holistic programme for organisational change. Management might decide to start small by redesigning one core process, such as product development or sales fulfilment, to increase the value offered to customers. A more ambitious change programme involves a whole business unit or the whole organisation, with business processes redesigned together with the organisation's structure, systems and procedures. The most elaborate change programme encompasses the total value network and includes the firm's strategic partners (such as resellers, vendors and complementors) in the change process. After all, the results from becoming focused on customers will be limited when channel partners remain product oriented.

To transform a technology- or product-oriented B2B firm into a value-creating organisation requires a comprehensive change programme, involving substantial resources and a long-term focus. Many managers underestimate the time required to significantly change an organisation and align business processes and supporting infrastructure elements with customer needs. All too often, impatient managers conclude that employees do not display the desired new behaviour and that therefore the change effort has failed. Implementing a value-creating organisation requires new attitudes and knowledge, new skills, an enabling infrastructure and an effective organisational change programme.

New attitudes and knowledge

The creation of superior value for customers requires changes in employees' attitudes. A technology-oriented culture, where everything revolves around the technical challenges of developing new products and ensuring smoothly running manufacturing processes, must be transformed into a market-oriented culture, in which all activities are determined by the customer's definition of superior value. Employees must rewire their mindsets and put the customer at the heart of their activities and decisions.

New knowledge plays a critical role in this transformation of an organisation's culture. In a typical B2B firm, many employees are unfamiliar with marketing and the concept of value creation. In addition, many firms are structured around business functions, such as marketing, R&D and manufacturing, each of which has developed into an island with its own language, priorities and habits. A comprehensive training and communication programme must explain the concepts of market orientation and value creation and how they contribute to improved firm performance. This ensures that all employees speak the same language and are conversant with key concepts such as value creation, superior value, target customers, competitive advantage and market segmentation. It is essential that the somewhat abstract concepts of 'market orientation' and 'value creation' are translated to the daily activities of individual employees. Otherwise, good intentions will not result in the desired behaviour.

The required attitudinal changes represent a wrenching change and many firms have discovered that not all employees are capable or willing to change their behaviour. A purchaser who has been successfully squeezing suppliers might be unable to treat them as partners in creating superior value for customers. Many firms will find that several employees either cannot keep up with the required changes or no longer feel at home in the firm's new culture.

New skills

Employees are only able to change and implement the desired new behaviour when they possess the required skills to do so. Product developers must no longer base their ideas for new products on the challenges of interesting new technologies, but on what customers need to improve their business performance. Successful B2B marketing is based on the customer's success: the more successful customers are, the more successful their vendors will be. The critical skills in a value-creating organisation are:

- *Interaction with market parties.* B2B firms interact with customers, suppliers, resellers and other market parties in their quest to create superior value. Employees, for example, must learn how to communicate with customers, create a seamless dialogue, implement relationship marketing and collaborate with customers in product development.

- *Interaction with other parts of the firm.* Interaction with market parties is only effective when the various parts of the organisation interact and collaborate effectively. Employees must learn about the perspectives and priorities of other departments or business units, improve their communication skills and learn to gather and disseminate market information.

- *Continuous improvement.* The creation of superior value is not a final state that the organisation needs to achieve, but a continuous journey. Changing customer needs and competitive positions require firms to be alert to changes in the marketplace and new opportunities to create superior value. This continuous improvement may be realised through periodic benchmark studies at other firms (who are not necessarily working in the same industry) and a user-friendly information system that captures information and experiences.

MINI CASE: CHANGING PEOPLE'S BEHAVIOUR

An organisation's culture and behaviour are closely related and one of the key questions is: should an organisation start with changing its culture (for instance, by sending employees to seminars about market orientation and value creation) or with changing the behaviour of its employees (for instance, by prescribing the new desired behaviour)? Changes in an organisation's culture are considered to be more fundamental and lasting, but when an organisation wants to achieve short-term results it is better to focus on changing people's behaviour.

An example is provided by Boeing. In the 1990s, Boeing developed the new jetliner 777, a huge development project that required billions of dollars and would generate income for the company for the next 25–30 years. To make sure that Boeing would develop an aircraft that its customers really wanted, in 1989 the company met with technical and planning specialists from potential airline customers in the US, Europe and Asia to discuss the aircraft's configuration. To develop the aircraft, Boeing used more than 200 design–build teams that included people from engineering design, finance, operations, manufacturing, customer support, suppliers and customers. In the words of Philip Condit, president of the Boeing company at the time, 'The success of our company is linked to the success of our airline customers. We cannot expect to be profitable unless we design and build the kind of equipment that gives them the competitive edge they need to grow and prosper. We have an obligation to listen to what our customers say, to work with them by asking the right questions, to determine their fundamental needs, and to develop solutions to those problems.'

But Boeing had never before cooperated so closely with customers in developing a new aircraft. For the development of the Boeing 777, a number of airlines were made part of Boeing's development teams. Boeing's engineers initially reacted very negatively to this new approach: 'You've got to be kidding. Do you realize what that means? It's tough to design an airplane. Did you think about what it would be like with a customer in there? It would be terrible!' But the experiment turned out to be a huge success. When customers were made part of the development teams, they were closely involved in the development process. Boeing engineers realised that they no longer needed to wonder how customers would react, because they could simply ask them. And that is how it happened that someone called out during a meeting: 'We can't go on with this meeting – where in the heck is the customer? Somebody go find the customer!'

Sources: Condit (1994) and Sabbagh (1996)

Enabling infrastructure

Implementing a value-creating organisation is not just a matter of learning some new techniques; it means acquiring a philosophy that radically changes the organisation. To be successful, firms must redesign all key elements of their infrastructure to support the new philosophy and enable the desired behaviour. This requires the elimination of barriers, such as inertia and resistance to change, and improving communication between departments and business units. The key elements of an enabling infrastructure are:

- *Role of top management.* Although successful implementation depends on the willingness of employees throughout the organisation to change their behaviour, top management plays a critical role by initiating and directing the change programme. Top management must communicate the need for change, decentralise responsibilities to cross-functional project teams, define new roles, tasks and responsibilities, allocate resources and function as role models.

- *Organisational memory.* To learn from experiences and obtained insights, firms need some kind of organisational memory that can be easily accessed and enhanced. Firms must design the required information system, communication channels and procedures, and protocols for registering results and experiences. But it is not all about information systems and procedures; an organisation's memory also depends on the commitment of key individuals and the use of cross-functional teams.

- *Evaluation and reward systems.* Employees will only change their behaviour when they benefit from doing so. This implies that firms must align their evaluation and reward systems with the desired behaviour. Salespeople, for example, should be rewarded on customer satisfaction and customer retention instead of sales, and product developers should be evaluated on the performance of the whole product development team. In some firms, salaries of sales representatives, sales managers and marketing managers are partly based on systematically measured customer satisfaction.

- *Training programmes.* Firms must design and implement training programmes to bridge the gap between employees' current skills and required market-oriented skills. Many key employees must be trained in basic marketing principles (especially market orientation and value creation), interaction with customers, communication and cooperation. Everybody must realise that they work for the customer and they must be taught how to implement a market orientation in their daily activities.

- *Organisation structure.* Successful implementation of value creation often also requires changes in an organisation's structure. Many firms tilt their organisations by changing a vertical structure (around business functions) into a horizontal one (around value-creating processes or customer groups).

Effective change programme

An effective **change programme**, designed to implement a value-creating organisation, requires both a short- and a long-term perspective. Changes in an organisation's culture will only be noticeable in the long run (frequently, only after several years), but short-term success is required to create commitment and momentum. Therefore, firms must design one or two pilot projects to jump-start the required changes. Such pilot projects must concern a clearly defined activity of limited scope (for instance, increasing the number of new product ideas generated by customers), have a high probability of quick and measurable success (for instance, the number of new product ideas from customers rather than the much more general and indirect success or profitability of new products) and be related to activities of individual employees (for instance, encouraging maintenance engineers to actively ask customers about product improvement suggestions).

The success of these pilot projects must be communicated extensively throughout the firm to create enthusiasm and momentum. Next, somewhat more complex or comprehensive follow-up projects must be initiated. Thus, the short-term success of one or two pilot projects creates the enthusiasm and commitment required for the long-term implementation of the change programme.

When this transformation process is designed and managed successfully, the end result is an organisation that effectively designs, develops and delivers superior value for customers and thus creates value for all its stakeholders.

Online
Learning **Centre**

When you have read this chapter, log on to the Online Learning Centre website at ***www.mcgraw-hill.co.uk/textbooks/biemans*** to explore chapter-by-chapter test questions, further reading and more online study tools.

Summary of Key Concepts

- Successful B2B firms create superior value for their customers and are strongly focused on customers. They are highly market oriented and a customer focus is the core of their corporate DNA.

- In practice, most B2B firms have a short-term product or sales orientation. They focus on products and their characteristics and do not look beyond the immediate sale.

- B2B vendors should be designed outside-in (starting with the customer's needs), but are usually designed inside-out (focusing on what is good for the organisation). An outside-in organisation is designed to create superior value for customers.

- Designing an outside-in organisation starts with the customer's needs and uses these to design the appropriate business processes and supporting infrastructure.

- A B2B firm that is highly market oriented may require a smaller marketing department. But every organisation needs marketing personnel who are dedicated to instilling a customer-oriented culture, making sure that all decisions ultimately serve the customer and developing the firm's marketing capability.

- Effective B2B marketing requires good cooperation between all departments in the organisation, but all too often departments are unable to work together.

- The largest differences in an organisation can be found between the firm's commercial side (marketing, sales) and its technical side (R&D, manufacturing). Different backgrounds, objectives and cultures often result in miscommunication, distrust and sometimes outright hostility.

- Even marketing and sales, however, are not always able to work together effectively. Although both departments are focused on customers and play complementary roles, the relationship between marketing and sales is not always a harmonious one.

- The keys to effective cooperation between departments are open communication, joint activities and training in each other's discipline.

- B2B firms that want to transform their product- or sales-driven organisation into a market-oriented one geared towards the creation of superior value for customers need to redesign many interrelated elements of their organisation (culture, structure, skills, systems and processes).

> ## 🔑 Key terms
>
> Change programme, p. 322
> Cross-functional teams, p. 318
> Customer experience, p. 308
> Customer touchpoints, p. 307
> Customer value, p. 307
> Customer-centric, p. 305
>
> Infrastructure, p. 310
> Interfunctional coordination, p. 313
> Process capabilities, p. 309
> Role of marketing, p. 311
> Value-creating organisation, p. 303

Discussion questions

1 Many B2B firms are not very market-oriented and are instead characterised by a strong product or sales orientation. But many of these short-term oriented firms still enjoy a good business performance in terms of sales and profits. Explain why many B2B firms manage to survive despite their short-term product or sales orientation.

2 The design of a market-oriented organisation must be based on customer needs and customer touchpoints. Select a specific B2B product and inventory all relevant customer touchpoints. How can a vendor inventory all relevant customer touchpoints?

3 One of marketing's key tasks is to promote an awareness of the customer's perspective. Describe a number of tools that marketing may use to promote a customer focus within the firm.

4 Small B2B firms, in particular, do not have the means for a separate marketing department and marketing activities are usually performed by the firm's CEO or sales manager. What problems are likely to occur in such a situation? How can a small firm solve these problems (or reduce their impact) without establishing a marketing department?

5 Despite many similarities between marketing and purchasing, the relationship between these two business functions is not always harmonious. What are the reasons for an ineffective marketing–purchasing interface? What are the advantages of effective collaboration between marketing and purchasing?

6 One suggestion to improve the relationship between marketing and R&D is to implement joint customer visits. What are the advantages of a joint customer visit by marketing and R&D for: (a) marketing, (b) R&D, (c) the selling organisation, and (d) the customer?

7 An important task of marketing at the corporate level is to promote a market orientation throughout the organisation. Which specific measures and activities can be used to promote a market orientation internally?

8 Describe several measures that a firm can take to encourage and improve interfunctional coordination and communication. Which of these measures would work best for small firms? And which of these measures would be more effective in large firms?

9 Describe a number of strategies or tools that a firm can use to create/improve the firm's organisational memory.

10 Effective programmes to implement a focus on creating superior value for customers often start with a limited pilot project. Consider the following two options for a pilot project: (a) implement changes for one specific group of customers, (b) implement changes for one specific business process. Which of these pilot projects is most likely to contribute to an improved market orientation in the firm? Justify your answer.

Further reading

Bund, Barbara E. (2006) *The Outside-In Corporation: How to Build a Customer-centric Organization for Breakthrough Results*, New York: McGraw-Hill.

Day, George S. (2003) Creating a superior customer-relating capability, *Sloan Management Review*, 44(3): 77–82.

Griffin, Abbie and John R. Hauser (1996) Integrating R&D and marketing: a review and analysis of the literature, *Journal of Product Innovation Management*, 13(3): 191–215.

Thompson, Harvey (2000) *The Customer-centered Enterprise: How IBM and Other World-class Companies Achieve Extraordinary Results by Putting Customers First*, New York: McGraw-Hill.

References

Ashkenas, Ron, Dave Ulrich, Todd Jick and Steve Kerr (1995) *The Boundaryless Organization: Breaking the Chains of Organizational Structure*, San Francisco, CA: Jossey-Bass.

Barabba, Vincent P. (1995) *Meeting of the Minds: Creating the Market-based Enterprise*, Boston, MA: Harvard Business School Press.

Beverland, Michael, Marion Steel and G. Peter Dapiran (2006) Cultural frames that drive sales and marketing apart: an exploratory study, *Journal of Business & Industrial Marketing*, 21(6): 386–94.

Biemans, Wim G., Maja Makovec Brenčič and Avinash Malshe (forthcoming) Marketing–Sales interface configurations in B2B firms, *Industrial Marketing Management*.

Bund, Barbara E. (2006) *The Outside-In Corporation: How to Build a Customer-centric Organization for Breakthrough Results*, New York: McGraw-Hill.

Condit, Philip M. (1994) Focusing on the customer: how Boeing does it, *Research-Technology Management*, 37(1): 33–37.

Crittenden, Victoria L., Lorraine R. Gardiner and Antonie Stam (1993) Reducing conflict between marketing and manufacturing, *Industrial Marketing Management*, 22(4): 299–309.

Day, George S. (2003) Creating a superior customer-relating capability, *Sloan Management Review*, 44(3): 77–82.

De Ruyter, Ko and Martin Wetzels (2000a) Determinants of a relational exchange orientation in the marketing–manufacturing interface: an empirical investigation, *Journal of Management Studies*, 37(2): 257–276.

De Ruyter, Ko and Martin Wetzels (2000b) The marketing–finance interface: a relational exchange perspective, *Journal of Business Research*, 50(2): 209–215.

Griffin, Abbie and John R. Hauser (1996) Integrating R&D and marketing: a review and analysis of the literature, *Journal of Product Innovation Management*, 13(3): 191–215.

Hammer, Michael (2007) The process audit, *Harvard Business Review*, 85(4): 111–123.

Hammer, Michael and James Champy (1993) *Reengineering the Corporation: A Manifesto for Business Revolution*, New York: HarperBusiness.

Hammer, Michael and Steven Stanton (1999) How process organizations *really* work, *Harvard Business Review*, 77(6): 108–118.

Kotler, Philip, Neil Rackham and Suj Krishnaswamy (2006) Ending the war between sales and marketing, *Harvard Business Review*, 84(7/8): 68–78.

Leenders, Mark A.A.M. and Berend Wierenga (2002) The effectiveness of different mechanisms for integrating marketing and R&D, *Journal of Product Innovation Management*, 19(4): 305–317.

Meyer, Christopher and Andre Schwager (2007) Understanding customer experience, *Harvard Business Review*, 85(2): 117–126.

Sabbagh, Karl (1996) *Twenty-first Century Jet: The Making and Marketing of the Boeing 777*, New York: Scribner.

Thompson, Harvey (2000) *The Customer-centered Enterprise: How IBM and Other World-class Companies Achieve Extraordinary Results by Putting Customers First*, New York: McGraw-Hill.

Webster, Frederick E., Jr. (1994) *Market-driven Management: Using the New Marketing Concept to Create a Customer-oriented Company*, New York: Wiley.

Workman, John P., Jr. (1993) Marketing's limited role in new product development in one computer systems firm, *Journal of Marketing Research*, 30(4): 405–421.

Note

[1] Aberdeen Group (2002) Bridging the divide: process, technology, and the marketing/sales interface, *Marketing Viewpoint*, 4 October, pp. 1–12.

Cases

Vekoma: Selling roller-coasters

Screaming people, the smell of candyfloss and the sound of roaring trains are not usually associated with B2B marketing. Yet, they are typical for the environment in which Vekoma's products are used. Vekoma is one of the world's largest roller-coaster manufacturers and its products are branded with colourful names such as Boomerang, Invertigo and Stingray. Vekoma's customers often rename their products with even more spectacular names; for instance, the Kentucky Kingdom Amusement Park painted the popular Boomerang blood red and promoted it as the 'Vampire'.

Source: Vekoma Rides Manufacturing. Used with permission.

History

Vekoma was founded in 1926 as Veld Koning Machinefabriek (Veld Koning Machine factory) and changed its strategic direction several times. It started out as a manufacturer of agricultural equipment such as harrows, ploughs and sowing machines. When the agricultural industry declined during the 1950s, Vekoma used its technical expertise for the construction of large steel structures for the mining industry. Ten years later they followed one of its largest customers, DSM (Dutch State Mines), into the petrochemical industry and started manufacturing industrial heaters and furnaces. Gradually, the design and manufacture of piping systems became the firm's core activity and in the 1970s the firm's management identified a new industry for their core expertise: roller-coasters. At present, Vekoma Rides Manufacturing is one of the world's largest manufacturers of roller-coasters and its products can be found throughout the world. For instance, Gardaland (Italy) features several Vekoma roller-coasters, including the spectacular Mammut that opened in 2008, which lasts four minutes and has 16 sudden changes of direction. And Walibi Belgium has no fewer than eight Vekoma coasters, including the wooden Werewolf and the LSM launch coaster Xpress. Vekoma distinguishes four major product groups:

- family coasters
- thrill and mega coasters
- indoor and custom-designed coasters
- attractions and specialities.

Design and manufacturing

Design, engineering and manufacturing of the roller-coasters is mostly done in-house, but, especially with large orders, manufacturing of non-strategic parts (such as stairs, stations, columns and straight pipes) may be outsourced to manufacturing partners. This flexibility in manufacturing is essential, because annual sales may fluctuate wildly: just a few extra orders for top-of-the-line coasters represent additional sales of several million euros!

Roller-coasters are no longer simple constructions with only limited variation. The development of the looping introduced a new element, but it did not stop at just one looping. Vekoma developed a coaster with no fewer than eight loopings that was mentioned in the *Guinness Book of Records*. In the spring of 2009, the Suzhou Giant Wheel Park in China opened a new Vekoma flying coaster. This Stingray includes a vertical loop, an outside loop, a double loop and a 180-degree roll, with riders flying face-down, parallel to the track. Another trend is indoor coasters. Asia has discovered Vekoma as a specialist in indoor roller-coasters and several custom-designed coasters are already being enjoyed by shopping mall visitors. In Korea can be found a shopping mall, where the mall's escalator goes right through the coaster's looping! To further enhance the roller-coaster experience, manufacturers add images, sounds, temperature differences and laser projections. A well-known example of such an enhanced coaster is Space Mountain in Disneyland Paris.

Source: Vekoma Rides Manufacturing. Used with permission.

Buying roller-coasters

Vekoma's customers are theme parks that purchase a wide variety of roller-coasters (including junior coasters for children), giant wheels, paratowers, sky shuttles, raging river safaris and panoramic flight simulators. The price of roller-coasters varies from €800,000 to €20 million. In the world of roller-coasters there is just a handful of global competitors and all major players know each other. Once a year, the International Association of Amusement Parks and Attractions (IAAPA) organises a large trade show, where all major manufacturers and customers meet. For Vekoma's customers, a roller-coaster is an important product that is capable of attracting many visitors. The earlier-mentioned Vampire was central to Kentucky Kingdom's advertising campaign and the opening of Space Mountain was also a much-publicised event. When purchasing a roller-coaster, customers first look at the relationship between price and value, which includes the coaster's capacity (number of people per hour). In addition, customers assess a coaster's:

- *Quality*: 95 per cent of which consists of safety (new roller-coasters are heavily regulated by the rules and regulations of EN, ASTM and governing bodies and tested extensively by Vekoma engineers).

- *Reliability*: because roller-coasters are typically heavily promoted, a broken-down coaster is a disaster.
- *Service*: to limit a coaster's downtime.
- *Financial aspects*: financing and leasing options.
- *Customisation*: ability to meet exact specifications.

While the price/quality ratio is most important, customer requirements vary widely and customers negotiate extensively about all relevant variables. In addition, many theme parks demand customisation to create a unique product. For instance, they want trains that match the overall theme of the park.

Theme parks are often family businesses, with a fixed core of only 20–30 employees and several hundred temporary employees. The purchase decision about a roller-coaster is usually made by the owner/director. Vekoma may only communicate with the owner/director, while in other cases extensive negotiations take place with the theme park's project manager and technical employees. Particularly when a theme park is looking for a unique concept, Vekoma must communicate with a team of people: the owner/director, a creative designer, a technical employee and someone from finance. To conduct these negotiations, Vekoma uses a sales team, consisting of salespeople, agents and possibly the firm's CEO, with a project manager coordinating all communications. The sales cycle typically lasts three to six months. Because theme parks are faced with increasing competition, their purchasing behaviour has become more professional over the years. The dominant role of the owner/director, making emotional purchasing decisions, is replaced by a professional management team that makes a largely rational purchasing decision.

Questions

1   Explain why Vekoma strives for both standardisation and customisation in manufacturing. What are the advantages of standardisation? What are the advantages of customisation? How can a manufacturer like Vekoma combine standardisation with customisation?

2   A theme park's buying centre typically consists of an owner/director, a creative designer, a technical person and someone from finance. Explain for all of these individuals, in detail, the selling arguments that Vekoma can utilise.

3   Is the decision to purchase a roller-coaster dominated by rational buying motives or emotional ones? Explain your answer.

4   How does buying a roller-coaster for the first time differ from a repeat purchase? What are the advantages for a theme park of buying the next roller-coaster also from Vekoma?

5   List several communication instruments that Vekoma can use in its marketing and sales process. Explain how they can be used and rank them according to their expected effectiveness.

Cater Inc.: Targeting the buying centre

Catering is usually one of the first processes that is outsourced to partners. Running a company cafeteria is not a core activity and increasing competition forces companies to outsource everything that is not considered core. Cater Inc. is a Stockholm-based firm specialising in managing catering processes from start to finish for all kinds of organisations in the Scandinavian countries. Cater Inc. has 7,500 employees and 1,285 contracts for 1,740 locations, where catering services are offered to almost 500,000 individuals. Its annual sales are approximately €450 million.

Cater Inc. distinguishes between three types of customer: companies, institutions and government agencies. Companies represent by far the largest part of annual sales, but there is no longer much growth potential in this market segment. All companies that want to outsource their catering have already done so by now. In contrast, many institutions have never considered outsourcing their catering, while increasing privatisation of government agencies also represents a potential for growth. The composition and size of the buying centre varies significantly between the three customer groups:

- In *companies*, the composition of the buying centre can sometimes be deduced from the number of tender copies requested. When a prospect only asks for two copies of a tender, Cater Inc. probably deals directly with the key decision-makers. But when four or more copies are requested, the buying centre and decision-making process may be quite complex. It is often difficult for Cater Inc. to get a good grip on such complex decision-making processes, because it usually deals with just one contact person (a facility manager or someone from the management team or from human resources). The job description of the contact person is an indicator of their role in the decision-making process.

- In *institutions*, the size and composition of the buying centre depends on the nature of the institution. In hospitals, someone from the management team usually conducts the negotiations, while in prisons Cater Inc. has to deal with a facility manager and a representative from the government.

- In *government agencies* different decision-making processes are also used. Some agencies purchase their catering services directly, while others use a central purchasing organisation. In the latter case, price is usually the most important buying motive (second to the quality of the catering service).

Negotiations with a prospect usually start when Cater Inc. is invited for an initial meeting, where the discussion focuses on the customer's wishes and requirements, such as the desired service level, pricing level, service personnel and free meals. Based on this discussion, Cater Inc. writes a catering proposal that details the service offered and its financial consequences. Most prospects invite several catering firms for an initial briefing. Two or three of them are invited to present their proposal to several employees of the prospect. Usually, the prospect will also demand a visit to one of Cater Inc.'s customers to experience its catering service in a real-life situation that matches the prospect's situation as closely as possible. When several catering firms are still in the running, such a customer visit may determine the eventual decision. After a caterer has been selected, negotiations focus on the details of the contract and the operational issues. This decision-making process takes approximately four to six months, while in extreme situations it may last as long as two years or just one week. The key buying motives are:

- effective management of personnel
- improved cost control
- improved quality.

Cater Inc. uses long-term contracts; its customers tend to be very loyal (the average length of a customer relationship is nine years). This is very different from some other countries, such as the US, where customers switch caterers on average once every three years. Scandinavian customers tend to be more forgiving towards their caterers; even when mistakes have been made, caterers usually get a chance to restore the relationship. This means that in 90 per cent of cases, the proposal is for a new customer, outsourcing its catering for the first time (rather than a customer switching caterers). When Cater Inc. is asked to write a proposal for a customer that considers switching caterers, the customer's current caterer usually goes to great lengths to keep its customer. In such situations, the customer frequently decides to give its current caterer a second chance. All this implies that the loss of a customer is taken very seriously.

Cater Inc.'s service offering and personal selling are its most important marketing instruments. Telemarketing does not work in this business; a personal approach is essential to acquire new customers. Prospects are only visited when an appointment has been made in advance; cold calling is not appreciated. Personal selling is supported by direct mail and participation in networks of facility managers. Ultimately, everything revolves around the effective management of personal relationships. This is also reflected in the emotional buying motives that often play a role in the final buying decision ('which caterer would I like to award the contract to?'). Services marketing is a matter of trust and trust is built through effective personal relationships.

Questions

1 Cater Inc. distinguishes between three market segments: companies, institutions and government agencies. Are these three market segments independent from each other? Describe the (potential) relationships that may exist between these three groups of customers.

2 When problems have occurred, the customer's caterer is usually given a second chance. What should Cater Inc. do when a serious problem has occurred with one of its customers to prevent a competitor from stealing this customer? What can Cater Inc. do to poach a customer from a competitor when that competitor has experienced a serious problem with that customer?

3 A key marketing instrument to win new customers is a persuasive catering proposal. List all elements that you would include in such a proposal. Describe for each of these elements whether you would offer them as fixed elements or whether their content can be negotiated.

4 The marketing of catering services strongly depends on effective relationship management. This means that Cater Inc. must invest in developing personal relationships with its customers. But the majority of sales efforts concern new customers. How can Cater Inc. use relationship management to win new customers?

This case is based on real information, but the name is fictitious.

WWSA: In search of a value proposition

Wolfgang Wiesel SA (WWSA) is a Swiss manufacturer of printing equipment for the graphic industry, specialising in printing large billboards, banners and XL posters. The company started out in Interlaken in the 1950s as a local manufacturer of all-purpose printing equipment, but real growth did not come until the firm's management decided, in 1987, to specialise in the graphic industry. The company moved its headquarters to Basel and grew into a major international player with sales offices, distributors and agents in 34 countries. Annual sales are approximately €230 million.

WWSA has traditionally focused on innovation as the engine of growth. Over the years the firm has developed and launched an impressive number of technological innovations that have contributed to the state of the art of printing in the graphic industry.

Too many products and no focus

Recently, WWSA's management has noticed that actual sales growth is no longer according to plan. In most of its major markets, sales are flat, while the total market still grows by 2–3 per cent each year. In 2010, WWSA decides to hire a consultant to take a closer look at the firm's business and find a way out of the slump. After several interviews with senior management and a few selected customers and industry experts, the consultant realises that, as a result of all these innovation efforts, WWSA simply has too many products. All these products serve specific niche customers with specific needs, but the whole portfolio lacks focus. Even worse, there appears to be no underlying theme to all the products offered to customers in the graphic industry. While every individual product still makes sense, the whole product range has grown to unwieldy proportions and it has become impossible to communicate a clear strategy to customers that communicates the firm's corporate identity. This is reflected in management's inability to state succinctly what makes WWSA's products unique. Similarly, WWSA's salespeople are unable to clearly explain to potential customers why they should buy from WWSA rather than from one of its competitors.

Developing a value proposition

To deal with this problem, WWSA needs to develop a clear value proposition for all of its major products. To jump-start this process, WWSA's management and the external consultant selected one of WWSA's key products that was launched five years ago but failed to command the level of sales that was projected: the XL Big Poster Printer. This is a specialised printer that can print very large posters, which are used to display advertising messages, hide scaffolding when a building is being renovated or increase the aesthetic value of blank concrete walls. These photo-realistic digital prints (with up to 300 dpi) allow advertisers to catch the eye of the target audience in highly frequented locations. The consultant guides WWSA through a systematic process in search of a suitable value proposition that can be used to persuade customers.

Step 1: Identifying potential value elements

The process starts with a small group of XL Big Poster Printer salespeople and other managers brainstorming all the elements of the printer that customers may value. This brainstorming session results in a list of eight potential value elements: fast turnaround time, low costs, consistent colour accuracy, large printing formats, near photographic quality on many different media types (high gloss, matte, canvas, silk, vinyl, cloth), high uptime, good product support and close dealer network.

Step 2: Identifying the next-best alternative

Having identified the potential value elements, the group of employees is asked to identify the next-best alternative: that is, the vendor that is perceived by customers as the most relevant competitor for this particular product. This turns out to be easy, since a new competitor arrived on the market four years ago and quickly established itself as a major player in the big poster segment.

Step 3: Identifying the key value elements

The next challenge is to identify those value elements that are really important to customers and where WWSA offers superior value compared to the next-best alternative. The management team starts with assessing both WWSA's and Competitor X's performance on all eight potential value elements. Initially, the management team assesses performance on all eight value elements only qualitatively. This results in the following table:

Value element	WWSA	Competitor X
Turnaround time	+	++
Costs	++	+
Colour accuracy	++	++
Printing formats	++	++
Quality on different media types	++	+
Uptime	++	+
Product support	–/+	+
Dealer network	–/+	+

Next, the management team conducts a series of face-to-face interviews with ten customers of big poster printing equipment. During these interviews, WWSA's team tries to get a better feeeling for the customer's perception of big poster printers and WWSA's and Competitor X's performance in this area. Based on these interviews, the team concludes that WWSA's just average performance in the areas of product support and dealer network does not really matter to customers. Customers typically have their own technical support staff to maintain and repair equipment and do not rely on manufacturers or dealers for product support. As a result of these interviews, it becomes clear that customers base their purchasing decisions on two key criteria: print quality on different media types and uptime.

Step 4: Formulating a value proposition

WWSA's team takes a closer look at the two criteria of print quality on different media types and uptime. They take an in-depth look at information from current customers and perform several calculations. Based on all of this, they conclude the following:

- On some media types, WWSA's printer provides better print quality than Competitor X's printer.
- WWSA's uptime is 98.4 per cent, compared to 94 per cent for Competitor X.

This results in the following value proposition: *WWSA's XL Big Poster Printer offers better quality at significantly higher uptime.*

Step 5: Formulating strategy

Based on the findings from this exercise, WWSA's management team wants to formulate a strategy to improve the sales and market share of their XL Big Poster Printer. However, a closer look at the data uncovers some troubling findings. First, while their printer provides better print quality on some media types, these concern only a few media types that are not commonly used by most customers. So, even though there is a competitive advantage here, it is only minimal. In addition, while the XL Big Poster Printer enjoys superior uptime, the problem is how to convince customers of this, since detailed data to support this claim are lacking. In fact, some members of WWSA's management team doubt that customers can be convinced of the benefits of the superior uptime and suggest that the XL Big Poster Printer should be discontinued, since customers perceive no significant difference in performance between the two alternative offerings. What should be done?

Questions

1 One problem is that customers do not see the difference in uptime. Indeed, Competitor X's salespeople will dispute the difference in uptime and will point to other advantages of their printer, such as its superior turnaround time and product support. How should WWSA deal with this problem?

2 How can WWSA substantiate its claim of superior uptime to potential customers?

3 Discuss reasons for discontinuing the XL Big Poster Printer. Next, discuss reasons for continuing with this product.

4 What kind of information does WWSA's management team need to resolve this situation? How can it get this information? What are the major problems that WWSA might encounter in collecting the required information?

5 How can WWSA use the experiences from this particular exercise to clean up its product range and make its offerings and accompanying strategy more focused?

This is a fictitious case, but based on real experiences of real firms. The case description is an amalgam of the experiences of several B2B firms trying to develop a competitive value proposition in competitive markets.

KPN: Learning from customers

KPN is the leading telecommunications and ICT service provider in the Netherlands, offering wireline and wireless telephony, internet and TV to consumers, and end-to-end telecommunications and ICT services to business customers.

(www.kpn.com).

At the end of 2008, KPN had more than 38 million customers in the Netherlands, Belgium and Germany. The company's 2008 sales were €14.6 billion, resulting in profits of €2.6 billion. KPN is convinced that satisfied customers are the drivers of profitable growth and the creation of value for its shareholders. This is especially true in B2B markets, where customers need telecommunications and ICT solutions to run their businesses. Not surprisingly, KPN's current strategy for business customers is built around a strong focus on what the customer wants. KPN has invested heavily in knowing its business customers and their underlying wants and needs.

Learning from large customers

Marketing policy is always based on information about customers. As a telecommunications and ICT service provider, KPN frequently interacts with customers and has access to a great deal of customer information. The challenge is to make sense of all this information and translate it into corporate-wide action to improve the customer's service experience. For KPN's large customers this is not really a problem: they are served directly by dedicated account managers and often have dedicated individuals or departments to deal with KPN. One-to-one interaction occurs almost on a daily basis, resulting in rich customer information and detailed insights into changing customer wants and needs. This rich customer information is quickly translated into effective marketing initiatives that increase the value offered to these large accounts.

Learning from small and medium-sized customers

Most customers are small and medium-sized businesses (SMEs: organisations with less than 150 employees), who infrequently interact with KPN on many different issues such as moving to a new location or upgrading their internet connection.

Because KPN has such a strong brand presence, all these customers already have certain expectations about KPN's service performance and it is up to KPN to live up to or exceed these expectations. KPN's learning from small and medium-sized customers focuses on improving its service performance and customer contacts, rather than obtaining suggestions about new product features. The products from telecommunication providers are increasingly similar and a provider's competitive advantage is no longer based on its products, but on the services offered to customers. Customers ask themselves, 'Which provider do I want to give my business to?' rather than, 'Which product characteristics do I need?'

KPN possesses a wealth of information about these SMEs in terms of their demographics (firm size, industry, geographical location) and buying behaviour (number of products bought, usage intensity). These data can be analysed to provide new insights, such as: Which customers buy the largest number of products? Which customers have the lowest churn? But while this represents a substantial amount of customer information, it is largely descriptive and does not answer the key question: Why do business customers continue to do business with KPN? This question is especially relevant for KPN's business customers because, as a result of its position as market leader, KPN already has a large customer base. The challenge is not to acquire new customers but to encourage existing customers to stay with KPN.

From customer satisfaction to Net Promoter Scores

During the years 2004–2008, KPN collected more information about its SME customers by using a customer satisfaction questionnaire. Every quarter the questionnaire was filled out by 3,000 customers, providing information about their satisfaction with various aspects of KPN's products and services. Gradually, however, people at KPN came to realise that customer satisfaction is not the key metric. After all, even satisfied customers were switching vendors, demonstrating that customer satisfaction does not always result in customer loyalty. That is why, in 2008, KPN started to experiment with a new metric: the *Net Promoter Score* (NPS). The NPS is based on the key question, 'How likely are you to recommend KPN to a colleague?' Customers are asked to provide a score on a scale from 0 to 10 and KPN's NPS is calculated as the percentage of promoters (customers scoring a 9 or 10) minus the percentage of detractors (customers scoring 0 to 6). This information is gathered by an outside market research firm, which conducts a business panel in the Dutch market.

But, helpful as all this information about NPS is, it still fails to explain what makes customers decide to stay with KPN. This realisation led KPN to initiate a survey that uses a standardised questionnaire to delve more deeply into the drivers of customer behaviour. Twice a year, the questionnaire is filled out by approximately 2,000 SMEs and 1,000 large customers. In addition to asking all kinds of questions about the KPN brand, its products, prices and services, the questionnaire also contains a number of NPS-related questions. This provides KPN with information about individual customers' propensity to recommend KPN to others.

Another source of customer information are the regular *process measurements* that measure the customer's experience with three key processes: service, delivery and billing. Twice a year, about 300 business customers who recently experienced one of these three key processes are asked to fill out a questionnaire containing detailed questions about their service experience. For the delivery process, for example, the questionnaire includes questions such as: Was the information complete when the project was carried out? Were no mistakes made when the project was carried out? Was the project carried out according to the predetermined schedule?

Finally, KPN collects *direct customer feedback* when customers contact KPN's customer service organisation. Each time a customer contacts the service centre, they are asked the question, 'Based on this contact, how likely is it that you would recommend KPN to a colleague (on a scale of 0–10)?' This type of customer feedback can concern not only the behaviour and knowledge of the service employee, but also the result. These measurements are an example of closed-loop feedback because the information is collected from customers, provided to KPN supervisors, analysed and discussed with individual service centre employees. It also provides KPN with the opportunity to fix the problem. When the customer agrees, the customer is contacted by the operational team manager to solve the problem. By solving the problem, KPN also retains the customer, increases loyalty and reduces churn. Thus, problems are quickly solved and KPN learns from the information received during the customer call backs by team managers. In addition, these call backs provide KPN with the information required to change the behaviour of individual employees on a weekly basis. Each month, several thousands of customers provide direct customer feedback to KPN.

From customer information to KPN action

Ultimately, the proof of the pudding is in how KPN manages to translate all the collected customer information into structural company-wide actions that systematically improve its processes and thus the value offered to customers. At present, KPN is still experimenting in this area. It is not difficult to collect information about one process for a small group of customers (for instance, about moving for customers of a given firm size) and use this information to improve this process for these customers. But KPN is a very large organisation and has a very large number of SME customers, who interact only infrequently with KPN about a large number of different issues. KPN's current challenge is to design a system and processes that facilitate the translation of customer information into effective marketing, sales and service activities that positively impact all relevant customers.

Questions

1 The twice-yearly questionnaire sent to SME customers provides KPN with scores of individual customers on the key question: 'High likely are you to recommend

KPN to a colleague?' How can KPN use this information to improve the effectiveness of its marketing, sales and service efforts?

2   KPN uses several different questionnaires to collect information about SME customers. An alternative approach would be to integrate all these instruments into one overall questionnaire. Discuss the advantages and disadvantages of this approach. Which approach would be better for KPN?

3   KPN's central objective is to obtain more insight into the drivers of their customers' behaviour. List the key issues that KPN should cover in a questionnaire aimed at achieving this objective.

4   Rather than using a standardised questionnaire, KPN could also use other methods to collect information about SME customers. Discuss the suitability of (a) customer focus groups and (b) observation of customers.

5   The remaining challenge for KPN is to translate all the collected customer information into effective marketing, sales and service activities. Consider the following three options: (a) select specific sub-processes and improve them before moving on to other sub-processes, (b) select specific customer groups and improve all services offered to them before moving on to other customer groups, and (c) select specific touch points, or moments of truth, and improve them before moving on to other touch points. Describe the advantages and disadvantages of these three approaches. Which approach would you prefer and why?

NNZ: Innovation in a trading company

NNZ is a family business that has been active in the field of agricultural and industrial packaging for more than 85 years. The company started out as a trading house selling jute bags, which were the primary packaging material for a large variety of products, such as grain, flour, coal and potatoes. After the Second World War, other packaging materials were introduced, first paper and later plastics, and in the 1960s NNZ started to manufacture its own plastic packaging. Although the firm had its roots in the agricultural sector, it also started to sell to industry. In the 1990s, both trading and manufacturing demanded substantial investment and management made the strategic decision to focus on trading and outsource manufacturing. NNZ invested primarily in growth by acquiring small local firms. Around 2000, the firm decided to consolidate its acquisitions by streamlining its operations, creating several new departments and building the corporate brand. In 2010, NNZ has grown into a company with 160 employees and 18 offices in 12 countries. The company has its headquarters in the northern part of the Netherlands, with branches in Europe, the US and Canada. Annual sales are approximately €100 million, 90 per cent of which is still realised in the agricultural sector.

Products

NNZ offers its agricultural and industrial customers a wide range of products. Agricultural customers require just-in-time deliveries, freshness, efficiency and responsible use of raw materials. Agricultural customers are served with products such as films, trays, net packaging, bio packaging, paper and cardboard packaging, PP sacks, jute bags, flexible bulk containers, transit packaging and various accessories (such as labels, clipping wire, strapping, seals and buckles). Industrial markets are faced with the challenges of increasing scale, globalisation, cost control, quality demands and limited stock. These customers are served with a range of flexible bulk containers, paper bags, PE packaging, PP sacks and bags and transit packaging.

NNZ and innovation

Even though NNZ is a trading company, it does have a Marketing and Innovation department. NNZ always believed very strongly in innovation and formulated the goal of introducing at least two new packagings per year. Marketing and Innovation collects factual information about markets, products, raw materials, packaging

Source: NNZ. Used with permission.

technologies and consumer trends. This information is saved in a knowledge management system, which forms the basis of the innovation policy that NNZ develops in close cooperation with its partners. One of NNZ's strengths is its cooperation with partners in many areas to offer optimum solutions to customers' packaging problems. NNZ forms the binding link in a network of buyers, suppliers, distributors, universities, research institutes and governments, hence its tagline: *NNZ, the packaging network*. NNZ uses its network of relationships to develop innovative solutions to customer packaging problems. For example, one customer mentioned the problem that potatoes sent in containers to countries with a warm climate tend to rot. The heat causes the air in the container to condense; the condensation drips on the potatoes and causes them to rot. NNZ used its Packaging Advisory Centre to brainstorm potential solutions. One of the ideas that came up was little bags filled with pellets that are packed with electronic equipment to absorb water. Although the pellets are chemical and cannot be used for potatoes, the basic idea looked promising. NNZ talked to Avebe (a local large starch company) and it turned out that they had an absorbing starch product that might be useful. Next, NNZ found a company that could impregnate blankets with the absorbing starch product, thus resulting in a blanket that can cover potatoes and absorb up to 30 litres of water. The product became a huge success and is currently prescribed for all transports of potatoes to countries with a warm climate.

In recent years this strategy of innovation through cooperation has led to a continuous stream of successful product innovations, including Carry Fresh®, Twin Bag®, Liqui-Sorb® and Power-Lift®. In addition, NNZ focuses on sustainability through its line of Ökopack products, made from renewable resources such as potato and corn starch. NNZ also uses the latest technologies to reduce the materials used in the production of packaging while maintaining or even improving their properties. Other innovations focus on improving the functional characteristics of packaging for consumers, such as better product protection, hygiene, convenience, presentation and shelf life.

Introducing concept packaging

The most recent development concerns the development of concept packaging. In the automotive industry it is common practice to develop concept cars: prototypes that showcase the latest features and technologies. In 2008, during a brainstorming session someone suggested borrowing this idea and developing concept packaging that shows the future of packaging. The basic idea is as follows: 'Over millions of years nature has perfected systems to package and protect its living organisms. What can we learn from her and can we mimic her designs to come up with the best possible packaging for various natural products?'[1] Fruit peel and potato skins are designed to protect fruit and potatoes. Similarly, NNZ thought it could imitate nature's packaging techniques (*biomimetic packaging*) to develop packaging that protects products from threats such as mechanical damage, dehydration, oxidation, greening, premature sprouting of tubers, bacterial and fungal infections and premature (over-)ripening of fruit. In addition, it should regulate gas exchange, indicate the ripeness or freshness of the product (for instance, through a series of coloured dots, similar to the battery indicator on a mobile phone), allow the product to be visible, but at the same time protect it from the influence of light.

Source: NNZ. Used with permission.

This concept is illustrated in the nearby figure for a film. The outer, water- and gas-permeable layer (1) is filled with various aromas (for instance, the smell of strawberries) that are released when the customer grabs or opens the packaging. In the case of strawberries, the sweet smell of the packaging will also reduce the consumer's need for sugar in the packaged strawberries, which results in a healthier final product. The inner, water-impermeable layer (3), connected with glue (2) to the outer layer, is filled with essential oils that limit the growth of micro-organisms; for instance, carvacrol from oregano protects potatoes. Measured diffusion of essential

---

[1] NNZ brochure, *The Evolution of Packaging*.

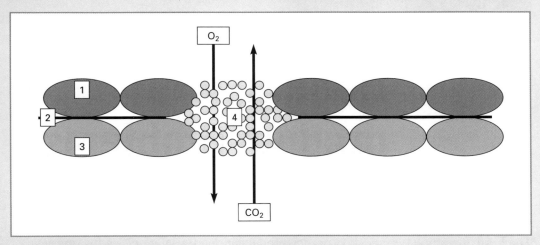

Source: NNZ. Used with permission.

oils from the bubbles of the inner layer slows down spoiling of the packaged product. Pores in the packaging (4), filled with hydrophobic grains, allow the exchange of oxygen, carbon dioxide and water vapour, but prevent the transport of liquid water.

It took NNZ four months to develop the concept packaging, which was introduced to great acclaim and interest during Fruitlogistica in February 2009. NNZ has contacted a business partner who is able to manufacture the developed innovative film and hopes to conduct the first tests with a finished product within two years.

Questions

1 Which criteria might NNZ use to select the first application to be tested?

2 Since NNZ is a trading company, it relies on business partners for manufacturing. List a number of criteria that NNZ could use in selecting suitable manufacturing partners for this new product.

3 While NNZ decided in the 1990s to outsource all manufacturing to strategic partners, there may be circumstances that make manufacturing of this product attractive. Discuss the advantages and disadvantages of both outsourcing manufacturing to partners and manufacturing the new packaging themselves.

4 Should NNZ stick to its outsourcing strategy for this innovative new packaging? What are the main reasons that would cause NNZ to start manufacturing the new packaging?

5 What are potential barriers that may prevent or limit the new packaging's success?

6 Develop a concept packaging strategy for NNZ that describes the key activities and decisions for the next five years.

Ford/Firestone: Dealing with product problems

The Ford/Firestone tyre recall is perhaps the most deadly safety crisis in American history. According to estimates, more than 250 deaths and 3,000 catastrophic injuries were associated with defective Firestone tyres. Most of the deaths occurred in accidents involving the Ford Explorer SUV, which tended to roll over when one of the tyres blew out.

In March 1990, Ford launched the Explorer. Ford internal documents show that company engineers recommended changing the product's design after it rolled over during tests conducted before introduction. But Ford only made minor changes and lowered the recommended air pressure to 26 psi, while the Firestone-recommended air pressure (as moulded into the tyre) was 35 psi. Soon after product launch, the first accidents occurred; the tyre's tread peeled off and the tyre then disintegrated, resulting in the vehicle rolling over if it was travelling at speed. The numerous deaths and injuries resulted in a complicated discussion between Ford and Firestone, with each party accusing the other of delivering a faulty product. This discussion continued for ten years and accidents kept happening.

In May 2000, the National Highway Transportation Safety Administration issued a letter to both companies requesting information about the high incidence of tyre failure on Ford Explorer vehicles. During July, Ford collected and analysed data on tyre failure. The data showed that 15-inch ATX and ATX II models and Wilderness AT tyres had very high failure rates, involving the tread peeling off. Many of these tyres were made at a Decatur, Illinois, plant. Based on these data, Ford estimated that the defect rate was 241 tyres per million for 15-inch ATX and ATX II tyres. But Ford also claimed that there were no defects in 16-inch tyres per million and only 2.3 incidents per million on other tyres. Nevertheless, on 9 August both companies decided on a product recall and several million tyres were replaced. But Ford and Firestone disagreed as to how to break the news to the public; ultimately questions were asked, but many remained unanswered.

Firestone executives continued to deny the problems and downplayed the significance of the failure. Indeed, they maintained that their tyres were not defective. In the words of one of their executives: 'Judging from the fact that most of the accidents occurred in southern states, we estimate that driving in high temperatures, at high speeds and under-tyre pressure are factors in these accidents.'

Ford openly disagreed with this suggestion and pointed out that rival company Goodyear also supplied nearly 500,000 tyres for Ford Explorers using the same specifications as Firestone was using, and there was no evidence of failure.

But Ford documents indicated that data showed that Firestone tyres installed on Explorer SUVs had little or no margin for safety in top-speed driving at the tyre pressures Ford recommended. Firestone emphasised the role of tyre pressure in the accidents and stated that a tyre pressure of 30 psi was needed. Ford denied all this and pointed out that Goodyear's recommendation of the lower pressure of 26 psi was maintained with a spotless record.

After 10 August, many consumers hurried to replace their tyres and Explorer sales plunged. An internal memo from Ford Venezuela said that the Ford Explorer turned over unexpectedly when the Firestone tyres lost their tread and that this did not happen with other SUVs in similar circumstances.

All in all, the Ford/Firestone tyre recall became a real nightmare, with a large number of deaths and injuries, huge costs for both companies, tremendous PR problems in the marketplace and a troubled relationship between two companies that had cooperated since the launch of the Ford Model T at the beginning of the twentieth century. Eventually, the relationship between Ford and Firestone was terminated.

Questions

1 The internet contains a large number of websites with detailed descriptions of the Ford/Firestone case. Write a chronological description of the major milestones in this complicated case.

2 Consider the case from Ford's perspective. What exactly happened? How did Ford management react to the situation? What were the results of these actions? Do you agree with Ford's reactions or should they have reacted differently?

3 Now consider the case from Firestone's perspective. What happened? How did Firestone react to the situation? What were the results of these actions? Do you agree with Firestone's reactions or should they have reacted differently?

4 Now look at the whole situation from the combined perspective of both Ford and Firestone as partners who jointly offered a product to customers. Make a list of all relevant parties in this situation. Describe a set of ideal reactions for each of these parties.

5 Did Ford and Firestone make a good decision when they decided to terminate their relationship? If yes, why? If no, what could they have done to save the relationship?

6 Would it have been an option to eliminate the Firestone brand in response to this crisis? Justify your answer.

7 What are the key B2B marketing lessons that can be learned from this case?

Based on information from www.firestone-tire-recall.com.

Philips Crypto: Pricing a completely new product

In the early 1990s, there was increasing use of electronic communication, especially fax machines, which were frequently used to send purchasing orders, product designs and financial statements. With increasing competition in many markets, the difference between competitive analysis and industrial espionage is not always clear. Hacking into computers and company telephones is no longer limited to eager computer enthusiasts and an increasing number of firms worry about the safety of their communications.

This is the backdrop against which Philips Crypto carved out a niche by selling advanced encryption products to governments and businesses, together with competitors such as Motorola, Ericsson and Siemens. Philips Crypto started as part of the Philips multinational by responding to the Dutch government's need for secure communications. Around 1990, all military activities were sold to Thomson, but the Dutch government declared Crypto to be of strategic importance. Approximately 60 per cent of Crypto's sales were to European government agencies, and the Dutch government designated Crypto its preferred vendor. The remaining 40 per cent consisted of sales to large multinational corporations that wanted to secure their communication networks.

The Crypto telephone

Crypto focused on secure communication, including speech, fax and data. At the beginning of the 1990s, fax communication was the most important market segment. Faxes contained detailed information that was often confidential in nature. One of Crypto's products was the Crypto telephone: a telephone that could be switched into crypto mode with an individual smart card that used a unique encryption key to encrypt communications. Each time an individual used the card, it generated a new unique key to encrypt the communication. At the receiving end of the line, a similar phone and smart card could be used to decrypt the communication. Thus, if the message was intercepted between sender and receiver, it was safely encrypted with the use of a unique key. The Crypto phone was sold for €5,000. Customers would typically order several Crypto telephones and a larger number of smart cards (which cost €50 each).

In the 1990s, Philips Crypto was approached by several large customers that wanted to obtain complete control over their secure communications. By using Crypto's telephones their communications would be secure, as long as people had no access to the algorithm assigning the unique encryption keys. This algorithm was part of Philips Crypto's key generation system that was used to produce the smart cards for customers. Several customers approached Philips Crypto wishing to purchase not only the telephones and smart cards, but also the heart of the system: the key generation system. The only problem was that Philips Crypto had never intended to sell the key generation system and thus management was faced with the question: at what price should we offer the key generation system to customers?

What resulted was a complex internal discussion about manufacturing costs, prices, estimated demand, investment in product development and marketing strategy. The following options were considered.

Option A: Manufacturing costs

This option uses the cost of manufacturing the key generation system, consisting of several standard components, such as a monitor, keyboard and printer, to calculate the price. These manufacturing costs were estimated at €10,000 per unit.

Option B: Development costs

The price of the key generation system may also be calculated, using the cost of developing the key generation system, including the complex software, and the level of expected demand. These development costs were estimated at €8 million, while expected demand was estimated at 100 units.

Option C: Perceived value

According to this option, the price of the key generation system should be based on the customer's perception of the value of the product.

Option D: Marketing strategy

Based on strategic considerations, management may also decide to give the key generation system away for free.

Questions

1 Option A is based on the manufacturing costs per unit. For which reasons would management use this method of price setting? What information do you need to

actually determine the price, using this method? What are the arguments *against* this method of price setting?

2 Option B is based on the investments in developing the key generation system and the required encryption software. According to this method of price setting, the development costs are divided by the level of expected demand to determine the price. How would you estimate the level of expected demand for this kind of product? What other information would you like to have, besides the development costs and expected demand?

3 Option C uses the customer's perceived value to determine the price. Management may estimate the customer's perceived value by simply ascertaining the customer's willingness to pay or by estimating the perceived value of the various elements of the offering. Which method would you prefer and why?

4 Option D suggests simply offering the key generation system for free. What are the reasons for following this strategy?

5 In the absence of a similar product offered by competitors, Philips Crypto could not base its price on the prices of the competition. How could Philips Crypto still include the influence of competitors in their pricing strategy?

6 Which price setting method do you prefer? Justify your answer.

While this case is based on factual information, all numbers are fictitious.

Index